60610
REF 220·7

Luton Sixth Form College
WITHDRAWN

Luton Sixth Form
COLLEGE

LIBRARY

THIS IS A REFERENCE
BOOK AND MUST NOT
BE REMOVED FROM
THE LIBRARY.

D1139090

00001897

The New Jerome Bible Handbook

Love the holy Scriptures, and wisdom
will love you. Love wisdom, and she
will keep you safe. Honour wisdom,
and she will embrace you.

(ST JEROME)

This handbook is named after St Jerome, the foremost Scripture scholar among the Church Fathers, a pioneer in biblical criticism.

Jerome lived from about AD 340 to 420. As a young man he dedicated his life to work on the Scriptures. He taught Hebrew to a group of women who met to study the Scriptures in the house of Marcella in Rome. He used his knowledge of Hebrew in his translation of the Old Testament into Latin, and he also consulted Jewish scholars on the meaning of the Hebrew. He also revised a Latin translation from the Greek of the New Testament. His translation, the Vulgate, became the accepted one for many centuries. He also wrote commentaries on many books of the Bible.

Raymond E. Brown, SS is Auburn Distinguished Professor Emeritus of Biblical Studies at Union Theological Seminary (NYC). A past President of the Studiorum Novi Testamenti Societas, he is the author of the Anchor Bible commentaries on the Gospel (2 vols) and Epistles of John, of *The Birth of the Messiah*, and of some fifteen other books on the Bible. A past member of the Pontifical Biblical Commission, he served from 1969 to 1992 as the only American Catholic member of the Faith and Order Commission of the World Council of Churches. He was elected to the American Academy of Arts and Sciences. Among his many honorary degrees are doctorates from the Universities of Uppsala, Edinburgh, Louvain and Glasgow.

Joseph A. Fitzmyer, SJ is Professor Emeritus of Biblical Studies at the Catholic University of America, Washington, DC. He has been a professor at Woodstock College, the University of Chicago, and Weston School of Theology, as well as Gasson Professor in the Theology Department at Boston College. He has served as President of the Studiorum Novi Testamenti Societas. At present he is a member of the Pontifical Biblical Commission. A specialist in New Testament Studies, the Dead Sea Scrolls, and the Aramaic language, he has published a commentary, *The Gospel According to Luke*, *The Genesis Apocryphon of Qumran Cave I*, and *The Aramaic Inscriptions of Sefire*, and many articles on biblical topics. In 1984 he was awarded the Burkitt Medal for Biblical Studies by the Royal Academy.

Roland E. Murphy, OCarm is G. W. Ivey Emeritus Professor of Duke University, Durham, NC. Previously, he was visiting Professor at Pittsburgh Theological Seminary, Yale University Divinity School, and the University of Notre Dame. He has also served on the editorial boards of several biblical and theological journals. Father Murphy's books include *Wisdom Literature, Wisdom Literature and Psalms, The Tree of Life* and *The Song of Songs*.

The New Jerome Bible Handbook

GEOFFREY
CHAPMAN

GEOFFREY CHAPMAN
An imprint of Cassell Publishers Limited
Villiers House, 41/47 Strand, London WC2N 5JE, England

© Geoffrey Chapman, an imprint of Cassell Publishers Limited, 1992

All rights reserved. No part of this publication may be reproduced or transmitted in
any form or by any means, electronic or mechanical including photocopying,
recording or any information storage or retrieval system, without prior permission in
writing from the publishers.

First published 1992

British Library Cataloguing-in-Publication Data
A catalogue record for this book is available from the British Library

ISBN 0-225-66642-1

Nihil obstat: Father John Deehan, LSS, *Censor*
Imprimatur: Monsignor David Norris, *V.G.*
Westminster, 7 July 1992
The *Nihil obstat* and *Imprimatur* are a declaration that a book or pamphlet is
considered to be free from doctrinal or moral error. It is not implied that those who
have granted the *Nihil obstat* and *Imprimatur* agree with the contents, opinions or
statements expressed.

The material in this handbook is based on *The New Jerome Biblical Commentary*
(ISBN 0-225-66640-5 paperback; 0-225-66588-3 hardback), and was compiled
with the full co-operation and help of the editors and original authors. *The New
Jerome Biblical Commentary* is published by Prentice Hall, Inc. in the United States
and by Geoffrey Chapman in Great Britain, © 1990, 1968 by Prentice Hall, Inc., a
division of Simon & Schuster.

Scripture quotations in the Highlights are from the New Revised Standard Version of
the Bible, copyright 1989 by the Division of Christian Education of the National
Council of the Churches of Christ in the USA. Used by permission.

00001897
60610
R8f 220.7

Cover photograph: BIPAC

Designed by Terry Jeavons

Typeset by Fakenham Photosetting Limited, Fakenham, Norfolk
Printed and bound in Great Britain by The Bath Press

Contents

WITHDRAWN

The New Testament

General Articles on the Bible

Introduction

The New Jerome Biblical Commentary holds a pre-eminent position in serious and academic Bible study. This *Bible Handbook* brings the fruits of this study outside the academic sphere to all those in parishes, courses and schools who read the Scriptures, in groups or individually. This simplification has been prepared with the help and advice of the three editors of *The New Jerome Biblical Commentary* and each article has been submitted for approval to its original author.

What this handbook offers

- *The New Jerome Biblical Commentary* (NJBC) introduction to every book of the Bible is given in simplified form.
- The outline of every book is included.
- A highlight from each book has been chosen to illustrate its character and style.
- Topical or general articles of the NJBC that offer basic information have been digested.
- Readers should refer to the NJBC itself for verse by verse commentary, bibliography, detailed arguments, and those topical articles that are highly specialized or involve considerable scholarly dispute.

The order of the books

The New Jerome Biblical Commentary has been followed. This is based on the editors' judgement of the order in which the books were written. To facilitate use of the handbook a list of the traditional order follows here, showing where each book may be found in the handbook.

The Old Testament

* The books thus marked, along with parts of Esther and
Daniel, are deuterocanonical (see page 323 below) and are
found in some Bibles designated as Apocrypha.

The New Testament

Biblical references are given in numbers which refer to chapters and after a colon to verses. Old Testament versification varies in English Bibles. In the Highlights of this handbook, NRSV versification is followed. Elsewhere the versification is that of the New American Bible, which follows the Hebrew. The difference is most notable in Psalms, where the Hebrew is often one verse different from NRSV.

The
Old Testament

Introduction to

the Pentateuch

What is the Pentateuch?

The material in this chapter is digested from NJBC article 1, 'Introduction to the Pentateuch', by Roland E. Murphy, OCarm.

The term Pentateuch means 'five containers', indicating the written leather or papyrus rolls that were kept in receptacles. In this case the five rolls are the first five books of the Bible: Genesis, Exodus, Leviticus, Numbers and Deuteronomy. Together they constitute the Law, which originally meant 'teaching'. The traditional division of the Hebrew Bible into Law (the Hebrew word is Torah), Prophets and Writings shows that the five books Genesis to Deuteronomy are to be understood as one unit.

A sweep of history is given from the creation of the world and humanity down to the words of Moses in the plains of Moab (his death and burial are recorded in Deuteronomy 34). The content can be summarized thus:

> primeval history (Genesis 1–11); period of the patriarchs (Genesis 12–36); Joseph story (Genesis 37–50); liberation from Egypt and journey to Sinai (Exodus 1–18); giving of laws at Sinai (Exodus 19–Numbers 10); journey from Sinai to Moab (Numbers 10–36); three speeches of Moses in the plains of Moab, with appendixes (Deuteronomy 1–34).

Another way of summarizing the content of the Pentateuch is by its five central themes:

> the patriarchal promises, guidance out of Egypt, guidance in the wilderness, the Sinai revelation, and guidance into the arable land.

Who wrote the Pentateuch?

For almost 2,000 years Moses was thought to be the author of the Pentateuch by both Jewish and Christian tradition. Today, however, it is generally agreed that he did not write it: Moses' death is recorded in Deuteronomy 34; the description of the land east of the Jordan as 'the other side' indicates the point of view of a resident of Palestine, which Moses never entered (Genesis 50:10); there are **anachronisms** such as the mention of Philistines (Genesis 26:14–18) or Chaldeans (Genesis 11:31). But the formation of the books is still shrouded in mystery.

> **anachronism** <
event placed at the wrong
time

One of the striking features which led early on to investigation of the books was the use of two different names for God: the general name for divinity, Elohim, and the sacred name of God, Yahweh. Each of the divine names, it was discovered, was associated with characteristic vocabulary, narrative styles and content which suggested different authors: J (for Yahwist) and E (for Elohist) began to emerge as likely sources in the actual text. Another telling argument was that the same events were told twice, such as the call of Moses (Exodus 3 and 6).

These differences in names and vocabulary, in style and content, within the Pentateuch were noticed and they needed an explanation. Were they the result of various written accounts being put together, or was it a question of 'fragments' that were eventually assembled? Or, another possibility, was there a basic story that was added to?

The documentary hypothesis

Finally, the 'documentary hypothesis' was developed. It recognizes four documents in the following sequence: J (9th century BC), E (8th century), D (Deuteronomist, 7th century) and P (Priestly, after the exile in Babylon). This is the classical dating proposed by J. Wellhausen; for dating preferred by other scholars see the chart in Chapter 65 (pages 329–30). The major *written* sources were eventually combined after the exile under the guiding hand of the P tradition. Each letter, J, E, D and P, stands either for an individual writer or, more probably, for a whole school of writers. There is a recognition that these 'documents' should be thought of as 'traditions' which incorporate any number of earlier spoken and written traditions.

Characteristics of the traditions J, E, D and P

It is helpful to know the usual characterization of the four traditions, with the proviso that these generalizations are not absolute. J speaks of God in a lively way, as if speaking of a human being, with vivid storytelling, and a creative theological vision of promise and fulfilment. J gives expression to the old traditions. The home of the J tradition is usually considered to be Judah (see map on page 30). E remains a problem. It has been considered to be merely inserted independent traditions, or an up-dating of J. It has been associated with the traditions of the Northern Kingdom (see page 374) and supposedly emphasizes morality and reflects the proper response of Israel: faith, and fear of the Lord. D is a very clear tradition. It insists on fear/love of God in terms of obedience to the divine commands and under threat of punishment. Its sermon style and its language give it a characteristic stamp, so that it is recognizable even when it appears outside the Pentateuch, as in Joshua 1:1–9; 23:3–16. P is another clearly marked strand. It is concerned with questions of cult and ritual (Leviticus), is interested in family trees (Genesis) and speaks of the presence of God in terms of glory (Exodus 16:10; 40:34–38).

It is generally agreed that Genesis–Deuteronomy never functioned as a complete Torah until the time of the exile. Before that time, several traditions, oral and written, including collections of prophetic oracles, would have provided guidance. It is undeniable that the Pentateuch contains old covenant traditions that formed the religious charter of the tribes that constituted the people of God.

Different literary forms within the Pentateuch

The traditional acceptance of authorship by Moses brought in its wake a rigid notion of history in the Pentateuch. It was

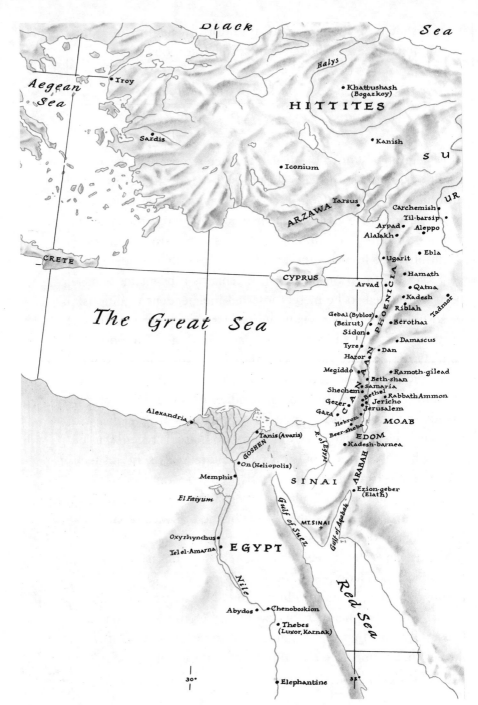

The ancient Near East. The New Jerome Biblical Commentary

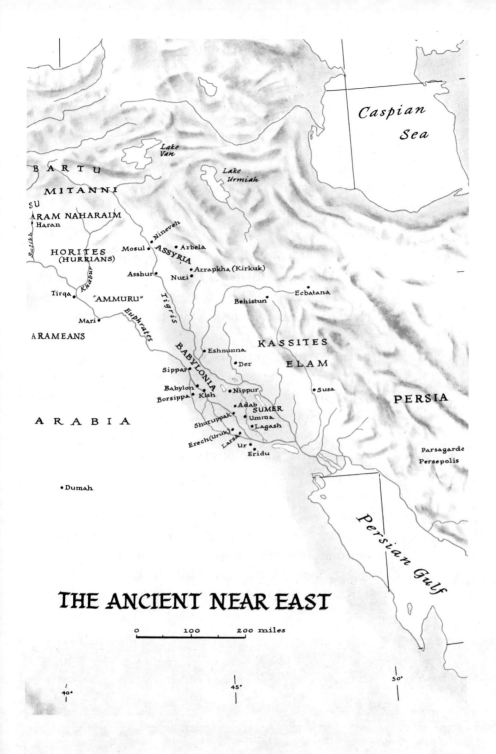

THE ANCIENT NEAR EAST

0   100   200 miles

believed that everything occurred in Exodus and Deuteronomy as Moses wrote it, for he would have been a first-hand witness. This equation of biblical truth with historical truth restricts the divine freedom to produce a literature that is as rich as the Old Testament in fact is. One must read the Pentateuch (not to mention the entire Old Testament) with an awareness of the various literary forms that are contained within it. Some forms are easier to recognize than others. Among them may be indicated the following (the list is far from complete):

- *Laws.*
- *Aetiology.* A story that provides an explanation for a certain name or situation. The aetiology can be wordplay which explains how something got its name, or a story which describes how a city came to be destroyed, for example.
- *Ritual.* A description of the way in which a community is to carry out (significant) ceremonies, such as the offering of tne firstfruits in Deuteronomy 26:1–11, or the prescriptions for sacrifices (Leviticus 1–7).
- *Genealogy.* A list that traces ancestral descent and/or relationship. It should be noted that ancient genealogies were not intended to be historical records. They include more than blood relationship, for they indicate the ties formed by commerce, geography, and other concerns.
- *Blessing.* A form of speech that imparts power upon someone. When the blessing is given on a deathbed (see Deuteronomy 33) it is also called a 'testament'.
- *Story.* This is a narrative with a plot that arouses interest

Royal standard from Ur, 3rd millennium BC. Inlaid stone and shell. This side shows peacetime activities, the other side war. Reproduced by courtesy of the Trustees of the British Museum

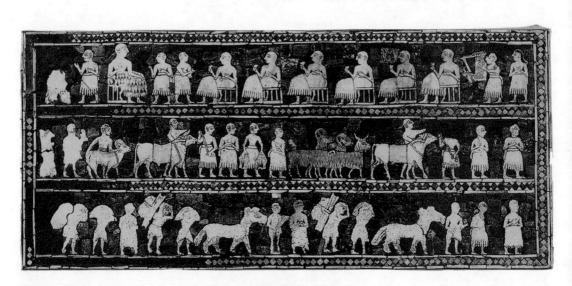

by creating a tension and resolving it. It may supply historical knowledge, or be simply for entertainment, employing certain folklore motifs, for example the story of Joseph.

- *History.* Obviously modern standards of history cannot be applied to the biblical record. Yet the Bible does supply history in various forms. It does record events of the past, but not precisely as they occurred or as a modern would record them. Sequence, cause-and-effect relationship, and selectivity are characteristic of historical writing. As a genre, history is to be found in the books of Kings, rather than in the Pentateuch.

Tradition history in the Pentateuch

Tradition history is the technical term given by scholars to the investigation of the stages that a given unit passes through on its way to being incorporated into a consecutive narrative. The process breaks the text down into units and traditions; it attempts to get behind the existing final form to what existed before. Thus, one can isolate certain literary forms, whether in oral or written tradition, which have been incorporated into a larger framework.

Literary analysis of the Pentateuch

This is the kind of analysis carried on by students of literature and applies to the whole Bible as much as to the five books in the Pentateuch. It does not ask questions about history. Its object is to appreciate the text as it stands now. Moreover, it believes that meaning is conveyed *through* the text, that meaning cannot be arrived at without taking into account all the characteristics of the text (sounds, **onomatopoeia**, catch words – in short, the functions of language that are employed to convey meaning).

> **onomatopoeia** <
a word which sounds like the thing it describes, e.g. swish

Historical questions put to the text yield history; literary questions put to the text yield literature; but both yield meaning. There is no reason to pit one against the other; they are in fact complementary. And they are both necessary for a theo-

13

logical interpretation of the religious literature that is the Torah.

The theological significance of the Pentateuch

It is obvious that the Torah contains the foundational events and theology of the people of God.

The marvel of the Pentateuch is that it is so many things at once:

- Torah, or the will of God for Israel;
- promise of the future of the people of God;
- the way to worship the Holy One;
- a story of human rebellion and divine redemption;
- the origins of the Judeo-Christian tradition.

THREE

Genesis

Title and composition

The material in this chapter is digested from NJBC article 2, 'Genesis', by Richard J. Clifford, SJ and Roland E. Murphy, OCarm.

This title comes from the word 'generation' and the final editor of the book, the P author (see Introduction to the Pentateuch, pages 8–9), in the 6th century BC during the exile in Babylon, organized his material into large blocks introduced by the words 'these are the generations of . . .'. The formula occurs ten times in Genesis and serves as a general guide through the stories.

Genesis is concerned with origins – of the world, of human beings, of Israel and its ancestors.

In Mesopotamian culture, the model for most of the stories in Genesis 1–11, scribes explored beginnings through stories, not through abstract reasoning. Most of the Mesopotamian stories of creation are brief, but there are several extended compositions that collect accounts of origins: the Gilgamesh Epic, Enuma Elish, and the Atrahasis story, which has the same basic

Part of the Atrahasis Epic, ca. 17th century BC

Part of the Creation Epic (Enuma Elish), 7th century BC

Part of the Gilgamesh Epic, 7th century BC

Baked clay tablets. Reproduced by courtesy of the Trustees of the British Museum

15

plot as Genesis 2–9. The biblical writers have produced a version of a common Mesopotamian story of the origins of the populated world, exploring major questions about God and humanity through story. The ancient East had a tolerance for different stories of the same event.

But Genesis is not a random collection of colourful episodes; it is a consciously planned narrative.

Genesis 1:11–11:26 describes the origin of the nations, showing how God created the world, a concept that in Genesis means the structured community of men and women, acting freely to fulfil their divine destiny to fill the world and possess their land.

In parallel but in contrast to the nations, Genesis 11:27–50:26 describes the origin of Israel (in the person of ancestors), showing how God created Israel, through fulfilling for the ancestors the human destiny of children and land. There are three blocks of tradition in the second segment: (A) Abraham and Sarah (11:27–25:18); (B) Jacob and his sons (25:19–36:43); and (C) Joseph and his brothers (37:1–50:26).

Significance

Genesis 2–9 seems to be introduced by Genesis 1 and carried forward by Genesis 10–11. Thus, Genesis 1–11 is a single story, an extended look at the world prior to Israel, a 'philosophical' and 'theological' explanation of the human race – its relation to God, its institutions (marriage, languages, racial and national divisions, metal working, animal husbandry etc.), its flaws, its destiny – and of God and God's justice and abiding fidelity to the human race. Modern readers, who are not used to taking stories seriously, often find it difficult to appreciate the meaning of these chapters. Some readers even end up concentrating on defending a 'literal interpretation' of chapters 1–3, in particular, against modern evolutionary theory, something that the ancient authors of Genesis, with their tolerance of different versions, would never have done.

The second half of Genesis tells of Israel's origins in its ancestors. *Abraham and Sarah* (11:27–25:18) labour under the same divine commands as the nations – to continue in existence through their descendants and to possess their land (Genesis

1:26–28). Their way is different, however: by direct relationship to their God in trust.

The double promise of descendants and land is repeated in the story of *Jacob* and his sons (25:19–36:43), but the emphasis falls rather on the blessing of the firstborn and the filling out of the number of sons to twelve, the number of the Israelite tribes. It is significant that Jacob, the father of the twelve, is called Israel (32:28; 35:10).

The last set of stories concerns the twelve brothers with the spotlight on *Joseph* (37:1–50:26). The ancient promise is repeated, but the real interest is the relationship of the brothers to each other and to Joseph, their leader–saviour.

How will this one family, torn by strife, maintain its unity in an alien land and relate to its chosen leader, Joseph? Psychological and family observations mark the story. The ancestral stories look forward to themes of later biblical literature: living with a just God's promise of increase and of land, the relations of the tribes, the relation of the leader to his people, Israel in Egypt.

Sumerian statuette, ca. 2900 BC, *of a woman worshipping. Reproduced by courtesy of the Trustees of the British Museum*

The covenant, however, makes Israel distinct from the nations, a people dwelling apart, reckoned among the nations (Numbers 23:9).

Finally, how historical are these ancestral stories? It is impossible to say. Because they have been revised and added to in the long course of their transmission, recovery of the 'original' stories is impossible because of the lack of sources outside the Bible itself.

Outline

(I) **The story of the nation (1:1–11:26)**
  (A) *Preamble: creation of the world (1:1–2:3)*
  (B) *The creation of the man and the woman, their offspring, and the spread of civilization (2:4–4:26)*
  (a) Creation of the man and woman (2:4–3:24)
  (b) Cain's murder of Abel (4:1–16)
  (c) Cain's descendants and the invention of culture (4:17–24)
  (d) Seth and introduction of worship (4:25–26)
  (C) *The generations before the flood (5:1–6:8)*
  (a) Genealogy from Adam to Noah (5:1–32)
  (b) Marriage of divine beings with women (6:1–8)

(D) *The flood and the renewed blessing (6:9–9:29)*
(a) The flood (6:9–9:17)
(b) The character of the sons of Noah (9:18–29)
(E) *The populating of the world and the prideful city (10:1–11:9)*
(a) Noah's descendants become landed peoples (10:1–31)
(b) The prideful city with the tower (10:32–11:9)
(F) *Genealogy from Shem to Terah (11:10–26)*

(II) **The story of the ancestors of Israel (11:27–50:26)**
(A) *The story of Abraham and Sarah (11:27–25:18)*
(a) The family of Terah in Haran (11:27–32)
(b) Abraham is called to journey to Canaan and is blessed (12:1–9)
(c) Abraham and Sarah in danger in Egypt (12:10–13:1)
(d) Abraham and Lot go their separate ways (13:2–18)
(e) Abraham defeats the kings and rescues Lot (14:1–24)
(f) God promises Abraham a son and land (15:1–21)
(g) Hagar bears Abraham a son (16:1–16)
(h) God's covenant with Abraham (17:1–27)
(i) The guests of Abraham and Lot (18:1–19:38)
  (i) Abraham and the three guests (18:1–15)
  (ii) Abraham bargains with God (18:16–33)
  (iii) The destruction of Sodom and the rescue of Lot (19:1–29)
  (iv) Lot the father of Moab and the Ammonites (19:30–38)
(j) Abraham and Abimelech (20:1–18)
(k) The birth of Isaac and the expulsion of Hagar and Ishmael (21:1–21)
(l) The treaty with Abimelech and the well at Beer-sheba (21:22–34)
(m) God tests Abraham (22:1–19)
(n) Nahor's descendants (22:20–24)
(o) Abraham buys a burial site for Sarah (23:1–20)
(p) A wife for Isaac (24:1–67)
(q) The descendants of Abraham (25:1–18)
  (i) The descendants of Abraham (25:1–6)
  (ii) The death and burial of Abraham (25:7–11)
  (iii) The descendants of Ishmael (25:12–18)
(B) *The story of Isaac and Jacob (25:19–36:43)*
(a) The birth of Esau and Jacob (25:19–34)
(b) Isaac stories (26:1–35)
(c) The blessing of Jacob (27:1–45)
(d) Jacob's departure for Paddan-aram (27:46–28:9)
(e) Jacob's vision at Bethel (28:10–22)
(f) Jacob's marriages (29:1–30)
(g) Jacob's children (29:31–30:24)

HIGHLIGHT

Jacob's dream at Bethel
Genesis 28:10–22

[10]Jacob left Beer-sheba and went toward Haran. [11]He came to a certain place and stayed there for the night, because the sun had set. Taking one of the stones of the place, he put it under his head and lay down in that place. [12]And he dreamed that there was a ladder set up on the earth, the top of it reaching to heaven; and the angels of God were ascending and descending on it. [13]And the Lord stood beside him and said, 'I am the Lord, the God of Abraham your father and the God of Isaac; the land on which you lie I will give to you and to your offspring; [14]and your offspring shall be like the dust of the earth, and you shall spread abroad to the west and to the east and to the north and to the south; and all the families of the earth shall be blessed in you and in your offspring. [15]Know that I am with you and will keep you wherever you go, and will bring you back to this land; for I will not leave you until I have done what I have promised you.' [16]Then Jacob woke from his sleep and said, 'Surely the Lord is in this place – and I did not know it!' [17]And he was afraid, and said, 'How awesome is this place! This is none other than the house of God, and this is the gate of heaven.'

[18]So Jacob rose early in the morning, and he took the stone that he had put under his head and set it up for a pillar and poured oil on the top of it. [19]He called that place Bethel; but the name of the city was Luz at the first. [20]Then Jacob made a vow, saying, 'If God will be with me, and will keep me in this way that I go, and will give me bread to eat and clothing to wear, [21]so that I come again to my father's house in peace, then the Lord shall be my God, [22]and this stone, which I have set up for a pillar, shall be God's house; and of all that you give me I will surely give one tenth to you.'

FOUR

Exodus

Title and composition

The title means literally 'going forth [from Egypt]', one of the main events narrated; the book was edited by the P author (see Introduction to the Pentateuch, pages 8–9) in the 6th century BC but it contains material from J, E and D sources, too. P arranges his traditions into two interlocking parts: the rescue of the Hebrews in Egypt from Pharaoh (1:1–15:21) and the journey from Egypt to Sinai (12:37–40:38). The journey is in twelve stages, each stage marked by the formula 'they departed from *place name A* and encamped at *place name B*'.

The material in this chapter is digested from NJBC article 3, 'Exodus', by Richard J. Clifford, SJ.

The route of the Exodus. The New Jerome Biblical Commentary

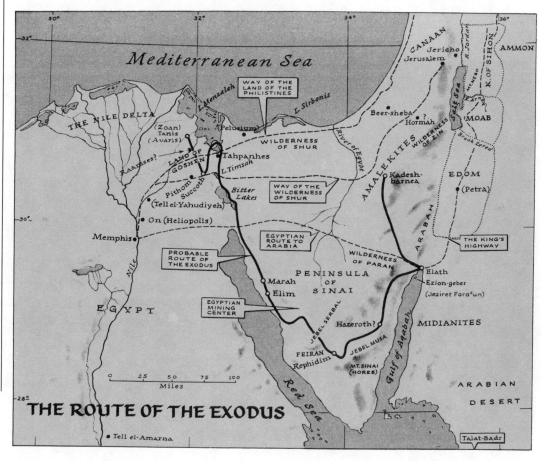

THE ROUTE OF THE EXODUS

Significance

Exodus has had a powerful hold on the imagination of later biblical authors and of Jewish and Christian thinkers. The book begins with the people in an alien land, forgetful of Yahweh's promises to them, oppressed by a cruel Pharaoh acting as a 'god' toward them by regulating every aspect of their life and keeping them slaves in Egypt. Yahweh defeats Pharaoh by a series of ten plagues and brings the people to his mountain, Sinai. At Sinai he confirms Moses as their leader, gives them his laws, establishes his dwelling, and sets them on their journey to his land Canaan.

In this task, Moses becomes the great servant of God, the model for the biblical portraits of Joshua, Jeremiah, Second Isaiah, and Jesus. Sharing in the people's plight, he is also close to God; by his mediation he brings people and God into faithful relationship. Exodus is a portrait of the community of God, called from false and demeaning slavery in an alien land to journey to the promised land.

Pharaoh Ramses II: the Exodus probably took place during his reign. Granite statue from Elephantine. Reproduced by courtesy of the Trustees of the British Museum

Egyptian wall painting of prisoners making bricks. Reproduced by courtesy of the Metropolitan Museum of Art, New York

Outline

    (vii) Judgements concerning responsibility for deposited
          property (22:7–15)

    (viii) Judgements concerning the seduction of a young
          woman (22:16–17)

    (ix) Commands about various social and cultic matters
         (22:18–23:19)

    (x)   The blessings of keeping the covenant (23:20–33)

(d) The ratification of the covenant (24:1–18)

(B) *Divine command to build and maintain the dwelling (chapters 25–31)*

(a) The people are to give the material for the dwelling (25:1–9)

(b) The Ark (25:10–22)

(c) The table (25:23–30)

(d) The lampstand (25:31–40)

(e) The dwelling (26:1–37)

(f) The altar (27:1–8)

(g) The court (27:9–19)

(h) The lamp (27:20–21)

(i) Priestly vestments (28:1–43)

(j) The consecration of priests (29:1–46)

(k) Appendix (30:1–31:17)

    (i)   Altar of incense (30:1–10)

    (ii)   Ransom ritual during a census (30:11–16)

    (iii) The bronze laver (30:17–21)

    (iv) The anointing oil (30:22–33)

    (v)   The incense (30:34–38)

    (vi) The selection of artisans (31:1–11)

    (vii) Affirmation of the sabbath (31:12–17)

(l) The tablets of the law are given to Moses (31:18)

(C) *Unfaithfulness and renewal of the covenant (chapters 32–34)*

(a) The people make new gods to go with them (32:1–6)

(b) Yahweh resolves to destroy the people (32:7–14)

(c) Moses breaks the tablets and punishes the people (32:15–35)

(d) The people lament when they learn Yahweh is not with them (33:1–6)

(e) Moses places the tent of meeting outside the camp (33:7–11)

(f) Appearance of Yahweh in response to Moses' plea (33:12–23)

(g) The remaking of the covenant (34:1–35)

(D) *Building of the dwelling and the descent of the glory (chapters 35–40)*

(a) The people build the dwelling (35:1–39:43)

(b) Dedication rites (40:1–38)

HIGHLIGHT

The Ten Commandments
Exodus 20:1–17

¹Then God spoke all these words: ²I am the Lord your God, who brought you out of the land of Egypt, out of the house of slavery; ³you shall have no other gods before me.

⁴You shall not make for yourself an idol, whether in the form of anything that is in heaven above, or that is on the earth beneath, or that is in the water under the earth. ⁵You shall not bow down to them or worship them; for I the Lord your God am a jealous God, punishing children for the iniquity of parents, to the third and the fourth generation of those who reject me, ⁶but showing steadfast love to the thousandth generation of those who love me and keep my commandments.

⁷You shall not make wrongful use of the name of the Lord your God, for the Lord will not acquit anyone who misuses his name.

⁸Remember the sabbath day, and keep it holy. ⁹Six days you shall labour and do all your work. ¹⁰But the seventh day is a sabbath to the Lord your God; you shall not do any work – you, your son or your daughter, your male or female slave, your livestock, or the alien resident in your towns. ¹¹For in six days the Lord made heaven and earth, the sea, and all that is in them, but rested the seventh day; therefore the Lord blessed the sabbath day and consecrated it.

¹²Honour your father and your mother, so that your days may be long in the land that the Lord your God is giving you.

¹³You shall not murder.

¹⁴You shall not commit adultery.

¹⁵You shall not steal.

¹⁶You shall not bear false witness against your neighbour.

¹⁷You shall not covet your neighbour's house; you shall not covet your neighbour's wife, or male or female slave, or ox, or donkey, or anything that belongs to your neighbour.

The material in this
chapter is digested
from NJBC article 4,
'Leviticus', by
Roland J. Faley,
TOR.

> **levitical** <

priests were descendants
of Levi, one of the sons of
Jacob

> **rubrics** <

instructions for liturgy

FIVE

Leviticus

Title and composition

The title of the book is highly appropriate because Leviticus
served as the liturgical handbook of the **levitical** priesthood. It
is almost wholly concerned with laws and **rubrics**, and the story
does not move ahead.

In its present form the book is to be dated to the period
after the return from exile, and is part of the P tradition (see
Introduction to the Pentateuch, pages 8–9). The P material
begins with the laws in Exodus 25–31 and 35–40 and continues in the book of Numbers.

Significance

Leviticus taught the Israelites the necessity of holiness in every
aspect of their lives.

Outline

(I) **The law of sacrifice (1:1–7:38)**
  (A) Types of sacrifice (1:1–5:26)
  (a) Holocausts (1:1–17)
  (b) Cereal offerings (2:1–16)
  (c) Peace offerings (3:1–17)
  (d) Sin offerings (4:1–5:13)
  (e) Guilt offerings (5:14–26)
  (B) The priest and sacrifice (6:1–7:38)
  (a) The daily holocaust (6:1–6)
  (b) The daily cereal offering (6:7–16)
  (c) Sin offerings (6:17–23)
  (d) Guilt offerings (7:1–10)
  (e) Peace offerings (7:11–21, 28–34)

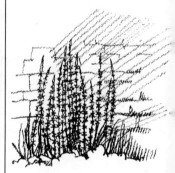

Hyssop

H I G H L I G H T

About justice
Leviticus 19:9–18

[9]When you reap the harvest of your land, you shall not reap to the very edges of your field, or gather the gleanings of your harvest. [10]You shall not strip your vineyard bare, or gather the fallen grapes of your vineyard; you shall leave them for the poor and the alien: I am the Lord your God.

[11]You shall not steal; you shall not deal falsely; and you shall not lie to one another. [12]And you shall not swear falsely by my name, profaning the name of your God: I am the Lord.

[13]You shall not defraud your neighbour; you shall not steal; and you shall not keep for yourself the wages of a labourer until morning. [14]You shall not revile the deaf or put a stumbling block before the blind; you shall fear your God: I am the Lord.

[15]You shall not render an unjust judgement; you shall not be partial to the poor or defer to the great: with justice you shall judge your neighbour. [16]You shall not go around as a slanderer among your people, and you shall not profit by the blood of your neighbour: I am the Lord.

[17]You shall not hate in your heart anyone of your kin; you shall reprove your neighbour, or you will incur guilt yourself. [18]You shall not take vengeance or bear a grudge against any of your people, but you shall love your neighbour as yourself: I am the Lord.

Numbers

Title and composition

The English title of the book refers to the census figures in chapters 1 and 26 as well as to arithmetical data elsewhere; but Numbers also contains extensive narrative, poetry and legal materials.

The problem of authorship is part of the overall question of the five books of the Pentateuch, but in Numbers there is a lot of Priestly (P) material including 1:1–10:28; 15; 17–19; 26–31; 33–36. Earlier, non-P material is found in 10:29–12:16 and 21–24. The remaining chapters have both P and earlier components (see Introduction to the Pentateuch, pages 8–9).

Significance

It is generally agreed by historians that the presentation of Israel's story as a march of all twelve tribes from Egypt, through the wilderness, around the Dead Sea, ending with a massive invasion of Canaan from the east, is a great simplification of what actually happened.

The author is much more concerned with later problems of theology and community organization than with presenting objective history

An important purpose of Numbers is to show how the religious practice and organization of Judaism after the exile goes back to the time of Moses and the wilderness. On a deeper level, Numbers shows the great blessing God gives his people by being among them. God has given worship to the people as a way of atoning for sin, so that the people can live near God without being destroyed by his terrifying holiness.

The material in this chapter is digested from NJBC article 5, 'Numbers', by Conrad E. L'Heureux.

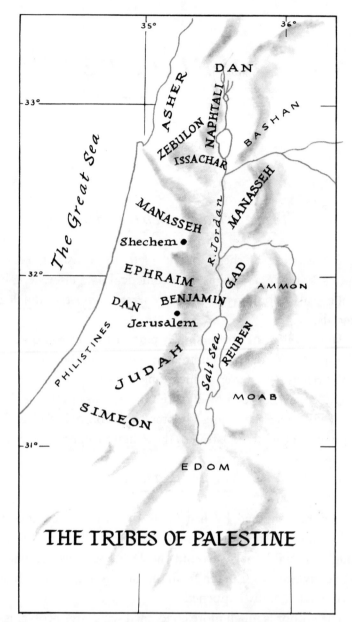

The tribes of Palestine. The New Jerome Biblical Commentary

The account of the time in the wilderness shows God's plan and care for his people, and gives examples of how people rebel against God and his appointed representatives.

Perhaps the most enduring teaching of Numbers is that it is possible to be God's people while still on the march, not yet at home. Liberated from slavery, they journey toward the land of promise.

Outline

(D) *From Kadesh to the plains of Moab (20:1–21:35)*
(a) The waters of Meribah (20:1–13)
(b) Negotiations with the king of Edom (20:14–21)
(c) Death of Aaron (20:22–29)
(d) Battle with the Canaanites at Hormah (21:1–3)
(e) The fiery serpents (21:4–9)
(f) Stages of the journey through Transjordan (21:10–20)
(g) The defeat of Sihon and Og (21:21–35)

(III) **On the plains of Moab: preparation for entry into the land (22:1–36:13)**
(A) *The story of Balaam (22:1–24:25)*
(a) Balaq sends for Balaam (22:1–21)
(b) Balaam's ass (22:21–35)
(c) Meeting of Balaam and Balaq (22:36–40)
(d) First oracle at Bamoth Baal (22:41–23:12)
(e) Second oracle at Mount Pisgah (23:13–26)
(f) Third oracle on Peor (23:27–24:9)
(g) Fourth oracle of Balaam (24:10–19)
(h) Concluding oracles (24:20–25)
(B) *Apostasy at Baal Peor (25:1–18)*
(C) *Preparation for conquest and division of the land (25:19–36:13)*
(a) The second census (25:19–26:65)
(b) The daughters of Zelophehad (27:1–11)
(c) Commissioning of Joshua (27:12–23)
(d) The ritual calendar (28:1–30:1)
(e) Vows made by women (30:2–17)
(f) The holy war against Midian (31:1–54)
(g) Settlement of Gad and Reuben (32:1–42)
(h) Overview of the desert itinerary (33:1–49)
(i) Apportionment of the land of Canaan (33:50–35:34)
(j) The daughters of Zelophehad (36:1–13)

HIGHLIGHT

The priests' blessing
Numbers 6:22–27

[22]The Lord spoke to Moses, saying: [23]Speak to Aaron and his sons, saying, Thus you shall bless the Israelites: You shall say to them, [24]The Lord bless you and keep you; [25]the Lord make his face to shine upon you, and be gracious to you; [26]the Lord lift up his countenance upon you, and give you peace.

[27]So they shall put my name on the Israelites, and I will bless them.

SEVEN

Deuteronomy

Title and composition

The material in this chapter is digested from NJBC article 6, 'Deuteronomy', by Joseph Blenkinsopp.

Deuteronomy means 'second law', an appropriate title because the law in Deuteronomy was intended to supersede the covenant code of law in Exodus 20:23–23:19. Moses' death in the final chapters of Deuteronomy rounds off the entire Pentateuch, which deals with the period up to the occupation of the promised land.

The theory that the law book found in about 621 BC in the reign of King Josiah during repair to the Temple (2 Kings 22:3–10) was an earlier version of our Deuteronomy has many supporters, but cannot be proved.

Significance

Deuteronomy is, first of all, a law book. The care to regulate life by law, one of the chief characteristics of Judaism, is seen in the adaptation of an ancient legal tradition to new situations (e.g. changes in the laws about slavery). The law in Deuteronomy repeats the message of the great prophets, e.g., about widows, fatherless, and aliens. The purpose of the law is to outline a level of moral performance compatible with Israel's God and Israel's high calling (e.g. 4:32–40). One of its most important consequences is the association between people and land, a permanent aspect of Jewish self-understanding often underestimated by Christians. Israel is a holy people (e.g. 7:6; 14:2) which expresses its fidelity to the one God in the *Shema,* 'Hear, O Israel' (6:4–9). The message of Deuteronomy can be summarized as: one God, one people, one sanctuary. It is understandable, therefore, that this most theological book of the Old

Testament has had an enormous influence on both Judaism and Christianity.

Vassal treaty from Nimrud, 672 BC; the covenants in the Old Testament have a literary form similar to such treaties. Reproduced by courtesy of the Trustees of the British Museum

Outline

(I) First address of Moses: from Horeb to Moab (1:1–4:49)
- (A) Introduction to the address (1:1–5)
- (B) Command to occupy the land (1:6–8)
- (C) Tribal and judicial organization (1:9–18)
- (D) The stay at Kadesh (1:19–46)
- (E) Passage through Edom, Moab, Ammon (2:1–25)
- (F) Conquest of Heshbon and Bashan (2:26–3:11)
- (G) Settlement of Transjordanian tribes (3:12–22)
- (H) Moses' unanswered prayer (3:23–29)
- (I) Prologue to the giving of the law (4:1–14)
- (J) On the danger of idolatry (4:15–31)
- (K) The unique vocation of Israel (4:32–40)
- (L) Appendix: cities of refuge (4:41–43)
- (M) Conclusion to the first address (4:44–49)

(II) Second address: introduction to the law book (5:1–11:32)
- (A) Summons (5:1–5)
- (B) The Ten Commandments (5:6–21)
- (C) Sequel to the Ten Commandments (5:22–6:3)
- (D) A law for life in the land (6:4–25)
- (E) Command to destroy the people of Canaan and their cults (7:1–11)
- (F) Prosperity in the land assured by fidelity to the law (7:12–26)
- (G) Historical recollection a counter to the temptations of the land (8:1–20)
- (H) Occupation of the land the work of God, not Israel (9:1–6)
- (I) Unfaithfulness at Horeb (9:7–24)
- (J) Intercession of Moses; second covenant (9:25–10:11)
- (K) Election and its consequences (10:12–11:1)
- (L) Remember your past! (11:2–25)
- (M) The two ways: blessing and curse (11:26–32)

(III) The law book (12:1–26:15)
- (A) The sanctuary law (12:1–27)
- (B) Laws about unfaithfulness (12:28–13:18)
- (C) Purity laws (14:1–21)
- (D) Periodic religious duties (14:22–16:17)
- (E) Offices and functions (16:18–18:22)
- (F) Homicide and related matters (19:1–21)
- (G) Rules for the conduct of war (20:1–21:14)
- (H) Miscellaneous laws (21:15–23:1)
- (I) Humanitarian and cultic laws (23:2–25:19)
- (J) Offering of the firstfruits (26:1–15)

(IV) **Conclusion to the giving of the law (26:16–28:69)**
- (A) *Commitment on both sides (26:16–19)*
- (B) *The Shechem covenant ritual (27:1–26)*
- (C) *Blessings and curses (28:1–69)*

(V) **Third address (29:1–30:20)**
- (A) *Lessons to be learned from history (29:1–8)*
- (B) *Charge to the covenanting community (29:9–28)*
- (C) *Reversal of fortune (30:1–14)*
- (D) *The two ways (30:15–20)*

(VI) **Last will, testament, and death of Moses (31:1–34:12)**
- (A) *Commissioning of Joshua (31:1–8)*
- (B) *Dispositions with respect to the law: Joshua commissioned (31:9–15)*
- (C) *Introduction to the Song (31:16–23)*
- (D) *The law placed in the sanctuary (31:24–29)*
- (E) *The Song of Moses (31:30–32:44)*
- (F) *Exhortation to observe the law (32:45–47)*
- (G) *Moses prepares for death (32:48–52)*
- (H) *Deathbed blessings of Moses (33:1–29)*
- (I) *Death of Moses; conclusion to the Pentateuch (34:1–12)*

HIGHLIGHT

The *Shema*
Deuteronomy 6:4–9

[4]Hear, O Israel: The Lord is our God, the Lord alone. [5]You shall love the Lord your God with all your heart, and with all your soul, and with all your might. [6]Keep these words that I am commanding you today in your heart. [7]Recite them to your children and talk about them when you are at home and when you are away, when you lie down and when you rise. [8]Bind them as a sign on your hand, fix them as an emblem on your forehead, [9]and write them on the doorposts of your house and on your gates.

EIGHT

Joshua

The Former Prophets

The material in this chapter is digested from NJBC article 7, 'Joshua', by Michael David Coogan.

This is the old title given to the books Joshua, Judges, 1–2 Samuel and 1–2 Kings, and they form a unit. They tell the story of Israel's life in its own land, after the Exodus, from the occupation under Joshua to the exile, but they must be understood more as a history of relations with God than political or social history, where they are frequently inaccurate.

Statue of Idri-mi, ruler of Alalakh in north Syria, inscribed with his autobiography, which mentions the land of Canaan, Hapiru (?Hebrew) warriors, and his wanderings, like those of Abraham and his descendants. Reproduced by courtesy of the Trustees of the British Museum

The text and its composition

Most scholars agree that in its present form the work is largely a product of the 7th century BC (the reign of Josiah), which was revised in the time of the exile in the light of the fall of Jerusalem in 587/586. Earlier critics had seen in Joshua a continuation of the various traditions found in the Pentateuch and sometimes referred to the first six books of the Bible as the Hexateuch.

Archaeological evidence shows that few if any of the major episodes in Joshua are historical. For example, neither Jericho

Drawing of the Israel stele of Pharaoh Merneptah (1211–1202 BC) from Thebes in Egypt, now in the Cairo Museum. It tells of Egyptian victories over the people (not land) of Israel, which suggests that the Israelites were a wandering, unsettled group at that time. Reproduced by permission of the British Library

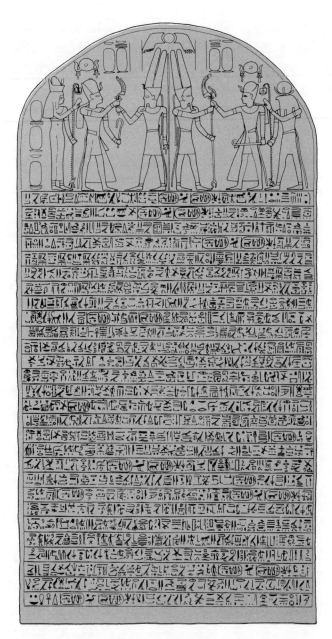

nor Ai nor Gibeon was occupied in the period when most scholars would date the appearance of Israel in Canaan, about 1200.
The picture of the total annihilation of the inhabitants of the
land, of a total Israelite conquest, did not apply to the time of
Joshua. It belongs to the period of the monarchy.

The authors write a kind of historical–theological fiction,
in order to present a picture of the ideal Israel under ideal
leadership. Various episodes show the consequences of failure
to observe the commands of Moses and comment on the
authors' own times. Underlying this is a profound belief: Yahweh had given Israel the land, and in order to keep it Israel had
to obey his law.

The author's purposes in writing the book of Joshua

Joshua acts like Moses:

Moses	Joshua
(1) sent spies to scout the land (Numbers 13; Deuteronomy 1:19–46)	sent spies to scout the land (Joshua 2)
(2) passed through the Red Sea on dry ground	crossed the Jordan as on dry ground
(3) celebrated the Passover	celebrated the Passover
(4) was told by a vision of a burning bush to remove his shoes (Exodus 3:5)	was told by a vision to remove his shoes (Joshua 5:15)
(5) held out 'God's rod' to prevail in battle	held out a sickle-sword to prevail in battle

There are several other parallels.

In addition to these parallels, there are a number of passages in which Joshua explicitly fulfils a command given by
Moses. These include his instruction to Reuben, Gad, and Eastern Manasseh to join the other tribes in the military conquest of
the land (1:12–18; see Numbers 32; Deuteronomy 3:12–20);
the erection of the altar on Mount Ebal (8:30–35; see Deuteronomy 27:1–26); the extermination of the inhabitants of the

land (11:15; see Deuteronomy 20:16) and of the Anakim (11:21; see Deuteronomy 9:2); the division of the land by lot (14:2; see Numbers 34:13); and the establishment of the cities of asylum (20; see Numbers 35:9–15; Deuteronomy 19:1–10) and the cities of the Levites (21:1–42; see Numbers 35:1–8).

One consequence of these parallels and fulfilments is that Joshua is presented as little more than a kind of carbon copy of Moses, and it is thus difficult to see behind the literary traditions to the historical Joshua. Unlike Moses, Joshua is the leader without flaw or hesitation; he is, in fact, deliberately portrayed as the ideal leader of Israel, one who keeps the teaching of Moses in its entirety (1:7–8; 11:15), and as such is the prototype of the ideal king of Israel, in particular David, Hezekiah and Josiah.

A final theme to be considered is the explanation of various features, known to the readers and hearers of the book of Joshua, by means of stories connected with the man Joshua. These stories are generally marked by the phrase 'to this day'; see 4:9; 5:9; 6:25; 7:26; 8:28, 29; 9:27; 10:27; 13:13; 14:14; 15:63; 16:10. The use of the phrase implies distance in time. The use of the phrase confirms that Joshua as a narrative developed long after the events described in it.

Did the man Joshua exist?

The existence of the parallels to Moses and fulfilments of what Moses commanded, described above, suggests that Joshua is a literary creation. The most that can be said is that Joshua was an Ephraimite (see 19:50; 24:30), perhaps originally a local hero who became the focus for the idealized reconstruction of early Israel. But he is not mentioned in 1 Samuel 12, or Nehemiah 9:6–31 or Psalms 78, 105, 106 or 136, all instances where Israel's history is recited.

The same is true of many events in Joshua: the fall of Jericho, the capture of Ai, the division of the land, and the covenant at Shechem are not mentioned in biblical sources apart from Joshua. However, in later Jewish tradition Joshua is an essential link in the handing on of the law from Moses, while for the pioneer Pilgrim settlers in America, in particular, Joshua served as a model and a divine guarantee: once again a group of

God's people escaped from oppression across a body of water to a 'providence plantation'. This belief continued to influence American history, and is seen in the many biblical place-names in New England and throughout the country.

Outline

(I) **Introduction (1:1–18)**
  (A) *The commissioning of Joshua (1:1–9)*
  (B) *Joshua's command to the people (1:10–11)*
  (C) *Instructions to the Transjordanian tribes (1:12–18)*

(II) **The conquest of the land (2:1–12:24)**
  (A) *Rahab and the spies (2:1–24)*
  (B) *The crossing of the Jordan (3:1–5:1)*
  (a) The crossing (3:1–17)
  (b) Memorials to the crossing (4:1–24)
  (c) The reaction of the kings (5:1)
  (C) *Ceremonies at Gilgal (5:2–12)*
  (a) Circumcision (5:2–9)
  (b) Passover (5:10–12)
  (D) *The destruction of Jericho (5:13–6:27)*
  (a) Prelude: God appears (5:13–15)
  (b) Instructions (6:1–7)
  (c) The procession and the fall of the walls (6:8–21)
  (d) Epilogue (6:22–26)
     (i) Rahab's family (6:22–25)
     (ii) The curse on Jericho (6:26)
  (e) Conclusion (6:27)
  (E) *The destruction of Ai (7:1–8:29)*
  (a) Achan's violation of the ban (7:1)
  (b) The first attack: defeat (7:2–5)
  (c) The discovery and punishment of Achan's sin (7:6–26)
  (d) The second attack: victory (8:1–29)
  (F) *Construction of the altar and reading of the teaching on Mount Ebal (8:30–35)*
  (G) *The reaction of the kings (9:1–2)*
  (H) *Covenant with Gibeon (9:3–27)*
  (I) *The southern campaign (10:1–43)*
  (a) Defeat of the coalition of five kings (10:1–27)
  (b) Defeat of the major cities (10:28–39)
  (c) Concluding summary (10:40–43)
  (J) *The defeat of the northern kings (11:1–15)*
  (K) *Summaries (11:16–12:24)*
  (a) Geographical summary (11:16–20)
  (b) The Anakim (11:21–22)

(c)   Final summary (11:23)
(d)   Lists of defeated kings (12:1–24)
    (i)   East of the Jordan (12:1–6)
    (ii) West of the Jordan (12:7–24)

(III) The division of the land (13:1–21:45)
  (A) Introduction (13:1–7)
  (B) East of the Jordan (13:8–33)
  (a)   Introduction (13:8–14)
  (b)   Reuben (13:15–23)
  (c)   Gad (13:24–28)
  (d)   Eastern Manasseh (13:29–31)
  (e)   Conclusion (13:32–33)
  (C) West of the Jordan (14:1–19:48)
  (a)   Introduction (14:1–5)
  (b)   Caleb's inheritance (Hebron) (14:6–15)
  (c)   Judah (15:1–63)
    (i)   Boundaries (15:1–12)
    (ii)   Caleb's share (15:13–19)
    (iii) City lists (15:20–62)
    (iv)   Jerusalem (15:63)
  (d)   Joseph (16:1–17:18)
    (i)   Introduction (16:1–4)
    (ii)   Ephraim (16:5–10)
    (iii) Western Manasseh (17:1–13)
    (iv)   Conclusion (17:14–18)
  (e)   The other tribes (18:1–19:48)
    (i)   Introduction (18:1–10)
    (ii)   Benjamin (18:11–28)
    (iii) Simeon (19:1–9)
    (iv)   Zebulun (19:10–16)
    (v)   Issachar (19:17–23)
    (vi)   Asher (19:24–31)
    (vii) Naphtali (19:32–39)
    (viii) Dan (19:40–48)
  (D) Conclusion (19:49–51)
  (a)   Joshua's land (19:49–50)
  (b)   Summary (19:51)
  (E) Cities of safety (20:1–9)
  (F) Cities of the Levites (21:1–42)
  (G) Summary (21:43–45)

(IV) Appendixes (22:1–24:33)
  (A) The Transjordanian tribes (22:1–34)
  (a)   Joshua's dismissal (22:1–9)
  (b)   The altar west of the Jordan (22:10–34)
    (i)   Construction and controversy (22:10–12)
    (ii)   Negotiation (22:13–31)
    (iii) Resolution (22:32–34)

HIGHLIGHT

God's promise to Joshua
Joshua 1:7–9

[7]Only be strong and very courageous, being careful to act in accordance with all the law that my servant Moses commanded you; do not turn from it to the right hand or to the left, so that you may be successful wherever you go. [8]This book of the law shall not depart out of your mouth; you shall meditate on it day and night, so that you may be careful to act in accordance with all that is written in it. For then you shall make your way prosperous, and then you shall be successful. [9]I hereby command you: Be strong and courageous; do not be frightened or dismayed, for the Lord your God is with you wherever you go.

NINE

Judges

The material in this chapter is digested from NJBC article 8, 'Judges', by M. O'Connor.

Historical and social setting of the book

Judges is concerned with the era between the death of Joshua and the rise of Saul. With Joshua's passing, the age dominated by Moses enters its decline; with Saul's rise, the age of David and the kings begins to take shape. It is a period of danger and uncertainty.

Both Judges and Joshua are major sources for the period between 1200 and 1050 BC. In the biblical view the major happening was the establishment of Israel as a people (2:6, 7; 5:11; 14:3; 20:2) or nation (2:20). Joshua presents the happening as a largely military event, whereas Judges sees it as a slower and more complex process. Judges views Israel as a federation, an association of tribes with no ongoing central authority: interim leadership was given by the judges. The stories tell of judges leading a tribe or group of tribes; the largest group is in the Song of Deborah and includes apparently all the northern tribes but not Judah or Simeon.

Early Israel was a largely agricultural and non-urban group, a peasant population. The leaders that arise in such systems are temporary, and their service is based not on inherited position (as a king's is) nor on permanent structures (such as election in an oligarchy or democracy). Max Weber (1864–1920), the German social scientist, called the basis for such leadership 'charisma', after the New Testament term for 'divine gift'.

Figure of the god Baal, 14th century BC, from Tartus on the Syrian coast

The significance of the book

The way to understand Judges is to see that Israel was living on a 'threshold' or 'border' of life, an experience sometimes described as 'liminal'. The book asks: How did Israel live without a great leader? How did Israel live with attacks from neighbours like the Philistines to the west or the Midianites to the south? How did the Canaanite city dwellers, who were already in the land, react to Israel and the changes Israel made? How did the groups and tribes of Israelites get on with each other? These are all questions about boundaries and about being on the threshold of something new. The most important threshold is the one that separates people from God, Israel from Yahweh. On one side of this threshold, nearer to God, are various divine messengers or angels: the stories of the angels of Bochim (Judges 2:1), Gideon (6:11–24), Manoah and his wife (13:2–23), and the curser of Meroz (5:23) are stories of the way Yahweh speaks to Israel. On the other side of the divine/human threshold, nearer to Israel, are various leaders known as the 'judges'. These dozen saviours of this or that tribe or groups of tribes put into practice the divine will and the divine plan. The judges are said to be 'raised up' by Yahweh, and are thereby associated with the actions of God. The Gideon story, combining divine revelation with judgeship, is the richest of the major stories in the book.

Outline

(I) **Prologues (1:1–3:6)**
  (A) *Argument (1:1–2:5)*
  (a) Three southern tribes (1:1–21)
  (b) Six northern tribes (1:22–36)
  (c) Divine rebuke (2:1–5)
  (B) *Preface (2:6–3:6)*
  (a) New generation (2:6–10)
  (b) Apostaśy (2:11–23)
  (c) Temptations (3:1–6)

(II) **Othniel–Abimelech (3:7–9:57)**
  (A) *Othniel (3:7–11)*
  (B) *Ehud (3:12–30)*
  (C) *Shamgar (3:31)*

Luton Sixth Form College Library

(D) Deborah and Baraq (4:1–24)
(E) Deborah's Song (5:1–31)
(F) Gideon's call (6:1–40)
(G) Gideon's victory (7:1–22)
(H) Gideon's supporters (7:23–8:3)
(I) Gideon's critics (8:4–21)
(J) Gideon's ephod (8:22–28)
(K) Gideon's family (8:29–35)
(L) Abimelech (9:1–57)

(III) Tola–Samson (10:1–16:31)
(A) Tola and Jair (10:1–5)
(B) Jephthah's enemies (10:6–18)
(C) Jephthah's call (11:1–11)
(D) Jephthah's victory (11:12–33)
(E) Jephthah's daughter (11:34–40)
(F) Jephthah's critics (12:1–7)
(G) Ibzan, Elon, and Abdon (12:8–15)
(H) Samson's birth (13:1–25)
(I) Samson's marriage (14:1–15:8)
(J) Samson's rampage (15:9–20)
(K) Samson's loves (16:1–22)
(L) Samson's death (16:23–31)

(IV) Epilogues (17:1–21:25)
(A) Dan and Micah (17:1–18:31)
(a) Micah's shrine (17:1–13)
(b) Dan's migration (18:1–31)
(B) From Gibeah to Shiloh (19:1–21:25)
(a) Outrage at Gibeah (19:1–30)
(b) Assembly at Mizpah (20:1–48)
(c) Rape at Jabesh-gilead and at Shiloh (21:1–25)

Philistine, with distinctive headdress. From a sculpture in the temple of Ramses III at Medinet Habu

HIGHLIGHT

Samson's death
Judges 16:23–31

[23]Now the lords of the Philistines gathered to offer a great sacrifice to their god Dagon, and to rejoice; for they said, 'Our god has given Samson our enemy into our hand.' [24]When the people saw him, they praised their god; for they said, 'Our god has given our enemy into our hand, the ravager of our country, who has killed many of us.' [25]And when their hearts were merry, they said, 'Call Samson, and let him entertain us.' So they called Samson out of the prison, and he performed for them. They made him stand between the pillars; [26]and Samson said to the attendant

who held him by the hand, 'Let me feel the pillars on which the house rests, so that I may lean against them.' [27]Now the house was full of men and women; all the lords of the Philistines were there, and on the roof there were about three thousand men and women, who looked on while Samson performed.

[28]Then Samson called to the Lord and said, 'Lord God, remember me and strengthen me only this once, O God, so that with this one act of revenge I may pay back the Philistines for my two eyes.' [29]And Samson grasped the two middle pillars on which the house rested, and he leaned his weight against them, his right hand on the one and his left hand on the other. [30]Then Samson said, 'Let me die with the Philistines.' He strained with all his might; and the house fell on the lords and all the people who were in it. So those he killed at his death were more than those he had killed during his life. [31]Then his brothers and all his family came down and took him and brought him up and buried him between Zorah and Eshtaol in the tomb of his father Manoah. He had judged Israel twenty years.

TEN

1–2 Samuel

The material in this chapter is digested from NJBC article 9, '1–2 Samuel', by Antony F. Campbell, SJ and James W. Flanagan.

Agate Philistine seal found at Dundrum, Ireland; 7th century BC. Reproduced by courtesy of the Trustees of the British Museum

The text and its composition

The contents were assembled over a period of hundreds of years, stretching from the beginnings of the monarchy and the end of the period of the judges (11th–10th centuries BC) to the exile and after (6th–5th centuries). Some passages are duplicated, others lack continuity. Some scholars have tried to explain the text using the same theory as for the Pentateuch. Others have talked about basic 'building blocks', originally independent narratives rather than continuous sources. These are:

(1) A possible prophetic record (1 Samuel 1–2 Kings 10)
(2) The Ark narrative (1 Samuel 4–6; 2 Samuel 6)
(3) Story of David's rise to power (1 Samuel 16–2 Samuel 5)
(4) Nathan's prophecy (2 Samuel 7)
(5) The report of the Ammonite war (2 Samuel 10)
(6) The succession narrative (2 Samuel 9–20; 1 Kings 1–2) (the story of David's later years).

Historical significance of 1–2 Samuel

The books deal with the period in which two significant elements came into prominence in Israel: one is the figure of the prophet; the other, the institution of kingship. 1 Samuel opens with the emergence of Samuel as a prophet to all Israel; 2 Samuel closes on the eve of the first dynastic transfer of royal power, from David to Solomon. The traditions that form 1–2 Samuel grapple with the interplay of these two forces and their implications for Israel's survival as a nation and its understanding of itself as people of God.

Outline

(I) **Hints of change (1 Samuel 1:1–7:17)**
  (A) *The emergence of a prophet (1:1–4:1a)*
  (a) Birth of Samuel (1:1–2:11)
  (b) Emergence of Samuel among the sons of Eli (2:12–3:18)
  (c) Recognition before all Israel (3:19–4:1a)
  (B) *The departure of the Ark (4:1b–7:1)*
  (a) Departure from Israel (4:1b–22)
  (b) Disaster in the land of the Philistines (5:1–12)
  (c) Return to Kiriath-jearim (6:1–7:1)
  (C) *The judgeship of Samuel (7:2–17)*

(II) **Introduction of a new epoch in Israel (1 Samuel 8:1–12:25)**
  (A) *Demand for a king (8:1–22)*
  (B) *Secret anointing of Saul as king-to-be (9:1–10:16)*
  (C) *Public acclamation of Saul as king (10:17–27)*
  (D) *Demonstration of Saul's kingly charisma (11:1–15)*
  (E) *Instruction of Israel by Samuel on ways of kingship (12:1–25)*

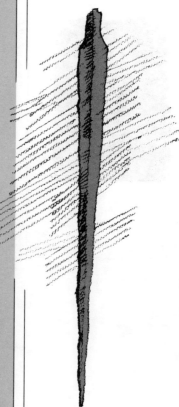

Iron two-edged
Philistine sword
blade

(III) **The beginnings of the kingdom (1 Samuel 13:1–2 Samuel 5:10)**
  (A) *Rejection of Israel's first king (13:1–15:35)*
  (a) First account of rejection (13:1–15a)
  (b) Battle at Michmash (13:15b–14:52)
  (c) Second account of rejection (15:1–35)
  (B) *Rise to power of Israel's second king (1 Samuel 16:1–2 Samuel 5:10)*
  (a) Secret anointing of David (16:1–13)
  (b) Demonstration of David's charisma (16:14–18:5)
  (c) Unfolding of David's rise and Saul's decline (18:6–31:13)
    (i) First signs (18:6–16)
    (ii) Conflict at court (18:17–21:1 [NRSV 20:42])
    (iii) Open rupture (21:2[1]–27:12)
    (iv) Ultimate failure of Saul (28:1–31:13)
  (d) Recognition of David's leadership (2 Samuel 1:1–5:10)
    (i) Report of Saul's and Jonathan's deaths (1:1–16)
    (ii) Elegy for Saul and Jonathan (1:17–27)
    (iii) David achieves power over Judah (2:1–7)
    (iv) Activity in the northern camp (2:8–11)
    (v) Hostilities erupt between David's and Saul's houses (2:12–3:1)
    (vi) Northern attempts at peace and leadership fail (3:2–4:12)

(1) Hebron genealogy (3:2–5)
(2) Abner's negotiations fail (3:6–39)
(3) Ishbaal falls (4:1–12)
(vii) David leads Israel (5:1–5)
(viii) Zion is chosen as administrative centre of the confederations (5:6–10)

(IV) David centralizes Yahweh's power in Jerusalem (2 Samuel 5:11–12:31)
(A) *Relocating the Ark and securing allegiances (5:11–8:18)*
(a) David secures his position (5:11–16)
(b) Philistine battles (5:17–25)
(c) Transfer of the Ark to Jerusalem (6:1–23)
(d) Oracle of Nathan and prayer of David (7:1–29)
(e) David subdues and allies with other nations to the east (8:1–14)
(f) David's administration (8:15–18)
(B) *Conflicts in David's palace (9:1–12:31)*
(a) Meribaal's protection and house arrest (9:1–13)
(b) David is tested by an eastern coalition (10:1–19 [+ 11:1 + 12:26–31])
(c) The Bathsheba affair, Nathan's judgement, and Solomon's birth (11:1–12:25)
(d) David assumes direct control of the Ammonites (12:26–31)

(V) David loses and regains Jerusalem (13:1–20:25)
(A) *Absalom challenges his father's sovereignty (13:1–19:9a)*
(a) The rape of Tamar and Absalom's revenge (13:1–39)
(b) Absalom's exile and reconciliation (14:1–33)
(c) Absalom's attempt at succession (15:1–12)
(d) David abandons Jerusalem and the Ark (15:13–16:14)
(e) Absalom's foolishness (16:15–17:23)
(f) David in exile (17:24–19:9a)
(B) *David processes to Jerusalem (19:9b–44)*
(C) *Further attempts to topple David (20:1–25)*

(VI) David prepares for Israel's future under Yahweh (21:1–24:25)
(A) *Suppression of the sons of Saul and their enemy, the Philistines (21:1–22)*
(a) David allows the massacre of Saul's house (21:1–14)
(b) Philistine unrest (21:15–22)
(B) *Praise and thanksgiving (22:1–23:7)*
(a) The Psalm of David (22:1–51)
(b) David's last words (23:1–7)

Slinger, 10th century
BC. *From a Hittite sculpture at Tell Halaf, northern Syria*

HIGHLIGHT

The anointing of David as king
I Samuel 16:1–13

¹The Lord said to Samuel, 'How long will you grieve over Saul? I have rejected him from being king over Israel. Fill your horn with oil and set out; I will send you to Jesse the Bethlehemite, for I have provided for myself a king among his sons.' ²Samuel said, 'How can I go? If Saul hears of it, he will kill me.' And the Lord said, 'Take a heifer with you, and say, "I have come to sacrifice to the Lord." ³Invite Jesse to the sacrifice, and I will show you what you shall do; and you shall anoint for me the one whom I name to you.' ⁴Samuel did what the Lord commanded, and came to Bethlehem. The elders of the city came to meet him trembling, and said, 'Do you come peaceably?' ⁵He said, 'Peaceably; I have come to sacrifice to the Lord; sanctify yourselves and come with me to the sacrifice.' And he sanctified Jesse and his sons and invited them to the sacrifice.

⁶When they came, he looked on Eliab and thought, 'Surely the Lord's anointed is now before the Lord.' ⁷But the Lord said to Samuel, 'Do not look on his appearance or on the height of his stature, because I have rejected him; for the Lord does not see as mortals see; they look on the outward appearance, but the Lord looks on the heart.' ⁸Then Jesse called Abinadab, and made him pass before Samuel. He said, 'Neither has the Lord chosen this one.' ⁹Then Jesse made Shammah pass by. And he said, 'Neither has the Lord chosen this one.' ¹⁰Jesse made seven of his sons pass before Samuel, and Samuel said to Jesse, 'The Lord has not chosen any of these.' ¹¹Samuel said to Jesse, 'Are all your sons here?' And he said, 'There remains yet the youngest, but he is keeping the sheep.' And Samuel said to Jesse, 'Send and bring him; for we will not sit down until he comes here.' ¹²He sent and brought him in. Now he was ruddy, and had beautiful eyes, and was handsome. The Lord said, 'Rise and anoint him; for this is the one.' ¹³Then Samuel took the horn of oil, and anointed him in the presence of his brothers; and the spirit of the Lord came mightily upon David from that day forward. Samuel then set out and went to Ramah.

1–2 Kings

The material in this chapter is digested from NJBC article 10, '1–2 Kings', by Jerome T. Walsh and Christopher T. Begg.

The text and its composition

The authors of the two books of the Kings are less interested in accurately chronicling events, no matter how important they may seem to a modern historian, than in explaining the tragic fate of Yahweh's people. They choose sources, arrange and modify them, expand and supplement them with this goal in mind, rather than with a view to accuracy, verifiability, or completeness. The sources used are many and varied, ranging from popular tales (1 Kings 3:16–27) and miracle stories (2 Kings 2) to archival records (1 Kings 4:7–19). In Kings, the writer cites three sources by name and repeatedly refers the reader to them for further information: The Acts of Solomon, The Chronicles of the Kings of Judah, and The Chronicles of the Kings of Israel. Unfortunately, all three are now lost.

The final version of Kings dates from the exile: 2 Kings 25:27 records the release of Jehoiachin from prison (*ca.* 560 BC) but the writer is unaware of the edict of Cyrus and the return from exile (538–537). Many scholars today, however, believe that the major work of shaping these books was done before the exile, perhaps in Josiah's reign (640–609), with the narrative being brought up to date during the exile.

The authors' purpose in writing 1–2 Kings

The purpose is to explain how Yahweh's people came to be in exile. The explanation, essentially, is that both Israel and Judah, in the person of their respective kings, were guilty of unfaithfulness to the worship of God so terrible that destruction was the only fit punishment. A number of subsidiary themes contribute to this explanation: the character of David and of Jeroboam I, the worship and the Temple, and the role of prophets.

David

(1) David is for Kings the ideal ruler of Judah. He was faithful and obedient to Yahweh (1 Kings 3:14); therefore Yahweh promised him an unending dynasty (1 Kings 8:25; cf. 2 Samuel 7:4–16). But beginning with Solomon, most of the southern kings fail to follow David's way (1 Kings 9:4–9; 11:4, 6; 15:3; 2 Kings 16:2); even those who are faithful are praised with reservations (1 Kings 15:11–14; 2 Kings 14:3–4); only Hezekiah and Josiah receive unqualified approval (1 Kings 18:3–5; 22:2; 23:25).

Jeroboam

Jeroboam I, by contrast, represents unfaithful Israel. Though chosen by Yahweh (1 Kings 11:26–40), Jeroboam became guilty of worshipping idols (12:26–31). This the writer calls the 'sin of Jeroboam', and he considers it the foundational evil of the Northern Kingdom. Israelite kings are condemned without exception, almost always for 'holding to the sin of Jeroboam'. Only Ahab is more roundly condemned for introducing the cult

The Black Obelisk from Nimrud, ca. 825 BC

Israelites pay tribute to Shalmaneser III of Assyria; detail from the Black Obelisk. Reproduced by courtesy of the Trustees of the British Museum

of Baal (1 Kings 16:30–33). These deviations led to Israel's destruction at the hands of Assyria, as the commentary on the fall of Samaria makes clear (2 Kings 17).

(2) Kings of both Judah and Israel are judged in terms of their faithfulness to the worship of God. In the north, the criterion for condemnation is the 'sin of Jeroboam'. In the south, the 'high places' (sacrificial sites on hilltops used in the pagan cult and perhaps in the popular cult of Yahweh as well) are the commonest aberration for which the kings are condemned, while reform of worship is a basis for praise (1 Kings 15:11–13; 22:46; 2 Kings 18:3–5, 22–23).

(3) The construction and dedication of the Temple are the centrepiece of the story of Solomon and that king's lasting glory, even though the judgement on Solomon is ultimately negative (1 Kings 11:9–13). The Temple remains a continuing topic of interest in Kings.

(4) Finally, the role of prophets in the unfolding history of Israel is a central concern. 1–2 Kings contain numerous prophetic narratives, including lengthy collections about Elijah and Elisha. Through the prophets Yahweh continually confronted the errant people to call them back to God's ways. The prophetic word could be an assurance of victory (1 Kings 20:13) or a promise of peace (2 Kings 7:1), a threat (1 Kings 22:17) or a condemnation (2 Kings 1:3–4). In every case it is Yahweh announcing in advance the plan of history – a plan that reaches fulfilment inexorably. Throughout 1–2 Kings are very many notices of fulfilled prophecies; the point is clear: Yahweh is in charge of history and 'reveals his counsels to his servants the prophets' (Amos 3:7).

Outline

(I) **The reign of Solomon (1 Kings 1:1–11:43)**
  (A) *Prophetic intervention into the royal succession (1:1–2:11)*
  (a) The king is cold (1:1–4)
  (b) Adonijah exalts himself (1:5–6)
  (c) Adonijah's faction gathers to celebrate (1:7–10)
  (d) Nathan plots to make Solomon king (1:11–14)
  (e) David decides for Solomon (1:15–37)

(I) *Prophetic intervention into the royal succession (11:26–40)*

(J) *Transition (11:41–43)*

(II) **Parallel history of the kingdoms of Israel and Judah (1 Kings 12:1–2 Kings 17:41)**

(A) *Jeroboam I of Israel (12:1–14:20)*

(a) Ahijah announces Jeroboam's kingship (11:26–43)

(b) Political disunity (12:1–20)

(c) A Judahite prophet's approval (12:21–25)

(d) Jeroboam's cultic innovations (12:26–31)

(e) A Judahite prophet's condemnation (12:32–13:10)

(f) Prophetic disunity; evaluation (13:11–14)

(g) Ahijah announces the end of Jeroboam's kingship (14:1–20)

(B) *Early kings of Judah and Israel (14:21–16:34)*

(a) Early kings of Judah (14:21–15:24)

    (i) Rehoboam (14:21–31)

    (ii) Abijam (15:1–8)

    (iii) Asa (15:9–24)

(b) Early kings of Israel (15:25–16:34)

    (i) Nadab (15:25–32)

    (ii) Baasha (15:33–16:7)

    (iii) Elah (16:8–14)

    (iv) Zimri; civil strife (16:15–22)

    (v) Omri (16:23–28)

    (vi) Ahab (16:29–34)

(C) *The story of Elijah the Tishbite (17:1–19:21)*

(a) Elijah decrees a drought (17:1–24)

(b) Elijah returns the rain (18:1–46)

    (i) Entrance (18:1–6)

    (ii) Elijah and the servant (18:7–16)

    (iii) Elijah and Ahab (18:17–20)

    (iv) Contest of the gods (18:21–40)

    (v) Elijah and Ahab (18:41–42a)

    (vi) Elijah and the servant (18:42b–45a)

    (vii) They leave (18:45b–46)

(c) Elijah runs from danger (19:1–21)

(D) *The downfall of Ahab (20:1–22:38)*

(a) Syria attacks Israel (20:1–43)

    (i) Ben-hadad demands tribute (20:1–11)

    (ii) The battle of Samaria (20:12–21)

    (iii) The battle of Aphek (20:22–30)

    (iv) Ben-hadad pleads for his life (20:31–34)

    (v) Prophetic narrative (20:35–43)

(b) Naboth's vineyard (21:1–29)

    (i) Naboth's murder (21:1–16)

    (ii) Prophetic narrative (21:17–29)

(III) Judah on its own (2 Kings 18:1–25:30)
  (A) Hezekiah (715–687) (18:1–20:21)
  (a) Introduction to Hezekiah's reign (18:1–12)
  (b) The Assyrian threat (18:13–19:37)
  (c) Two appended narratives and conclusion (20:1–21)
  (B) Manasseh (687–642) and Amon (642–640)
    (21:1–26)
  (C) Josiah (640–609) (22:1–23:30)
  (D) Jehoahaz (609) and Jehoiakim (609–598)
    (23:31–24:7)
  (E) Jehoiachin (598–597) and Zedekiah (597–587)
    (24:8–25:30)

HIGHLIGHT

Elijah and the widow's son
I Kings 17:17–24

[17]After this the son of the woman, the mistress of the house, became ill; his illness was so severe that there was no breath left in him. [18]She then said to Elijah, 'What have you against me, O man of God? You have come to me to bring my sin to remembrance, and to cause the death of my son!' [19]But he said to her, 'Give me your son.' He took him from her bosom, carried him up into the upper chamber where he was lodging, and laid him on his own bed. [20]He cried out to the Lord, 'O Lord my God, have you brought calamity even upon the widow with whom I am staying, by killing her son?' [21]Then he stretched himself upon the child three times, and cried out to the Lord, 'O Lord my God, let this child's life come into him again.' [22]The Lord listened to the voice of Elijah; the life of the child came into him again, and he revived. [23]Elijah took the child, brought him down from the upper chamber into the house, and gave him to his mother; then Elijah said, 'See, your son is alive.' [24]So the woman said to Elijah, 'Now I know that you are a man of God, and that the word of the Lord in your mouth is truth.'

TWELVE

Introduction to

Prophetic

Literature

The nature of prophecy

Although Israelite prophecy was something special, we must recognize that it was part of a wider human culture. Most religions, if not all, have produced the phenomenon of prophecy either continuously or at some stage in their development. By prophecy we understand not specifically or even principally the forecasting of the future – a fairly late conception of what is essential to prophecy – but rather the interpretation of the mind and will of God. It is not the nature of biblical prophecy to see the future like a photograph. Prediction was, indeed, often part of the prophetic message, but prediction was permitted to the prophet always in terms of what he knew and what would be understood by his hearers. Isaiah's prophecy of Sennacherib's invasion (10:27–34) is a classical example: the prophecy was fulfilled, but under circumstances not expected by the prophet.

The means of prophetic communication were dreams, visions, ecstatic or mystical experiences, and various divinatory practices. The oracles of Balaam in Numbers 22–24 were regarded as true prophecies from Yahweh, although biblical traditions classified Balaam with the enemies of God and his people (Numbers 31:8, 16; Joshua 13:22; 2 Peter 2:15; Jude 11; Revelation 2:14). The same person might prophesy both truth and falsehood, depending on whether or not he had been touched by the Spirit of God.

The material in this chapter is digested from NJBC article 11, 'Introduction to Prophetic Literature', by Bruce Vawter, CM.

True and false prophets abound not only in ancient times, in the Old Testament and New Testament, within and without the people of God, but also in later times.

Prophecy in the ancient Near East

In the ancient Near East, of which Israel was a tiny part, it was a routine hazard to encounter the effects of ecstatic prophecy; they continued to be an embarrassment to Paul over a thousand years later (Acts 16:16–18). The graphic story told in 1 Kings 18:19–40 shows the character of ecstatic prophecy among the Canaanites in the time of Elijah. The behaviour of these Canaanites must have been very like that of the bands of ecstatic prophets of Yahweh mentioned in 1 Samuel 10:5–7, 10–13; 19:18–24 in the time of Saul.

Detail of an Assyrian relief showing Sargon II (king 721–705 BC), who conquered Samaria. Reproduced by courtesy of the Egyptian Museum, Turin

Prophet and priest

The Near Eastern pattern makes little or no distinction between prophet and priest. But in Israel, the difference between the two was well defined. The Israelite priesthood was **hereditary** and **hierarchical**, whereas prophecy was **charismatic**; prophets like Ezekiel and Jeremiah might also be priests, but there is no indication that such a man as Amos was a priest – indeed, many indications are against it. Yet, it is hard to separate the priestly from the prophetic functions of Samuel in the story of 1 Samuel 9:11–26. Throughout he is called 'the seer', and in 1 Samuel 19:18–24 we see that he heads a band of ecstatic prophets; yet some of his main duties are to bless the sacrifice on the 'high place' and to preside at the sacrificial meal. There was, indeed, in the ancient Near East, of which Israel was a small part, a fairly consistent pattern of prophecy – or inspired men and women who in various ways spoke the word of God to their fellow believers, whether of Babylonia, Canaan, or Israel. The recognition of this common pattern does not detract from, but instead enhances, the unique qualities of biblical prophecy.

> **hereditary** <
handed down in a family

> **hierarchical** <
controlled by the priests

> **charismatic** <
free, not controlled

Early prophecy in Israel

Biblical tradition traces the origins of Israelite prophecy to Moses, yet we must admit that we do not hear much about prophets before the late period of the judges and the early monarchy, when they are mentioned in connection with the Philistine wars. This is not surprising, because a major function of these ecstatic prophets seems to have been to stimulate patriotic and religious fervour. Usually these men prophesied in groups whose experiences are described in such passages as 1 Samuel 10:6–8, 10–13. Hence, they are often given the name 'sons of the prophets', which has been variously interpreted as 'members of prophetic guilds', 'professional prophets', and 'prophetic disciples'.

'Cult' and 'court' prophets

These prophets are found attached to the sanctuaries as 'cult' prophets or serving the king as 'court' prophets. They wore a distinctive dress of haircloth (2 Kings 1:18; Zechariah 13:4) and often bore other distinguishing marks (Zechariah 13:6), possibly at times a **tonsure** (2 Kings 2:23).

The ecstatic experience transformed the prophet, made him 'another man' (1 Samuel 10:6). In such a state, his antics could become grotesque, so that he could be called 'a madman' (2 Kings 9:11), while his profession was regarded as hardly in keeping with responsible, respectable citizenship (1 Samuel 10:11).

Classical prophecy in Israel

By 'classical prophecy' we mean the prophecy of those whom the Old Testament has taught us to regard as examples of what is distinctive about Israelite prophets – all that separates them from the Near Eastern pattern. These prophets are those whose teaching has been preserved in the Old Testament and especially those whose names appear at the head of the prophetic books.

False and true prophets

The distinction between false and true prophecy in the days of the classical prophets was not always clear. Possession of the ecstatic prophetic 'spirit' was no sure criterion: prophets might be touched by the spirit and still prophesy falsehood, and most of the classical prophets give no signs of having been ecstatics.

The fulfilment of prophecy, even if it had been always evident to the prophet's contemporaries, was not an infallible sign, as Deuteronomy 13:2ff. shows; moreover, true prophecy apparently often went unfulfilled, discouraging even the prophet himself (cf. Jeremiah 20:7ff.). When the prophet Hananiah prophesied his own wishful thinking in predicting the end of the Babylonian exile in two years and the restoration of Jeconiah (Jeremiah 28:1ff.), Jeremiah could offer only his conviction of the truth of his own contrary prophecy. 'Amen! Thus may Yahweh do! May he fulfil the things you have prophesied ...' Wistfully Jeremiah said this, for he would very much have preferred to prophesy as Hananiah did; however, he knew he could not, for such was not the word of Yahweh.

The prophet's authority

The classical prophets could offer their contemporaries only the testimony of the prophetic word itself; it is the word itself that must find a response in the heart tuned to the reception of God's word. Their own conviction of the truth of their prophecy rests on the same foundations; therefore, the story of the prophetic call, the experience of the divine presence, plays a prominent role in the records of the literary prophets. This testimony constitutes their credentials, both for themselves and for those to whom they have been sent. The prophetic speech attributed to Nathan in 2 Samuel 12:1ff., a fearless revelation of the moral will of Yahweh, the God of Israel's covenant, is to be the characteristic of classical prophecy, setting it apart from all the other prophecy, both of Israel and its neighbours. In like manner, Elijah denounces Ahab's sin in 1 Kings 21:17–24, in language worthy of an Amos or a Jeremiah.

The classical prophets best known to us are the so-called literary prophets of the 8th, 7th and 6th centuries BC. In a roughly chronological order, these are Amos, Hosea, Isaiah, Micah, Nahum, Zephaniah, Habakkuk, Jeremiah, and Ezekiel. Classical prophecy should not be limited to these great names, however. There are other literary prophets whose names we do not know. One of these is a prophet of the exile whom we call Second Isaiah.

Prophecy in Israel after the exile

During the exile Israel was given a new vision of its relationship with Yahweh through the great prophets Jeremiah, Ezekiel and Second Isaiah. Prophecy after the exile, by comparison, lacks much of the vigour and spontaneity of the 'classical' prophets. These later prophets, listed in chronological order, are the prophet or prophets responsible for the final section of Isaiah, Haggai, Zechariah (chapters 1–8), Malachi, Obadiah, Joel, and the anonymous prophets who produced Zechariah 9–11, 12–14. In general, the prophets after the exile could take a more 'optimistic' view of Israel's destiny than could the prophets before, for the doom had now come and gone, and a new

> **apocalyptic** <
revelation about the end
of the world
(see Chapter 19)

hope could be found in the figure of the Servant of the Lord revealed by Isaiah.

Zechariah and Malachi show a concern for the Temple, the law, and matters of worship that cannot be discovered in a pre-exilic prophet. This concern, however, is a continuation of Ezekiel's. Third Isaiah also has been greatly influenced by Ezekiel and the Second Isaiah. The bold **apocalyptic** imagery of Zechariah, Joel, and the Isaiah supplements (Isaiah 24–27, 34–35) was foreshadowed in Ezekiel, whom many regard as the father of apocalyptic.

The disappearance of prophecy in Israel was as unobtrusive as its beginning; it would be impossible to decide who was the last Old Testament prophet. In the last 200 years BC, the wisdom writers carried on the tradition inherited from prophecy without, however, claiming to possess the prophetic spirit.

The distinctive character of Israelite prophecy

There is no non-Israelite parallel for classical prophecy, either in form or in content. Israelite prophecy broke with the ancient pattern when it began to produce prophets who not only spoke from the Israelite institutions but also judged them and became their conscience.

The prophets' attitude to the Temple and its sacrifices

The prophets were concerned that sacrifices had lost their meaning. These sacrifices, say Amos and Jeremiah, Yahweh did not command. Love, not sacrifice, is the will of God, says Hosea; or, as we might rephrase it, there can be no true sacrifice without love.

Jeremiah went to the Temple that he denounced, as did Isaiah before him. Ezekiel, however, who clearly believed in the restoration of Jerusalem's Temple, nevertheless knew full well that Yahweh himself was the true sanctuary who alone could give any meaning to the Temple built with hands (cf. 11:16).

The prophetic attitude to the Temple worship was like the prophetic attitude to everything – forms were always secondary to the realities they signified.

The prophets' attitude to the monarchy

The prophets' attitude to the monarchy showed a concern for spiritual realities and a lack of interest in forms as such. Prophecy never headed any movement in Israel to replace the monarchy with another form of government. This is fortunate, for there is no indication that the prophetic tradition ever possessed either the taste or the talent for practical politics. It is surely not by accident that nowhere in the biblical traditions is it recorded that Solomon either sought the advice of prophecy or received a prophetic oracle. Of course, this was as it should have been. The function of prophecy was to form the conscience of a people, not to dictate its politics. The work of prophecy was to make the kingship of Israel truly Israelite.

Religion and morality

The prophetic connection of religion with morality is also something unique. The prophets found the basis for this connection in the common tradition they shared with their contemporaries, but they strengthened the connection so that it could never again be broken.

The prophets were not moralists, statesmen, or politicians; they were prophets. Their function was to reveal the mind of God, which they understood as others did not. It was the function of others to translate the prophetic word into plans of action whether for personal or public life. The tragedy of Israel was that it had priests who would not know God and his law, rulers who made their laws apart from God, and a people who would not heed the prophetic word.

Do we have the prophets' original words?

The answer to this question is not simple, nor is there a single answer in every case.

In general, we probably have good reason to think that in most cases we have a substantial transcription of the prophet's original words. It is not unthinkable that in some instances these have actually been written by the prophet himself. Writing was not really necessary, however, as the poetic structure itself enabled the prophet's words to be remembered and passed on.

The most characteristically prophetic of the material found in the prophetic books is the oracle – i.e., the revelation of Yahweh. The oracle is ordinarily a brief poetic utterance, although oracles of a similar kind have often been joined into a larger unity, sometimes by the prophet himself but usually by an editor. To underline the divine origin of the oracle, the prophet has often prefaced, concluded, or interlarded it with appropriate reminders: 'So says Yahweh'; 'Yahweh speaks', etc. However, the prophet may just as easily speak in his own name as the accredited spokesman for God.

Our concern with the prophetic literature is not merely the interest we have in an ancient religious phenomenon. Prophecy not only was, but still is, the word of God. If all Scripture is the word of God, that is pre-eminently true of the prophecy in which God chose to speak directly with his people. It is, furthermore, not just a record, but the living word of a living God.

We must recognize two things. First, the prophetic word is greater than the prophet, which the prophets themselves would have been the first to acknowledge. We know of this greatness from the New Testament fulfilment, which is a continually living and growing reality.

Second, the prophetic word is the word of Isaiah, or Amos, or Jeremiah, or perhaps a man whose name we do not know – a man, in any case, who was personally involved in the word, who lived for it and was prepared to die for it. If we are to take in this message as God has delivered it to us, we must take it in as it has come through the prophets of Israel. Anything less is not the prophetic word.

THIRTEEN

Amos

The prophet and his times

Amos is the first of the prophets whose oracles have come down to us in the form of a book. According to 1:1 he was from the small town of Tekoa in the hill country of Judah just south of the Israel–Judah border. The extent of his prophetic career is uncertain. He prophesied at Bethel, one of the main centres of worship in the Northern Kingdom, near the Israel–Judah border (7:10–17), and perhaps elsewhere as well. He was active in the reigns of Uzziah of Judah (783–742 BC) and Jeroboam II of Israel (786–746) (1:1). By trade he was a breeder of livestock and a 'tender of mulberry figs' (7:14) whose job was to puncture the immature fruit to make it turn sweet. Although Amos undoubtedly prophesied at religious centres (7:10–14) and was familiar with the language of worship (4:4; 5:4–5, 14), his precise relationship to the priests is not known.

The material in this chapter is digested from NJBC article 13, 'Amos', by Michael L. Barré, SS.

Historical events in the time of Amos

Amos's career took place during a period of great material prosperity for Israel, but also a period of social and religious corruption. Politically, it was the calm before the storm – or rather, between the storms. During the second half of the 9th century Israel had felt the military might of Assyria: Shalmaneser III (859–825) exacted tribute from Jehu. After this, Assyrian power in the area weakened until the rise of Tiglath-pileser III (745–727). In 721 Samaria, the capital of the Northern Kingdom, fell.

The message of Amos

Four interrelated themes are of central importance in the book:

(1) Judgement

Of all the classical prophets, Amos's message is the least hopeful. Israel's fate – destruction – is certain, inescapable, total. Although Amos never refers directly to the Sinai covenant, this concept lies at the heart of his message of judgement. Yahweh had acknowledged Israel as his covenant people (3:1–2), but they had abused this privilege. Therefore, Yahweh was dissolving the covenant (cf. Hosea 1:9) and declaring war on Israel, who had now become his enemy. Like the messages of the other prophets, Amos's harsh words were directed in a particular way against the leadership – king (7:10–11), priests (7:16–17), and upper classes (4:1–3; 6:1). But the coming judgement would affect the entire people, for Israelite thought tends to perceive the nation as a unity, with a common destiny.

Ivory decorations from the palace of Ahab in Samaria, like those Amos protested against. Now in the Palestine Archaeological Museum, Jerusalem. Reproduced by courtesy of the Israel Antiquities Authority

(2) Social justice

A distinctive feature of Israelite religion was the connection between the relationship to one's neighbour and to God established by the covenant. The quality of a person's relationship to God depended to some extent on how a person related to fellow members of the community. At the time of Amos many among Israel's powerful had chosen to ignore this aspect of Israelite religion and to treat the disadvantaged as they wished. Wealthy landowners oppressed the less fortunate, taking over the landholdings of many poor Israelites. The prophet expresses Yahweh's distress at the maltreatment of these people (2:7; 4:1; 5:7, 11, 24; 8:4–6). This is the ultimate reason for Yahweh's decision to execute judgement on his people.

(3) The cult

There was no lack of religious fervour in Israel during this time (5:21–24). Amos mentions major worship centres – Bethel (3:14; 4:4; 5:5, 6; 7:10, 13), Gilgal (4:4; 5:5), and Dan (8:4) – and at times imitates the language of the cult (4:4–5; 5:4–6, 14). Those who disregarded the covenant and took advantage of the poor continued to go through the motions of worshipping the covenant God. Merchants were careful not to do business on days forbidden by divine law (8:4–8). Amos denounces this **hypocrisy**, at times with bitter irony (4:4–5). Unlike his near-contemporary Hosea, he has little to say on the question of worshipping other gods. In his view, the foremost sin involved in the religious life of Israel was its separation from concern for the neighbour (5:21–24).

> **hypocrisy** <
claiming to be religious but disregarding the teachings of the religion

(4) The word

Israel turned a deaf ear to the prophets who reproached them for their disloyalty and even tried to silence them (2:12; 7:12–13). In the eyes of Amos, this was a particularly grave offence, since it amounted to a rejection of Yahweh himself. The punishment would be a loss of the guiding word of Yahweh (8:11–12).

Outline

(I) **Editorial introduction (1:1–2)**
    (A) *The author (1.1)*
    (B) *Opening verse (1:2)*

(II) **Oracles against the nations (1:3–2:16)**
    (A) *Damascus (1:3–5)*
    (B) *Gaza (1:6–8)*
    (C) *Tyre (1:9–10)*
    (D) *Edom (1:11–12)*
    (E) *Ammon (1:13–15)*
    (F) *Moab (2:1–3)*
    (G) *Judah (2:4–5)*
    (H) *Israel (2:6–16)*

(III) **Three summonses to hear Yahweh's word (3:1–5:17)**
    (A) *People of Israel (3:1–15)*
    (a) Israel as Yahweh's covenant partner (3:1–2)
    (b) The source of the prophetic word (3:3–8)
    (c) Evil Samaria and its fate (3:9–11 + 12)
    (d) The houses of the wicked (3:13–15)
    (B) *Cows of Bashan (4:1–13)*
    (a) Oppression of the poor (4:1–3)
    (b) The cult and transgression (4:4–5)
    (c) Litany of unrepentance (4:6–12)
    (d) Hymn (4:13)
    (C) *House of Israel (5:1–17)*
    (a) Lamentation over Israel (5:2–3)
    (b) Seeking Yahweh (5:4–6)
    (c) Hymn (5:8–9)
    (d) Haters of righteousness (5:7, 10–13)
    (e) Seeking good (5:14–15)
    (f) Lamentation over Israel (5:16–17)

(IV) **Three warnings (5:18–6:14)**
    (A) *Warning to those who desire the day of Yahweh (5:18–20)*
    (B) *Israel's corrupt worship (5:21–27)*
    (C) *Warning to those secure in their riches (6:1–3)*
    (D) *Warning to the idle rich (6:4–7)*
    (E) *Devastation and aftermath (6:8–10)*
    (F) *The fruits of Israel's depravity (6:11–14)*

(V) **Five visions (7:1–9:10)**
    (A) *First vision: locusts (7:1–3)*
    (B) *Second vision: fire (7:4–6)*
    (C) *Third vision: plumb line (7:7–9)*
    (D) *Biographical interlude (7:10–17)*

HIGHLIGHT

Amos 5:21–24

[21]I hate, I despise your festivals,
 and I take no delight in your solemn assemblies.
[22]Even though you offer me your burnt offerings and grain
  offerings,
 I will not accept them;
 and the offerings of well-being of your fatted animals
 I will not look upon.
[23]Take away from me the noise of your songs;
 I will not listen to the melody of your harps.
[24]But let justice roll down like waters,
 and righteousness like an everflowing stream.

Hosea

The material in this chapter is digested from NJBC article 14, 'Hosea', by Dennis J. McCarthy, SJ, revised by Roland E. Murphy, OCarm.

The prophet and his times

We know nothing of Hosea, son of Beeri, except what we can learn from the book that collects his prophetic speeches. He spoke his oracles in the last days of Israel, the northern of the two kingdoms into which the Hebrews had divided themselves after the days of Solomon. We learn that his activity extended from the prosperous reign of Jeroboam II into the disastrous times that followed and saw the final disappearance of Israel from the political scene. All this is reflected in his oracles, which give us the date of their origin, from *ca.* 750 until after 732 BC.

Historical events in the time of Hosea

Assyria did not threaten Israel during the first half of the 8th century. In this breathing space the dynasty of Jehu was able to establish itself firmly in Israel, and under Jeroboam II (786–746) it expanded the kingdom to its greatest extent and raised it to its greatest heights of material prosperity.

However, Jeroboam's death corresponded closely to the accession of a vigorous king in Assyria, Tiglath-pileser III (745–727). The renewed pressure which that monarch soon applied to the states of Syria and Palestine revealed the hollowness of Israel's power. The political life of the nation deteriorated to a succession of palace revolutions, assassinations, and dynastic changes. In the 20 years between Jeroboam's death and the end of the kingdom six kings reigned in Israel.

The message of Hosea

This violent and ever-changing history is reflected on every page of his book. He condemns the empty pomp of Israel's purely external cult as well as the pride of the people in its wealth and military power. His message may be summarized:

● Against the kings of Israel

He has harsh words for the self-seeking of Israel's kings and leaders, their quarrels and plots, and the never-ending revolutions and changes of government. The prophet's quarrel is not with the idea of monarchy among the Hebrews; it is with the monarchy of the Northern Kingdom, which separated the nation from Judah and the legitimate kingship of David, at the same time founding the paganizing sanctuaries of Dan and Bethel. He holds up the threat of exile and final destruction, fulfilled to the letter in Israel's last days.

● Against the Baals

The political folly and the anarchy of Israel's last days were not Hosea's chief concern. He knew that they were only symptoms of the fundamental disorder: Israel had forsaken Yahweh, its true king and its salvation, to take up the cult of the fertility gods of Canaan, the Baals, so that it attributed its prosperity to this cult and not to Yahweh. The pervasive sin was that Yahweh was considered a god of the same kind as the Baals, bound to the land and a giver of agricultural plenty. His worship was performed with rites borrowed from the sanctuaries of the Baals. Such was the religion that Hosea saw around him masquerading as Yahwism, and against this he protested.

He is preoccupied with Israel's rejection of Yahweh, so that 'lie' and 'falsity' become characteristic words for sin in his vocabulary (cf. 7:1, 3; 10:2, 13; 11:12; 12:2, 8, 12). He repeatedly returns to the thought that Israel through its history has forgotten again and again the God who saved it from Egyptian slavery, strengthened it, and made it a nation. Even when the nation has seemed to return to Yahweh, Hosea sees it as lip service, insincere repentance filled with a proud confidence in its own deserts (e.g., 5:15–7:2).

Hosea draws a very clear conclusion: The people that has

turned away from its true God, Yahweh, must suffer punishment.

● **For the true traditions of Yahwism**
Again and again Hosea appeals to history, to the evidence that Yahweh has indeed been Israel's saviour. The vehicle for this is a formula like 'I am Yahweh who brought you out of Egypt'.

● **For Yahweh's union with Israel**
The richness of Hosea's idea of the true character of union with God is best evident in the image peculiarly his own, i.e., the presentation of Yahweh and Israel as husband and wife (chapters 1–3). His own experience of the marriage union, characterized by a tender, understanding love and an unshakeable fidelity despite his wife's unfaithfulness, provides an image of Yahweh's union with Israel. He knows that Yahweh's love is unchanging no matter how the partner breaks faith.

Hope for the future
Finally, Hosea holds out hope for the future. Warning and judgement are the heart of his message, but he also promises a future restoration that will finally bring Israel to Yahweh.

Outline

(I) **Hosea's marriage (1–3)**
  (A) *The prophet's children (1:2–2:3)*
  (B) *Accusation of the faithless wife (2:4–17)*
  (C) *Reconciliation (2:18–25)*
  (D) *The prophet and his wife (3:1–5)*

(II) **Condemnation of Hosea's contemporaries (4:1–9:9)**
  (A) *Yahweh's accusation of Israel (4:1–3)*
  (B) *Accusation of the leaders of Israel (4:4–5:7)*
  (C) *Political upheavals (5:8–14)*
  (D) *False repentance (5:15–7:2)*
  (E) *Corruption of the monarchy (7:3–12)*
  (F) *Lament over Israel (7:13–16)*
  (G) *Sins in politics and cult (8:1–14)*
  (H) *Exile without worship (9:1–6)*
  (I) *Rejection of the prophet (9:7–9)*

(III) Sin and history (9:10–14:1)
    (A) Sin and decline (9:10–17)
    (B) Punishment of unfaithfulness to God (10:1–8)
    (C) False confidence (10:9–15)
    (D) Love overcomes ingratitude (11:1–11)
    (E) Israel's perfidy (12:1–15)
    (F) Death sentence (13:1–14:1)

(IV) Epilogue: repentance and salvation (14:2–9)

HIGHLIGHT

The prophet and his wife
Hosea 3:1–5

[1]The Lord said to me again, 'Go, love a woman who has a lover and is an adulteress, just as the Lord loves the people of Israel, though they turn to other gods and love raisin cakes.' [2]So I bought her for fifteen shekels of silver and a homer of barley and a measure of wine. [3]And I said to her, 'You must remain as mine for many days; you shall not play the whore, you shall not have intercourse with a man, nor I with you.' [4]For the Israelites shall remain many days without king or prince, without sacrifice or pillar, without ephod or teraphim. [5]Afterward the Israelites shall return and seek the Lord their God, and David their king; they shall come in awe to the Lord and to his goodness in the latter days.

The material in this
chapter is digested
from NJBC article
15, 'Isaiah 1–39', by
Joseph Jensen, OSB
and William H.
Irwin, CSB.

FIFTEEN

Isaiah 1–39

How many Isaiahs were there?

The book of Isaiah consists of 66 chapters, but the actual words of Isaiah are found mainly in chapters 1–11 (largely from the reign of Ahaz) and 28–32 (largely from the days of Hezekiah). Authentic words of Isaiah are also found among the 'Oracles against the Nations' (chapters 13–23) and perhaps also in the historical appendix (chapters 24–27). Chapters 40–55 and 56–66 are collections that date from the time of the exile in Babylon and after it. In this book these collections are called Second Isaiah and Third Isaiah (see Chapter 21).

The prophet and his times

Isaiah was called to be a prophet 'in the year King Uzziah died' (6:1), i.e., in 742 BC. This was shortly after the accession in Assyria of Tiglath-pileser III (745–727), who was followed by other able and vigorous kings: indeed, the period of Isaiah's prophetic ministry was overshadowed by the irresistible power of Assyria and its plans for world empire.

Isaiah's prophetic ministry took place in and around Jerusalem. Little is known of his personal life. His devotion to Jerusalem traditions and the literary quality of his compositions suggest that he was from an upper-class family and was highly educated. He was married to a prophetess (8:3) and had two sons with symbolic names (7:3; 8:3, 18).

Some of Isaiah's oracles may have been given in the days of Jotham (750–735), perhaps some of those that relate to social justice and pagan practices, though such materials are difficult to date. Oracles that can be dated securely relate mainly to political crises that occurred under Ahaz (735–715) and Hezekiah (715–687).

Six-sided clay prism inscribed with an account of the military campaigns of Sennacherib (king of Assyria 705–681 BC), including his siege of Jerusalem. Reproduced by courtesy of the Trustees of the British Museum

77

In 735 Syria and Israel invaded Judah in an attempt to force it into the anti-Assyrian coalition. This led to the Assyrian conquest of Israel (733) and Syria (732), with Judah becoming an Assyrian slave-state in the process (2 Kings 16:7–9); most of the materials in 7:1–8:18 relate to this time.

There may have been a period of silence, but Isaiah spoke out again to protest at Egypt's attempt to press Judah to revolt against Assyria in 714 and possibly earlier (20:1–6; 18:1–6 probably also dates from this period and possibly some of chapter 19). The temptation was renewed at the death of Sargon II in 705, but now Isaiah's fervent, sometimes bitter, words failed to move Hezekiah, who revolted together with other small states, with promise of help from Egypt. The revolt was crushed in 701 with great devastation in Judah; Hezekiah had to surrender and pay a huge fine (22:1–14; 2 Kings 18:13–16). None of Isaiah's oracles can be securely dated after 701, and his ministry may have ended about that time.

*Entrance to the
Gihon spring in
Jerusalem, a vital part
of the city's ancient
water supply*

Isaiah's teaching

About holiness

Isaiah believed strongly in the holiness and kingly power of the God of Israel, both of which he experienced in his first vision (6:1–13); 'the Holy One of Israel' was his favourite title for Yahweh, whose 'glory' did not abide merely in Jerusalem but filled the whole earth (6:3).

About social justice

Oppression of weaker members of society offended God's holiness, and so Isaiah speaks vehemently concerning social justice (1:10–17, 21–26; 3:13–15; 5:1–10, 20–23; 10:1–4) and of the punishment for rejecting God's instruction (5:24).

About God's plan in history

God's power is such that all lies under his control, including the destinies of the mightiest nations, who are instruments of his policy (5:26–29; 7:18–19, 20; 10:5–6). Yahweh has a plan which he carries out in history with supreme wisdom (28:23–29) and power (14:26–27). All human plans are doomed to futility (7:4–7; 8:9–10). Thus, Isaiah thought it folly for Judah to attempt to carve out its own destiny, especially when this involved turning to Assyria (for help against Syria and Israel) or Egypt (for help in revolting against Assyria). To trust in Yahweh's help and protection is faith, whereas to fail to do so is lack of faith (7:9b; 8:17; 28:16–17; 30:1–5, 15; 31:1–3). Because the royal advisers, acting on purely human wisdom, led the kings Ahaz and Hezekiah into paths contrary to those advocated by Isaiah, he has a special attack on these so-called wise (5:18–19; 6:9–10; 29:13–14, 15–16). This same group was responsible for the administration of justice and are condemned for their failure to live up to the high ideals in which they were trained.

About pride and judgement

Isaiah saw pride as the greatest sin; it is the contradiction of faith and brings judgement (2:11–12, 17; 3:16; 5:15–16; 9:8–9; 10:7–16, 33; 28:1–4, 22; 29:5). Thus Isaiah sees Yahweh's intention to bring punishment on Israel and Judah (3:1–4:1; 5:25, 26–29; 6:11–13; 9:7–20). Such punishment can, however, prepare the way for restoration (1:21–26). Thus, Isaiah opened a door for hope.

Outline

(I) An introductory collection (1:1–31)
  (A) *The inscription (1:1)*
  (B) *Yahweh's complaint against his senseless children (1:2–3)*
  (C) *Jerusalem chastised (1:4–9)*
  (D) *Worship and justice (1:10–17)*
  (E) *The choice (1:18–20)*
  (F) *Purifying judgement on Jerusalem (1:21–28)*
  (G) *Crime and punishment (1:29–31)*

(II) Concerning Judah and Israel: Part I (2:1–5:30)
  (A) *Zion, focus of future peace (2:2–4)*
  (B) *The day of the Lord's judgement (2:6–22)*
  (C) *Disintegration of leadership and people (3:1–12)*
  (D) *Yahweh accuses the leaders (3:13–15)*
  (E) *Fate of the women of Jerusalem (3:16–4:1)*
  (F) *Jerusalem purified and protected (4:2–6)*
  (G) *Song of the Lord's vineyard (5:1–7)*
  (H) *Series of woes ([10:1–4] + 5:8–24)*
  (I) *Yahweh's outstretched hand (5:25–30)*

(III) Isaiah's memoirs (6:1–8:18 [9:6])
  (A) *Isaiah's call (6:1–13)*
  (B) *Encounter with Ahaz (7:1–9)*
  (C) *The sign of Immanuel (7:10–17)*
  (D) *Some fragments (7:18–25)*
  (E) *Maher-shalal-hash-baz (8:1–4)*
  (F) *The waters of Shiloah (8:5–8)*
  (G) *Vain plans of nations (8:9–10)*
  (H) *Isaiah conspires with Yahweh (8:11–15)*
  (I) *Waiting for the Lord (8:16–18)*
  (J) *Two additions (8:19–22)*
  (K) *Prince of Peace (8:23–9:6)*

(IV) Concerning Judah and Israel: Part II (9:7–12:6)
  (A) *Yahweh's outstretched hand (9:7–20 + 5:25–30)*
  (B) *Woe against oppressive rulers (10:1–4)*
  (C) *Woe against Assyria (10:5–15)*
  (D) *Some completions (10:16–27a)*
  (E) *Enemy advance (10:27b–34)*

(F) The future king (11:1–9)
(G) Later additions (11:10–16)
(H) A concluding song of thanksgiving (12:1–6)

(V) Oracles against the nations (13:1–23:18)

(A) Oracle against Babylon (13:1–22)
(B) The Gentiles and Israel's restoration (14:1–2)
(C) Taunting song against the king of Babylon (14:3–23)
(D) Yahweh's plan for Assyria (14:24–27)
(E) Warning to Philistia (14:28–32)
(F) Concerning Moab (15:1–16:14)
(G) Against Syria and Israel (17:1–11)
(H) Attack and deliverance (17:12–14)
(I) Embassy from Egypt (18:1–7)
(J) Concerning Egypt (19:1–25)
(K) Isaiah a sign and portent to Egypt (20:1–6)
(L) On the fall of Babylon (21:1–10)
(M) Concerning Dumah, Dedan, and Kedar (21:11–17)
(N) Oracle on the valley of vision (22:1–14)
(O) Shebna and Eliakim (22:15–25)
(P) Concerning Tyre (23:1–18)

(VI) The Apocalypse of Isaiah (24:1–27:13)

(A) Earth's final downfall (24:1–20)
(B) Yahweh's triumph in prophecy and song (24:21–27:1)
(a) Yahweh's Kingship (24:21–23)
(b) Hymn to Yahweh, safe refuge (25:1–5)
(c) The banquet on Mount Zion (25:6–10a)
(d) On Moab (25:10b–12)
(e) Prayer for deliverance (26:1–27:1)
(C) Vineyard and city revisited (27:2–13)
(a) Second song of the vineyard (27:2–6)
(b) The future of Jacob (27:7–13)

(VII) Oracles in Hezekiah's reign reinterpreted by promises of future salvation (28:1–33:24)

(A) Against Samaria (28:1–6)
(B) Against the ruling classes in Jerusalem (28:7–22)
(C) Ariel (29:1–8)
(D) Two speeches against the people's 'unknowing' (29:9–16)
(E) Salvation as reversal of the present situation (29:17–21)
(F) Jacob's future (29:22–24)
(G) Woe to rebellious sons (30:1–5)
(H) The burden of the beast(s) of the south (30:6–7)
(I) A testimony to the perils of rejecting the Holy One of Israel (30:8–17)
(J) Those who wait for Yahweh (30:18–26)

HIGHLIGHT

Isaiah's call
Isaiah 6:1–9

[1]In the year that King Uzziah died, I saw the Lord sitting on a throne, high and lofty; and the hem of his robe filled the temple. [2]Seraphs were in attendance above him; each had six wings: with two they covered their faces, and with two they covered their feet, and with two they flew. [3]And one called to another and said:
'Holy, holy, holy is the Lord of hosts;
the whole earth is full of his glory.'
[4]The pivots on the thresholds shook at the voices of those who called, and the house filled with smoke. [5]And I said: 'Woe is me! I am lost, for I am a man of unclean lips, and I live among a people of unclean lips; yet my eyes have seen the King, the Lord of hosts!'
[6]Then one of the seraphs flew to me, holding a live coal that had been taken from the altar with a pair of tongs. [7]The seraph touched my mouth with it and said: 'Now that this has touched your lips, your guilt has departed and your sin is blotted out.'
[8]Then I heard the voice of the Lord saying, 'Whom shall I send, and who will go for us?' And I said, 'Here am I; send me!' [9]And he said, 'Go and say to this people:
"Keep listening, but do not comprehend;
keep looking, but do not understand."'

SIXTEEN
Micah

The prophet and his times

The material in this chapter is digested from NJBC article 16, 'Micah', by Léo Laberge, OMI.

Micah was the last of the four prophets of the 8th century BC. The fall of Samaria (721) is used in his preaching as an example for Jerusalem. Micah came from the south-west of Judah, from Moresheth-gath. His reputation as a prophet of doom was preserved (see Jeremiah 26:18–19). His preaching is more concerned with sin and punishment than with politics or matters of worship. In his concern for social justice, he does not fear princes, prophets or priests. Not being a member of such groups, he affirms his independence through his message.

Historical events in the time of Micah

The times were bad. The Assyrian armies of Tiglath-pileser III conquered Damascus in 732 (with a part of Israel), and Samaria in 722. Ashdod fell in 711. Sennacherib was occupying part

Winged human figures. Ivory decoration from the palace of Ahab in Samaria. Reproduced by courtesy of the Palestine Archaeological Museum, Jerusalem

of the coastal land, menacing Moresheth and the area; see 1:10–15. Jerusalem was besieged in 701. Danger was not only external. Prophets, priests and judges accepted bribes; merchants cheated. There were pagan cults alongside the worship of Yahweh. There are oracles of doom followed by oracles of promise (doom: 1:2 to 3:12; 6:1 to 7:6; promise: 2:12–13; chapters 4–5). The concluding verses (7:8–20) seem to be a 'liturgical text' from the days after the exile.

The prophet's message

The people's rejection of God

Sin is the reason for the coming punishment. The Assyrian king is an unconscious instrument of God's wrath. A false sense of security (3:11: 'Is not the Lord in our midst?') has replaced allegiance to God.

Social justice

Like Hosea, Amos, and Isaiah, Micah is concerned with social justice and with the wickedness of all leaders, political and spiritual. While princes and merchants cheat and rob the poor and humble, especially women and children, priests and prophets adapt their words to please their audience. The leaders mistake evil for good and good for evil. Prophecy is rejected and sacrifices have no relation to God.

Covenant

The covenant is ignored and the Lord must turn his face away from the people and abandon them to their fate.

Hope

However, a message of hope is inserted in the middle of the book. The Temple shall become once again the centre of the land and of the world. People will come there in procession. A remnant will be the origin of a new Israel, and its leader will be a true shepherd, a bringer of peace in the name of the Lord. Thus, Bethlehem and Jerusalem will be renewed and the sources of sin will be eliminated.

The final verses of the book give us an example of the

liturgy to be performed: having confessed their sin, the people no longer ask: 'Where is Yahweh, your God?' A new exodus is taking place. God's wrath has abated and a new era is beginning. God's steadfast love will be shown to Jacob and Abraham, thus realizing the promise given to the fathers in the days of old.

Outline

(I) **The judgement of the Lord against his people (1:1–2:11)**
    (A) *The author (1:1)*
    (B) *Accusation against Samaria and Judah (1:2–7)*
    (C) *Lamentation (1:8–16)*
    (a) The dire situation of Jerusalem (1:8–9)
    (b) The fate of the southern cities (1:10–16)
    (D) *Social sins (2:1–11)*
    (a) Woe-oracle against the oppressors (2:1–5)
    (b) Rejection of prophecy (2:6–11)

(II) **A remnant will return (2:12–13)**

(III) **Condemnation of the leaders (3:1–12)**
    (A) *Against the perverse leaders (3:1–4)*
    (B) *Against the prophets (3:5–7), with a statement concerning Micah's mission (3:8)*
    (C) *Against the leaders, prophets and priests included (3:9–12)*

(IV) **A new dwelling place for God in a renewed Israel (4:1–5:14)**
    (A) *All nations will come to the Mount of the Lord's house (4:1–5)*
    (B) *The Lord as King of the assembled remnant (4:6–8)*
    (C) *Destruction and exile (4:9–14)*
    (D) *A Messiah from Bethlehem (5:1–3)*
    (E) *Peace: deliverance from Assyria (5:4–5)*
    (F) *The remnant of Jacob in the midst of nations (5:6–8)*
    (G) *Destruction of the causes of sin (5:9–14)*

(V) **Accusation and condemnation of Israel (6:1–7:7)**
    (A) *Yahweh's lawsuit against Israel (6:1–8)*
    (a) Address (6:1–2)
    (b) Lamentation based on the mighty deeds of Yahweh (6:3–5)
    (c) True religion (6:6–7)
    (d) The answer (6:8)
    (B) *Jerusalem is punished for its sin (6:9–16)*

(C) *Lamentation (7:1–7)*
(a) Social injustice and consequent punishment by God (7:1–6)
(b) Attitude of the prophet (7:7)

(VI) A liturgy of faith (7:8–20)
   (A) *Confession of sin and address to the enemy (7:8–10)*
   (B) *God's answer: a new Jerusalem (7:11–13)*
   (C) *A prayer to God for his people and concerning the other nations (7:14–17)*
   (D) *A hymn to God, who pardons and who is faithful (7:18–20)*

HIGHLIGHT

Jerusalem's punishment
Micah 6:6–8

⁶"With what shall I come before the Lord,
   and bow myself before God on high?
Shall I come before him with burnt offerings,
   with calves a year old?
⁷Will the Lord be pleased with thousands of rams,
   with ten thousands of rivers of oil?
Shall I give my firstborn for my transgression,
   the fruit of my body for the sin of my soul?'
⁸He has told you, O mortal, what is good;
   and what does the Lord require of you
but to do justice, and to love kindness,
and to walk humbly with your God?

SEVENTEEN

Zephaniah,

Nahum,

Habakkuk

ZEPHANIAH

Historical background

The book comes mainly from words of the prophet in Josiah's reign (640–609 BC).

A century earlier Assyria had conquered Judah, and Judah had been a vassal state of Assyria ever since. But Assyria's power was collapsing and Babylon was becoming more powerful.

Message

In this world of political turmoil Zephaniah sees the fate of nations in God's hands. The dominant theme is the Day of the Lord, when God will destroy the enemy nations, and punish his own people especially for their false worship. But because the rebellious and arrogant will be destroyed, the effect will be purification and the forming of a smaller people, more pleasing to God (2:3; 3:11–13).

The material in this chapter is digested from NJBC article 17, 'Zephaniah, Nahum, Habakkuk', by Thomas P. Wahl, OSB, Irene Nowell, OSB and Anthony R. Ceresko, OSFS.

Outline

(I) Title (1:1)

(II) Oracles of doom (1:2–18)
    (A) Universal destruction (1:2–3)
    (B) Judah and Jerusalem (1:4–18)
    (a) Canaanite cult (1:4–6)
    (b) Coming day of sacrifice (1:7–9)
    (c) Invasion of the city (1:10–13)
        (i) Breakthrough (1:10–11)
        (ii) Looting of the scoffers (1:12–13)
    (d) Day of Yahweh (1:14–18)

(III) Exhortations based on threats against the nations (2:1–15)
    (A) Exhortations (2:1–3)
    (B) Reasons: oracles against the nations (2:4–15)
    (a) Philistines (2:4–7)
    (b) Moab and Ammon (2:8–11)
    (c) Assyrians (2:[12] 13–15)

(IV) Salvation of Jerusalem and Judah (3:1–20)
    (A) Oracle I (3:1–5)
    (B) Oracle II (3:6–8)
    (C) Threat becomes promise (3:9–20)
    (a) Service of Yahweh from nations (3:9–10)
    (b) Moral recovery of Jerusalem/Judah (3:11–13)
    (c) Summons to rejoicing (3:14–15)
    (d) Oracle of reassurance to Jerusalem (3:16–17)
    (e) Oracle: change of fortunes (3:18–20)

HIGHLIGHT

The day of Yahweh
Zephaniah 1:14–18

[14]The great day of the Lord is near,
    near and hastening fast;
the sound of the day of the Lord is bitter,
    the warrior cries aloud there.
[15]That day will be a day of wrath,
    a day of distress and anguish,
a day of ruin and devastation,
    a day of darkness and gloom,
a day of clouds and thick darkness,

> [16] a day of trumpet blast and battle cry
> against the fortified cities
> and against the lofty battlements.
> [17] I will bring such distress upon people
> that they shall walk like the blind;
> because they have sinned against the Lord,
> their blood shall be poured out like dust,
> and their flesh like dung.
> [18] Neither their silver nor their gold
> will be able to save them
> on the day of the Lord's wrath;
> in the fire of his passion
> the whole earth shall be consumed;
> for a full, a terrible end
> he will make of all the inhabitants of the earth.

NAHUM

Historical background

Very little is known about the prophet himself, and the date of the prophecy is equally vague. It is likely that Nahum wrote in Judah close to 612, during the reform of Josiah, before the death of Josiah (609) and before the evidence of Babylonian imperial might quenched the spirit of optimism surrounding the fall of Assyria.

Message

The prophecy of Nahum comes from a poet of great skill. The work is a combination of many forms. The whole prophecy is similar to other oracles against foreign nations. But it contains a partial **acrostic** poem (1:2–8), a funeral lament ('woe', 3:1–7), and a taunt-song (3:8–19). Several images are drawn of Nineveh: pool (2:9), den of lions (2:12–14), prostitute (3:4–6), yielding fig trees (3:12), swarm of locusts (3:15–17). There is one message: God will execute vengeance against Nineveh. The destruction of the oppressor will bring joy to God's people and to all who have suffered Assyria's cruelty. The fall of Nineveh is an act of divine justice. Assyria has plundered the nations and

> **acrostic** <
a poem in which the individual lines open with successive letters of the alphabet

89

torn them like prey for its voracious appetite; now Assyria in turn will be plundered and become the prey of another.

Nahum has been criticized for his glee over the fall of the enemy and for the corresponding absence of any criticism of his own people (contrast his contemporary, Jeremiah). His prophecy, however, is only intended to make one statement: God who is faithful has not abandoned Judah. The enemy will not prevail forever; the punishment will come to an end. The good news is already proclaimed; feasts of thanksgiving should be celebrated (2:1).

Outline

(I) Title (1:1)

(II) Appearance of the divine avenger (1:2–8)

(III) Oracles of hope (1:9–2:1)

(IV) The fall of Nineveh (2:2–14)
    (A) Introduction (2:2–3)
    (B) Description of the battle from inside the city (2:4–10)
    (C) The fate of the lion (2:11–14)

(V) Final destruction (3:1–19)
    (A) Funeral lament for the harlot city (3:1–7)
    (B) Taunting song (3:8–19)
    (a) Comparison to Thebes (3:8–11)
    (b) Futility of defence (3:12–15a)
    (c) Comparison to locust swarm (3:15b–17)
    (d) Final destiny (3:18–19)

HABAKKUK

Historical background

The book tells us only the prophet's name. The main clue to the date of his prophecies comes from the mention in 1:6 of the Chaldeans, a people from southern Mesopotamia who, with their centre at Babylon, replaced the Assyrians as the masters of the ancient Near East in the late 7th–early 6th centuries. This plus the obvious turmoil on both the national and international

*Last part of a scroll from Qumran containing a commentary on Habakkuk.
Reproduced by courtesy of the Israel Museum, Jerusalem*

scene has led scholars to date the prophecies themselves somewhere between the beginning of Assyria's decline after 626 and
the fall of Jerusalem in 587. The woes in 2:6–20 and the canticle in chapter 3 make some scholars believe this book was
composed for use in the Temple worship. Habakkuk has in fact
arranged his material not to write a history book but to stress
his message: the power of God over human history and the call
to trust and faithfulness (see 2:4).

Message

Habakkuk makes an important and original contribution to
Israel's reflection on the nature of God and of God's ways with
Israel. The book begins with a question which the prophet
dares to direct to God, raising doubts about divine justice and
God's treatment of the wicked. The question represents a first
step in an attempt to deal with a breakdown of order and
justice, a situation to which God seems implicitly to agree by
silence and apparent inaction. But despite the doubts the prophet expresses, there is an underlying attitude of faith and trust.
This is especially due to the canticle in chapter 3, which, with
its ringing affirmation of God's absolute power over creation
and history, places the disturbing events recounted in chapters
1–2 in the wider context of God's saving design. Thus, the key
sentence in 2:4 advises confidence and trust in God's faithfulness, and the book repeatedly condemns all forms of
oppression and exploitation as well as the pride and arrogance
that stand opposed to the humble faith demanded by God.

Outline

(I) **Dialogue between the prophet and God (1:1–2:5)**
    (A) *The first exchange (1:2–11)*
    (a) The prophet's complaint: there is no justice (1:2–4)
    (b) The Lord's response (1:5–11)
    (B) *The second exchange (1:12–2:5)*
    (a) The prophet's complaint (1:12–17)
    (b) The Lord's response (2:1–5)

(II) **The five woes (2:6–20)**
    (A) *Introduction (2:6a)*
    (B) *The first woe: against arrogant greed (2:6b–8)*
    (C) *The second woe: against presumption (2:9–11)*
    (D) *The third woe: against pride and violence (2:12–14)*
    (E) *The fourth woe: against the degradation of human dignity (2:15–17)*
    (F) *The fifth woe: against idolatry (2:18–20)*

(III) **The canticle of Habakkuk (3:1–19)**
    (A) *Title (3:1)*
    (B) *Introduction: fear and salvation (3:2)*
    (C) *God appears (3:3–15)*
    (a) Part I: God's appearance and the reaction of creation (3:3–7)
    (b) Part II: the battle with the forces of chaos (3:8–15)
        (i) Preparation for the battle (3:8–9a)
        (ii) The reaction of nature (3:9b–11a)
        (iii) The charge into battle (3:11b–13a)
        (iv) The victory (3:13b–15)
    (D) *Conclusion: fear and salvation (3:16–19)*
    (a) Fear (3:16–17)
    (b) Salvation (3:18–19)

HIGHLIGHT

God's battle with the forces of chaos
Habakkuk 3:8–15

[8]Was your wrath against the rivers, O Lord?
    Or your anger against the rivers,
    or your rage against the sea,
when you drove your horses,
    your chariots to victory?
[9]You brandished your naked bow,
    sated were the arrows at your command.   *Selah*

You split the earth with rivers.
¹⁰The mountains saw you, and writhed;
a torrent of water swept by;
the deep gave forth its voice.
The sun raised high its hands;
¹¹the moon stood still in its exalted place,
at the light of your arrows speeding by,
at the gleam of your flashing spear.
¹²In fury you trod the earth,
in anger you trampled nations.
¹³You came forth to save your people,
to save your anointed.
You crushed the head of the wicked house,
laying it bare from foundation to roof.   *Selah*
¹⁴You pierced with his own arrows the head of his warriors,
who came like a whirlwind to scatter us,
gloating as if ready to devour the poor who were in hiding.
¹⁵You trampled the sea with your horses,
churning the mighty waters.

EIGHTEEN

Jeremiah

The material in this chapter is digested from NJBC article 18, 'Jeremiah', by Guy P. Couturier, CSC.

Jeremiah's time

Jeremiah lived in a very troubled time. His country, Judah, was under the control of the Assyrian empire, and this led people to an interest in the religion of the foreign rulers, which was idolatry.

But during the reign of King Josiah (640–609 BC), the Book of the Law, which is a part of the Book of Deuteronomy, was discovered in the Temple, and Josiah led a thorough reform in Judah. Some people had remained faithful to the covenant with Yahweh and they supported the king's new policy. In a solemn ceremony the covenant was renewed, and all the high places where idolatry was practised were destroyed, leaving Jerusalem as the centre for true worship. After Josiah's death in battle, other kings ruled. King Zedekiah rebelled against Babylon, but failed. Jerusalem was destroyed and many of the people were taken as prisoners to exile in Babylon. Some Judeans escaped to Egypt, taking Jeremiah with them.

Jeremiah's mission

Yahweh called Jeremiah to be a prophet to Judah and to the nations in the midst of these events; his ministry lasted 40 years (see 1:1–3). During this time other prophets were also at work: Zephaniah, Habakkuk, Nahum and Ezekiel.

Jeremiah's message was to define true religion, and to proclaim the wars which were to come as a punishment for the wrongdoing of Judah. In chapters 1–6 he reminds them that the covenant is basically a matter of love between Yahweh and Israel – like the love between a man and woman in marriage.

This love is expressed through a sincere conversion to true justice as expressed in the laws of the covenant.

Later, when people returned to idolatry, Jeremiah gave a solemn warning of the war to come. The prophet had to face opposition and persecution; he then went through a crisis about his faith and his mission, which he described in lyric poems, called his confessions (see 11:18ff.). These poems are scattered in chapters 11–20.

When Jerusalem was destroyed he escaped to Egypt, where he died about ten years later. Most of his oracles were preserved by Baruch, who inserted them in narratives recording the circumstances (chapters 27–29 and 32–45). Jeremiah, then, understood that a true change of heart could only be brought about by Yahweh. And that one day Israel and Judah would be reunited.

Literary forms

There are various kinds of writing in the book of Jeremiah:

- Oracles
- Biographical narratives about the message and life of Jeremiah, written by Baruch
- Deuteronomic speeches: these are usually introduced by the words, 'The message that came to Jeremiah from the Lord'. These are in the style of the Deuteronomic reformers.

Outline

(I) Title (1:1–3)

(II) Oracles against Judah and Jerusalem (1:4–25:38)
    (A) Call of Jeremiah (1:4–19)
    (a) The dialogue (1:4–10, 17–19)
    (b) The visions (1:11–16)
    (B) Early oracles under Josiah (2:1–6:30)
    (a) A lawsuit against Israel (2:1–37)
    (b) The return of the apostate (3:1–4:2)
        (i) The poem on conversion (3:1–5, 19–25; 4:1–2)
        (ii) Two additions (3:6–18)

(c) Evil of Judah and evil of war (4:3–6:30)
    (i) The invasion (4:3–31)
    (ii) The moral corruption (5:1–31)
    (iii) The correction (6:1–30)
(C) *The ministry under Jehoiakim (7:1–20:18)*
(a) The mistaken covenant (7:1–10:25)
    (i) The Temple discourse (7:1–8:3)
    (1) The Temple (7:2–15)
    (2) The Queen of Heaven (7:16–20)
    (3) Religion and sacrifice (7:21–28)
    (4) False cult and punishment (7:29–8:3)
    (ii) New and old (8:4–10:25)
     (1) Universal estrangement (8:4–12)
     (2) The sacked vineyard (8:13–17)
     (3) The prophet's lament (8:18–23)
     (4) An attempt at evasion (9:1–8)
     (5) Dirge over the land (9:9–21)
     (6) True wisdom (9:22–23)
     (7) Circumcision is worthless (9:24–25)
     (8) A satire on idolatry (10:1–16)
     (9) In full flight! (10:17–22)
     (10) Jeremiah's prayer (10:23–25)
(b) The broken covenant (11:1–13:27)
    (i) Jeremiah and the covenant (11:1–14)
    (ii) Misplaced sayings (11:15–17)
    (iii) The plot against Jeremiah (11:18–12:6)
    (iv) Yahweh's complaint (12:7–13)
    (v) Death or life for Judah's neighbours (12:14–17)
    (vi) Two parabolic discourses (13:1–14)
    (1) The rotten loincloth (13:1–11)
    (2) The broken wineflasks (13:12–14)
    (vii) Threatening words (13:15–27)
    (1) The dark night (13:15–17)
    (2) The exile (13:18–19)
    (3) Incurable sickness (13:20–27)
(c) Crime and punishment (14:1–17:27)
    (i) The great drought (14:1–15:9)
    (1) Drought (14:1–16)
    (2) Lament (14:17–15:4)
    (3) Tragedy (15:5–9)
    (ii) The renewal of the call (15:10–21)
    (iii) Jeremiah's celibacy (16:1–13, 16–18)
    (iv) Scattered fragments (16:14–15, 19–21; 17:1–18)
    (1) Return from exile (16:14–15)
    (2) Conversion of the heathen (16:19–21)
    (3) Judah's guilt (17:1–4)
    (4) Wisdom sayings (17:5–11)
    (5) The source of life (17:12–13)

(iii) Personal responsibility (31:29–30)
(iv) The new covenant (31:31–34)
(v) The stability of Israel (31:35–37)
(vi) The rebuilding of Jerusalem (31:38–40)
(D) The restoration of Judah (32:1–33:26)
(a) A pledge of restoration (32:1–44)
(i) The purchase of a field (32:1–15)
(ii) Jeremiah's prayer (32:16–25)
(iii) The Lord's answer (32:26–44)
(b) More on the restoration of Jerusalem and Judah (33:1–26)
(i) Jerusalem and Judah restored (33:1–13)
(ii) An anthology on messianism (33:14–26)
(E) The conditions for salvation (34:1–35:19)
(a) Zedekiah's fate (34:1–7)
(b) A dishonest deal (34:8–22)
(c) The example of the Rechabites (35:1–19)

(IV) Martyrdom of Jeremiah (36:1–45:5)
(A) The scroll of 605–604 (36:1–32)
(B) Zedekiah and the prophet (37:1–38:28a)
(a) Zedekiah consults Jeremiah (37:1–10)
(b) Jeremiah is arrested (37:11–16)
(c) A new consultation (37:17–21)
(d) Jeremiah in the muddy cistern (38:1–13)
(e) Zedekiah's last interview with Jeremiah (38:14–28a)
(C) The fall of Jerusalem (38:28b–39:18)
(D) A tragedy in Mizpah (40:1–41:18)
(a) Jeremiah at Mizpah (40:1–6)
(b) The colony at Mizpah (40:7–12)
(c) The assassination of Gedaliah (40:13–41:3)
(d) The assassination of pilgrims (41:4–10)
(e) Flight and panic (41:11–18)
(E) Sojourn in Egypt (42:1–44:30)
(a) Search for guidance (42:1–6)
(b) The divine answer (42:7–18)
(c) The refusal to stay home (42:19–43:7)
(d) Nebuchadnezzar in Egypt (43:8–13)
(e) Jeremiah's last words (44:1–30)
(F) The consolation of Baruch (45:1–5)

(V) Oracles against the nations (46:1–51:64)
(A) Against Egypt (46:1–28)
(a) The battle of Carchemish (46:2–12)
(b) The invasion of Egypt (46:13–28)
(B) Against Philistia (47:1–7)
(C) Against Moab (48:1–47)
(D) Against Ammon (49:1–6)
(E) Against Edom (49:7–22)

HIGHLIGHT

The new covenant
Jeremiah 31:31–34

[31]The days are surely coming, says the Lord, when I will make a new covenant with the house of Israel and the house of Judah. [32]It will not be like the covenant that I made with their ancestors when I took them by the hand to bring them out of the land of Egypt – a covenant that they broke, though I was their husband, says the Lord. [33]But this is the covenant that I will make with the house of Israel after those days, says the Lord: I will put my law within them, and I will write it on their hearts; and I will be their God, and they shall be my people. [34]No longer shall they teach one another, or say to each other, 'Know the Lord', for they shall all know me, from the least of them to the greatest, says the Lord; for I will forgive their iniquity, and remember their sin no more.

NINETEEN

Old Testament

Apocalypticism

and Eschatology

The material in this
chapter is digested
from NJBC article
19, 'Old Testament
Apocalypticism and
Eschatology', by
John J. Collins.

Definitions

The two words 'eschatology' and 'apocalypticism' are used by scholars and, although they are sometimes ambiguous, need to be studied if we are to understand how prophecy developed historically in the history of the Jewish people.

Eschatology

Eschatology is literally the doctrine of the last things.

National eschatology – a concern for the future of Israel.

Cosmic eschatology – a concern for the future of the world.

These cannot be clearly separated, even in the prophets before the exile. The cosmic eschatology uses the language of worship, and sees God as the judge of all the earth (Psalm 98:8–9).

Personal eschatology – a concern for the fate of the individual after death – does not become important until the end of the Old Testament period.

Apocalyptic

Apocalyptic comes from the word 'apocalypse', which means 'revelation'. The last book of the Bible is called Revelation, or The Apocalypse. Although all the Bible is revelation from God, the word 'apocalyptic' is used for a revelation through visions of heavenly mysteries, often related to the end of the world.

Most Jewish apocalyptic writing was produced about 200 BC–AD 100 and includes the book of Daniel.

Early Post-exilic Prophecy

Second Isaiah

Before the exile prophets had prophesied salvation and destruction, but their chief emphasis was on judgement; after the exile they emphasized final and lasting salvation. Second Isaiah saw the return from exile in Babylon as the start of a new liberation and transformation of Israel.

Haggai

Haggai also believed that the return from exile would lead to transformation, but as time passed he began to say that though this had not happened yet, it would come to pass in the future. He also introduced the expectation of a Messiah.

Zechariah 1–8

Zechariah also expects the Messiah; his visions are explained to him by an angel, as in later apocalypse. Like the other prophets of the day, Zechariah predicted that 'my cities shall again overflow with prosperity' (1:17) and that the Lord himself would dwell among them (2:14–15). In this vision there are two 'anointed ones' (Messiahs) who stand before the Lord – Zerubbabel and the high priest Joshua.

Ezekiel 40–48

Ezekiel has a similar vision of the restored Jerusalem, which the prophet is shown by a guiding angel. In Ezekiel's vision, however, the Messiah figure is a 'prince' and there is no mention of an individual high priest.

Third Isaiah

Perhaps the most striking eschatological passage is 65:17: 'Lo, I am about to create new heavens and a new earth'. This sentence is repeated in Revelation 21:1.

The idea of a new creation is more radical than anything before it: but the details are not new. In the new creation people will live longer, and in peace and plenty in this life as we know it.

Oracles of uncertain date

After Haggai and Zechariah the most significant passages about eschatology give no sign of their date. They include:

Malachi
Malachi criticized corrupt priesthood, mixed marriages and divorce. He predicted: 'Suddenly there will come to the Temple the Lord whom you seek' (3:1).

His main contribution is the angel or messenger who will prepare the way before the Lord (3:1). In 3:23–24 this messenger is said to be Elijah the prophet.

Joel
Joel uses the idea of the Day of the Lord, in chapters 1 and 2 to describe a plague of locusts, but in chapters 3 and 4 (which may be by a different prophet) to events concerned with the last days.

Ezekiel 38–39
The prophecy is not concerned with real geography or history but with the end of all history.

Zechariah 9–14
The dominant theme is 'the destruction of all nations that come against Jerusalem' (12:9). We do not know whether these oracles were inspired by specific events or simply reflect the resentment of a small and powerless people.

Isaiah 24–27
This writing uses traditions about a rebellion by the host of heaven, which is never told in the Bible, although there are a few possible references to it in the Psalms (see Psalm 82).

Apocalypticism

Daniel

Daniel is distinguished by his ability to interpret dreams and mysterious signs (e.g., the writing on the wall) more successfully than the professional Babylonian diviners and wise men, because of the revelation he receives from his God.

The continuity of apocalypticism with biblical prophecy is most evident in Daniel 7, the central vision of the book, composed in the heat of the persecution of the Jews by Antiochus Epiphanes. There Daniel reports his famous vision of four beasts rising from the sea and one like a son of man riding on the clouds of heaven. This imagery is derived from the myth of God's battle with the sea monster (Isaiah 27:1; 51:9–11).

Three other features, taken in combination, further distinguish Daniel as 'apocalyptic' over against earlier prophecy: (1) Daniel consistently receives his revelation from an angel, whether through interpretation of a vision (chapters 7 and 8), interpretation of Scripture (chapter 9) or direct speech (chapters 10–12). (2) The revelations cover a wide sweep of history, most of which was already past by the time Daniel was actually written. (3) The historical review in Daniel 11 culminates in 12:1–3 with the resurrection of the dead. This is the first (and only) passage in the Hebrew Bible that speaks clearly of personal afterlife.

The spread of apocalyptic ideas

The writing of apocalypses continued off and on well into the Christian era. The ideas they contain include interest in heavenly mysteries, a sense of participation in the angelic world, and expectation of a final battle between the Sons of Light and Sons of Darkness, led by their respective angels.

Other ideas that were originally characteristic of the apocalypses came to be more widely accepted. Belief in resurrection was accepted by the Pharisees and others and gradually entered the mainstream of Jewish faith, although it was still rejected by the Sadducees in the 1st century AD.

Their influence on Christianity

The main historical importance of apocalypticism is that it set the stage for the origin of Christianity. Apocalypticism has been called 'the mother of Christian theology'. Whether Jesus himself should be understood as an eschatological prophet or apocalyptic preacher is disputed. There is no doubt that his followers drew heavily on the understanding of history that had been developed in 'historical' apocalypses of the Daniel type. For Paul, the resurrection of Jesus was the firstfruits of the general resurrection (1 Corinthians 15:20), which was therefore imminent. Indeed, the resurrection of Jesus was only credible in the context of an apocalyptic eschatological scenario: 'If the dead are not raised, then Christ has not been raised' (1 Corinthians 15:16).

The early gospel writers drew directly on Daniel 7 and cast Jesus in the role of the Son of Man who would come on the clouds of heaven. The first generation of Christians did not use the literary form of the apocalypse, perhaps because of their heightened sense of the immediate presence of the Spirit. By the end of the 1st century, however, the form appears in the book of Revelation. After that it flourished in Christian circles.

The key to understanding the apocalyptic tradition lies in the realization that apocalypses are more poetry than dogma. They are works of imagination, which cannot be regarded as sources of factual information. Their value lies in their ability to envision alternatives to the world of present experience and so to provide hope and consolation. As such they speak to enduring human needs and are a vital part of the Western religious heritage.

TWENTY

Ezekiel

The text of Ezekiel

The material in this chapter is digested from NJBC article 20, 'Ezekiel', by Lawrence Boadt, CSP.

No prophetic book poses more of a question than does Ezekiel. It combines prophetic oracles with legal reflections, prose and poetry, extremely detailed historical descriptions with highly imaginative mythological allusions, sober judgement and wild vision, sermonizing with vivid dramatic presentation. This leads to a wealth of material and a breadth of vision far greater than in other prophetic books. We have barely begun to understand the complexity and depth of this prophet, who preached at the worst of times and the most decisive of times in Israel's long history.

The book is largely composed from Ezekiel's own preaching with extensive editing by disciples working in the exile and shortly afterwards. Fifteen dates are given in the book which allow us to connect it with known historical events of the period 593–573 BC.

The historical background to Ezekiel's ministry

The prophetic ministry of Ezekiel must be understood against the turbulent background of the last days of Judah as an independent state. Ezekiel claims to have begun his ministry in 593 among the Judean exiles in the land of Babylon (1:2). His last dated prophecy falls in 571 (29:17). Presumably he was one of the 8,000 prisoners brought to Babylon when Jerusalem was conquered by Nebuchadnezzar in 598 (2 Kings 24:16). Babylon had conquered Jerusalem in 598 and had taken the new king Jehoiachin to Babylon with the prisoners. But they left Zede-

The city of Babylon. Reconstruction by Eckhard Unger. Reproduced by courtesy of the State Museums, Berlin

kiah, the young king's uncle, as king-regent in Jerusalem; he rebelled and this led to the complete destruction of all the cities of Judah. Ezekiel seems to have opposed the rebellion, and the ambitions of the ruling class in Jerusalem. He believed that Israel should be faithful to Yahweh as a community, whether they were politically independent or not.

The theology of the book

Ezekiel believes that God punishes unfaithfulness to the covenant with political disaster, as Isaiah and Jeremiah did also. He speaks of unfaithfulness to the covenant as adultery and prostitution. He believed (like Jeremiah) that God's will was not a war of independence built on human pride and political motives, but a faithfulness to God under Babylonian rule. So he saw the defeat by Babylon as God's correction. He develops traditional themes in a unique way:

(a) Yahweh is Lord of all nations and events.
(b) Yahweh is holy.
(c) Worship and moral holiness are very important.
(d) Each generation is responsible for its own acts.
(e) God intends to restore Israel out of a totally free gift of grace.

Outline

(I) **Oracles of judgement (1:1–24:27)**
    (A) The call to prophecy (1:1–3:27)
    (a) The vision of God (1:1–28a)
        (i) The author (1:1–3)
        (ii) The chariot vision (1:4–28a)
    (b) The call of the prophet (1:28b–3:11)
    (c) The commission to be watchman (3:12–21)
    (d) The prophet constrained (3:22–27)
    (B) Symbolic actions and oracles (4:1–7:27)
    (a) Three symbolic actions (4:1–5:4)
        (i) The siege map and lying on the side (4:1–8)
        (ii) Eating unclean bread (4:9–17)
        (iii) Cutting off the beard (5:1–4)
    (b) Oracles of judgement (5:5–7:27)
        (i) Oracle against Jerusalem (5:5–17)
        (ii) Oracle against the mountains (6:1–14)
        (iii) Oracle against the whole land (7:1–27)
    (C) The vision of the end of the Temple (8:1–11:25)
    (a) The vision of the Temple abominations (8:1–18)
    (b) The angels of judgement (9:1–11)
    (c) The cherubim throne returns (10:1–22)
    (d) The oracle of destruction for the city (11:1–25)
    (D) Condemnation of all: people and leaders (12:1–14:23)
    (a) The coming exile (12:1–28)
        (i) Symbolic attempt to escape (12:1–16)
        (ii) The food of exiles (12:17–20)
        (iii) The proverb of the long day (12:21–28)

(b) Condemnation of the prophets (13:1–23)
     (i) False prophets (13:1–16)
     (ii) False prophetesses (13:17–23)
(c) Idolatry and unfaithfulness (14:1–23)
     (i) Punishment of idolators (14:1–11)
     (ii) Need for personal righteousness (14:12–23)
(E) Allegories and metaphors of judgement (15:1–19:14)
(a) The allegory of the vine wood (15:1–8)
(b) Jerusalem as the unfaithful wife (16:1–63)
     (i) Jerusalem the harlot (16:1–43)
     (ii) Her sisters Sodom and Samaria (16:44–58)
     (iii) The covenant restored (16:59–63)
(c) The allegory of the eagles (17:1–24)
(d) A law case for individual responsibility (18:1–32)
     (i) A proverb for three generations (18:1–20)
     (ii) Conversion and mercy (18:21–32)
(e) Two laments over Zedekiah (19:1–14)
     (i) The lioness and her cubs (19:1–9)
     (ii) The sceptre of vine wood (19:10–14)
(F) Indictment and condemnation (20:1–24:27)
(a) Israel's history of infidelity (20:1–44)
     (i) Past history of rebellion (20:1–31)
     (ii) Divine judgement (20:32–44)
(b) Oracles of the sword (20:45–21:32)
     (i) A sword against the south (20:45–49, 21:1–7)
     (ii) The sword polished for slaughter (21:8–17)
     (iii) The sword of the king of Babylon (21:18–27)
     (iv) The sword against the Ammonites (21:28–32)
(c) Legal charges against Jerusalem (22:1–31)
     (i) A city of defilement and blood (22:1–16)
     (ii) Divine wrath in punishment (22:17–22)
     (iii) All classes are guilty (22:23–31)
(d) The allegory of the two sisters (23:1–49)
     (i) The allegory of Oholah and Oholibah (23:1–35)
     (ii) Interpretation for Jerusalem (23:36–49)
(e) Two signs of the end (24:1–27)
     (i) The allegory of the boiling pot (24:1–14)
     (ii) The death of Ezekiel's wife (24:15–27)

(II) Oracles against foreign nations (25:1–32:32)
  (A) Oracles against Israel's small neighbours (25:1–17)
  (a) Oracle against Ammon (25:1–7)
  (b) Oracle against Moab (25:8–11)
  (c) Oracle against Edom (25:12–14)
  (d) Oracle against the Philistines (25:15–17)
  (B) Oracles against Tyre (26:1–28:19)
  (a) Tyre destroyed by Babylon's tidal wave (26:1–21)
  (b) The wreck of the great ship Tyre (27:1–36)

The valley of dry bones
Ezekiel 37:1–14

¹The hand of the Lord came upon me, and he brought me out by the spirit of the Lord and set me down in the middle of a valley; it was full of bones. ²He led me all around them; there were very many lying in the valley, and they were very dry. ³He said to me, 'Mortal, can these bones live?' I answered, 'O Lord God, you know.' ⁴Then he said to me, 'Prophesy to these bones, and say to them: O dry bones, hear the word of the Lord. ⁵Thus says the Lord God to these bones: I will cause breath to enter you, and you shall live. ⁶I will lay sinews on you, and will cause flesh to come upon you, and cover you with skin, and put breath in you, and you shall live; and you shall know that I am the Lord.'

⁷So I prophesied as I had been commanded; and as I prophesied, suddenly there was a noise, a rattling, and the bones came together, bone to its bone. ⁸I looked, and there were sinews on them, and flesh had come upon them, and skin had covered them; but there was no breath in them. ⁹Then he said to me, 'Prophesy to the breath, prophesy, mortal, and say to the breath: Thus says the Lord God: Come from the four winds, O breath, and breathe upon these slain, that they may live.' ¹⁰I prophesied as he commanded me, and the breath came into them, and they lived, and stood on their feet, a vast multitude.

¹¹Then he said to me, 'Mortal, these bones are the whole house of Israel. They say, "Our bones are dried up, and our hope is lost; we are cut off completely." ¹²Therefore prophesy, and say to them, Thus says the Lord God: I am going to open your graves, and bring you up from your graves, O my people; and I will bring you back to the land of Israel. ¹³And you shall know that I am the Lord, when I open your graves, and bring you up from your graves, O my people. ¹⁴I will put my spirit within you, and you shall live, and I will place you in your own land; then you shall know that I, the Lord, have spoken, and I have done it, says the Lord.'

Second Isaiah
and Third Isaiah

Three authors – and an editor

The material in this chapter is digested from NJBC article 21, 'Deutero-Isaiah and Trito-Isaiah', by Carroll Stuhlmueller, CP.

Until the 18th century, it was thought that Isaiah of Jerusalem (see page 76) wrote all 66 chapters of the book under his name, but we can now identify at least three authors: for 1–39; 40–55; 56–66. Scholars maintain that chapters 40–55 were written by a man who lived some 150 years later than the 'First' Isaiah, during the Babylonian exile, about the year 550 BC (in chapters 41 and 45 Cyrus is already on the march). They named this second Isaiah simply that: 'Second' or 'Deutero'-Isaiah. Chapters 56–66 were written after the exile by another author, called 'Third' or 'Trito'-Isaiah. In Third Isaiah Israel is back again in its own land, and the problems are different from those pictured in Isaiah 1–39.

Baked clay cylinder from Babylon, 6th century BC, relating Cyrus's conquest of the city in 539 BC. Reproduced by courtesy of the Trustees of the British Museum

Finally, there was an editor for the entire book of Isaiah as we now have it. This person not only drew principally upon the oral and written traditions of three individuals but also included some of the reflections and teaching of their disciples. The editor centred the entire book on Jerusalem. Somehow the first Temple had to be destroyed and in the process the people purified of false hopes in externals. Yet even the new Temple is itself tarnished by unworthy leaders. This sad, sinful situation leads to its final opening to the Gentiles. The editor has allowed all major sections to open with a sympathetic attitude toward the Gentiles: 11:10–16; 23:17–18; 27:12–13; 33:17–24; 35:5–6; 49:6; 56:1–8; 66:18–21.

The religious message of Second Isaiah

The poetry reveals someone thoughtful, earnest, optimistic, and sympathetic. So sturdy was his faith in the God of history that every episode contributed to the redemption of Israel (44:24–45:7).

The prophet places ancient traditions in a cosmic setting, so that the new exodus levels mountains or strikes flowing water in the heights (40:3–5; 41:17–20). The covenant with Moses is expanded into a world covenant by mentioning the covenants with Noah (54:9) and with Abraham and Sarah (51:1–3), and in the latter case Second Isaiah sees the garden of paradise emerge before his eyes. The spirit of the liturgy breaks forth into new life through hymns, laments, and proclamation of the word. His themes are:

The new exodus
I.e., from Babylon to the promised land of Israel (Isaiah 40:3–11; 43:1–7, 14–21).

First and last
An entire series of poems is dedicated to first and last, mostly in the literary form of argument or trial speech (41:1–5; 41:21–29 + 42:8–9; 42:12–31; 43:8–13; 44:6–8; 45:18–22; 46:9–13; 48:1–11, 12–19). These discuss the fulfilment of earlier pro-

phecies, the first things, and therefore the necessary fulfilment of the final or last prophecy which ushers in an extraordinary age for Israel.

Yahweh creator

This theme is introduced as an indication of the exceptionally new nature of what is about to happen to Israel in the future. See for instance 41:17–20; 48:12–13.

The justice of God

Because every divine promise is on the point of fulfilment, Second and Third Isaiah praise God for a 'just' or complete fulfilment of all divine promises (41:2, 16; 42:6; 61:3; 62:11–12).

The power of the divine word

From his opening statements (40:5, 8) to his final verses (55:10–11) Second Isaiah dwells more than any other prophet upon the power of the divine word.

Jerusalem

For Second and Third Isaiah Jerusalem occupies a central role. At times the prophet sees Jerusalem as announcing Israel's return across the desert to its own land (40:9–10), at other times as a lonely widow who will become the happy mother of many children (54:1–10; 65:17–25). Only once, in a very disputed line (44:28b), does Second Isaiah mention the Temple. Third Isaiah bitterly condemns the greedy Temple leaders of the post-exilic age (56:9–57:13).

The four 'servant' poems

These are to be found at 42:1–7; 49:1–7; 50:4–9; 52:13–53:12. When the four major songs are studied within the context of other servant passages in 40–66, the personality and mission of the servant become more complex: (a) in a positive sense, the servant refers to a beloved and chosen one, redeemed by Yahweh, whether this be Israel (41:8, 9; 43:10; 44:1, 2, 21), Israel under the name of Jacob (45:4; 48:20), or the prophet and his disciples (42:1; 49:3, 6), as contemplated by other Israelites or foreigners (50:10, 52:13, 53:11), or by the foreigner Cyrus (44:26); (b) in a negative sense, the servant is the people Israel – blind, deaf, and despoiled (42:19), the slave of kings (49:7) – burdened by its sins (43:23), or Yahweh burdened by Israel's sins (43:27).

Outline

(I) **Book of comfort (40:1–55:13)**
   (A) *Overture (40:1–31)*
   (a) Commissioning of the prophet (40:1–11)
   (b) Disputations with Israel (40:12–31)
   (B) *Prophetic fulfilment in the new exodus (41:1–48:22)*
   (a) The servant hears and is saved (41:1–44:23)
     (i) Israel's salvation acclaimed and defended (41:1–42:13)
     (1) Champion of justice (41:1–20)
     (2) Military and peaceful ways of justice (41:21–42:13)
     (ii) Yahweh, redeemer and re-creator (42:14–44:23)
     (1) The blind and deaf servant (42:14–43:21)
     (2) Yahweh alone saves (43:22–44:23)
   (b) Cyrus, anointed liberator (44:24–47:15)
     (i) Commissioning of Cyrus (44:24–45:13)
     (1) Disputation over world events (44:24–28)
     (2) Commissioning of Cyrus (45:1–8)
     (3) Disputation with Israel (45:9–13)
     (ii) The Lord's decree (45:14–25)
     (iii) Trial against Israel (46:1–13)
     (iv) Taunt against Babylon (47:1–15)
   (c) Conclusion (48:1–22)
     (i) Yahweh, first and last (48:1–16)
     (ii) Message of promise (48:17–19)
     (iii) Concluding hymn (48:20–22)
   (C) *Comforting Zion (49:1–54:17)*
   (a) From sorrow to redemption (49:1–51:8)
     (i) Commissioning of servant prophet (49:1–7)
     (ii) Announcement of the new exodus (49:8–13)
     (iii) Announcement of salvation for Zion (49:14–26)
     (iv) Confidence of the servant prophet (50:1–11)
     (v) Promise of salvation (51:1–8)
   (b) Comforting the mourners (51:9–52:12)
     (i) Lament and comfort (51:9–52:6)
     (ii) Messenger of salvation (52:7–10)
     (iii) Conclusion: a new exodus (52:11–12)
   (c) Thanksgiving for servant prophet (52:13–53:12)

(d) Zion, mother and spouse (54:1–17)
(D) *Conclusion to the book of comfort (55:1–13)*

(II) **Struggle for new Temple and new leadership**
     (56:1–66:24)
     (A) *Oracle of Temple worship for outsiders (56:1–8)*
     (B) *Struggle for true leadership (56:9–59:21)*
     (a) False leaders; some faithful people (56:9–57:13)
     (b) Comforting the faithful (57:14–21)
     (c) True and false fasting (58:1–14)
     (d) Indictment, lament, and victory (59:1–21)
     (C) *The glorious new Zion (60:1–62:12)*
     (a) Glory of the new Zion (60:1–22)
     (b) Anointing of the prophet (61:1–3)
     (c) Glory of the new Zion (61:4–62:9)
     (d) Final reflection (62:10–12)
     (D) *From sorrow to a new heaven and new earth*
         (63:1–66:16)
     (a) The solitary conqueror (63:1–6)
     (b) Confession of sin (63:7–64:11)
     (c) True and false servants (65:1–25)
     (d) Controversy over the new Temple (66:1–16)
     (E) *Foreigners at home in God's house (66:17–24)*

HIGHLIGHT

The servant who suffers
Isaiah 53:3–6

³He was despised and rejected by others;
    a man of suffering and acquainted with infirmity;
  and as one from whom others hide their faces
    he was despised, and we held him of no account.
⁴Surely he has borne our infirmities
    and carried our diseases;
  yet we accounted him stricken,
    struck down by God, and afflicted.
⁵But he was wounded for our transgressions,
    crushed for our iniquities;
  upon him was the punishment that made us whole,
    and by his bruises we are healed.
⁶All we like sheep have gone astray;
    we have all turned to our own way,
  and the Lord has laid on him
    the iniquity of us all.

TWENTY-TWO

Haggai,

Zechariah,

Malachi

The material in this
chapter is digested
from NJBC article
22, 'Haggai,
Zechariah,
Malachi', by Aelred
Cody, OSB.

HAGGAI

The prophet and his situation

The oracles were all delivered in the beginning of Darius I's long reign over the Persian empire (521–486 BC). Darius renewed the policies, introduced by Cyrus (d. 530), which allowed persons deported by the Babylonians to return to their homelands, and which aimed at conciliating the loyalty of the empire's subject peoples by allowing them a certain amount of local government and by granting them freedom to practise their own religions.

It is generally assumed that Haggai was one of the exiled Judeans who had recently returned to Judah, but we have no evidence confirming that. In Ezra 5:1–2; 6:14 we are told that he was successful in moving the Judeans to action in rebuilding the Temple, but for Haggai the Temple's importance lay not so much in its being a place of worship as in its being the place of Yahweh's presence on earth. For Haggai, the future is the future of Judah, restored with a ruler descended from David and with God once again dwelling in his earthly Temple.

HIGHLIGHT

God's signet ring
Haggai 2:20–23

[20]The word of the Lord came a second time to Haggai on the twenty-fourth day of the month: [21]Speak to Zerubbabel, governor of Judah, saying, I am about to shake the heavens and the earth, [22]and to overthrow the throne of kingdoms; I am about to destroy the strength of the kingdoms of the nations, and overthrow the chariots and their riders; and the horses and their riders shall fall, every one by the sword of a comrade. [23]On that day, says the Lord of hosts, I will take you, O Zerubbabel my servant, son of Shealtiel, says the Lord, and make you like a signet ring; for I have chosen you, says the Lord of hosts.

ZECHARIAH

The relationship between chapters 1–8 and 9–14

The differences between Zechariah 1–8 and Zechariah 9–14 are great enough for most scholars to see them as two distinct and originally independent works. The apocalyptic vision of a future time in which conflict will end with victory on the side of those who are faithful to God is characteristic only of the second part.

Yet certain passages in both parts show some similarity in topic or outlook. They share a view of Jerusalem at the centre of the world's destiny, linked to a universalistic view of other nations turning towards Jerusalem in a coming age. They share a desire for purifying Judean society, and a common concern with the community's leadership. The final editor who put the parts together to form our present book may have done so partly because of the topical similarities which he saw in them here and there.

The prophet and his situation: chapters 1–8

We may guess that Zechariah was a responsible member of priestly circles and the establishment more generally. He was active at least as early as 520 (Zechariah 1:1) and at least as late as the beginning of the following century (Nehemiah 12:16). The historical situation when Zechariah began to see his visions and hear the word of God was the same as that which provided the setting for Haggai. Both in Haggai and in Zechariah we find emphasis on Jerusalem as the place of God's dwelling, on the importance of reconstructing the Temple, on the role of Joshua and Zerubbabel.

The prophet and his situation: chapters 9–14

There have been vast differences of opinion among scholars trying to find the historical situations in which the oracles of chapters 9–14 were uttered, so that we might understand those oracles better. They have been referred to the period before 721, or to the latter years of the kingdom of Judah or, more commonly, to a period after the arrival of the armies of Alexander the Great in the Near East in 333.

Outline

(I) Zechariah 1–8
  (A) Prologue (1:1–6)
  (B) Eight night visions and their oracles (1:7–6:15)
  (a) The coloured horses and the horsemen (1:7–17)

HIGHLIGHT

Zechariah 6:1–8

[1] And again I looked up and saw four chariots coming out from between two mountains – mountains of bronze. [2] The first chariot had red horses, the second chariot black horses, [3] the third chariot white horses, and the fourth chariot dappled grey horses. [4] Then I said to the angel who talked with me, 'What are these, my Lord?' [5] The angel answered me, 'These are the four winds of heaven going out, after presenting themselves before the Lord of all the earth. [6] The chariot with the black horses goes toward the north country, the white ones go toward the west country, and the dappled ones go toward the south country.' [7] When the steeds came out, they were impatient to get off and patrol the earth. And he said, 'Go, patrol the earth.' So they patrolled the earth. [8] Then he cried out to me, 'Lo, those who go toward the north country have set my spirit at rest in the north country.'

MALACHI

The prophet and his situation

We know nothing of the author's life, but from his small book we learn something of the kind of person he was. Despite his attacks on priests (1:6–2:4), he was favourable to the levitical priesthood (2:4–7), and he insisted on the people's obligation to contribute to the expenses of the Temple and the support of the personnel (3:6–12). He had a humane concern for the wife who suffers rejection (2:14–16), for the people of Judah who wonder about God's love for them (1:2–5), and he was sure that those who wrong the defenceless would eventually receive punishment from God (3:5). He had a religious sense of God's honour (1:6–14) and of the transcendence which enables God to enforce his will wherever he wishes (1:5).

Although we have no way of dating Malachi precisely, it is surely more recent than 515, because it presupposes the Temple already built, with its regular system of worship functioning. The regional administrator or governor of the Persian period is mentioned in 1:8. Some of the problems mentioned are among those troubling Nehemiah and reformed by Ezra – foreign wives (Malachi 2:10–12; Nehemiah 13:3, 23–30; Ezra 9:1–15; 10:1–43) and inadequate Temple administration (Malachi 1:6–2:9; 3:6–12; Nehemiah 12:44–47; 13:10–14). The new age, imminent in Haggai and Zechariah, has not come, and one senses a certain disillusionment in what the people say in Malachi 2:17–3:5; 3:13–15. In Malachi new hope is held out, but the coming age is no longer presented as something necessarily soon to be.

Outline

(I) **The six oracles (1:1–3:21)**
- (A) *God's preferential love for Israel (1:2–5)*
- (B) *Cultic offences (1:6–2:9)*
- (C) *Mixed marriages and divorce (2:10–16)*
- (D) *God will purify and justly judge (2:17–3:5)*
- (E) *Tithes for God, blessings for the people (3:6–12)*
- (F) *Those who fear God will come out ahead (3:13–21)*

(II) **The two appendixes (3:22–24)**

HIGHLIGHT

Malachi 3:1–5

¹See, I am sending my messenger to prepare the way before me, and the Lord whom you seek will suddenly come to his temple. The messenger of the covenant in whom you delight – indeed, he is coming, says the Lord of hosts. ²But who can endure the day of his coming, and who can stand when he appears?

For he is like a refiner's fire and like fullers' soap; ³he will sit as a refiner and purifier of silver, and he will purify the descendants of Levi and refine them like gold and silver, until they present offerings to the Lord in righteousness. ⁴Then the offering of Judah and Jerusalem will be pleasing to the Lord as in the days of old and as in former years.

⁵Then I will draw near to you for judgement; I will be swift to bear witness against the sorcerers, against the adulterers, against those who swear falsely, against those who oppress the hired workers in their wages, the widow and the orphan, against those who thrust aside the alien, and do not fear me, says the Lord of hosts.

TWENTY-THREE

The Chronicler:

1–2 Chronicles,

Ezra, Nehemiah

The material in this chapter is digested from NJBC article 23, 'The Chronicler: 1–2 Chronicles, Ezra, Nehemiah', by Robert North, SJ.

What are 1–2 Chronicles about?

They are a book (or books) of history. Partly they are a dull, dry listing of genealogies, partly a collection of lively sermons. Neither of these types exactly fits our definition of history, but then every history is different. 1–2 Chronicles/Ezra/Nehemiah is the third major history in the Bible: the other two are the Pentateuch and the Former Prophets (see pages 13, 37). The principal block of Chronicles sets forth the achievement of David, chiefly the regulation of the Temple worship. Both David's rise to power in displacing Saul and the story of the succession to David's throne are omitted. Chronicles was written to glorify and consolidate the ritual and dynastic authority of the Davidic covenant, almost wholly ignoring the covenant of Moses and Sinai so largely focused elsewhere in the Bible. Not only David but Solomon too is glorified, and these two along with two other 'approved' kings (out of 21) occupy 480 of the 822 verses.

There is general agreement that the author of Chronicles is a Levite cantor whose own genealogy is probably that given in 1 Chronicles 3:19–24; in general he mentions Levites 100 times; in Ezra and Nehemiah they are mentioned 60 times; by contrast they are mentioned twice only in 1–2 Samuel and but once in 1–2 Kings! More broadly still, the concern for a live worship ritual in Chronicles is perhaps its chief message for our century.

Ezra and Nehemiah considered alongside 1-2 Chronicles

The prevalent opinion among scholars is that the Chronicler wrote (or rather added to his compilation) the materials in Ezra and Nehemiah – although some scholars deny this.

The first statement made about Ezra in the book which bears his name is that he and some other latecomers finally leave Babylon in the seventh year of King Artaxerxes (Ezra 7:7). If the king in question is Artaxerxes I this gives a date of 458 BC. But if Artaxerxes II is referred to, the date would be 398. Other scholars believe that Ezra 7:7–8 should read '37th' year (of Artaxerxes I) which would mean 428.

1-2 CHRONICLES

Outline

(I) Threshold genealogies (1 Chronicles 1:1–9:44)
- *(A) The Semites in the family of nations (1:1–54)*
- *(B) The twelve tribes (2:1–7:40)*
- (a) Judah's line (2:1–4:23)
  - (i) Judah to Jesse (2:3–17)
  - (ii) First Caleb saga (2:18–41)
  - (iii) Two variant Caleb sagas (2:42–55)
  - (iv) David's own line (3:1–24)
  - (v) Three more Caleb sagas (4:1–23)
- (b) Rest of the SE tribal alliance (4:24–5:26)
- (c) The Levites (6:1–81)
  - (i) Moses and Samuel (6:1–30)
  - (ii) Lineage of the Levite choir (6:31–48)
  - (iii) Zadokite legitimacy (6:49–53)
  - (iv) The Levite settlements (6:54–81)
- (d) Pre-David northern elements (7:1–40)
- *(C) Saul/Jerusalem setting (8:1–9:44)*

(II) David's empire (10:1–29:30)
- *(A) Legitimacy of the succession (10:1–11:9)*
- *(B) David's militia (11:10–12:40)*
- *(C) Theocratic consolidation (13:1–17:27)*
- (a) Recovery of the Ark (13:1–14)
- (b) Building up the house of David (14:1–17)
- (c) Tabernacle inauguration (15:1–16:43)
- (d) Temple project deferred (17:1–27)

Drawing of reliefs from the palace of Sennacherib at Nineveh, showing the siege of Lachish in 701 BC (see 2 Chronicles 32:9). Reproduced by permission of the British Library

(D) *Empire-building wars (18:1–21:7)*
(a) East-Jordan campaigns (18:2–20:3)
(b) Philistine episodes (20:4–8)
(c) The fateful census (21:1–7)
(E) *Temple under way (21:8–29:30)*
(a) Religious import of the census (21:8–22:1)
(b) David's plans (22:2–19)
(c) The Levite personnel (23:1–27:34)
(d) David's entailed abdication (28:1–29:30)

(III) **Solomon's reign (2 Chronicles 1:1–9:31)**
(A) *The inauguration at Gibeon (1:1–17)*
(B) *The Temple (2:1–7:22)*
(a) Contracts and building (2:1–3:17)
(b) Minor furnishings (4:1–22)
(c) Enthronement of the Ark (5:1–7:22)
(C) *Solomon's civil rule (8:1–9:31)*
(a) Commerce and urban renewal (8:1–16)
(b) Fleet and fringe benefits (8:17–9:31)

(IV) **Kings of Judah-without-Israel (2 Chronicles 10:1–36:23)**
(A) *The first Israelite dynasty (10:1–16:14)*
(a) Rehoboam causes trouble (10:1–12:16)
(b) The end of Jeroboam (13:1–22)
(c) Asa outlives Jeroboam's dynasty (14:1–16:14)
(B) *The century of social unrest (17:1–25:28)*
(a) Jehoshaphat (870–852?) (17:1–20:37)
(b) Athaliah (841–835) (21:1–23:21)
(c) Joash (835–797), Amaziah (797–792) (24:1–25:28)
(C) *Rise of book prophecy (26:1–32:33)*
(a) Uzziah's architecture and leprosy (26:1–23)
(b) Isaiah's royal antagonists (27:1–28:27)
(c) Hezekiah's reconciling move (29:1–32:33)
(D) *Judah's disillusionment (33:1–36:23)*
(a) Not-so-wicked Manasseh (33:1–25)
(b) Josiah (34:1–35:27)
(c) The Babylonian puppets (36:1–23)

EZRA AND NEHEMIAH

Outline

(I) **The second Temple (Ezra 1:1–6:22)**
(A) *Cyrus and the return (1:1–11)*
(B) *Zerubbabel and the list (2:1–70)*
(C) *Laying the cornerstone (3:1–13)*

(D) *Interruption: the Samaritans (4:1–24)*
(E) *Prophetic nudge to completion (5:1–6:22)*

(II) Ezra's return and Torah (Ezra 7:1–10:44)
 (A) *Ezra's priestly scribal activity (7:1–28)*
 (B) *Rounding up the convoy (8:1–31)*
 (C) *The situation in Jerusalem (8:32–10:44)*

(III) Rearmament of Jerusalem (Nehemiah 1:1–7:72)
 (A) *Susa report and sequel (1:1–2:11)*
 (a) The Jerusalem disaster (1:1–10)
 (b) Nehemiah's plea granted (2:1–11)
 (B) *Programme of reconstruction (2:12–3:32)*
 (a) Wall inspection by night (2:12–20)
 (b) The local chapter masons (3:1–32)
 (C) *Triumphalism (4:1–7:72)*
 (a) Embattled persistence (4:1–23)
 (b) Social justice reform (5:1–19)
 (c) Dramatic completion of the mission (6:1–7:72)

(IV) Ezra's Torah promulgated (Nehemiah 7:73–9:38)

(V) Nehemiah's reform (Nehemiah 10:1–13:31)
 (A) *The pledge (10:1–39)*
 (B) *Repopulating Jerusalem (11:1–12:26)*
 (C) *Solemn dedication of the wall (12:27–13:14)*
 (D) *Nehemiah as defender of the faith (13:15–31)*

HIGHLIGHT

Cyrus and the return
Ezra 1:1–11

[1]In the first year of King Cyrus of Persia, in order that the word of the Lord by the mouth of Jeremiah might be accomplished, the Lord stirred up the spirit of King Cyrus of Persia so that he sent a herald throughout all his kingdom, and also in a written edict declared:

[2]"Thus says King Cyrus of Persia: The Lord, the God of heaven, has given me all the kingdoms of the earth, and he has charged me to build him a house at Jerusalem in Judah. [3]And of those among you who are of his people – may their God be with them! – are now permitted to go up to Jerusalem in Judah, and rebuild the house of the Lord, the God of Israel – he is the God who is in Jerusalem; [4]and let all survivors, in whatever place they reside, be assisted by the people of their place with silver and gold, with

goods and with animals, besides freewill offerings for the house of God in Jerusalem.'

[5]The heads of the families of Judah and Benjamin, and the priests and the Levites – everyone whose spirit God had stirred – got ready to go up and rebuild the house of the Lord in Jerusalem. [6]All their neighbours aided them with silver vessels, with gold, with goods, with animals, and with valuable gifts, besides all that was freely offered. [7]King Cyrus himself brought out the vessels of the house of the Lord that Nebuchadnezzar had carried away from Jerusalem and placed in the house of his gods. [8]King Cyrus of Persia had them released into the charge of Mithredath the treasurer, who counted them out to Sheshbazzar the prince of Judah. [9]And this was the inventory: gold basins, thirty; silver basins, one thousand; knives, twenty-nine; [10]gold bowls, thirty; other silver bowls, four hundred and ten; other vessels, one thousand; [11]the total of the gold and silver vessels was five thousand four hundred. All these Sheshbazzar brought up, when the exiles were brought up from Babylonia to Jerusalem.

Joel, Obadiah

The material in this chapter is digested from NJBC article 24, 'Joel, Obadiah', by Elias D. Mallon.

JOEL

The author of Joel

Joel had a deep appreciation for the worship conducted in the Temple (1:8–9; 2:27; 4:16–17). The book contains liturgical terms such as vegetable offering and libation, fast and solemn assembly (1:14; 2:12, 15). Temple personnel such as priests (1:9, 13; 2:17), ministers of Yahweh (1:9; 2:17), ministers of the altar (1:13), and 'ministers of my God' (1:13) appear.

The date of Joel

The book was written after the rebuilding of the Temple in 515 BC and before the destruction of Sidon in 343, and after the time of Obadiah and Malachi. A date between the last half of the 5th and the first half of the 4th century seems best to fit the context.

The book of Joel and its message

The book falls into two large sections. The first (1–2) deals with the locust plague and drought, the second (3–4) is eschatological (see page 100). The book nevertheless remains both a theological and artistic unit.

Joel develops a theme of reversal of fortunes. Chapters 1–2 deal with the immediate crisis of the locusts and drought; chapter 1 presents the effects which the locusts have on the countryside and the crops. This has a direct effect on the worship in the Temple. The people who are immediately affected – harvesters, farmers, priests and Temple ministers – are called to lament.

Locusts

Theologically the message is one of hope built on experience.
The devastation visited upon Israel by the locusts and drought
was immense. However, if Yahweh responded to Israel's heart-
felt lament and removed this particular disaster, it was a sign
that Yahweh had not abandoned his people; God was still in
their midst.

Outline

(I) **The locust plague (1:1–2:17)**
    (A) *The attack on the countryside (1:1–20)*
    (a) Immediate effects (1:1–4)
    (b) Calls to lament (1:5–14)
        (i) 'Wake up, drunkards!' (1:5–7)
        (ii) 'Wail!' (1:8–10)
        (iii) 'Be ashamed, farmers!' (1:11–12)
        (iv) 'Gird yourselves, priests!' (1:13–14)
    (c) Lament for 'the Day' (1:15–18)
    (d) Prayer to Yahweh (1:19–20)
    (B) *The attack on the city (2:1–17)*
    (a) The military metaphor (2:1–11)
    (b) Calls to repent (2:12–17)

(II) **The plague interpreted (2:18–4:21)**
    (A) *The end of the plague and the restoration (2:18–26)*
    (B) *The purpose of the plague (2:27)*
    (C) *Effects of Yahweh's presence in the midst of Israel
        (3:1–4:21)*
    (a) Cosmic 'spiritual' effects on Israel (3:1–5)
    (b) Reversal of fortune (4:1–21)
        (i) Judgement of the nations in the valley of
            Jehoshaphat (4:1–3)
        (ii) Additional oracle against Tyre, Sidon, and
            Philistia (4:4–8)
        (iii) War against the nations (4:9–11)
        (iv) Judgement of the nations in the valley of
            Jehoshaphat (4:12–17)
        (v) Judah and Jerusalem compared with Edom and
            Egypt (4:18–21)

OBADIAH

Background

Edom was a neighbouring country, related to Judah through Esau and Jacob, but the relationship between the two countries had hardly ever been friendly.

During the last days of the kingdom of Judah, Judah and Edom were involved with others in a plot against Babylon. The result was disastrous: Judah and Jerusalem were destroyed. It is not certain that Edom actively took part in the destruction of Jerusalem, but the people of Judah believed that they had been betrayed by Edom and this bitterness was expressed in this book, and in Psalm 137:7.

The date

The book must have been written after the destruction of Jerusalem in 587 BC and before Edom was conquered by the Nabateans in 312. But most of it is probably as early as the 5th century.

Outline

(I) Oracle against Edom (1–14, 15b)
  (A) Edom is doomed (1–9)
  (B) Reasons for Edom's destruction (10–14, 15b)

(II) Day of Yahweh, punishment of nations (15a, 16–21)

HIGHLIGHT

Joel 2:1–3

¹Blow the trumpet in Zion;
  sound the alarm on my holy mountain!
Let all the inhabitants of the land tremble,
  for the day of the Lord is coming, it is near –
²a day of darkness and gloom,
  a day of clouds and thick darkness!

Like blackness spread upon the mountains
    a great and powerful army comes;
their like has never been from of old,
    nor will be again after them
    in ages to come.
[3]Fire devours in front of them,
    and behind them a flame burns.
Before them the land is like the garden of Eden,
    but after them a desolate wilderness,
    and nothing escapes them.

Stone carving of Darius I, king of Persia 521–486 BC

TWENTY-FIVE

Daniel

Title and contents

The material in this chapter is digested from NJBC article 25, 'Daniel', by Louis F. Hartman, CSSR, revised by Alexander A. Di Lella, OFM.

The book is named not after its author but after the leading character, who is presented here as living in Babylonia during the reign of the last kings of the Neo-Babylonian empire and their first successors, the early kings of the Medes and the Persians – i.e., most of the 6th century BC. The name Daniel means 'my judge is God'.

The first part contains six stories about Daniel and his three companions at the royal court in Babylonia. *The second part* (chapters 7–12) tells in symbolic visions of the four kingdoms under which God's people, the Jews, would live from the Babylonian conquest of Judea until God's establishment of his kingdom for them.

An appendix, chapters 13–14, contains three other stories. Since these appear only in the Greek Old Testament, they are left out of some Bibles.

Historical background

Coin of Ptolemy I (king of Egypt 304–283/282 BC)

Nebuchadnezzar, king of Babylon, had taken over most of the Assyrian empire including the Northern Kingdom, Israel; in 587 he conquered Judah as well. However, in 539 Cyrus the Great of Persia conquered Babylon, and the Persians ruled the whole area until conquered by the Greeks under Alexander the Great in 331.

In the third century Palestine was governed by the Ptolemies of Egypt, and in the second century by the Greek dynasty of the Seleucids, whose capital was at Antioch in Syria.

For the Jews Nebuchadnezzar's conquest meant that many

of them were deported to exile in Babylon between 598 and 582. After Cyrus conquered Babylon, they were allowed to return to their homeland. They had a certain amount of religious and political freedom under the Persians and the Ptolemies, but the Seleucid ruler Antiochus IV Epiphanes tried to force them to abandon their religion and to practise pagan worship. This led to the armed revolt told of in Maccabees.

The conflict between the religion of the Jews and the paganism of their foreign rulers is the theme of Daniel. But the book of Daniel takes the view that God had long foreseen this and allowed it: to show the superiority of Israel's wisdom and to show that in the end the God of Israel is the ruler of history and will eventually establish his kingdom on earth.

What kind of literature is this book?

There are two kinds of literature in this book which seem strange to modern readers.

(1) THE TELLING OF A STORY TO GIVE A MORAL LESSON: this is seen in chapters 1–6; 13–14. It is not claimed that these stories about Daniel are true history, and no one knows whether Daniel was a real character about whom popular legends grew, or whether he was a figure of folklore.

(2) APOCALYPTIC WRITING: this is fantastic writing concerning mysterious 'revelation' about the past, the present and the future. Events of the past are presented as prophecies of future happenings, to give an interpretation of history as if from God's point of view. (See page 100.)

When was it written?

The beliefs and interests of the author show that he lived long after the exile; and his detailed description of the profanation of the Temple by Antiochus IV Epiphanes, together with his expectation that such an evil man would come to a bad end, suggest that it was written shortly before Antiochus's death in 164.

The book was written to encourage the Jews to remain faithful to their religion in spite of two temptations: one was to be impressed by the worldly culture of Hellenism (the Greek-speaking world); the other was to give in when those who would not accept the pagan religion of Antiochus IV Epiphanes were persecuted.

The importance of Daniel

Chapters 7–12 are the first clear example of apocalyptic writing in its fullest development, and it was to have tremendous influence in the next few centuries.

Also significant are the important role of angels as messengers of God, and the clear teaching on the resurrection of the dead, which is unique in the Hebrew Old Testament.

The expectation of the Messiah in Daniel brings Israel's hope of salvation to the final stage before its full realization in the New Testament.

Outline

(I) **Exploits of Daniel and his companions at the Babylonian court (1:1–6:29)**
  (A) *The food test (1:1–21)*
  (B) *Nebuchadnezzar's dream of the composite statue (2:1–49)*
  (C) *Daniel's companions in the fiery furnace (3:1–97)*
  (D) *Nebuchadnezzar's dream of the great tree (3:98[31]–4:34)*
  (E) *The writing on the wall at Belshazzar's feast (5:1–6:1)*
  (F) *Daniel in the lions' den (6:2–29)*

(II) **Daniel's apocalyptic visions (7:1–12:13)**
  (A) *The four beasts (7:1–28)*
  (B) *The ram and the he-goat (8:1–27)*
  (C) *The interpretation of the 70 weeks (9:1–27)*
  (D) *The revelation of the Hellenistic wars (10:1–12:13)*

(III) **Other exploits of Daniel (13:1–14:42)**
  (A) *Daniel's rescue of the chaste Susanna (13:1–64)*
  (B) *Daniel and the priests of Bel (14:1–22)*
  (C) *Daniel's destruction of the dragon (14:23–42)*

HIGHLIGHT

Daniel 7:13–14

[13]As I watched in the night visions,
  I saw one like a human being
    coming with the clouds of heaven.
  And he came to the Ancient One
    and was presented before him.
[14]To him was given dominion
    and glory and kingship,
  that all peoples, nations, and languages
    should serve him.
  His dominion is an everlasting dominion
    that shall not pass away,
  and his kingship is one
    that shall never be destroyed.

TWENTY-SIX

1–2 Maccabees

Are Maccabees part of Scripture?

The material in this chapter is digested from NJBC article 26, '1–2 Maccabees', by Neil J. McEleney, CSP.

There are four books known by the title 'Maccabees'. All four owe their name to Judas Maccabeus, the third son of the priest Mattathias, who began the Jewish revolt against the Seleucids in 167 BC.

The earliest explicit Christian reference to these books is in Clement of Alexandria, near the beginning of the 3rd century AD. First-century and subsequent Judaism omitted these books from those held sacred.

In the Roman Catholic Church 1 and 2 Maccabees have, since antiquity, been part of the canon of Scripture, i.e., those books placed in the Bible; Protestant Christianity, however, does not consider 1 and 2 Maccabees to be canonical literature, although it accords these works a special place among the apocrypha.

The authors' purpose in writing

Although 1 Maccabees is a historical work, it is meant to convey a lesson. Probably intended to show God at work in Jewish history in the Seleucid empire as he was earlier in Jewish history, it depicts his saving action in the Maccabean struggle against paganism. The lesson of Mattathias and his sons is there for every true Israelite to learn. Fidelity to the law and faith in God achieved more than the size of one's army or the strength of one's arm (2:61–64). The Maccabees' efforts won independence and a kingdom, and prepared the way for God's future intervention (4:46; 14:41). All Israel should look to their example.

Similarly, 2 Maccabees is intended to instruct and to edify. It seeks to strengthen Jewish faith everywhere by the heroic example of persecuted brethren (6:31).

Teaching

The teaching of 2 Maccabees belongs to the Pharisees' school while the thought of 1 Maccabees is closer to that of the Sadducees.

1 MACCABEES

*Seleucid coin,
showing a war
elephant*

Outline
(I) Preamble (1:1–64) (A) *Alexander and the Diadochi (1:1–10)* (B) *Hellenizers (1:11–15)* (C) *Antiochus's first campaign in Egypt (1:16–19)* (D) *Antiochus despoils the Temple (1:20–24a)* (E) *Dirge (1:24b–28)* (F) *Apollonius attacks Jerusalem (1:29–35)* (G) *Dirge (1:36–40)* (H) *Antiochus proscribes Judaism and imposes pagan practices (1:41–51a)* (I) *The execution of Antiochus's edict (1:51b–64)* **(II) Mattathias begins active resistance (2:1–70)** (A) *Mattathias's lament (2:1–14)* (B) *Resistance flares (2:15–28)* (C) *The slaughter on the Sabbath and its sequel (2:29–41)* (D) *The Hasideans (2:42–48)* (E) *Mattathias's testament (2:49–70)* **(III) Judas Maccabeus takes command of the struggle (3:1–9:22)** (A) *Praise of Judas (3:1–9)* (B) *Judas defeats Apollonius and Seron (3:10–26)* (C) *Antiochus goes east (3:27–37)* (D) *Judas defeats Gorgias and Nicanor (3:38–4:27)* (E) *Judas defeats Lysias at Beth-zur (4:28–35)* (F) *The purification and dedication of the Temple (4:36–61)* (G) *Judas battles with neighbouring peoples (5:1–68)* (a) *Idumea (5:3–5; 2 Maccabees 10:14–23)* (b) *Ammon (5:6–8; 2 Maccabees 8:30–33?)*

(H) Renewal of the alliances with Rome and Sparta
(14:16–24)
(I) Decree of the Jews honouring Simon (14:25–49)
(J) Antiochus VII grants privileges to Simon and besieges
Trypho (15:1–14)
(K) The return of the embassy sent to Rome (15:15–24)
(L) Antiochus breaks his alliance with Simon (15:25–36)
(M) John Hyrcanus and Judas defeat Cendebaeus
(15:37–16:10)
(N) The murder of Simon and his two sons (16:11–22)
(O) Conclusion to 1 Maccabees (16:23–24)

2 MACCABEES

Outline

(I) Letters to the Jews of Egypt (1:1–2:18)
(A) The first letter (1:1–10a)
(B) The second letter (1:10b–2:18)

(II) The epitomist's preface (2:19–32)

(III) The decline of the high priesthood (3:1–4:50)
(A) The episode of Heliodorus (3:1–40)
(B) Simon's plot against Onias (4:1–6)
(C) Jason the high priest introduces Hellenism (4:7–20)
(D) Antiochus is received by Jason in Jerusalem (4:21–22)
(E) Menelaus as high priest (4:23–50)

(IV) Antiochus Epiphanes and the imposition of Hellenism
(5:1–7:42)
(A) Antiochus ravages Jerusalem (5:1–14)
(B) Antiochus despoils the Temple (5:15–23a)
(C) Apollonius attacks Jerusalem (5:23b–26)
(D) Judas Maccabeus in the desert (5:27)
(E) Antiochus imposes Hellenism (6:1–11)
(F) The writer's understanding (6:12–17)
(G) The martyrdom of Eleazar (6:18–31)
(H) The martyrdom of the mother and her seven sons
(7:1–42)

(V) The triumph of Judaism under Judas Maccabeus
(8:1–10:9)
(A) Judas organizes resistance to the persecution (8:1–7)
(B) Judas defeats Nicanor and Gorgias (8:8–29, 34–36)
(C) Judas's other victories (8:30–33)

HIGHLIGHT

Mattathias's testament
I Maccabees 2:49–70

[49]Now the days drew near for Mattathias to die, and he said to his sons, 'Arrogance and scorn have now become strong; it is a time of ruin and furious anger. [50]Now, my children, show zeal for the law, and give your lives for the covenant of our ancestors.

[51]'Remember the deeds of the ancestors, which they did in their generations; and you will receive great honour and an everlasting name. [52]Was not Abraham found faithful when tested, and it was reckoned to him as righteousness? [53]Joseph in the time of his distress kept the commandment, and became lord of Egypt. [54]Phinehas our ancestor, because he was deeply zealous, received the covenant of everlasting priesthood. [55]Joshua, because he fulfilled the command, became a judge in Israel. [56]Caleb, because he testified in the assembly, received an inheritance in the land. [57]David, because he was merciful, inherited the throne of the kingdom forever. [58]Elijah, because of great zeal for the law, was taken up into heaven. [59]Hannaniah, Azariah, and Mishael believed and were saved from the flame. [60]Daniel, because of his innocence, was delivered from the mouth of the lions.

[61]'And so observe, from generation to generation, that none of those who put their trust in him will lack strength. [62]Do not fear the words of sinners, for their splendour will turn into dung and worms. [63]Today they will be exalted, but tomorrow they will not

be found, because they will have returned to the dust, and their plans will have perished. [64]My children, be courageous and grow strong in the law, for by it you will gain honour.

[65]'Here is your brother Simeon who, I know, is wise in counsel; always listen to him; he shall be your father. [66]Judas Maccabeus has been a mighty warrior from his youth; he shall command the army for you and fight the battle against the peoples. [67]You shall rally around you all who observe the law, and avenge the wrong done to your people. [68]Pay back the Gentiles in full, and obey the commands of the law.'

[69]Then he blessed them, and was gathered to his ancestors. [70]He died in the one hundred and forty-sixth year and was buried in the tomb of his ancestors at Modein. And all Israel mourned for him with great lamentation.

Introduction to

Wisdom

Literature

Background

The material in this
chapter is digested
from NJBC article
27, 'Introduction to
Wisdom Literature',
by Roland E.
Murphy, OCarm.

Wisdom literature was an international phenomenon in the ancient world. The biblical books fit into this literary and philosophical development, and were influenced by it in varying degrees. Scholars are able to compare the biblical writings with other texts, principally from Egypt and Mesopotamia. However, in spite of parallels between the biblical and other writings, biblical wisdom retains its own individual stamp.

The wisdom literature of the Bible:
introduction

About three-quarters of the 400 occurrences of the word 'wisdom' in the Old Testament appear in just five books, usually classified as 'wisdom literature': Proverbs, Job, Ecclesiastes, Sirach and Wisdom. In addition, the counsels in Tobit 4:3–21; 12:6–13, and the poem in Baruch 3:9–4:4 should be mentioned. There has been considerable discussion of wisdom influence on other books, such as the Joseph story (Genesis 37–51), but 'wisdom' is a wide-ranging term, describing the skill of an artisan (Exodus 36:8), royal judgement (1 Kings 3:28), cleverness (Proverbs 30:24–28), proper rules of conduct (Proverbs 2:1–22), piety (Proverbs 9:10; Job 1:1), a way of coping with life.

Certain general features are characteristic of this literature:

(1) An absence of any reference to the sacred traditions, such as the promises to Abraham, Isaac and Jacob, Exodus, Sinai, covenant, etc. (2) A certain international style. This is shown by the appearance of non-Israelites, such as Agur and Lemuel in Proverbs 30–31 and Job with his three friends, by the explicit comparison of Solomon's wisdom with that of the people of the East and of Egypt (1 Kings 4:29–34 [5:9–14]).

Wisdom is both content and style. The content can be summed up in one word: life. The goal of wisdom is the good life, here and now, marked by long life, prosperity, and prestige, as recalled in Job 30:2–20. A necessary ingredient is a proper relationship to God; indeed, fear of the Lord leads to wisdom (Proverbs 9:10; 1:7; Job 28:28; Psalm 111:10; Sirach 1:16).

The content can also be described in terms of (1) justice, as when Solomon prayed for and received a 'listening heart' (1 Kings 3:9, 12); (2) nature, a knowledge of which is attributed to Solomon (1 Kings 4:33 [5:13]) and which is illustrated in Proverbs 30:15–33 and Job 38–41; (3) theological wisdom, in which the sages reflected more intensely on the nature of wisdom (Proverbs 8; Sirach 24); (4) experiential wisdom, the broadest and most common category. Experiential wisdom is a human response to environment, an attempt to understand and cope with it. Successful insights are captured in pithy sayings. Pride goes before a fall (Proverbs 16:18; 18:12). A quarrel should be checked at once (Proverbs 17:12); laziness leads to poverty (Proverbs 10:4). The wisdom literature of the Bible reflects on a wide area of life in order to provide insights into the way things are and the way they should be. The lessons consist of simple observations as well as moral exhortation. Compared with the commandments of the Torah, the teaching deals with the formation of character. Control of the tongue and of all the appetites is the ideal.

Origins

What are the origins of wisdom literature? Each book has its own particular history, but how did the wisdom movement originate? At the present time it seems best to recognize two sources: (1) the clan or tribe within which lessons would have been transmitted in the home; (2) the court school(s), in which more technical instruction was available. For neither view is there any direct evidence.

In wisdom literature, the 'saying' is a sentence, drawn from experience and usually expressed in a short pithy form; when it establishes itself among a community it may be called a 'proverb'. Usually, the saying characterizes a particular act or attitude as wise or foolish.

The saying can also be put in the form of a command (compare Proverbs 16:3 with 16:20), or a prohibition; frequently a reason is added to strengthen a prohibition (Proverbs 3:1–2; 22:22–23).

• JOB is unique; it partakes of various forms derived from litigation and from the Psalms as well as from the sayings of wisdom literature.

• QOHELETH employs many forms, but the reflection based on experience ('I have seen' and 'I know' occur very often) is characteristic. The style of his reflection is clear from such phrases as 'I said in my heart' (1:16–17; 2:1, 15; 3:17). He also makes use of an example story (9:13–16). Qoheleth is also known as Ecclesiastes.

• THE WISDOM OF SOLOMON is difficult to classify. Within it are to be found sayings, admonitions, and even prayers (Wisdom 9:1–18).

Key theological aspects

Retribution

Wisdom and folly are practical virtues. The attitude and actions of the wise beget prosperity; folly leads to disaster. This optimistic doctrine was not presented without reservations but it was the dominant view, and it shared in the general biblical belief in divine retribution (Deuteronomy 28, 30; the prophets).

Creation

Wisdom theology has rightly been characterized as 'creation theology'. That is to say, the created world is the source of wisdom's insights. The 'environment' ranges through the entire realm of creation from humans to ants to trees. Job tells his friends to go to the beasts and birds, to reptiles and fish, to learn the activity of God in all that happens (12:7–9). The series of comparisons in Proverbs 30:15–31 draws on the observation of humans and animals. Human experience becomes the basis of all comments: parent to child, master to servant, equal to equal. One must learn from human experience how to live and thus ensure development of character. Creation not only offers the raw material for human development. It also serves as a line of communication for God, as Psalm 19 indicates.

The personification of Wisdom

The figure of Lady Wisdom emerges clearly in Proverbs 1, 8 and 9. In chapter 1 she speaks in the style of an Old Testament prophet, threatening her audience, should they not heed her; she will laugh at their doom, just as the Lord laughs at his enemies (1:26). But she also offers peace and security to those who obey her. In Proverbs 9 there is a change of tone, as she invites the 'simple' to the banquet she has prepared (9:1–6). This is in stark contrast to the meal prepared by Dame Folly (9:13–18), who offers bread and water, and stolen, at that! The lengthiest personification occurs in 8:3–36, where again Lady Wisdom speaks in public, and in an encouraging vein. The truth she proclaims is more valuable than silver or gold, and she loves those who love her (8:17). No fewer than six times does she affirm her existence before creation (8:22–26). Wisdom 7:22 understands her to be actively engaged in creation. Her precise role remains unclear. She is distinct from the works of creation, yet somehow present. However, she does have a role in the created world, for her delight is to be with human beings (8:31). The nature of her dealings with human beings can be inferred from her preaching and teaching in chapters 1, 8, 9, and especially from her promise of life in 8:32: 'the one who finds me finds life'. The interpretation of wisdom as a communication of God is continued in the Christian tradition: Christ is called the wisdom of God in 1 Corinthians 1:24; and Hebrews 1:3 seems to reflect Wisdom 7:25–26. The role of Lady Wisdom in the development of Christology is an important chapter in the history of theology.

Proverbs

The book

The material in this chapter is digested from NJBC article 28, 'Proverbs', by Thomas P. McCreesh, OP.

Proverbs is a collection of short two-line sayings (chapters 10–29). It opens with long poetic instructions (chapters 1–9) and ends with a section of longer sayings and short poems (30–31).

It was probably formed in two stages: first proverbs were collected by families or clans. Then, under Solomon and other kings, the collecting and editing of traditional wisdom was encouraged. The book is a special editing of some of these earlier materials.

A probable date is the late 6th or early 5th century BC: the personified wisdom (Proverbs 8) probably lies behind the portrait of wisdom in Sirach 24, so it must be earlier than Sirach. Also, the proverbs dealing with the king would suggest it was written not long after the time of the kings.

'Instructions' and 'proverbs'

● Instructions are advice given by a teacher or sage to a student ('son') and appear in chapters 1–9; 22:17–24:22 and 31:1–9. They are probably modelled on Egyptian parallels.
● Proverbs are statements expressing truth in a striking and memorable way.

Interpreting the book

The work seems easy to understand, but actually conceals deep and profound insights.

The nature of wisdom

Wisdom is not a secret knowledge reserved for the few, but can be sought by all. It is found through the difficult process of making well-informed choices in life. The reason the author is writing in the first place is that he considers there is a need to inform, train and persuade the young about these right choices. Wisdom is also at the service of others. It recognizes limits, ambiguities, and uncertainties. For example, the statement of one proverb is often modified, even denied, by the advice of another (26:4–5). And the ultimate guarantee of wisdom is the Lord, against whom no wisdom or counsel can stand (21:30).

Wisdom as symbolized

The instructions (chapters 1–9) describe wisdom as a woman who is courted. This is an apt symbol since wisdom must be sought out and cherished with dedication and devotion. Her call must be discerned amid appeals of pleasure and easy success, which are the ways of folly. Once gained, though, she will be faithful to her followers, building up their houses with peace and prosperity, like the good wife in 31:10–31. Wisdom is a gift from God meant to be the goal for all human searching.

Teaching

Wisdom mediates between God and the world. She was present at creation, she is the source of all meaning about this world. Coming from God, she is also a revelation of God and a call from him to the world. The heart of this wisdom is 'the fear of the Lord' which opens us to what God reveals and to respond to him. But this divine communication comes not only as knowledge but also as love. It is a divine appeal through creation which draws and embraces us. Thus, Christian theology has applied the figure of Wisdom to Jesus who, as the Incarnate Word of God, is the mediator between God and this world (1 Corinthians 1:24).

Outline

(I) **Prologue (1:1–9:18)**
   (A) *Introduction (1:1–33)*
   (a) Title and purpose (1:1–7)
   (b) First instruction: warning about sinners (1:8–19)
   (c) First speech of personified wisdom (1:20–33)
   (B) *The benefits of wisdom (2:1–7:27)*
   (a) Second instruction: wisdom's benefits (2:1–22)
   (b) Third instruction: fidelity toward the Lord (3:1–12)
   (c) Fourth instruction: the value of wisdom (3:13–26)
   (d) Fifth instruction: right conduct (3:27–35)
   (e) Sixth instruction: exhortation to get wisdom (4:1–9)
   (f) Seventh instruction: the two ways (4:10–27)
   (g) Eighth instruction: warning against adultery (5:1–23)
   (h) Interlude: four warnings (6:1–19)
   (i) Ninth instruction: warning against adultery (6:20–35)
   (j) Tenth instruction: warning against adultery (7:1–27)
   (C) *Second speech of personified wisdom (8:1–36)*
   (D) *Invitations to the banquets (9:1–18)*
   (a) Invitation to the banquet of wisdom (9:1–6)
   (b) Interlude: six proverbs (9:7–12)
   (c) Invitation to the banquet of folly (9:13–18)

(II) **The major collections of proverbs (10:1–29:27)**
   (A) *First collection of proverbs of Solomon (10:1–22:16)*
   (B) *Sayings of the wise (22:17–24:22)*
   (C) *Other sayings of the wise (24:23–34)*
   (D) *Second collection of proverbs of Solomon (25:1–29:27)*

(III) **Smaller collections of proverbs (30:1–31:9)**
   (A) *Sayings of Agur (30:1–14)*
   (B) *Numerical proverbs (30:15–33)*
   (C) *Sayings of Lemuel (31:1–9)*

(IV) **Acrostic poem on the good wife (31:10–31)**

HIGHLIGHT

Right conduct
Proverbs 3:27–35

[27]Do not withhold good from those to whom it is due,
   when it is in your power to do it.
[28]Do not say to your neighbour, 'Go, and come again,
   tomorrow I will give it' – when you have it with you.

[29]Do not plan harm against your neighbour
    who lives trustingly beside you.
[30]Do not quarrel with anyone without cause,
    when no harm has been done to you.
[31]Do not envy the violent
    and do not choose any of their ways;
[32]for the perverse are an abomination to the Lord,
    but the upright are in his confidence.
[33]The Lord's curse is on the house of the wicked,
    but he blesses the abode of the righteous.
[34]Toward the scorners he is scornful,
    but to the humble he shows favour.
[35]The wise will inherit honour,
    but stubborn fools, disgrace.

Canticle of Canticles, also known as Song of Songs or Song of Solomon

Title and date

The title in verse 1 – Song of Songs or Canticle of Canticles – is the way the Hebrew language says 'the greatest', so it is The Greatest Song. This is a collection of songs or poems; its unity is emphasized by the statement that Solomon is its author, perhaps because his name appears in 3:7ff. and 8:1ff.

It is generally agreed that it dates from after the exile, though individual poems might have been composed much earlier.

Structure and content

The work is dramatic in the sense that there is dialogue between the following speakers: a woman, a man, and the Daughters of Jerusalem. The main speaker is the woman; the man appears as both shepherd (1:7) and king (1:4, 12). It has been portrayed as a drama with two main characters (Solomon and the Shulammite), or even three (Solomon attempts to woo the Shulammite

The material in this chapter is digested from NJBC article 29, 'Canticle of Canticles', by Roland E. Murphy, OCarm.

151

from her country lover), but this latter view is generally rejected. There are several refrains (e.g., 2:7; 3:5; 8:4; 2:6; 8:3); very many words and phrases are repeated, and the same themes consistently appear. On the other hand, there are sudden shifts in dialogue (2:13–15; 3:5–6) and scene (5:1–2) that are hard to explain. There are poems of yearning (1:2–4; 2:14–15), teasing (1:7–8; 2:15), admiration (1:15–2:3; 4:9–5:1; 6:4–7), reminiscence (2:8–13), boast (6:8–10), and description of physical beauty (4:1–7; 5:10–16; 7:1–6). Similar forms appear in the love songs of ancient Egypt.

Interpretation

Traditionally, both Jewish and Christian interpretation of the Canticle of Canticles has been religious: the book is about the love of the Lord for his people; or, for Christians, the love of Christ for the church (or the individual soul). This view was supported by the theme of the marriage between the Lord and Israel (Hosea 1–3; Isaiah 62:5).

This interpretation contains the important basic insight that human love should not be seen as separate from divine love. But it can be taken too far, in finding religious meaning for every detail of the book.

Scholars nowadays would say the book is literally about human sexual love. Even though they may disagree about the number of characters, or the structure, or the dramatic nature of the work, most agree on this point: it seems to be the obvious meaning of the language. But that is not all it means: it recognizes another dimension to human love, as sharing somehow in divine love.

Imagery

There are many images drawn from the fields: gazelles and hinds, doves and foxes, sheep and goats. The gifts of nature abound: wine and vineyard, cedars and cypresses, figs and pomegranates. The imagery is drawn from many worlds. Not only places but also persons become transfigured. There is a 'make-believe' character about love, an idealization that knows no bounds when lovers speak about each other.

So they speak of a 'tower of ivory' (7:5) and of lips that drip choice myrrh (5:13). The modern reader has to adjust somewhat to the imagery because it is both representative and evocative, as the comparison of the woman's hair to a flock of goats streaming down Mount Gilead. The poetry and images are present for the enjoyment of imagination. Love has created a world of its own.

Myrrh

Outline

(I) The title (1:1)

(II) Introduction (1:2–6)

(III) Dialogue between lovers (1:7–2:7)

(IV) Reminiscence (2:8–17)

(V) Loss and discovery (3:1–5)

(VI) Solomon's wedding procession (3:6–11)

(VII) Dialogue between lovers (4:1–5:1)

(VIII) Dialogue between the woman and the Daughters (5:2–6:3)

(IX) Dialogue between lovers (6:4–12)

(X) A dialogue (7:1–8:4)

(XI) Appendixes (8:5–14)

HIGHLIGHT

Canticle of Canticles 8:6–7

⁶Set me as a seal upon your heart,
as a seal upon your arm;
for love is strong as death,
passion fierce as the grave.
Its flashes are flashes of fire,
a raging flame.
⁷Many waters cannot quench love,
neither can floods drown it.
If one offered for love all the wealth of his house,
it would be utterly scorned.

THIRTY

Job

The material in this chapter is digested from NJBC article 30, 'Job', by R. A. F. MacKenzie, SJ, revised by Roland E. Murphy, OCarm.

The structure of Job

The structure of the book of Job is essential for understanding it. Job was known in Hebrew tradition as a holy man and the story of his trial and restoration is found in the prologue (chapters 1–2) and epilogue (42:7–17) that form the framework. The poetic dialogue (chapters 3–31) deals with the problem of the meaning of suffering in the life of a just man. It is literature, not a report of an actual debate. In a series of speeches Job defends himself against the charges of the three friends who think they are defending God. In chapters 29–31 he ends the debate with a formal protestation of his innocence and issues a challenge to God. At this point Elihu intervenes to speak against Job (chapters 32–37). Finally, the Lord appears to deliver two speeches (chapters 38–41), and Job gives his final reaction (42:1–6). The author knew, perhaps better than modern readers, that suffering is a mystery, but he comes to it with all the wisdom available for his time.

The language and date of the book

The book of Job uses a number of rare words, which often make the meaning hard to grasp.

The date of the book is unknown but it is usually thought to be after the exile. The question is complicated by the claims of some scholars that portions of the work are later additions. There are no historical allusions within the book.

The concept of 'justice' in the book of Job

That Yahweh was just and the source of justice had always been believed. But this justice could be seen in two very different ways.

(1) A saving justice

From the viewpoint of the helpless and oppressed, justice is liberation, salvation; the early 'judges' are heroes and champions, deliverers of Yahweh's people from oppression. In the experience of the exodus from Egypt, Yahweh's was a saving justice; his intervention produced justice, by which all have what they ought to have. His covenant partners, naturally, ought to have security and well-being.

(2) A punishing justice

But if these covenant partners were disloyal and became his enemies, then they ought to experience the other side of justice, which is destruction. And that, according to the Deuteronomist and the prophets, is what befell Judah in the exile. Hence, after the exile, there was increasing insistence on loyalty to Yahweh, by the ritual and social observance of a detailed external law. At the same time, the wisdom teachers stressed that there are moral laws that govern life. These can be known, and, by prudent choice and blameless behaviour, one can live in harmony with them and be assured of happiness and success. The emphasis of the authors of Proverbs on their equation – wisdom = virtuous living = 'success' – no doubt helped people to form good habits. But for the thinker it made the problem of 'justice' in human life more difficult.

The author's message and purpose

The author undertook to show that the problem of suffering was wrongly posed: God may have other purposes than merely the exercise of punishing justice. As his medium he chose an old story that was no doubt familiar to his contemporaries.

The dialogue between the Lord and Satan has been interpreted as a crude representation of a divinity who cruelly permits the torture of his creation. This fails to see the deep issues that lie in the text. Satan's question is one of the most important in the Bible: Do humans serve God for themselves and their own profit?

Job and his friends are 'true believers', but they speak for humankind in general, in the face of a God known indeed by revelation to Israel, but to whom these men are related only by the fact that they are his creatures. They expect no salvation from God other than individual well-being in this life. Only Job is groping for a more intimate and permanent relationship, based not on the mere exchange of gifts or services but on a communion of love. The friends never talk to God; only Job does.

Outline of the book

1–2	Job						
	3	Eliphaz	Job	Bildad	Job	Zophar	Job
		4–5	6–7	8	9–10	11	12–14
		15	16–17	18	19	20	21
		22	23 – – – – – – – – – 27				28
	29–31	Elihu					
			32 – – – – – – – – – 37				
	The Lord	38 – – – – – – – – 39			40:1–5	Job	
	The Lord	40:6 – – – – – – – – 41:34			42:1–6	Job	
42:7–17							

[R. A. F. MacK.]

For readers unfamiliar with the text of Job:

(1) The book is framed by a prologue (1–2) and an epilogue (42:7–17), both in prose. The rest of the text, apart from a few phrases, is in verse.

(2) The debate between Job and the friends is framed by Job's two soliloquies (speeches in which Job is expressing his thoughts, to himself) (chapter 3 and chapters 29–31). In between, the friends (Eliphaz, Bildad and Zophar) speak in

turn, and Job makes a response between every two speeches. This pattern is followed twice (chapters 4–14, and 15–21), and a repeat of this pattern begins with chapter 22 (Eliphaz). Unfortunately chapters 23–27 are difficult to restore as the text has been damaged. If it continued the pattern described above, it contained Job's seventh response, Bildad's third speech, Job's eighth response and Zophar's third speech. Thus there were nine speeches by the friends and eight responses by Job, plus his two soliloquies: ten against nine.

(3) Chapter 28 is a separate poem, not part of the dialogue. (4) The Elihu speeches (chapters 32–37) appear to be a supplement, inserted in the book after its 'first edition'. It is not clear if they are the work of the original author or of a later writer.

H I G H L I G H T

Job's complaint
Job 10:1b–3

'I loathe my life;
   I will give free utterance to my complaint;
  I will speak in the bitterness of my soul.
²I will say to God, Do not condemn me;
   let me know why you contend against me.
³Does it seem good to you to oppress,
   to despise the work of your hands
   and favour the schemes of the wicked?'

Ecclesiastes

(Qoheleth)

The material in this chapter is digested from NJBC article 31, 'Ecclesiastes (Qoheleth)', by Addison G. Wright, SS.

The date, authorship and title of the book

The book is the work of an unknown Jewish writer after the exile. Most scholars date it to the 3rd century BC.

The author is stated to be Solomon (1:1, 12) but the language of the book makes this impossible, as well as the fact that the author speaks as someone without power to correct oppression. The author calls himself 'Qoheleth', a term that remains a mystery, but probably means one who has some relationship to an assembly or congregation (e.g. a teacher). One author is responsible for the work (1:1–12:8), and an editor/disciple has added an epilogue (12:9–14).

Its structure

In this book structure is of the utmost importance. The book can be made to say many different things depending upon how one divides it into units. The structure that the author intended to give to his book has finally been recovered. (See outline below for a breakdown of the literary and numerical structure of the book.)

The thought of the book

Qoheleth represents the sceptical side of Israelite wisdom. He does not reject the wisdom movement, but he does challenge some of its cherished beliefs. He believes in

- God
- an ethical code
- God's judgement on human behaviour.

He does not believe in

- an afterlife.

He rejects

- any theology that does not fit with experience
- the traditional belief in retribution, because human experience is that sometimes the good suffer and the wicked are not punished
- total absorption in work because it robs one of enjoyment, and it does not always bring good results.

He believes

- enjoyment is the thing to seek in life
- we should enjoy what is at hand and not long for the unattainable.

The book needs to be complemented by the other voices of Scripture, but its voice is of considerable importance.

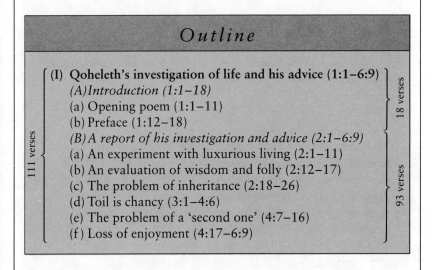

Outline

111 verses

(I) **Qoheleth's investigation of life and his advice (1:1–6:9)**
  (A) Introduction (1:1–18) } 18 verses
  (a) Opening poem (1:1–11)
  (b) Preface (1:12–18)
  (B) A report of his investigation and advice (2:1–6:9)
  (a) An experiment with luxurious living (2:1–11)
  (b) An evaluation of wisdom and folly (2:12–17)
  (c) The problem of inheritance (2:18–26) } 93 verses
  (d) Toil is chancy (3:1–4:6)
  (e) The problem of a 'second one' (4:7–16)
  (f) Loss of enjoyment (4:17–6:9)

(II) **The inadequacy of other advice and of our knowledge of the future (6:10–12:14)**

    (A) Introduction (6:10–12)

    (B) The development of the two topics (7:1–11:6)

    (a) No one can find out what is good to do (7:1–8:17)

        (i) Critique of advice to seek sorrow and adversity (7:1–14)

        (ii) Critique of advice to avoid ethical extremes (7:15–24)

        (iii) Critique of advice on women (7:25–29)

        (iv) Critique of advice to heed authority (8:1–17)

    (b) No one knows the future (9:1–11:6)

        (i) The time of misfortune is not known (9:1–12)

        (ii) Events in general are unpredictable (9:13–10:15)

        (iii) You know not what evil may happen (10:16–11:2)

        (iv) You know not what good may happen (11:3–6)

    (C) Conclusion (11:7–12:14)

    (a) Closing poem on enjoyment, youth, and old age (11:7–12:8)

    (b) Epilogue (12:9–14)

111 verses

93 verses

18 verses

HIGHLIGHT

Wisdom and folly
Ecclesiastes 2:12–17

[12]So I turned to consider wisdom and madness and folly; for what can the one do who comes after the king? Only what has already been done. [13]Then I saw that wisdom excels folly as light excels darkness.

[14]The wise have eyes in their head,
    but fools walk in darkness.

Yet I perceived that the same fate befalls all of them. [15]Then I said to myself, 'What happens to the fool will happen to me also; why then have I been so very wise?' And I said to myself that this also is vanity. [16]For there is no enduring remembrance of the wise or of fools, seeing that in those days to come all will have been long forgotten. How can the wise die just like fools? [17]So I hated life, because what is done under the sun was grievous to me; for all is vanity and the chasing after wind.

Ecclesiastes 9:7–10

[7]Go, eat your bread with enjoyment, and drink your wine with a merry heart; for God has long ago approved what you do. [8]Let

your garments always be white; do not let oil be lacking on your head. ⁹Enjoy life with the wife whom you love, all the days of your vain life that are given you under the sun, because that is your portion in life and in your toil at which you toil under the sun. ¹⁰Whatever your hand finds to do, do with your might; for there is no work or thought or knowledge or wisdom in Sheol, to which you are going.

THIRTY-TWO

Sirach

The material in this chapter is digested from NJBC article 32, 'Sirach', by Alexander A. Di Lella, OFM.

The book and its author

Sirach is one of the rare biblical works that was actually composed by the author who is named in 50:27. One of the longest books in the Bible, Sirach contains the longest portion of Israelite wisdom literature to come down to us.

The title 'Ecclesiasticus' which probably means the 'ecclesiastical [or church] book' is found in a number of translations of the Bible. There is little doubt that the entire book was composed by one author, Ben Sira, who lived during the 3rd and early 2nd centuries BC. A native of Jerusalem (50:27 in the Greek version), he devoted his life to the study of the Law, Prophets, and Writings (cf. the foreword) and became a highly respected scribe and teacher, who ran an academy for young Jewish men (51:23–30). In his extensive travels (34:12–13) he came in contact with other cultures and wisdom traditions and acquired 'much cleverness' (34:11); and he did not hesitate to utilize what he had learned as long as he could make it fit his Jewish heritage and tradition (39:1–11).

Ben Sira wrote his book not for personal gain (51:25) but 'for all who seek instruction' (33:18). He did not intend to write a systematic attack on **Hellenism**, which had made its impact felt throughout the Near East. Rather, his purpose was to demonstrate that the Jewish way of life was superior to Greek culture and that true wisdom was to be found primarily in Jerusalem, and not in Athens. Hence, the good Jew should not give in to the temptation to follow the Greek way of life.

He employs a wide range of literary forms including proverbs, comparisons, hymns of praise, prayers of petition, autobiographical narrative and lists. He often composes units of 22

> Hellenism <
Greek culture

lines (the number of letters in the Hebrew alphabet – or by way of variation 23 lines) to signal the opening or closing of a part of the book, to show the unity of a section, or simply to add elegance.

It is virtually impossible to outline the book because, except for chapters 44–50 ('Praise of the ancestors of old'), Ben Sira seems to have had no clear plan for arranging the various subjects about which he wrote his thoughts and exhortations. He dealt with some of the same topics in different parts of the book; e.g., children in 7:23–25; 16:1–4; 22:3–4; 25:7; 30:1–13; 41:5–10; and parents in 3:1–16; 7:27–28; 23:14; 41:17. Since the book is basically a compilation of notes that Ben Sira accumulated over many years of teaching, it is not surprising that there is little order in the presentation of topics. The outline below is little more than a description of the contents of the book.

Outline

(I) Foreword or prologue

(II) Part I (1:1–4:10)
    (A) *Introduction: the origin of wisdom (1:1–10)*
    (B) *Fear of the Lord as wisdom for humans (1:11–30)*
    (C) *Trust in God (2:1–18)*
    (D) *Honour due to one's parents (3:1–16)*
    (E) *Humility (3:17–24)*
    (F) *Docility, almsgiving, social conduct (3:25–4:10)*

(III) Part II (4:11–6:17)
    (A) *Rewards and warning of wisdom (4:11–19)*
    (B) *Cowardice (4:20–31)*
    (C) *Presumption, duplicity, unruly passions (5:1–6:4)*
    (D) *True and false friendship (6:5–17)*

(IV) Part III (6:18–14:19)
    (A) *Exhortation to strive for wisdom (6:18–37)*
    (B) *Conduct toward God and neighbour (7:1–17)*
    (C) *Family life, religion, and charity (7:18–36)*
    (D) *Prudence in one's affairs (8:1–19)*
    (E) *About women and the choice of friends (9:1–16)*
    (F) *About rulers and pride (9:17–10:18)*
    (G) *The believer's true glory (10:19–11:6)*
    (H) *Providence and trust in God (11:7–28)*

(I) Care in choosing one's friends (11:29–12:18)
(J) Rich and poor (13:1–14:2)
(K) The use of wealth (14:3–19)

(V) Part IV (14:20–23:27)
(A) Wisdom and her blessings (14:20–15:10)
(B) Free will and responsibility (15:11–16:23)
(C) God's wisdom as seen in humans (16:24–18:14)
(D) Prudential warnings (18:15–19:17)
(E) Wisdom and folly in word and deed (19:18–20:32)
(F) Various kinds of sin and folly (21:1–22:18)
(G) Preserving friendship (22:19–26)
(H) Against destructive sins (22:27–23:27)

(VI) Part V (24:1–33:18)
(A) Praise of wisdom (24:1–33)
(B) Gifts that bring joy (25:1–12)
(C) Wicked and virtuous women (25:13–26:18[27])
(D) Dangers to integrity and friendship (26:28–27:21)
(E) Malice, anger, vengeance, evil tongue (27:22–28:26)
(F) Loans, alms, surety (29:1–20)
(G) Frugality and training of children (29:21–30:13)
(H) Health, cheerfulness, riches (30:14–31:11)
(I) Food, wine, banquets (31:12–32:13)
(J) Providence of God (32:14–33:18)

(VII) Part VI (33:19–38:23)
(A) Property and servants (33:19–33)
(B) Trust in the Lord and not in dreams (34:1–20)
(C) True worship of God and his response (34:21–36:22)
(D) Choice of associates (36:23–37:15)
(E) Wisdom and temperance (37:16–31)
(F) Sickness and death (38:1–23)

(VIII) Part VII (38:24–43:33)
(A) Vocations of skilled worker and scribe (38:24–39:11)
(B) Praise of God the Creator (39:12–35)
(C) Miseries and joys of life (40:1–41:13)
(D) True and false shame; care of daughters
    (41:14–42:14)
(E) The works of God in nature (42:15–43:33)

(IX) Part VIII (44:1–50:24)
(A) Praise of Israel's great ancestors (44:1–15)
(B) The early patriarchs (44:16–23e)
(C) Moses, Aaron, Phinehas (44:23f–45:26)
(D) Joshua, Caleb, the Judges, Samuel (46:1–20)
(E) Nathan, David, Solomon (47:1–22)
(F) Elijah and Elisha (47:23–48:15d)
(G) Hezekiah and Isaiah (48:15e–25)

H I G H L I G H T

Ancestral praise
Sirach 44:1–15

¹Let us now sing the praises of famous men,
   our ancestors in their generations.
²The Lord apportioned to them great glory,
   his majesty from the beginning.
³There were those who ruled in their kingdoms,
   and made a name for themselves by their valour;
those who gave counsel because they were intelligent;
   those who spoke in prophetic oracles;
⁴those who led the people by their counsels
   and by their knowledge of the people's lore;
   they were wise in their words of instruction;
⁵those who composed musical tunes,
   or put verses in writing;
⁶rich men endowed with resources,
   living peacefully in their homes –
⁷all these were honoured in their generations,
   and were the pride of their times.
⁸Some of them have left behind a name,
   so that others declare their praise.
⁹But of others there is no memory;
   they have perished as though they had never existed;
they have become as though they had never been born,
   they and their children after them.
¹⁰But these also were godly men,
   whose righteous deeds have not been forgotten;
¹¹their wealth will remain with their descendants,
   and their inheritance with their children's children.
¹²Their descendants stand by the covenants;
   their children also, for their sake.
¹³Their offspring will continue forever,
   and their glory will never be blotted out.

[14]Their bodies are buried in peace,
  but their name lives on generation after generation.
[15]The assembly declares their wisdom,
  and the congregation proclaims their praise.

Wisdom

'The Book of Wisdom' or 'The Wisdom of Solomon' is not in the Hebrew Bible and is known to us only in the Greek. It is generally held today that Greek was the original language, despite the claim that it was written by Solomon.

The author of the book remains anonymous, and the most we can say is that he was a learned Greek-speaking Jew and probably a teacher, and that he was familiar with Greek philosophy, rhetoric, and culture.

It was probably written in the last half of the 1st century BC. So it is the last of the Old Testament books. The place of composition is apparently Egypt, probably Alexandria, the great intellectual and scientific centre of the Mediterranean world and one of the largest Jewish centres outside the Holy Land. The thought of Wisdom closely resembles that of other Jewish-Alexandrian works of the same period. Other indications are the emphasis on Egypt and its relationship to Israel in chapters 11–19, and the attack on animal worship (prevalent at the time in Egypt) in chapters 13–15.

The author's purpose

The book is a practical appeal that learning should have an impact on a person's moral life.

The book incorporates lectures (1:1–6:9; 13–15), philosophical inquiry (6:10–9:18), proof from example (10) and comparisons (11–19). The poetry, well-sustained in 1–5 and 9, is at times truly impressive. The author wanted to strengthen the faith of his fellow Jews in Alexandria. Living in the midst of pagans, the Jewish community was in frequent contact with the new Greek society. Discoveries in science were opening up to

The material in this chapter is digested from NJBC article 33, 'Wisdom', by Addison G. Wright, SS.

> **scepticism** <
a philosophy which
questions all belief

> **anti-Semitism** <
hatred and persecution of
Jews

> **retribution** <
just punishment

people the beauty and mystery of the world around them
(7:17–20). A variety of religions and philosophical systems
offered wisdom or salvation or a view on the real meaning of
life. There existed the new cosmopolitan and individualistic
mentality, **scepticism**, and dissatisfaction with traditional ideas.
It was a time of crisis for faith, which some Jews had abandoned (2:12), replacing it with pagan religions, secular philoso-
phies, or their own superficial versions of these (2:1–20); other
Jews were in danger of following their example.

The problems created for the Jews by the intellectual
atmosphere were increased by an age-old problem that afflic-
tions and **anti-Semitism** had evoked once again – **retribution**.
How is it that the wicked and godless prosper and the just
suffer? How and where does God give justice?

It was to these issues that our author addressed himself,
and for solutions he searched the Scriptures. The 19 chapters of
Wisdom contain many lines and connected passages that the
author has drawn from fruitful meditation on the earlier sacred
books.

In addition, throughout the book he expresses himself in a
vocabulary highly influenced by contemporary Greek philosophy, religion, and science.

Ideas

The book seems to have been addressed to Jewish students and
intellectuals who shared the author's wide background. Only
they would have been able to understand the allusions.

Why do the evil go unpunished?

Wisdom looks forward to life after death, and in the opening
chapters the author situates the problem of retribution in that
context. According to the traditional view, beyond the grave
was a weak and pale existence in Sheol separated from God;
reward and retribution were to be in this world, with long life,
a large family, riches and prestige for the just, and misfortune
for the wicked. This theory was not borne out by the hard facts
of experience, and various ideas had been put forward to
explain this (Job, Second Isaiah, Ecclesiastes). Some psalms

had expressed a hope of a life with God beyond the grave for the individual (Psalms 49:16; 73:23–24), and Isaiah 26:19; Daniel 12:2; 2 Maccabees 7 show a form of resurrection belief. Wisdom builds on these and other texts, states the reward of life with God, reassesses the problem of the suffering of the just and the value of children and old age in the light of his beliefs, and presents the most extensive discussion on the subject in the Old Testament.

Why believe in life after death?

The author may have been aided in his thinking on future life by the Greek concepts of body and soul. However, his reasoning process is Jewish, for he believes in immortality not because of the nature of the soul, but as a gift from God to the righteous.

The body

There is no mention of a resurrection of the body in Wisdom as there is in so many other writings of the period. It would seem that Wisdom does not envision a resurrection of the body.

The afterlife

In discussing the events of the afterlife, the author is understandably vague.

The book presumes a separation of the just and the wicked at death; the just are in the hand of God and at peace (3:1–3) and the wicked go to Sheol, which is a place of torment.

He sets forth Solomon's quest for Wisdom as a model for the reader, and describes who Wisdom is and how she came to be. The author shows his Jewish audience that they are not barbarians, as has been said, and that they have no reason to envy the wisdom of the pagans, since they themselves possess true wisdom. He reminds us that Wisdom teaches above all the righteousness that is God's pleasure (9–10).

In the second half (11:2–19:22), the author recalls the precision with which God saved Israel and punished the Egyptians at the Exodus and how God 'stands by his people in every time and circumstance' (19:22).

Outline

(I) The praises of Wisdom (1:1–11:1)
- *(A) Immortality is the reward of Wisdom (1:1–6:21)*
- (a) Exhortation to justice (1:1–15)
- (b) The wicked invite death (speech of the wicked) (1:16–2:24)
- (c) The hidden counsels of God (3:1–4:19)
  - (i) Suffering (3:1–12)
  - (ii) Childlessness (3:13–4:6)
  - (iii) Early death (4:7–19)
- (b') The judgement (speech of the wicked) (4:20–5:23)
- (a') Exhortation to seek Wisdom (6:1–21)
- *(B) The nature of Wisdom and Solomon's quest for her (6:22–11:1)*
- (a) Introduction (6:22–25)
- (b) Solomon's speech (7:1–8:21)
  - (i) Solomon is like other men (7:1–6)
  - (ii) Solomon prayed and Wisdom and riches came to him (7:7–12)
  - (iii) Solomon prays for help to speak of Wisdom (7:13–22a)
  - (iv) The nature of Wisdom (7:22b–8:1)
  - (iii') Solomon sought Wisdom, the source of knowledge (8:2–8)
  - (ii') Solomon sought Wisdom as his counsellor and comfort (8:9–16)
  - (i') Solomon realizes that Wisdom is a gift of God (8:17–21)
- (c) Solomon's prayer for Wisdom (9:1–18)
- (d) Transitional section: Wisdom saves her own (10:1–11:1)

(II) God's fidelity to his people in the Exodus (11:2–19:22)
- *(A) Introductory narrative (11:2–4)*
- *(B) Theme: Israel is benefited by the very things that punish Egypt (11:5)*
- *(C) Illustration of the theme in pictures (11:6–19:22)*
- (a) First picture: water from the rock instead of the plague of the Nile (11:6–14)
- (b) Second picture: quail instead of the plague of little animals (11:15–16:15)
  - (i) (11:15–16) plus digression on God's power and mercy (11:17–12:22)

(ii) (12:23–27) plus digression on false worship (13:1–15:17)

(iii) (15:18–16:4) plus digression on the serpents in the desert (16:5–15)

(c) Third picture: the elements bring favour to Israel instead of punishment (16:16–29)

(d) Fourth picture: the pillar of fire instead of the plague of darkness (17:1–18:4)

(e) Fifth picture: the tenth plague and the Exodus by which God punished the Egyptians and glorified Israel (18:5–19:22)

HIGHLIGHT

Wisdom 3:1–9

1 But the souls of the righteous are in the hand of God,
   and no torment will ever touch them.
2 In the eyes of the foolish they seemed to have died,
   and their departure was thought to be a disaster,
3 and their going from us to be their destruction;
   but they are at peace.
4 For though in the sight of others they were punished,
   their hope is full of immortality.
5 Having been disciplined a little, they will receive great good,
   because God tested them and found them worthy of himself;
6 like gold in the furnace he tried them,
   and like a sacrificial burnt offering he accepted them.
7 In the time of their visitation they will shine forth,
   and will run like sparks through the stubble.
8 They will govern nations and rule over peoples,
   and the Lord will reign over them forever.
9 Those who trust in him will understand truth,
   and the faithful will abide with him in love,
   because grace and mercy are upon his holy ones,
   and he watches over his elect.

Psalms

The material in this chapter is digested from NJBC article 34, 'Psalms', by John S. Kselman, SS and Michael L. Barré, SS.

The Psalter

The book of Psalms is also called the Psalter; it is a collection of hymns used in worship. The psalms in the Psalter are arranged in five parts – which was a Jewish tradition – like the five books of the law (Genesis, Exodus, Leviticus, Numbers, Deuteronomy). There are more laments in the first half and more songs of praise in the second half.

Reconstruction of a kinnor or harp, of the kind played by David.
Reproduced by courtesy of the Haifa Museum of Music and Ethnology

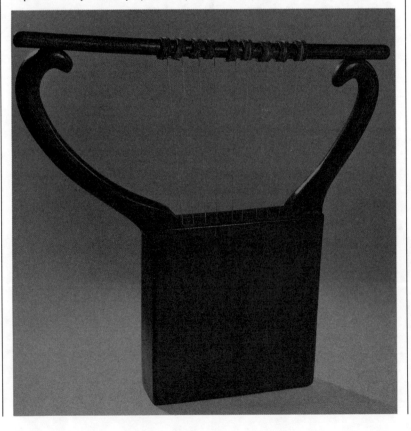

The five parts are arranged as follows:

Psalm 1 is a wisdom poem describing the joy of the right-eous in the study of the law of God.

Psalms 2–41 form the first part, ending with a doxology (praise and glory to God) at Psalm 41:14.

Psalms 42–72 are the second part, ending with a doxology (72:18–20).

Psalms 73–89 are the third part, ending with a doxology (89:53).

Psalms 90–106 are the fourth part, ending with a doxology (106:48).

Psalms 107–150 are the fifth part: this has a different form, and it is possible that the original collection ended with Psalm 119 – a wisdom psalm about God's law which matches Psalm 1 at the beginning and so may have been the end; after this come the pilgrimage songs (120–134) and other material.

Types of psalm

Scholars in the 20th century have been able to compare the psalms with a growing amount of similar literature from the ancient Near East. By comparing their vocabulary, style and imagery their meaning has been better understood.

A study of the Babylonian worship and myths, which cen-tred on a new year festival, has led some scholars to believe that the Jews also had a new year's festival celebrated in September–October, a feast of thanksgiving for the harvest with the sym-bolic enthronement of Yahweh, in which his dominion over the world was proclaimed and renewed. Many of the psalms are thus seen to have had an origin in worship.

(a) Hymns of praise
These include Psalms 8; 19; 29; 33; 65–66[1–12]; 100; 104–105; 111; 113–114; 117; 135–136; 145–146; 148–150; some would also include here the 'Songs of Zion' (Psalms 46; 48; 76; 84; 87) and the 'Enthronement psalms' (Psalms 47; 93; 95–99). There are other hymns of praise in the Old Testament outside the Psalter.

The typical hymn consists of three parts.

(1) The introduction sets the tone of praise. It usually mentions the intention of praising or blessing Yahweh or invites others to do so.

(2) The main body flows from the introduction and gives the reasons for praising God. In some psalms the connection is made explicitly by the word 'for' (Psalms 33; 100; 117; 135–136; 147–149) as is often found in the thanksgiving psalms.

(3) Many of these psalms have a recognizable conclusion, though it varies. It may repeat the language or thought of the introduction (Psalms 8; 103–104; 135–136) or contain a wish or a blessing (Psalms 29; 33; 146; 148).

(b) Laments

These are the largest category, including about 40 individual laments and at least a dozen national or communal laments. The standard format of these psalms includes the following elements:

(1) calling on God's name
(2) a description of present need
(3) prayer for help and deliverance
(4) reasons why God should help the one praying
(5) vow to offer praise or sacrifice when the petition is heard
(6) grateful praise to God.

A prominent feature of the lament is the sudden shift from the lament itself – elements (1) to (5) – to the concluding confession of praise for God's help (6). The language of praise is usually in the past tense, with the psalmist praising God for help that seems already to have been given.

Two subtypes are related to and perhaps developed from the lament: 'psalms of trust' and 'thanksgiving psalms'. When the emphasis in the psalm is on the expressions of confidence and trust that occur in a lament psalm, it can be called a psalm of trust. Similarly, the thanksgiving that concludes many of the laments can so predominate that the poem is classified as a 'psalm of thanksgiving'. The psalmist can give thanks for specific benefits such as recovery from serious illness (Psalms 30; 116) or forgiveness of sins (Psalms 32; 103). There are both individual (Psalms 9–10; 30; 32; 34; 41; 92; 103; 116; 118; 138) and communal thanksgiving psalms (Psalms 65–68; 124). It is not always possible to distinguish a psalm of trust from a lament, or a thanksgiving psalm from a hymn of praise.

(c) Royal psalms

This heading covers a number of types of psalms. There are royal laments (144:1–11), royal thanksgiving songs (Psalms 18; 21; 118), etc. Royal psalms are those in which the king is the speaker (e.g., Psalms 2; 21; 45; 110). A number of psalms are generally recognized as royal, but there are different views on exactly how many.

(d) Wisdom psalms

By their form and content these show connections with Old Testament wisdom literature. Many scholars would agree that at least the following are wisdom psalms: 1; 34; 37; 49; 112; 128. Others would add 32; 73; 111; 127. Characteristics of wisdom psalms are:

- the formula 'Happy the one who . . .'
- a teacher speaking to a pupil or 'son'
- proverbs
- themes such as the righteous and the wicked
- advice on how to live
- concern with reward and punishment.

(e) Liturgical psalms

The liturgical setting of the psalms in general is widely recognized today. Individual psalms may allude to some aspect of the worship of Israel; but only a few complete psalms are generally recognized as deriving from worship such as entrance liturgies (Psalms 15; 24:3–6; Isaiah 33:14b–16; [cf. Jeremiah 7:2–15; Micah 6:6–8]). This group was probably part of a rite of entrance to the Temple. Would-be worshippers stood at the gate of the Temple, asking who was worthy to enter the Temple (Psalms 15:1; 24:3). The fixed response by the priests described the behaviour of the morally upright person, focusing on the relationship with one's neighbour (Psalms 15:2–5a; 24:4) and concluding with the assurance that such a person would be permitted access to God (Psalms 15:5b; 24:5–6). Psalm 24 (verses 7–10) may also reflect a liturgical sequence – namely, a procession into the Temple. Psalm 134 may also be considered a liturgical psalm. It consists of an exhortation to bless Yahweh and a concluding priestly blessing.

(f) Historical psalms

A number of psalms contain accounts of God's great works in the history of Israel. These would include Psalms 78; 105–106; 135–136. Since this classification is based on subject matter rather than structure, psalms of this type may also belong to other categories (Psalm 78 = wisdom; Psalm 105; 135–136 = hymns). The psalms in this category tell different parts of 'salvation history' and for different purposes. Psalms 78 and 106 contrast the history of Israel's rebellion with God's graciousness; Psalm 105 praises Yahweh for his faithfulness to the covenant.

The teaching of the psalms

The picture of God in the psalms is not basically different from that in the rest of the Old Testament. He is saviour and creator. Psalms about creation include Psalms 74, 89, 104, 136. Psalms in which Yahweh is saviour or refuge include 28, 42, 62, 71, 78, 14, 46, 48, 57, 59, 62.

The Psalter has been called the songbook of the Temple, so it is not surprising that the Temple is important.

Israelites had no clear belief in life after death, and this is reflected in the psalms. At the end of life was a shadowy existence in Sheol, away from God's presence.

God's justice and righteousness are constantly emphasized.

HIGHLIGHT

Psalm 23

¹The Lord is my shepherd, I shall not want.
²   He makes me lie down in green pastures;
he leads me beside still waters;
³   he restores my soul.
He leads me in right paths
    for his name's sake.
⁴Even though I walk through the darkest valley,
    I fear no evil;
for you are with me;
    your rod and your staff—
    they comfort me.
⁵You prepare a table before me
    in the presence of my enemies;
you anoint my head with oil;
    my cup overflows.
⁶Surely goodness and mercy shall follow me
    all the days of my life,
and I shall dwell in the house of the Lord
    my whole life long.

Ruth

The material in this
chapter is digested
from NJBC article
35, 'Ruth', by Alice
L. Laffey.

The book and its date

Most scholars agree the book of Ruth is fiction, a short story, set in history. The story is historically possible, but scholars believe it was written for several purposes:

- it holds up to its readers models: heroines and a hero,
- it shows how a non-Israelite can become a faithful worshipper of Yahweh,
- it justifies the custom of levirate marriage.

Levirate marriage was a custom which gave a family the chance to have children and continue its existence, when the husband had died before having children. The dead man's brother, or nearest male relative, would marry the dead man's widow so that she could bear a child who would be considered the dead man's child. This allowed his family to continue and his property to be passed on.

Ruth was probably written at a time when Jews were intermarrying with non-Jews, and many considered this wrong. It would have borne witness that non-Jewish people were not to be condemned. After all, a Moabite woman was King David's great-grandmother. The story refers to 'the days when judges were judging'. Since the early monarchy followed the period of the judges, the story may have originated in the early monarchy, in the reign of David or Solomon. The basic story may have circulated orally centuries before its written version.

*Lapis lazuli Moabite
seal found at Ur in
Babylonia; 7th
century* BC.
*Reproduced by
courtesy of the
Trustees of the British
Museum*

The theme of loyalty and faithfulness

Faithfulness to the covenant in the book of Ruth echoes Israel's covenant with Yahweh. They are God's people, and Yahweh is their God. Naomi asks God to provide for the well-being of her daughters-in-law; her words to Ruth about Boaz are a prayer that God will bless him. Likewise, Boaz's words to Ruth are a prayer that God will bless her.

The characters' relationships with one another show a faithfulness which is grounded in the firm conviction that Yahweh will be faithful to his covenant people. Orpah and Ruth remain faithful to their widowed mother-in-law. Even though Orpah eventually returns home to Moab, she had been willing to accompany Naomi to Judah. Naomi praises such loyalty. Boaz shows his faithfulness by allowing a widow to gather the remnants of his harvest (Deuteronomy 24:19–21) and by protecting the widows of his dead relatives' family. Ruth, who comes to accept Israel's God, will seek a levirate marriage.

Outline

(I) **Act I: famine, Moab, and death (1:1–22)**
  (A) *Introduction: three widowed women (1:1–7)*
  (B) *The action: relationship and return (1:8–21)*
  (C) *Narrative transition (1:22)*

(II) **Act II: Ruth encounters Boaz (2:1–23)**
  (A) *Introduction (2:1)*
  (B) *Scene one: Ruth and Boaz (2:2–16)*
  (C) *Narrative transition (2:17–18)*
  (D) *Scene two: Naomi and Ruth (2:19–22)*
  (E) *Narrative transition (2:23)*

(III) **Act III: Boaz encounters Ruth (3:1–18)**
  (A) *Scene one: Naomi and Ruth (3:1–5)*
  (B) *Narrative transition (3:6–8)*
  (C) *Scene two: Ruth and Boaz (3:9–13)*
  (D) *Narrative transition (3:14–15)*
  (E) *Scene three: Naomi and Ruth (3:16–18)*

(IV) **Act IV: the resolution (4:1–17)**
  (A) *The closer kinsman-redeemer (4:1–12)*
  (B) *Climax (4:13)*
  (C) *Conclusion (4:14–17)*

(V) **Appendix (4:18–22)**

HIGHLIGHT

Ruth 1:15–18

[15]So she said, 'See, your sister-in-law has gone back to her people
and to her gods; return after your sister-in-law.' [16]But Ruth said,
   'Do not press me to leave you
      or to turn back from following you!
   Where you go, I will go;
      Where you lodge, I will lodge;
   your people shall be my people,
      and your God my God.
[17]Where you die, I will die –
      there will I be buried.
   May the Lord do thus and so to me,
      and more as well,
   if even death parts me from you!'
[18]When Naomi saw that she was determined to go with her, she
said no more to her.

Lamentations

Historical setting and composition

The material in this chapter is digested from NJBC article 36, 'Lamentations', by Michael D. Guinan, OFM.

In the year 587 BC the Babylonians destroyed Jerusalem and its Temple and deported a large segment of the population, leaving only the poorest and the weakest (2 Kings 24:8–25:30, Jeremiah 39; 52). The five poems corresponding to the five chapters of Lamentations were almost certainly composed in Palestine in response to this crisis in the political, social, and religious life of ancient Israel. Since some kind of ritual mourning continued to be carried out at the site of the Temple after its destruction (Jeremiah 41:4–5; Zechariah 7:1–5; 8:18–19), it is possible that these laments were used there.

The poems themselves are anonymous. Although it is possible that more than one author is involved, the overall style, content, and vocabulary point rather to one.

The lines are arranged into stanzas based on the 22-letter Hebrew alphabet. Similar **acrostics** occur elsewhere in the Old Testament (Sirach 32:4). The exact purpose of the acrostic device is unclear; various suggestions have been made. It helped the memory in public recitation, taught the alphabet, showed the skill of the author, expressed completeness. The five laments present an A + B + C + B' + A' arrangement. Chapters 1 and 5 are more general descriptions of the disaster; chapters 2 and 4 describe the details of death and destruction. Chapter 3 stands in the centre, and its content is confession of sin and trust in the goodness of God.

> **acrostics** <
see page 89

Israel had just gone through a terrible experience in its recent history. How could the people respond to this? There were several ways:

first, to return to worship of the gods of Canaan;
second, to worship the gods of Babylon since they seemed to be stronger;
third, to be faithful to their own God, Yahweh, and try to understand why Yahweh had let this happen to them.

The writer of Lamentations is looking for a way to help the people be faithful to Yahweh.

- The present. First he looks at the present situation – there has been death, and grief is the only appropriate response.
- The past. In the past Yahweh had led them out of Egypt, made a covenant with them at Sinai, and led them to their inheritance in Canaan. If they remained faithful to this covenant, they could expect blessing; if they were disobedient, the covenant curse would follow (Deuteronomy 28).
- Sin. Israel had become the enemy of Yahweh because of sin, and this is the real cause of the destruction. All have sinned, but the religious leaders are the most responsible.
- The future. Israel laments and confesses; these are acts of faith. The poet prays for God to 'be near and redeem my life' (3:57–58) and tells Zion 'Your punishment is complete . . . he will not exile you again' (4:22). Yahweh 'does not cast off forever' (3:31). In 3:56–61 the poet is sure that Yahweh has heard his prayers. Yahweh still sits on his throne for ever (5:19). In spite of the great pain of recent events, the door to God's mercy is still open.

Outline

(I) The desolation of Zion (1:1–22)
  (A) *Lament over Zion (1:1–11)*
  (B) *Lament of Zion (1:12–22)*

(II) The day of Yahweh's wrath (2:1–22)
  (A) *The Lord's day of wrath (2:1–10)*
  (B) *The poet and Zion respond (2:11–22)*

(III) Out of the depths I cry (3:1–66)
  (A) *Loneliness (3:1–20)*
  (B) *Memory and reflection (3:21–39)*
  (C) *Experience of reconnection (3:40–66)*

(IV) The city revisited (4:1–22)
  (A) *The distress of the city (4:1–16)*
  (B) *Our futile hope (4:17–22)*

(V) The prayer of the people (5:1–22)

HIGHLIGHT

Lamentations 3:55–59

[55] I called on your name, O Lord,
    from the depths of the pit;
[56] you heard my plea, 'Do not close your ear
    to my cry for help, but give me relief!'
[57] You came near when I called on you;
    you said, 'Do not fear!'
[58] You have taken up my cause, O Lord,
    you have redeemed my life.
[59] You have seen the wrong done to me, O Lord;
    judge my cause.

Baruch

The material in this chapter is digested from NJBC article 37, 'Baruch', by Aloysius Fitzgerald, FSC.

The nature of the book

Baruch is a collection of several distinct pieces, grouped together because all are too short to stand alone and all are set against the background of the fall of Jerusalem in 587 BC. The introduction to the confession and prayer of Baruch indicates that he composed it five years after the destruction of Jerusalem by Nebuchadnezzar, i.e. in 582 (1:2). But the various parts of the book may be dated much later, somewhere before AD 70 and after 300 BC. The authors are unknown.

The history Baruch presents is not even history in the sense that events in the books of Kings are history. There is something of a contradiction between the prayer in 2:26, which presumes the Temple is in ruins, and the introduction, which presumes that the Temple is standing and that normal worship is carried on there (1:10, 14). Belshazzar is not the son of Nebuchadnezzar (604–562; 1:11–12), but of Nabonidus (555–539), the last Chaldean king. The Babylon described in 6:14, 48 is not the great city of Nebuchadnezzar.

Outline

(I) **Confession and prayer of Baruch (1:1–3:8)**
    (A) *Narrator's introduction (1:1–14)*
    (B) *The confession (1:15–2:10)*
    (C) *The prayer (2:11–3:8)*

(II) **A wisdom poem (3:9–4:4)**
    (A) *The importance of wisdom (3:9–14)*
    (B) *No man can find wisdom (3:15–31)*
    (C) *Wisdom is the law (3:32–4:4)*

(III) **A prophetic address (4:5–5:9)**
  (A) *The prophet addresses the Jews throughout the world (4:5–9a)*
  (B) *Jerusalem addresses her neighbours (4:9b–16)*
  (C) *Jerusalem addresses the Jews throughout the world (4:17–29)*
  (D) *The prophet addresses Jerusalem (4:30–5:9)*

(IV) **The letter of Jeremiah (6:1–72)**

HIGHLIGHT

Wisdom's importance
Baruch 3:9–14

9Hear the commandments of life, O Israel;
  give ear, and learn wisdom!
10Why is it, O Israel, why is it that you are in the land of your
    enemies,
  that you are growing old in a foreign country,
 that you are defiled with the dead,
11 that you are counted among those in Hades?
12You have forsaken the fountain of wisdom.
13If you had walked in the way of God,
  you would be living in peace forever.
14Learn where there is wisdom,
  where there is strength,
  where there is understanding,
 so that you may at the same time discern
  where there is length of days, and life,
  where there is light for the eyes, and peace.

The material in this
chapter is digested
from NJBC article
38, 'Tobit, Judith,
Esther', by Irene
Nowell, OSB, Toni
Craven and
Demetrius Dumm,
OSB.

THIRTY-EIGHT

Tobit, Judith,

Esther

TOBIT

Date and structure

The most probable date for the writing of Tobit is between 200
and 180 BC. It is not certain where it was written, whether
Palestine, Egypt or Mesopotamia. Tobit is best described as a
Hebrew romance. That it is fiction is shown by several characteristics such as historical inaccuracy and literary manipulation
of time and character. Two folktales, 'The Grateful Dead' and
'The Monster in the Bridal Chamber', provide the structure of
the plot. The form of the successful quest in the central part of
the book is in the style of romance.

Its message

The book has an educative purpose. The tale of the two families
joined by marriage is told both to teach and to entertain. The
message of the book, illustrated through ordinary faithful lives,
is that God is indeed both just and free. Suffering is not a
punishment but a test. God does, in the long run, reward the
just and punish the wicked. The believer is called upon to trust
God and to mirror in daily life the justice, mercy, and freedom
of God.

Outline

HIGHLIGHT

Tobit's blindness is cured and he sees his son
Tobit 11:13–15a

[13]Next, with both his hands he peeled off the white films from the corners of his eyes. Then Tobit saw his son and threw his arms around him, [14]and he wept and said to him, 'I see you, my son, the light of my eyes!' Then he said,
   'Blessed be God,
      and blessed be his great name,
      and blessed be all his holy angels.
   May his holy name be blessed
      throughout all the ages.
[15]Though he afflicted me,
      he has had mercy upon me,
      Now I see my son Tobias!'

JUDITH
Date and author

Judith was written by an author about whom virtually nothing is known, but who most scholars believe was a Palestinian Jew within the tradition of the Pharisees. Because Judith is fiction and contains historical and geographical inaccuracies, it is difficult to date its composition. Most likely it was composed early in the 1st century BC during the late Hasmonean period, or perhaps during the reign of John Hyrcanus (135–104).

The teaching of the book

God in Judith is portrayed as the one true transcendent God of heaven and earth (5:8; 6:19), the unfathomable (8:14) ruler and creator of the universe (9:12; 13:18). God of the ancestors (7:28; 9:2) and champion of the weak (9:11), the Lord shows mercy to the faithful (16:15) and crushes enemies through the agency of a female (9:10; 13:15; 16:5).

Concern for physical survival and the continuance of the Jerusalem Temple worship in the face of fear and the existence of evil (misinterpreted as punishment for sin) leads to a prophetic call for trust in the God of tradition.

Though the high priest, Joakim, has religious and military authority (4:6–8), Judith, the widow, leads the people to triumph. She shows a right relationship with God in ways that shatter narrow orthodoxy. It is unconventional in ancient Israel that a woman chops off a man's head (13:8), lies for the sake of her people and the sanctuary of their God (11:8), criticizes the theology of the male leaders of her community (8:9–34), delegates the management of her household to another woman (8:10), and refuses to marry (16:22). Judith conserves traditions as old as Exodus and serves as an example of human liberation. Judith upholds the fundamental truths that faith does not depend on visible results (8:17) and that God's 'might is not in numbers' (9:11).

Outline

(I) **Nebuchadnezzar's eastern campaign and revenge against the disobedient western nations (1:1–7:32)**

(A) *Introduction to Nebuchadnezzar and his campaign against Arphaxad (1:1–16)*

(B) *Nebuchadnezzar commissions Holofernes to take vengeance on the disobedient nations (2:1–13)*

(C) *Holofernes attacks the western nations (2:14–7:32)*

(a) The campaign against the disobedient nations; the people surrender (2:14–3:10)

(b) Israel hears and is 'greatly terrified', Joakim orders war preparations (4:1–15)

(c) Holofernes talks with Achior; Achior is expelled from the Assyrian camp (5:1–6:11)

(c') Achior is received into Bethulia; he talks with the people of Israel (6:12–21)

(b') Holofernes orders war preparations; Israel sees and is 'greatly terrified' (7:1–5)

(a') The campaign against Bethulia; the people want to surrender (7:6–32)

(II) **Judith achieves Yahweh's triumph over Assyria (8:1–16:25)**

(A) *Introduction to Judith (8:1–8)*

(B) *Judith plans to save Israel (8:9–10:9a)*

(C) *Judith and her maid leave Bethulia (10:9b–10)*

(D) *Judith overcomes Holofernes (10:11–13:10a)*

(C') *Judith and her maid return to Bethulia (13:10b–11)*

(B') *Judith plans the destruction of Israel's enemy (13:12–16:20)*

(A') *Conclusion about Judith (16:21–25)*

HIGHLIGHT

Holofernes declares war against Israel
Judith 7:1–5

[1]The next day Holofernes ordered his whole army, and all the allies who had joined him, to break camp and move against Bethulia, and to seize the passes up into the hill country and make war on the Israelites. [2]So all their warriors marched off that day; their fighting forces numbered one hundred and seventy thousand infantry and twelve thousand cavalry, not counting the baggage and the foot soldiers handling it, a very great multitude. [3]They encamped in the valley near Bethulia, beside the spring, and they

> spread out in breadth over Dothan as far as Balbaim and in length
> from Bethulia to Cyamon, which faces Esdraelon.
>
> ⁴When the Israelites saw their vast numbers, they were greatly
> terrified and said to one another, 'They will now strip clean the
> whole land; neither the high mountains nor the valleys nor the
> hills will bear their weight.' ⁵Yet they all seized their weapons, and
> when they had kindled fires on their towers, they remained on
> guard all that night.

ESTHER

The text and its date

The nucleus of the Hebrew story may go back to the 5th century BC, with later editing in the Greek period. Greek additions were made in the 2nd century BC in Egypt. The book of Esther may reflect remembrances of a real or threatened **pogrom** against the Jews in the Persian empire or even a historical Mordecai and Esther with influence at the Persian court. Moreover, the description of Persian customs is generally faithful to what is known about that culture.

> **pogrom** <
a massacre of Jews

However, the story as it now exists is a fictional story, told for more or less religious purposes and expressing well-known themes of Old Testament wisdom literature. Mordecai and Esther are classic examples of the righteous wise who seem helpless but who eventually turn the tables on clever schemers like Haman.

The Greek additions are religious and devotional commentary composed out of the religious convictions and fertile imaginations of later translators/authors.

Message

THE HEBREW STORY describes the dramatic deliverance of the Jews from the power of a great empire that found them guilty of being different.

Like most writings after the exile, Esther is concerned with the painful and urgent problem of how to be a faithful Jew in a foreign environment. One common solution to this problem was the creation of Jewish areas where the faithful could be protected against the pagan world and nourish a very explicit piety. Esther has a different emphasis: the Jews must participate in the affairs of state; they must appreciate the good elements in non-Jewish society and co-operate wherever possible; they must take responsibility and not wait for God to provide some miraculous solution.

To highlight this theme of personal responsibility, God is represented as hidden while the personal courage and resourcefulness of Mordecai and Esther are given full play. Esther goes beyond the hurt pride and stubbornness of Mordecai to rely on personal talent, diplomacy, and a trust in the basic fairness of life. The relatively slow pace of the story (eleven months between edict and execution [3:13], two banquets for the king and Haman [5:4, 8]) may very well be, in this perspective, a reminder to the Jews to be patient and persistent as they strive to be true to their calling in difficult circumstances.

THE GREEK ADDITIONS The sections added by the Greek translator/author change the focus of the book and affect its teaching. Where the emphasis had been on the courage and resourcefulness of Mordecai and Esther it is now shifted to the intervention of God. Indeed, not only is the subtlety of the Hebrew story lost but the religious emphasis is so overdone as to be somewhat tedious. The Greek sections move away from the broad-mindedness of the original by suggesting narrow racial perspectives and by adopting attitudes hostile to non-Jews.

Outline

(I) Prologue: Mordecai's dream (A:1–17 [11:2–12:6])

(II) Esther replaces Queen Vashti (1:1–2:23)

(III) Haman plots to destroy the Jews (3:1–15; B:1–7 [13:1–7])

(IV) Esther and Mordecai plead for help (4:1–16; C:1–30 [13:8–14:19])

(V) Deliverance is prepared (D:1–16 [15:1–16]; 5:1–14)

(VI) A dramatic reversal of fortunes (6:1–8:12; E:1–24 [16:1–24]; 8:13–9:19)

> **deuterocanonical** <
see page 323

(VII) The feast of Purim (9:20–10:3)

(VIII) Epilogue: interpretation of Mordecai's dream (F:1–11
    [10:4–11:1])

Note: the letters above refer to **deuterocanonical** Greek
material added to the text.

HIGHLIGHT

Purim
Esther 10:4–13

⁴And Mordecai said, 'These things have come from God; ⁵for I
remember the dream that I had concerning these matters, and
none of them has failed to be fulfilled. ⁶There was the little spring
that became a river, and there was light and sun and abundant
water – the river is Esther, whom the king married and made
queen. ⁷The two dragons are Haman and myself. ⁸The nations are
those that gathered to destroy the name of the Jews. ⁹And my
nation, this is Israel, who cried out to God and were saved. The
Lord has saved his people; the Lord has rescued us from all these
evils; God has done great signs and wonders, wonders that have
never happened among the nations. ¹⁰For this purpose he made
two lots, one for the people of God and one for all the nations,
¹¹and these two lots came to the hour and moment and day of
decision before God and among all the nations. ¹²And God
remembered his people and vindicated his inheritance. ¹³So they
will observe these days in the month of Adar, on the fourteenth
and fifteenth of that month, with an assembly and joy and gladness
before God, from generation to generation forever among his
people Israel.

THIRTY-NINE

Jonah

A unique book

The material in this chapter is digested from NJBC article 39, 'Jonah', by Anthony C. Ceresko, OSFS.

This book probably dates from the period after the exile. The author is clearly not trying to give a historical account. The issues with which he deals – the mercy and justice of God – as well as the obvious exaggerations the book contains indicate that he has another purpose in mind: to tell a story.

It is a story, however, that has not been written simply to entertain. The central role is given to God. Also, the description of the relationships between God and Jonah, and between God and the pagan sailors and Ninevites, emphasizes a particular world-view. It may be described as a **parable**.

In Jonah we find a caricature of a prophet. There is certainly irony in this, and even satire, which may reflect something of the disillusionment with prophecy during this period. But it also reflects a profound humility. The author turns the audience's gaze away from the prophetic messengers themselves to the One whose messengers they were, the One who is able to achieve his ends even in spite of envoys like Jonah.

> **parable** <
a story which illustrates an idea

Interpretation

Contrary to popular opinion, the importance of the work lies neither in the 'miracle' of the 72 hours in the belly of a fish nor in Jesus' reference to the 'sign of Jonah' in his preaching. It is important for two things:

(1) Prophecy
Although the only oracle that Jonah delivers is a brief and blunt announcement of coming destruction (3:4), the book as a

whole emphasizes the possibility and desirability of repentance as well as the merciful and forgiving nature of God.

(2) The mystery of God

In Jonah, the central human character in the book, the author draws not a cardboard character but a real human being who, despite his obvious failings, manages to evoke sympathy in his struggle to understand the God he serves. At the root of Jonah's sometimes inexplicable actions and argumentative character, one can begin to recognize a sincere striving to reconcile the concept of a just God with the reality of God's mercy. In asking us to view the problem through the eyes of this reluctant prophet, the author brings us close to the mystery of God.

Outline

(I) **First mission (1:1–2:11)**
    (A) Jonah and the sailors (1:1–16)
    (a) Jonah's flight (1:1–3)
    (b) The storm (1:4–16)
    (B) Jonah and the great fish (2:1–11)

(II) **Seond mission (3:1–4:11)**
    (A) The conversion of Nineveh (3:1–10)
    (a) The action of the prophet (3:1–4)
    (b) The reaction of the city (3:5–10)
    (B) God's attempt to convert Jonah (4:1–11)

HIGHLIGHT

A lesson for Jonah
Jonah 4:1–11

[1]But this was very displeasing to Jonah, and he became angry. [2]He prayed to the Lord and said, 'O Lord! Is not this what I said while I was still in my own country? That is why I fled to Tarshish at the beginning; for I knew that you are a gracious God and merciful, slow to anger, and abounding in steadfast love, and ready to relent from punishing. [3]And now, O Lord, please take my life from me, for it is better for me to die than to live.' [4]And the Lord said, 'Is it right for you to be angry?' [5]Then Jonah went out of the city and sat down east of the city, and made a booth for himself there. He

sat under it in the shade, waiting to see what would become of the city.

⁶The Lord God appointed a bush, and made it come up over Jonah, to give shade over his head, to save him from his discomfort; so Jonah was very happy about the bush. ⁷But when dawn came up the next day, God appointed a worm that attacked the bush, so that it withered. ⁸When the sun rose, God prepared a sultry east wind, and the sun beat down on the head of Jonah so that he was faint and asked that he might die. He said, 'It is better for me to die than to live.'

⁹But God said to Jonah, 'Is it right for you to be angry about the bush?' And he said, 'Yes, angry enough to die.' ¹⁰Then the Lord said, 'You are concerned about the bush, for which you did not labour and which you did not grow; it came into being in a night and perished in a night. ¹¹And should I not be concerned about Nineveh, that great city, in which there are more than a hundred and twenty thousand persons who do not know their right hand from their left, and also many animals?'

The
New Testament

The Gospel

According to

Mark

Who wrote the book: when and where?

The material in this chapter is digested from NJBC article 41, 'The Gospel According to Mark', by Daniel J. Harrington, SJ.

Nothing in the Gospel identifies its author by name. The Gospel is traditionally thought to have been written by Mark the 'interpreter of Peter' in Rome after Peter's death (about AD 64–67). Peter appears in many incidents in the Gospel and could have been a source of information about sayings and deeds of Jesus. Nevertheless, it is better not to assume that Peter was Mark's only informant about Jesus' public ministry.

That Mark wrote in Rome is suggested by Latin words in the Greek text and by the atmosphere of impending persecution that pervades the Gospel. Since Mark 13 speaks as if the Jerusalem Temple had not yet been destroyed the Gospel was most likely composed before AD 70. A setting in the 60s at Rome seems best, for then the Christian community lived under the threat (or reality) of persecution and looked upon the start of revolt in Palestine as a source of potential trouble for the Jewish (and even Gentile) Christians at Rome.

A tightly structured narrative

(a) Geography

The geographical aspect features the movement from Galilee to Jerusalem. After the prologue (1:1–15), the first half of the

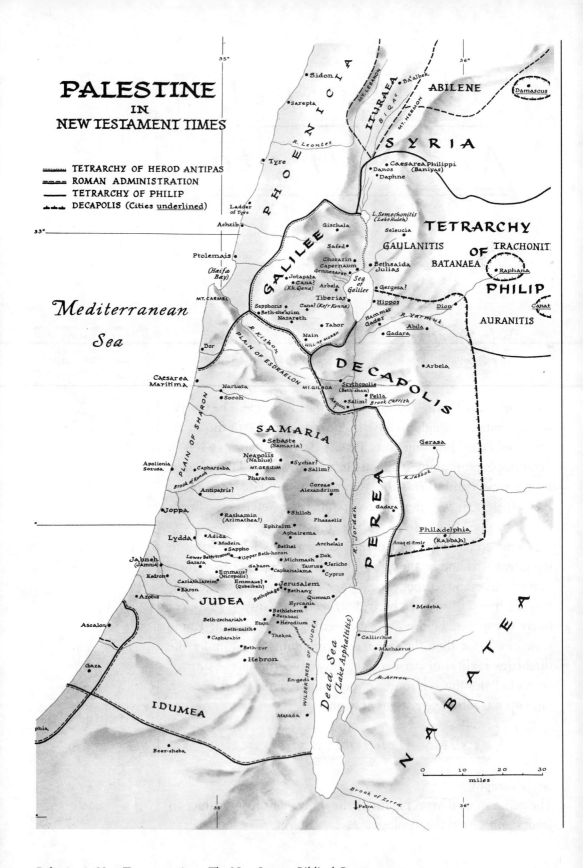

Palestine in New Testament times. The New Jerome Biblical Commentary

Gospel describes Jesus' activity in Galilee and beyond (1:16–8:21). The second half focuses on Jerusalem: the journey from Galilee to Jerusalem (8:22–10:52), Jesus' symbolic actions and teachings during the first part of passion week in Jerusalem (11:1–13:37), and his passion and death there (14:1–16:8).

(b) Theology

The Gospel highlights the authority of Jesus. Once we know who Jesus is (1:1–15), we see his authority revealed in his actions and his words (1:16–3:6), his rejection by his own people (3:7–6:6a), and the misunderstanding of him even by his disciples (6:6b–8:21). On the way up to Jerusalem (8:22–10:52), Jesus clarifies the nature of his authority and spells out its consequences for his followers. At Jerusalem he encounters resistance to his teaching (11:1–13:37) and meets a cruel and tragic death at the hands of those who reject his authority (14:1–16:8).

(c) A new kind of literature

Mark was the first to write a Gospel, the 'good news' about God's action in Jesus Christ. As the first one to write an account of Jesus' ministry in an orderly fashion, Mark appears to have created a model followed and developed by other evangelists.

Mark had various kinds of traditions to use: sayings, parables, controversies, healing stories and other miracles, and probably a passion narrative. Some of these traditions may also have been grouped: controversies (2:1–3:6), seed parables (4:1–34), miracles (4:35–5:43), etc. Mark gave an order and a plot to these sayings and incidents, connected them with linking passages, and added comments for the sake of his readers.

(d) Mark's purpose

Mark wrote his Gospel to deepen the faith of the members of his community. By showing them how the traditions about Jesus related to their belief in the saving significance of the cross and resurrection, the evangelist strengthened them to face persecution and resist the temptations of their world.

Mark's teaching

(a) The kingdom

The focus of Mark's teaching is the focus of Jesus' teaching – the kingdom of God. What is taught about who Jesus is and discipleship (response to Jesus) takes its framework from the kingdom of God. The opening prologue of the Gospel (1:1–15) leads up to a sample of Jesus' preaching: 'The time is fulfilled, and the kingdom of God has drawn near. Repent and believe in the good news.'

In Judaism of Jesus' time the 'kingdom of God' referred to the display of God's lordship at the end of history and its acknowledgement by all creation.

Much of Jesus' teaching (especially the parables) aimed at deepening the people's understanding of the coming kingdom and preparing for it. Even his healings appear as signs of what life in God's kingdom will be like. That kingdom is now largely hidden, though in Jesus it is begun.

While Jesus taught about the kingdom of God in parables, his own life was really the parable of the kingdom. Mark's

Reconstructed ruins of the synagogue at Capernaum built ca. AD 200, *on the site of the earlier one in which Jesus spoke and worked*

message is that whoever wishes to understand the kingdom must look at Jesus the healer, the teacher, and the crucified-and-risen one.

The large amount of space devoted to healings and exorcisms proves that Mark knew and revered Jesus as a wonder-worker. The miracles are balanced by teaching in both word and deed.

But the way in which Mark has outlined the story of Jesus suggests that the passion and death were its climax. Without the cross, the portrayals of Jesus as wonder-worker and teacher are unbalanced and without purpose. Within this framework, Mark made use of the Old Testament titles available: Messiah, Son of God, Son of Man, Lord, Son of David, Suffering Servant, and Suffering Just One.

(b) The messianic secret

A peculiar feature of Mark's Gospel is often called 'the messianic secret', from the several instances in which Jesus commands people to be silent about his action or identity (see 1:34, 44; 3:12; 5:43; 7:36; 8:26, 30; 9:9). Jesus in his public ministry neither claimed to be the Messiah nor was recognized as such. Jesus, indeed, does not take to himself the title of Messiah without serious qualification (see 8:27–38). Mark shows that the real meaning of Jesus' messiahship became clear only with his death and resurrection. In some Jewish circles the longed-for Messiah had political and military functions, and Mark may have been unwilling to provoke the Roman authorities. However, the commands to silence and the development of Jesus' messiahship in Mark are more complex than this.

(c) Discipleship

Mark's ideal of discipleship is 'being with' Jesus, sharing his mission of preaching and healing (3:14–15). As the narrative proceeds, the disciples repeatedly fail to understand Jesus (6:52; 8:14–21). On the way to Jerusalem Jesus predicts his passion and resurrection three times (8:31; 9:31; 10:33–34); each time the disciples misunderstand (8:32–33; 9:32–37; 10:35–45). The passion narrative turns on the betrayal of Jesus by Judas (14:17–21; 14:43–52) and the denial of Jesus by Peter (14:26–31; 14:54, 66–72). In the first half of the Gospel the disciples are portrayed as examples to be imitated; in the second half, they are examples to be avoided. The effect of this is to highlight Jesus as the only one who deserves imitation.

Outline

(I) Prologue (1:1–15)

(II) Jesus' authority is revealed in Galilee (1:16–3:6)
(A) Call of the first disciples (1:16–20)
(B) The eventful day in Capernaum (1:21–45)
(a) Teaching and healing at Capernaum (1:21–28)
(b) Healing of Peter's mother-in-law (1:29–31)
(c) Evening healings (1:32–34)
(d) Jesus' temporary withdrawal (1:35–39)
(e) Healing of the leper (1:40–45)
(C) Five conflict stories (2:1–3:6)
(a) Healing of a paralytic and forgiveness of sin (2:1–12)
(b) Call of Levi (2:13–17)
(c) Question about fasting (2:18–22)
(d) Work on the sabbath (2:23–28)
(e) Healing on the sabbath (3:1–6)

(III) Jesus is rejected in Galilee (3:7–6:6a)
(A) Positive responses (3:7–19a)
(a) People come to Jesus (3:7–12)
(b) Appointment of the Twelve (3:13–19a)
(B) Negative responses (3:19b–35)
(C) Parables and explanations (4:1–34)
(a) Setting (4:1–2)
(b) Parable of the seeds (4:3–9)
(c) Parables' purpose (4:10–12)
(d) Explanation (4:13–20)
(e) Sayings (4:21–25)
(f) Parable of the growing seed (4:26–29)
(g) Parable of the mustard seed (4:30–32)
(h) Summary (4:33–34)
(D) Three miraculous actions (4:35–5:43)
(a) Stilling the storm (4:35–41)
(b) Exorcizing a demon (5:1–20)
(c) Healing the sick (5:21–43)
(E) Rejection of Jesus by his own people (6:1–6a)

(IV) Jesus misunderstood by disciples in Galilee and beyond (6:6b–8:21)
(A) The disciples' mission and John's death (6:6b–34)
(a) The disciples' mission (6:6b–13)
(b) John's death (6:14–29)

(c) The disciples' return (6:30–34)

(B) *Acts of power and a controversy (6:35–7:23)*

(a) Feeding the five thousand (6:35–44)

(b) Walking on the waters (6:45–52)

(c) Healing the sick (6:53–56)

(d) Controversy about ritual purity (7:1–23)

(C) *More acts of power and a controversy (7:24–8:21)*

(a) Healing a Gentile woman's daughter (7:24–30)

(b) Healing a man incapable of hearing and speaking properly (7:31–37)

(c) Feeding the four thousand (8:1–10)

(d) Controversy about signs (8:11–21)

(V) **Jesus instructs his disciples on the way to Jerusalem (8:22–10:52)**

(A) *Healing a blind man (8:22–26)*

(B) *Jesus the Christ (8:27–30)*

(C) *First instruction on who Christ is and discipleship (8:31–9:29)*

(a) First passion prediction and its consequences for discipleship (8:31–38)

(b) Jesus' transfiguration and the Elijah question (9:1–13)

(c) Healing a possessed boy (9:14–29)

(D) *Second instruction on who Christ is and discipleship (9:30–10:31)*

(a) Second passion prediction and its consequences for discipleship (9:30–50)

(b) Jesus' teaching on marriage and divorce (10:1–12)

(c) Jesus' blessing of the children (10:13–16)

(d) Jesus' teachings about riches (10:17–31)

(E) *Third instruction on who Christ is and discipleship (10:32–45)*

(a) Third passion prediction (10:32–34)

(b) Its consequences for discipleship (10:35–45)

(F) *Healing blind Bartimaeus (10:46–52)*

(VI) **The first part of passion week in Jerusalem (11:1–13:37)**

(A) *Entrance on the first day (11:1–11)*

(B) *Prophetic teachings on the second day (11:12–19)*

(C) *More teachings on the third day (11:20–13:37)*

(a) Explanations (11:20–26)

(b) Controversies (11:27–12:37)

    (i) Jesus' authority (11:27–33)

    (ii) Parable of the vineyard (12:1–12)

    (iii) Taxes to Caesar (12:13–17)

    (iv) Resurrection (12:18–27)

    (v) The great commandment (12:28–34)

    (vi) David's son (12:35–37)

(c) Scribes and a widow (12:38–44)

(d) Jesus' final discourse (13:1–37)
    (i)   Introduction (13:1–4)
    (ii) Beginning of the sufferings (13:5–13)
    (iii) The great tribulation (13:14–23)
    (iv) Triumph of the Son of Man (13:24–27)
    (v) Exhortation to confidence and vigilance
        (13:28–37)

(VII) Jesus' death in Jerusalem (14:1–16:20)
  (A) The anointing and the Last Supper (14:1–31)
  (a) Plotting and anointing (14:1–11)
  (b) Arrangements for the Passover meal (14:12–16)
  (c) The Last Supper (14:17–31)
    (i)   Prediction of Judas's treachery (14:17–21)
    (ii) The supper (14:22–25)
    (iii) Prediction of Peter's denial (14:26–31)
  (B) Jesus' prayer and arrest (14:32–52)
  (a) Gethsemane (14:32–42)
  (b) Arrest (14:43–52)
  (C) The trials (14:53–15:15)
  (a) Trial before the high priest; Peter's denial (14:53–72)
  (b) The trial before Pilate (15:1–15)
  (D) The crucifixion and death (15:16–47)
  (a) The mockery (15:16–20)
  (b) The crucifixion (15:21–32)
  (c) The death of Jesus (15:33–39)
  (d) The burial (15:40–47)
  (E) The empty tomb (16:1–8)
  (F) Later endings (16:9–20)

HIGHLIGHT

Prediction of the passion and its consequences for a disciple
Mark 10:32–45

[32]They were on the road, going up to Jerusalem, and Jesus was walking ahead of them; they were amazed, and those who followed were afraid. He took the twelve aside again and began to tell them what was to happen to him, [33]saying, 'See, we are going up to Jerusalem, and the Son of Man will be handed over to the chief priests and the scribes, and they will condemn him to death; then they will hand him over to the Gentiles; [34]they will mock him, and spit upon him, and flog him, and kill him; and after three days he will rise again.'
[35]James and John, the sons of Zebedee, came forward to him and said to him, 'Teacher, we want you to do for us whatever we

ask of you.' [36]And he said to them, 'What is it you want me to do for you?' [37]And they said to him, 'Grant us to sit, one at your right hand and one at your left, in your glory.' [38]But Jesus said to them, 'You do not know what you are asking. Are you able to drink the cup that I drink, or be baptized with the baptism that I am baptized with?' [39]They replied, 'We are able.' Then Jesus said to them, 'The cup that I drink you will drink; and with the baptism with which I am baptized, you will be baptized; [40]but to sit at my right hand or my left is not mine to grant, but it is for those for whom it has been prepared.' [41]And when the ten heard it, they began to be indignant at James and John. [42]And Jesus called them to him and said to them, 'You know that those who are supposed to rule over the Gentiles lord it over them, and their great men exercise authority over them. [43]But it shall not be so among you; but whoever would be great among you must be your servant, [44]and whoever would be first among you must be slave of all. [45]For the Son of Man also came not to be served but to serve, and to give his life as a ransom for many.'

FORTY-ONE

The Gospel

According to

Matthew

The material in this chapter is digested from NJBC article 42, 'The Gospel According to Matthew', by Benedict T. Viviano, OP.

Who was Matthew?

This Gospel early acquired prestige not only because of its own merits (e.g., the Sermon on the Mount, chapters 5–7) but because it bore the name of an apostle (mentioned 9:9; 10:3). But, since the author of the final Greek text seems to have copied (with modifications) the whole Gospel according to Mark, it is now usually thought unlikely that it is the work of an eyewitness apostle. Why would an eyewitness need to copy from someone who was not? The Gospel as we have it combines the earliest Gospel, Mark, with an early collection of sayings of Jesus (Q), which is also used in the Gospel according to Luke.

So who wrote the full Gospel in Greek as it has come down to us? We must look to the Gospel itself for information. The writer was an early Christian teacher, church leader and (perhaps) converted rabbi. The story of the call of the tax collector (9:9–13) is probably less significant than 13:52 – the description of the scribe who might be the writer himself.

But the Gospel may, instead, have been produced by an early school of biblical studies, backed and accepted by a major local church. The Gospel contains some internal contradictions or puzzles, e.g., on the Gentile mission (cf. 15:24; 10:6 with 28:19), which could be explained as representing different currents of opinion within the same community.

A Jewish Gospel?

Does Matthew stand inside or outside Judaism? If one sup-
poses, as now seems likely, that Matthew's community had
recently been driven out of Judaism by the rabbis through a ban
(*ca.* AD 80), it is still possible that many leading members of the
community felt themselves to be Jewish. This feeling of belonging, and indeed of being the true Israel, would explain the harsh
words against the rabbis in chapter 23. It is a bitter family feud.
Thus, the Gospel represents a predominantly Jewish-Christian
outlook.

Date

Matthew must have been composed after Mark (AD 64–67) and
before AD 110, since it seems to be known to Ignatius of Antioch. If the writer was reacting to the rabbis of Jamnia (AD 75–
90), it would be reasonable to date the Gospel between 80 and
90, and later rather than earlier within that decade.

Matthew's purpose in writing his Gospel

The writer both passes on traditions he has received from the
early church about Jesus and the Christian life and, at the same
time, shapes those traditions into new combinations with new
emphases. He has a number of purposes in writing: to instruct
and encourage members of his community; perhaps to provide
liturgical reading and sermon material; but also to offer a missionary address to outsiders of good will, as well as attacks on
hostile critics and rivals. He has used two main kinds of
material, stories and teaching, to achieve these various ends.

Matthew has gathered Jesus' teaching into five great discourses showing his interest and creativity. They are:

- the Sermon on the Mount (chapters 5–7)
- the Missionary Discourse (10)
- the Parable Discourse (13)
- the Community Discourse (18)
- the Apocalyptic Judgement Discourses (23–25).

Christians have been quick to find in the discourses the masterpieces of the Gospel. We can see that Matthew's primary intent was to write a handbook for church leaders to assist them in preaching, teaching, worship, mission, and argument. But he has inserted this handbook into the story of a living person, Jesus Christ, to keep it focused on Christ and his kingdom as the good news of salvation.

Matthew's teaching

(a) Introduction
This Gospel has two focuses, Jesus as the Christ and the coming of the kingdom of God which Jesus proclaims.

The two themes are closest together at the beginning of the Gospel, where Jesus is set forth as royal Son of God and Immanuel, God with us, and at the end, where Jesus is given all (divine) authority as Son of Man over the kingdom of God, in heaven and on earth.

Recent studies have shown that the title Son of God is especially important, occurring at crucial moments in the story: the baptism (3:17), Peter's confession (16:16, representing the confession or faith of the church), the transfiguration (17:5), and the trial and the cross (26:63; 27:40, 43, 54). Fitting in with this role is the title Son of David (10 times in Matthew, e.g., 9:27). With this title Jesus is seen as a new Solomon, as healer and wise man. Jesus speaks as wisdom incarnate in 11:25–30 and in 23:37–39. Equally, if not more, important is the public title of Jesus as the Son of Man, which runs through the Gospel, leading up to chapter 28:18–20. This title is based on the mysterious figure of Daniel 7:13–14, where it is also connected with the kingdom theme.

(b) The kingdom
The kingdom of heaven is the great object of hope, prayer (6:10), and proclamation (3:2; 4:17), which unifies the entire Gospel, especially the five great discourses, and provides its eschatological goal. It contains God's promise of salvation to redeemed humanity, on earth as in heaven, in time and eternity, socially and politically as well as personally. It entails justice (6:33), peace (5:9), and joy (13:44).

> eschatological <
see Chapter 19

Because of its moral content it leads naturally to two other themes in Matthew's Gospel: justice (or righteousness) and the law. Justice is a special emphasis in Matthew (3:15; 5:6, 10, 20; 6:1, 33; 21:32) and refers for the most part to the human response of obedience to the Father's will. The law is affirmed as of abiding significance (5:17–20), but, although some ceremonial precepts are maintained (sabbath observance, 12:1–8), or even encouraged (23:23), the way the Pharisees interpreted the law is firmly rejected in favour of Jesus' interpretation. In fact, Jesus speaks mainly about ethical precepts, the Ten Commandments and the great commandments of the love of God and neighbour.

Denarius of Tiberius Caesar, emperor AD *14–37*

(c) The church

First there are apostles with Peter at their head (10:2), who share the authority of Christ himself (10:40; 9:8). After them come prophets, scribes, and sages (10:41; 13:52; 23:34). As a court of final appeal there is Peter (16:19). Since power is dangerous, though necessary, the leaders need humility (18:1–9). Matthew has no illusions about the church. Anyone can fall (even Peter, 26:69–75); prophets can be false (7:15); and the church is a mixture of saint and sinner until the final sorting out (13:36–43; 22:11–14; 25). Nevertheless, the church is called to worldwide mission (28:18–20). The style of apostolic or missionary life is described in 9:36–11:1. God is united with his people through Jesus Christ (1:23 and 28:18–20). The outcasts of old Israel (21:31–32), together with the Gentile converts, become the new people of God (21:43).

(d) Use of the Old Testament

Matthew has a series of 10 (some count 11 or 12) Old Testament quotations introduced by a formula like 'This happened to fulfil what was spoken by the Lord through the prophet' (1:23; 2:15, 18, 23; 4:15–16; 8:17; 12:18–21; 13:35; 21:5; 27:9–10). Almost half occur in the infancy story; the others relate to Jesus' public ministry, entry into Jerusalem, passion and death. As a whole, they reflect Matthew's conviction that Jesus came 'not to destroy but to fulfil' (5:17) the promises made of old. They also suggest Matthew's conviction that one could find explanations of the puzzling or shocking aspects of

Jesus' story, especially his death on the cross and the rejection of his mission by Jewish leaders and their followers, through consulting the Old Testament.

Outline

(I) Birth and beginnings (1:1–4:22)
    (A) *The genealogy of Jesus (1:1–17)*
    (B) *The birth of Jesus (1:18–25)*
    (C) *The visit of the wise men (2:1–12)*
    (D) *The flight to Egypt (2:13–15)*
    (E) *The slaughter of the innocents (2:16–18)*
    (F) *The return from Egypt (2:19–23)*
    (G) *The preaching of John the Baptist (3:1–12)*
    (H) *The baptism of Jesus (3:13–17)*
    (I) *The temptation of Jesus (4:1–11)*
    (J) *The beginning of the Galilean ministry (4:12–17)*
    (K) *The call of the disciples (4:18–22)*

(II) The Sermon on the Mount (4:23–7:29)
    (A) *Introduction (4:23–5:2)*
    (B) *The opening (5:3–16)*
    (a) Beatitudes (5:3–12)
    (b) Salt and light (5:13–16)
    (C) *The new ethic: hypertheses (5:17–48)*
    (a) The higher righteousness (5:17–20)
    (b) Anger (5:21–26)
    (c) Adultery (5:27–30)
    (d) Divorce (5:31–32)
    (e) Oaths (5:33–37)
    (f) Retaliation (5:38–42)
    (g) Love of enemies (5:43–48)
    (D) *Reformation of works of piety (6:1–18)*
    (a) Almsgiving (6:1–4)
    (b) Prayer (6:5–15)
    (c) Fasting (6:16–18)
    (E) *Further instructions (6:19–7:12)*
    (a) Treasure in heaven (6:19–21)
    (b) The single eye (6:22–23)
    (c) God and mammon (6:24)
    (d) On care and anxiety (6:25–34)
    (e) Judging others (7:1–6)
    (f) Ask, seek, knock (7:7–12)
    (F) *Conclusion of the Sermon (7:13–27)*
    (a) The narrow gate (7:13–14)
    (b) Bearing fruit (7:15–20)

(c) An episode in the last judgement described (7:21–23)
(d) Houses built on rock and sand (7:24–27)

(III) Authority and invitation (8:1–9:38)
(A) *The cleansing of a leper (8:1–4)*
(B) *The cure of the centurion's servant (8:5–13)*
(C) *The healing of Peter's mother-in-law (8:14–15)*
(D) *The sick healed at evening (8:16–17)*
(E) *On following Jesus (8:18–22)*
(F) *Stilling the storm (8:23–27)*
(G) *The cure of the Gadarene demoniacs (8:28–34)*
(H) *The healing of the paralytic (9:1–8)*
(I) *The call of Matthew the tax collector (9:9–13)*
(J) *The question about fasting (9:14–17)*
(K) *The healing of a ruler's daughter (9:18–26)*
(L) *The healing of two blind men (9:27–31)*
(M) *The healing of a dumb demoniac (9:32–34)*
(N) *The compassion of Jesus (9:35–38)*

(IV) Mission discourse (10:1–42)
(A) *The mission of the Twelve Apostles (10:1–4)*
(B) *The commissioning of the Twelve (10:5–16)*
(C) *How to face future persecutions (10:17–25)*
(D) *Appropriate and inappropriate fear (10:26–31)*
(E) *Confessing Jesus before people (10:32–39)*
(F) *Rewards of discipleship (10:40–42)*

(V) Rejection by this generation (11:1–12:50)
(A) *John the Baptist and Jesus (11:1–19)*
(B) *Woes on the cities (11:20–24)*
(C) *Cry of jubilee and Saviour's call (11:25–30)*
(D) *Plucking ears of grain on the sabbath (12:1–8)*
(E) *Healing the man with the withered hand (12:9–14)*
(F) *The chosen servant (12:15–21)*
(G) *Jesus and Beelzebul (12:22–32)*
(H) *A tree and its fruits (12:33–37)*
(I) *The sign of Jonah (12:38–42)*
(J) *The return of the evil spirit (12:43–45)*
(K) *Jesus' family (12:46–50)*

(VI) Parables of the kingdom (13:1–52)
(A) *The parable of the sower (13:1–9)*
(B) *The purpose of the parables (13:10–17)*
(C) *The parable of the sower explained (13:18–23)*
(D) *The parable of the weeds among the wheat (13:24–30)*
(E) *The parables of the mustard seed and the leaven (13:31–33)*
(F) *Jesus' use of parables (13:34–35)*

(G) *The interpretation of the parable of the weeds (13:36–43)*

(H) *The parables of the treasure, the pearl, and the dragnet (13:44–50)*

(I) *Old and new (13:51–52)*

(VII) **Acknowledgement by disciples (13:53–17:27)**

(A) *The rejection of Jesus in his own country (13:53–58)*

(B) *The death of John the Baptist (14:1–12)*

(C) *The feeding of the five thousand (14:13–21)*

(D) *Walking on the water (14:22–33)*

(E) *The healing of the sick in Gennesaret (14:34–36)*

(F) *Jesus and the tradition of the Pharisees on purity and vows (15:1–20)*

(G) *The Canaanite woman's faith (15:21–28)*

(H) *The healing of many people (15:29–31)*

(I) *The feeding of the four thousand (15:32–39)*

(J) *The demand for a sign (16:1–4)*

(K) *The leaven of the Pharisees and Sadducees (16:5–12)*

(L) *Peter's confession (16:13–20)*

(M) *First prediction of the passion and sayings on discipleship (16:21–28)*

(N) *The transfiguration (17:1–13)*

(O) *The healing of the moonstruck boy (17:14–20)*

(P) *Second passion prediction (17:22–23)*

(Q) *The coin in the fish's mouth (17:24–27)*

(VIII) **Community discourse (18:1–35)**

(A) *True greatness (18:1–5)*

(B) *Leaders who cause little ones to sin (18:6–9)*

(C) *The parable of the lost sheep (18:10–14)*

(D) *Trial procedures (18:15–20)*

(E) *The parable of the unforgiving servant (18:21–35)*

(IX) **Authority and invitation (19:1–22:46)**

(A) *Teaching about divorce (19:1–12)*

(B) *Little children blessed (19:13–15)*

(C) *The rich young man (19:16–30)*

(D) *The parable of the labourers in the vineyard (20:1–16)*

(E) *The third prediction of the passion (20:17–19)*

(F) *The request of the sons of Zebedee (20:20–28)*

(G) *The healing of two blind men (20:29–34)*

(H) *The triumphant entry into Jerusalem (21:1–11)*

(I) *The cleansing of the Temple (21:12–17)*

(J) *The cursing of the fig tree (21:18–22)*

(K) *The authority of Jesus questioned (21:23–27)*

(L) *The parable of the two sons (21:28–32)*

(M) *The parable of the vineyard and the wicked tenants (21:33–46)*

(N) *The parable of the marriage feast (22:1–14)*
(O) *Paying taxes to Caesar (22:15–22)*
(P) *The question about the resurrection (22:23–33)*
(Q) *The great commandment (22:34–40)*
(R) *The question about David's son (22:41–46)*

(X) Woes and eschatological discourse (23:1–25:46)
(A) *Woes against the scribes and Pharisees (23:1–36)*
(B) *The lament over Jerusalem (23:37–39)*
(C) *The eschatological discourse (24:1–25:46)*
(a) The destruction of the Temple and the beginning of the woes (24:1–14)
(b) The great tribulation (24:15–28)
(c) The coming of the Son of Man (24:29–31)
(d) The lesson of the fig tree (24:32–35)
(e) The unknown day and hour (24:36–44)
(f) The faithful or the unfaithful servant (24:45–51)
(g) The wise and foolish virgins (25:1–13)
(h) The parable of the talents (25:14–30)
(i) The judgement of the nations (25:31–46)

(XI) Death and rebirth (26:1–28:20)
(A) *The suffering and death of Jesus (26:1–27:66)*
(a) The plot to kill Jesus (26:1–5)
(b) The anointing at Bethany (26:6–13)
(c) Judas' agreement to betray Jesus (26:14–16)
(d) The Passover with the disciples (26:17–25)
(e) The institution of the Lord's Supper (26:26–30)
(f) Peter's denial foretold (26:31–35)
(g) The prayer in Gethsemane (26:36–46)
(h) The betrayal and arrest of Jesus (26:47–56)
(i) Jesus before the Sanhedrin (26:57–68)
(j) Peter's denial of Jesus (26:69–75)
(k) Jesus brought before Pilate (27:1–2)
(l) The death of Judas (27:3–10)
(m) Jesus questioned by Pilate (27:11–14)
(n) Jesus sentenced to die (27:15–26)
(o) The soldiers mock Jesus (27:27–31)
(p) The crucifixion of Jesus (27:32–44)
(q) The death of Jesus (27:45–56)
(r) The burial of Jesus (27:57–61)
(s) The guard at the tomb (27:62–66)
(B) *The Resurrection and the commission to preach the gospel (28:1–20)*
(a) The Resurrection of Jesus (28:1–10)
(b) The report of the guard (28:11–15)
(c) The commission to preach the gospel (28:16–20)

HIGHLIGHT

The Beatitudes
Matthew 5:3–12

[3]'Blessed are the poor in spirit, for theirs is the kingdom of heaven.

[4]'Blessed are those who mourn, for they will be comforted.

[5]'Blessed are the meek, for they will inherit the earth.

[6]'Blessed are those who hunger and thirst for righteousness, for they will be filled.

[7]'Blessed are the merciful, for they will receive mercy.

[8]'Blessed are the pure in heart, for they will see God.

[9]'Blessed are the peacemakers, for they will be called children of God.

[10]'Blessed are those who are persecuted for righteousness' sake, for theirs is the kingdom of heaven.

[11]'Blessed are you when people revile you and persecute you and utter all kinds of evil against you falsely on my account. [12]Rejoice and be glad, for your reward is great in heaven, for in the same way they persecuted the prophets who were before you.'

FORTY-TWO

The Gospel

According to

Luke

The author

The material in this chapter is digested from NJBC article 43, 'The Gospel According to Luke', by Robert J. Karris, OFM.

Among the traditions in the early church concerning the writer of this Gospel, we can deduce from the New Testament that he was a physician, and a companion or colleague of Paul. One should accept the tradition that Luke composed this Gospel (as well as Acts), for there seems no reason why anyone in the ancient church would invent this and make a relatively obscure figure the author of a Gospel. Luke was from Antioch in Syria. Since Luke in Acts shows little knowledge of Paul's theology and none of Paul's letters, it seems that his association with Paul was early, before Paul's theology was fully developed, before Paul engaged in serious letter writing to his communities, and before the Jerusalem 'Council'.

The date of Luke's Gospel

Luke used Mark, which was written a little before the Jewish War of AD 66–70. Luke 21:5–38 presupposes that Jerusalem has been destroyed; thus he wrote after AD 70. Luke–Acts does not reflect knowledge of the bitter persecution of Christians from the latter part of Domitian's rule (AD 81–96). From these considerations one arrives at a date of AD 80–85 for the composition of Luke–Acts.

Bronze head of the Roman emperor Augustus. Reproduced by courtesy of the Trustees of the British Museum

Tombstone of Q. Aemilius Secundus which mentions a census ordered by Quirinius, the Roman governor of Syria. Reproduced by courtesy of the Archaeological Museum, Venice

Luke's literary style

The talents of Luke, artist and theologian, are many. He is a master of Greek and he uses his sources creatively. In his account of Jesus' ministry he uses Mark, the sayings source Q, and his own special material. He adopts some 60 per cent of Mark but omits unnecessary material. For example, he takes over only one of Mark's feeding stories.

Luke's teaching

(a) His audience

Writing in Syrian Antioch, Luke addresses a primarily Gentile audience with well-to-do members who are painfully rethinking their mission in a hostile environment. Internal and external controversies contribute to the hostile environment. The key question of Luke's communities is this: if God has not been faithful to the promises made to God's chosen people and has allowed their holy city and Temple to be destroyed, what reason do Gentile Christians have to think that God will be faithful to promises made to them? Luke's answer takes the form of a story, which we find in the two books Luke and Acts. In them, Luke demonstrates that God through Jesus was faithful to promises made to Israel, but in an unexpected way: to include Gentiles, the unclean, the poor, women, Samaritans, rich tax collectors, and other outcasts, as well as elect people who have repented of their initial rejection of Jesus, God's prophet and Chosen One.

(b) Continuity with the old

In his Gospel Luke depicts a Jesus who is an upholder of the law (see, e.g., 16:17). Paul, too, in Acts defends himself against accusations that he is against the law and the Temple. In narrating God's establishment of **the new Israel**, Luke tells how Jesus selected Twelve (6:12–16) and how this Twelve was restored after the death of Judas (Acts 1:15–26). The Gospel begins in Jerusalem and in the Temple. Acts 1–3 details the origins of the new Israel in Jerusalem and in the Temple. From Jerusalem God's word goes out to all the nations (Acts 1:8).

> **the new Israel** <
the early Christian church

(c) Controversies

Luke battles on two fronts:

INTERNALLY Here, he attacks Jewish Christians who seek to apply over-strict entrance requirements to those who want to join the new Israel. These Jewish Christians are the 'Pharisees' of the Gospel, who object to Jesus' eating habits and association with sinners and tax collectors. Against them Luke develops his view that those who believe in Jesus are the children of Abraham (e.g. 13:10–17; 19:1–10) and therefore heirs of God's promises.

The lame, blind, and maimed now belong to this elect group (see 14:13, 21) as well as well-to-do Gentile Christians who share their possessions with those in need (6:17–49).

Finally, in the new Israel the outcast class, women, plays a prominent role (e.g. 7:36–50).

EXTERNALLY The main external problems which Luke's communities face are those of harassment, primarily from local Jewish synagogue leaders. (See 21:11–19 and the problems of Peter, John, Stephen, Barnabas, and Paul in Acts.) As the sermons of Peter, Stephen and Paul further indicate, these problems involve the interpretation of Scripture, especially how Jesus is the fulfilment of God's promises. And such Scripture interpretation is of no small concern for the mission to Jews.

(d) Jesus' mission

Jesus' mission is an inclusive one as he seeks out the lost and sinners and restores them to union with God.

● THE NEW ISRAEL The people, however, are not as stubborn and blind in their rejection of Jesus as their leaders. They contemplate the meaning of Jesus' crucifixion (23:35) and ultimately repent of their sin of rejecting Jesus in preference for Barabbas (23:48). From these repentant people Jesus forms the bond of continuity between the old Israel and the new believers.

● REJECTED PROPHET Luke's theme of the rejected prophet brings out a further side of his portrayal of Jesus. The Old Testament had told of: God's mercy in sending a prophet; rejection of the prophet; punishment; sending of another prophet. Jesus may have been rejected by the religious leaders, but such rejection does not close the door to God's offers of mercy.

● MERCY After punishment comes another offer of mercy. Luke narrates this further offer of mercy (e.g., in Acts 2), which records the repentance of 3,000 Jewish people from all over the world after Peter's Pentecost sermon. These help to form the new Israel.

Papyrus from Egypt, AD 104, ordering people to return to their homes for a census. Reproduced by permission of the British Library

• FAITHFULNESS There is a final nuance to Luke's portrait of Jesus, and this deals with the faithfulness of Jesus' God. Luke begins his Gospel with this theme as he tells how promises have been fulfilled in the birth of Jesus; he ends it with the theme as he tells how God has fulfilled promises in raising Jesus from the dead. This God will surely be faithful to promises made to Jesus' followers who journey from all corners of the globe to take up their places at the heavenly banquet with Abraham, Isaac and Jacob.

Outline

(I) Preface (1:1–4)

(II) Dawn of God's fulfilment of promise (1:5–2:52)
  (A) *Gabriel's annunciation of the birth of John to Zechariah in the Temple (1:5–25)*
  (B) *Gabriel's annunciation of the birth of Jesus to Mary in obscure Nazareth (1:26–38)*
  (C) *Elizabeth's and Mary's pronouncements about the meaning of Jesus in God's plan of salvation (1:39–56)*
  (A') *Zechariah's pronouncement of the meaning of John in God's plan of salvation (1:57–80)*
  (B') *The angels' pronouncement about the meaning of the baby Jesus lying in the manger (2:1–20)*
  (C') *Simeon's pronouncement of the meaning of the baby Jesus who has come into the Temple (2:21–40)*
  (D) *Bridge passage: conclusion to Luke's overture, Jesus' pronouncement about himself, and anticipation of the future journey of Jesus, God's son, from Galilee to Jerusalem (2:41–52)*

(III) Preparation for Jesus' public ministry (3:1–4:13)
  (A) *John the Baptist's preaching (3:1–20)*
  (B) *Jesus' baptism (3:21–22)*
  (C) *Jesus, culmination of God's plan in creation and salvation history (3:23–38)*
  (D) *Jesus, God's son and servant, conquers the devil (4:1–13)*

(IV) Jesus' Galilean ministry (4:14–9:50)
  (A) *Anticipatory description of Jesus' Galilean ministry (4:14–15)*
  (B) *God's promises fulfilled in Jesus for all (4:16–30)*
  (C) *God's kingdom restores men and women to wholeness (4:31–44)*

(D) *Positive response to Jesus' kingdom message (5:1–11)*

(E) *Jesus' boundary-breaking ministry for outcasts (5:12–16)*

(F) *Religious leaders oppose Jesus' kingdom message (5:17–6:11)*

(a) Jesus' power to forgive sins (5:17–26)

(b) Jesus' mission is for sinners (5:27–32)

(c) Jesus is the bridegroom and provider of new wine (5:33–39)

(d) The sabbath is subordinate to Jesus (6:1–5)

(e) Compassionate Jesus cures on the sabbath (6:6–11)

(G) *The gathering of the new Israel (6:12–49)*

(a) Jesus' selection of Twelve Apostles (6:12–16)

(b) The Sermon on the Plain (6:17–49)

(H) *Jesus' kingdom message is for men and women and shatters the boundaries of clean and unclean (7:1–9:6)*

(a) Unclean Gentiles are open to Jesus' kingdom message (7:1–10)

(b) God's prophet, Jesus, has compassion on a widow (7:11–17)

(c) The roles of John and Jesus in God's plan of salvation (7:18–35)

(d) A woman sinner responds to God's gift of forgiveness (7:36–50)

(e) The women disciples of Jesus (8:1–3)

(f) Diverse ways of hearing God's word (8:4–21)

(g) Jesus conquers chaos (8:22–25)

(h) Jesus restores a demented Gentile to human community (8:26–39)

(i) Jesus' power goes beyond ritual purity and gives life to two women (8:40–56)

(j) The Twelve continue Jesus' kingdom mission (9:1–6)

(I) *Responses to Jesus as his Galilean ministry draws to a close (9:7–50)*

(a) The fate of Jesus' forerunner is his fate and that of his disciples (9:7–9)

(b) Jesus' gift of food is linked to his cross (9:10–17)

(c) The cross in the lives of the Messiah and his disciples (9:18–27)

(d) Jesus' transfiguration and the divine confirmation of the way of the cross (9:28–36)

(e) How the cross interprets Jesus' merciful deeds (9:37–45)

(f) The disciples' misunderstanding of the meaning of following Jesus (9:46–50)

(V) **Jesus' journey to Jerusalem (9:51–19:27)**

(A) *First part of instruction on the meaning of the Christian way (9:51–13:21)*

(a) The Samaritan rejection and non-retaliation (9:51–56)

(b) The cost of discipleship (9:57–62)

(c) Jesus' teaching about mission (10:1–24)

(d) The Christian mission and observance of the law (10:25–37)

(e) Discipleship for men and women (10:38–42)

(f) Jesus' disciples and prayer (11:1–13)

(g) Controversies reveal the meaning of Jesus' journey (11:14–36)

(h) Almsgiving makes one clean before God (11:37–54)

(i) Disciples meet with external and internal opposition (12:1–59)

(j) All need to repent (13:1–9)

(k) An illustration of the nature of God's kingdom (13:11–17)

(l) Despite opposition God's kingdom grows (13:18–21)

(B) *Second part of instruction on the meaning of the Christian way (13:22–17:10)*

(a) The need for repentance stressed again (13:22–30)

(b) Jesus obediently journeys to Jerusalem (13:31–35)

(c) The inclusive nature of Jesus' kingdom banquet (14:1–24)

(d) The demands of discipleship repeated (14:25–35)

(e) God's mercy for sinners thrice illustrated (15:1–32)

(f) The necessity of sharing possessions with the needy (16:1–31)

(g) The inward renewal of disciples (17:1–10)

(C) *Third part of instruction on the meaning of the Christian way (17:11–19:27)*

(a) The gratitude and faith of a Samaritan leper (17:11–19)

(b) Fidelity while waiting for the coming of the Son of Man (17:20–18:8)

(c) Disciples must depend on God rather than on themselves (18:9–17)

(d) The wealthy have great difficulty entering God's kingdom (18:18–30)

(e) Jesus' passion and vindication predicted again (18:31–34)

(f) Summaries of Jesus' ministry to the outcasts (18:35–19:10)

(g) Disciples must take risks in following Jesus the King (19:11–27)

(VI) **Jerusalem rejects God's prophet and Son and Temple (19:28–21:38)**

   (A) *Jesus takes over the Jerusalem Temple (19:28–48)*

   (a) Jesus is hailed as King (19:28–40)

(b) Jesus weeps over Jerusalem (19:41–44)

(c) Jesus takes possession of the Temple and is the Temple (19:45–46)

(d) The responses of the people and religious leaders to Jesus (19:47–48)

(B) *Jesus affirms his authority to speak for God (20:1–21:4)*

(a) Jesus is a prophet commissioned by God (20:1–8)

(b) Jesus is God's Son and the cornerstone of the new Israel (20:9–19)

(c) Jesus truly teaches the way of God (20:20–26)

(d) Jesus' God is the God who gives and sustains life beyond the grave (20:27–40)

(e) Jesus the Messiah is David's son and Lord (20:41–44)

(f) Worship of God and a life-style of justice (20:45–21:4)

(C) *The consequences for Jerusalem for not heeding God's prophet (21:5–38)*

(VII) Jesus' last meal and association with sinners (22:1–23:56a)

(A) *Jesus' farewell discourse at a meal (22:1–38)*

(a) Preparation for Jesus' farewell discourse to his disciples (22:1–13)

(b) The eucharist as Jesus' legacy to the church (22:14–20)

(c) Will future disciples betray Jesus? (22:21–23)

(d) The meaning of leadership in Luke's communities (22:24–30)

(e) Peter's role in the church (22:31–34)

(f) The justification for the changed missionary praxis of Luke's communities (22:35–38)

(B) *Jesus' fidelity and disciples' failure during trial (22:39–71)*

(a) Jesus and his disciples contrasted in prayer (22:39–46)

(b) Infidelity and fidelity contrasted (22:47–53)

(c) The fidelity of Jesus, Son of God, and of Peter contrasted (22:54–71)

(C) *To the end, the innocent Jesus associates with sinners (23:1–56a)*

(a) The wronged and righteous Jesus is handed over to crucifixion (23:1–25)

(b) Jesus, rejected prophet, calls for repentance (23:26–31)

(c) Jesus, among sinners, prays for forgiveness (23:32–34)

(d) Negative and positive responses to Jesus (23:35–49)

(e) Jesus is given a kingly burial (23:50–56a)

HIGHLIGHT

The Magnificat
Luke 1:46–55

[46]And Mary said,
  'My soul magnifies the Lord,
[47]and my spirit rejoices in God my Saviour,
[48]for he has looked with favour on the lowliness of his servant.
    Surely, from now on all generations will call me blessed;
[49]for the Mighty One has done great things for me,
    and holy is his name.
[50]His mercy is for those who fear him
    from generation to generation.
[51]He has shown strength with his arm;
    he has scattered the proud in the thoughts of their hearts.
[52]He has brought down the powerful from their thrones,
    and lifted up the lowly;
[53]he has filled the hungry with good things,
    and sent the rich away empty.
[54]He has helped his servant Israel,
    in remembrance of his mercy,
[55]according to the promise he made to our ancestors,
    to Abraham and to his descendants forever.'

FORTY-THREE

Acts of the Apostles

The material in this chapter is digested from NJBC article 44, 'Acts of the Apostles', by Richard J. Dillon.

The author of Acts

The identity of the author is not given in the text. But Acts, like Luke, is dedicated to Theophilus, and it is generally accepted that Acts is by the same author.

However, there is disagreement as to whether this author is the same Luke who accompanied Paul on some of his missionary journeys. The author uses the word 'we' (in Acts 16: 10–17; 20:5–8, 13–15; 21:1–18; 27:1–28:16); this may mean that he was with Paul on these occasions. The problem with this is that there are considerable differences between the portrait of Paul in the Acts and Paul's firsthand testimonies in his authentic letters.

Place and date of writing

The great importance given to Paul in the Acts suggests that it was written in a community which was part of Paul's mission territory, but one where the personal legend of the apostle was known far better than his writings. It is widely accepted that Acts was written somewhere between AD 80 and 90.

Luke's purpose in writing Acts

The crucial questions are:
(1) why Luke produced this companion volume to his Gospel; and
(2) what the two-volume combination was meant to accomplish.

The opening words of Luke and Acts are the most reliable

Coin of Nero, emperor AD 54–68

clues to the character and purpose of Luke's work: Luke–Acts has been written to help Christians to understand themselves more clearly, not as an evangelistic address to outsiders.

To judge by his prologues, Luke intended to write history. Luke shows the persistent rejection of the gospel by Jewish audiences, and the gradual formation of a predominantly Gentile Christendom by a mission which nevertheless still made Jews its first audience. His readers' problem was: how could non-Jews find value in Christianity, which had its roots in Judaism but which most Jews rejected? To answer this, Luke had to show the historical relationship between Israel and Jesus on the one hand (the Gospel) and between Jesus and the church on the other (Acts), and thus to demonstrate the full scope of the divine plan in which the church of the present proves to be the fruit of God's plan for Israel (cf. 15:14–21).

Luke's way of presenting his material

The author concentrates on bringing historical reality vividly before the eyes of the reader by concentrating on particular events and mostly ignoring the chronological sequence between them. The clearest example of these freestanding dramatic episodes are the Pentecost account (chapter 2), Stephen's martyrdom (chapters 6–7), the Cornelius conversion (chapter 10), the Jerusalem agreement (chapter 15), Paul's Athens mission (17:16–34), and successive trials (chapters 21–26).

The centrepiece of most of these great scenes is a speech, whether a mission sermon (chapters 2, 17), a prophetic indictment (chapter 7), a commentary on the event being described (chapters 10, 15), or a defence before public authority (chapters 22, 26). The speeches in Acts all have Luke as their author and his readers as their audience; whether the audience on the scene would have grasped the argument is often beside the point (e.g. 17:22–31!).

The so-called missionary discourses, six to Jewish audiences (2:14–39; 3:12–26; 4:9–12; 5:29–32; 10:34–43; 13:16–41), two to Gentiles (14:15–17; 17:22–31), do not preach the gospel directly but illustrate, together with their settings, how the preaching of the apostles and its reception

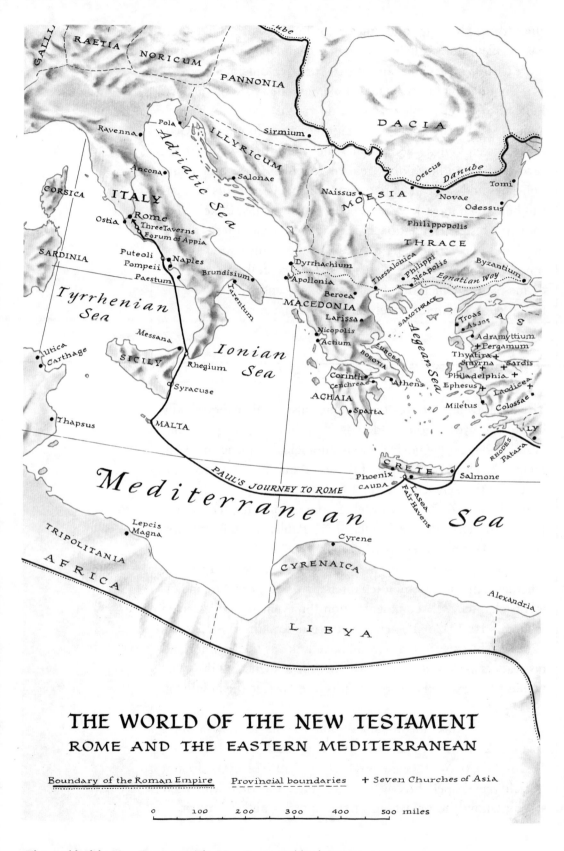

THE WORLD OF THE NEW TESTAMENT
ROME AND THE EASTERN MEDITERRANEAN

Boundary of the Roman Empire   Provincial boundaries   + Seven Churches of Asia

0   100   200   300   400   500 miles

The world of the New Testament. The New Jerome Biblical Commentary

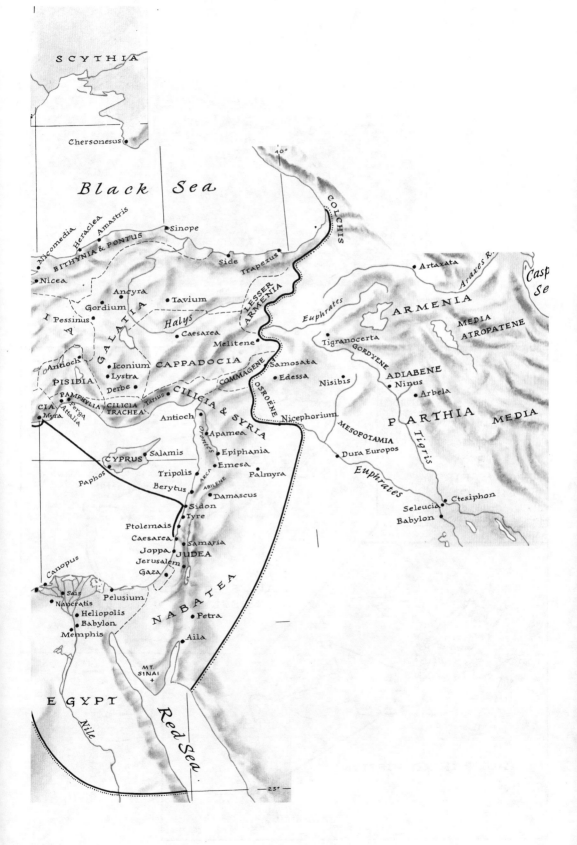

The Acropolis, Athens

The missions of Paul.
The New Jerome Biblical Commentary

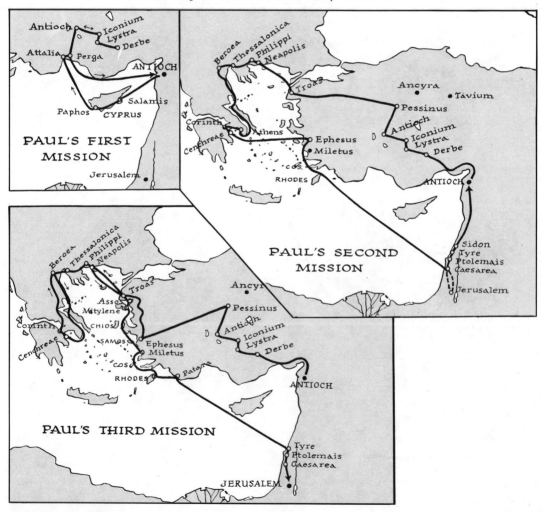

PAUL'S FIRST MISSION

PAUL'S SECOND MISSION

PAUL'S THIRD MISSION

carried earliest Christian history toward the outcome intended by God.

The sources of Acts

Luke was a resourceful Greek historian; but the sources of his information are not yet known. After chapter 15, above all in the reports of Paul's second and third mission journeys, there was perhaps a travel diary written by a companion of Paul.

Outline

(I) Introduction to the era of the church (1:1–26)
(A) Witnesses' commission and Jesus' ascension (1:1–14)
(a) Preface (1:1–8)
(b) The ascension (1:9–14)
(B) The restoration of the Twelve (1:15–26)

(II) The mission in Jerusalem (2:1–5:42)
(A) The appeal to Israel (2:1–3:26)
(a) The Pentecost event (2:1–13)
(b) The Pentecost sermon (2:14–41)
(c) First major summary (2:42–47)
(d) The healing in the Temple (3:1–11)
(e) Peter's Temple sermon (3:12–26)
(B) The life and trials of the apostolic church (4:1–5:42)
(a) Peter and John before the Sanhedrin (4:1–22)
(b) The Apostles' prayer (4:23–31)
(c) Second major summary (4:32–35)
(d) Singular cases (4:36–5:11)
(e) Third major summary (5:12–16)
(f) The second persecution (5:17–42)

(III) The mission's outward path from Jerusalem (6:1–15:35)
(A) The Hellenists and their message (6:1–8:40)
(a) The commission of the seven (6:1–7)
(b) The testimony of Stephen (6:8–8:3)
   (i) Mission and trial (6:8–7:1)
   (ii) The speech of Stephen (7:2–53)
   (iii) The martyrdom of Stephen (7:54–8:3)
(c) Philip and the advance of the word (8:4–40)
   (i) The gospel's triumph in Samaria (8:4–25)
   (ii) Philip and the Ethiopian eunuch (8:26–40)
(B) The persecutor becomes the persecuted (9:1–31)
(a) The conversion of Saul (9:1–19a)
(b) Saul's preaching and peril in Damascus (9:19b–25)

(c)   Saul's confrontations in Jerusalem (9:26–31)

(C) Peter as missionary (9:32–11:18)

(a)   Miracles in Lydda and Joppa (9:32–43)

(b)   The conversion of Cornelius and his household (10:1–11:18)

    (i)   The vision of Cornelius (10:1–8)

    (ii) The vision of Peter (10:9–16)

    (iii) Reception of the messengers (10:17–23a)

    (iv) Proceedings in Cornelius's house (10:23b–48)

    (v) Peter's accounting at Jerusalem (11:1–18)

(D) Between Jerusalem and Antioch (11:19–12:25)

(a)   The first church of the Gentile mission (11:19–30)

(b)   Herod's persecution and Peter's escape (12:1–25)

(E) The first missionary journey of Paul (13:1–14:28)

(a)   Prelude to the journey (13:1–3)

(b)   A contest won by Paul in Cyprus (13:4–12)

(c)   Mission and rejection at Pisidian Antioch (13:13–52)

    (i)   Visit to a synagogue and sermon (13:13–43)

    (ii) Missionaries turn to the Gentiles (13:44–52)

(d)   Mixed receptions in central Asia Minor (14:1–20)

    (i)   Iconium (14:1–7)

    (ii) Lystra and Derbe (14:8–20)

(e)   Return to Antioch (14:21–28)

(F) The Jerusalem conference and resolution (15:1–35)

(a)   Prehistory (15:1–5)

(b)   Peter's appeal to precedent (15:6–12)

(c)   James' confirmation and amendments (15:13–21)

(d)   Resolution (15:22–29)

(e)   Aftermath (15:30–35)

(IV) Paul's path to Rome (15:36–28:31)

(A) The major missions of Paul (15:36–20:38)

(a)   Mission journeys resumed (15:36–41)

(b)   The road to Europe (16:1–10)

    (i)   Timothy's circumcision (16:1–5)

    (ii) Paul's vision (16:6–10)

(c)   The mission in Greece (16:11–18:17)

    (i)   The evangelization of Philippi (16:11–40)

    (ii) Paul in Thessalonica and Beroea (17:1–15)

    (iii) Paul in Athens (17:16–34)

    (iv) Paul in Corinth (18:1–17)

(d)   Return to Antioch and journeys resumed (18:18–23)

(e)   The mission in Ephesus (18:24–19:40)

    (i)   The ministry of Apollos (18:24–28)

    (ii) Paul and the Baptist's disciples (19:1–7)

    (iii) Paul's mighty word and wonders in Ephesus (19:8–20)

HIGHLIGHT

The conversion of Paul
Acts 9:1–19a

Luke tells this as a major event in the mission, the conversion of
that fearsome enemy who was to become the greatest missionary
and the hero of the rest of the book. Paul's conversion stands
with the conversion of Cornelius's household at the pivotal centre
of the history of Acts; each of these events has extraordinary
importance and each is retold twice afterwards by the person
concerned. Paul tells his story a second and third time in his
speeches of self-defence (Acts 22:3–21; 26:2–23). The first telling,

in chapter 9, is likely to be closest to the original story. This is the story of a conversion, not a vocation. It points to Paul's future as a persecuted Christian witness.

[1]Meanwhile Saul, still breathing threats and murder against the disciples of the Lord, went to the high priest [2]and asked him for letters to the synagogues at Damascus, so that if he found any who belonged to the Way, men or women, he might bring them bound to Jerusalem. [3]Now as he was going along and approaching Damascus, suddenly a light from heaven flashed around him. [4]He fell to the ground and heard a voice saying to him, 'Saul, Saul, why do you persecute me?' [5]He asked, 'Who are you, Lord?' The reply came, 'I am Jesus, whom you are persecuting. [6]But get up and enter the city, and you will be told what you are to do.' [7]The men who were travelling with him stood speechless because they heard the voice but saw no one. [8]Saul got up from the ground, and though his eyes were open, he could see nothing; so they led him by the hand and brought him into Damascus. [9]For three days he was without sight, and neither ate nor drank.

[10]Now there was a disciple in Damascus named Ananias. The Lord said to him in a vision, 'Ananias.' He answered, 'Here I am, Lord.' [11]The Lord said to him, 'Get up and go to the street called Straight, and at the house of Judas look for a man of Tarsus named Saul. At this moment he is praying, [12]and he has seen in a vision a man named Ananias come in and lay his hands on him so that he might regain his sight.' [13]But Ananias answered, 'Lord, I have heard from many about this man, how much evil he has done to your saints in Jerusalem; [14]and here he has authority from the chief priests to bind all who invoke your name.' [15]But the Lord said to him, 'Go, for he is an instrument whom I have chosen to bring my name before Gentiles and kings and before the people of Israel; [16]I myself will show him how much he must suffer for the sake of my name.' [17]So Ananias went and entered the house. He laid his hands on Saul and said, 'Brother Saul, the Lord Jesus, who appeared to you on your way here, has sent me so that you may regain your sight and be filled with the Holy Spirit.' [18]And immediately something like scales fell from his eyes, and his sight was restored. Then he got up and was baptized, [19]and after taking some food, he regained his strength.

FORTY-FOUR

Introduction to

the New

Testament

Epistles

'Epistles' or 'letters'

The material in this chapter is digested from NJBC article 45, 'Introduction to the New Testament Epistles', by Joseph A. Fitzmyer, SJ.

Letter writing is a very ancient practice and was very popular in the Greek world of the 1st century AD. Both Paul and the later Christian writers use the letter for a religious purpose.

There is a difference between a 'letter' and an 'epistle'. A letter is something non-literary, a means of communication between persons who are separated from each other. It is both confidential and personal in its nature, although in style, tone and form it can be as frank and familiar as conversation. An epistle is an artistic, literary form and is written for a wide audience.

Paul's writings are for the most part letters, not literary epistles. They were composed for an occasion, often in haste, and mostly in complete independence of each other. Philemon is a private letter sent to an individual; Galatians a letter addressed to a group of local churches with Paul's personal concern for his converts. Similarly, 1 Corinthians, 1 Thessalonians, Philippians, despite all the great truths they discuss, are basically 'letters' handling concrete issues in the churches addressed. Much of the difficulty of 2 Corinthians comes from the fact that it is a letter: it contains many allusions no longer fully understood and yet so expressive of Paul's feelings about his relations with that church.

Of the genuine letters of Paul, Romans comes closest to being an epistle sent to a church that Paul had not yet evangelized; it might best be called an essay-letter.

Paul rarely wrote his letters as a private individual; he was an apostle, a missionary, a preacher. His letters were sent to communities and individuals to build up Christian churches. He used the letter form as a means of spreading his understanding of the Christian gospel and especially of applying it to the concrete problems that arose in areas that he could not then visit personally.

The form of Paul's letters

Paul's letters share features with Greek, Roman and Jewish letters of his time:

● **Opening formula**
'Paul ... (plus co-writer) to ...' 'Grace and Peace ...' (1 Thessalonians 1:1; Galatians 1:3; Philippians 1:2). The formula may be Paul's way of summarizing the good news of the Christian era, the spiritual gifts he begs for his readers.

● **Thanksgiving**
In this section Paul is usually at prayer. Often it is difficult to decide where the thanksgiving ends and the body of the letter begins (1 Thessalonians).

● **Message**
This reflects early Christian preaching. The letter is usually divided into two parts – one presenting truths of the Christian message, the other giving instructions for Christian behaviour.

● **Conclusion and final greeting**
The final section often contains personal news or specific advice for individuals. It is followed by a blessing. 'The grace of our Lord Jesus Christ be with you' (1 Thessalonians 5:28; Galatians 6:18; Philippians 4:23; 1 Corinthians 16:23; 2 Corinthians 13:13; Romans 16:20, [24]; Philemon 25).

Other types of material

Into his letters Paul often introduced other types of material:

- the early Christian apostolic proclamation (1 Thessalonians 1:9–10; 1 Corinthians 15:1–7; Romans 1:3–4; 4:25; 10:8–9)
- homilies and sermons (Romans 1:18–32)
- a list of vices and virtues (Galatians 5:19–24)
- hymns (Philippians 2:6–11; Romans 8:31–39; 1 Corinthians 13:1–13)
- liturgical phrases (1 Corinthians 11:24–25; 12:3; 16:22)
- Jewish statements of faith (Galatians 4:21–31; 2 Corinthians 3:4–18; Romans 4:1–24)
- proof texts from the Old Testament (Romans 3:10–18; 15:9–12)
- judgement and rebuke (Romans 2:1–3:9)

In many cases the material was derived from the young church's growing tradition but was reshaped by Paul's own preaching and teaching.

Letters in the New Testament attributed to Paul

There are 13 attributed by name to Paul:

(1) GENUINE WRITINGS: 1 Thessalonians, Galatians, Philippians, 1 and 2 Corinthians, Romans, Philemon.

(2) DOUBTFULLY GENUINE WRITINGS (probably written by a disciple): 2 Thessalonians, Colossians, Ephesians.

(3) NOT WRITTEN BY PAUL: Titus, 1 and 2 Timothy.

Hebrews does not bear Paul's name, even though it was often regarded as part of the collection of Paul's works in early church tradition. No one knows who wrote it. (See also the chapters on individual letters, especially page 292.)

Several passages suggest that Paul wrote other letters beyond the 13 attributed to him. In 1 Corinthians 5:9 Paul refers to a letter previously written to the Corinthian church; 2 Corinthians 2:3–4 mentions a 'letter written in tears', composed apparently between 1 Corinthians and 2 Corinthians. The 'letter written in tears' may be part of 2 Corinthians (see page 256). In Colossians 4:16 a letter to the Laodiceans is mentioned. It is debated whether Romans 16 was intended as a separate letter, and Philippians is possibly also made up of more than one letter. Paul himself was aware (2 Corinthians 10:10) that some of his letters were being widely read and causing comments. By the end of the 1st century AD the letters were already being gathered into a **corpus**.

> **corpus** <
a recognized collection of someone's work

Of the 13 letters, Philippians, Philemon, Colossians and Ephesians are often called the 'Captivity' letters because imprisonment is mentioned in them. 'Pastoral' letters is the title for 1 and 2 Timothy and Titus because of their concern for church organization and discipline.

The order of Paul's letters in the modern Bible is not chronological. Length is most likely to be the factor governing their order: each letter decreases in length from Romans to Philemon; and letters to churches precede letters to individuals.

The other letters

(1) Hebrews. Like a sermon and very theological in discussion, it is quite unlike the letters of Paul and has no opening formula. (2) The 'Catholic' Epistles. James, 1 and 2 Peter and Jude are homilies in letter form and are better thought of as epistles; 1 John lacks all the features of a biblical letter; 2 and 3 John are letters to the 'chosen lady and her children'.

Were the New Testament letters written or dictated?

Four ways of letter writing were used in ancient times:

(1) to write oneself
(2) to dictate word for word, syllable for syllable
(3) to dictate the sense, leaving the formulation to a secretary
(4) to have someone write in one's name, without indicating the contents.

The most commonly used modes were (1) and (3). Ancient writers complained that dictation was wearying, especially when the scribe was not skilled.

What method did Paul use? Romans 16:22 suggests dictation to Tertius. In 1 Corinthians 16:21 Paul adds the greeting in his own hand, which may imply that the rest was dictated. See too Galatians 6:11, where he compares his handwriting with that of the trained scribe, who has written what preceded. Cf. 2 Thessalonians 3:17; Colossians 4:18. Was the dictation of the sort (2) or (3)? Impossible to say. The latter could explain the difference in style in the doubtfully genuine writings. Philemon 19 may mean that Paul has written the whole letter in his own hand.

Inconsistencies of style, and the variations in the use of words, may be explained by dictation; distractions must have occurred that would also have affected the style. A long letter like Romans or 1 Corinthians would scarcely have been finished in one sitting or one day. Little can be said about the writing of other New Testament epistles. 1 Peter 5:12 may imply writing by Silvanus as scribe.

Did the New Testament writers dictate to scribes who used shorthand? Shorthand was known in the Roman world, but it is usually thought that it was not practised by Greek scribes before *ca.* AD 155.

FORTY-FIVE

The First Letter

to the

Thessalonians

The material in this
chapter is digested
from NJBC article
46, 'The First Letter
to the
Thessalonians', by
Raymond F. Collins.

The church at Thessalonica

Thessalonica was a port and capital city of Macedonia, in the north of what is now Greece. At the time of Paul it was a thriving commercial centre. Commerce attracted a cosmopolitan population. The Jewish population of Thessalonica had a synagogue, in which according to Acts 17:1–2 Paul preached. Isis, Serapis, Osiris, and Anubis were among the Oriental deities venerated, but there was also some emperor worship.

Inscription from a Roman gateway in Thessalonica; 2nd century AD. It mentions the 'rulers of the city' (see Acts 17:6, 8). Reproduced by courtesy of the Trustees of the British Museum

According to Acts, Paul, Silvanus and Timothy came to Thessalonica during Paul's second mission journey, most probably in AD 50. Having been expelled from Philippi (Acts 16:16–40), almost 100 miles east of Thessalonica, they passed through Amphipolis and Apollonia but did not stay in either of these places, apparently because neither of them had a synagogue. The Jewish population of Thessalonica was, however, large enough to support one. In Acts Luke relates that Paul and his companions found lodging in the house of Jason, that he preached in the synagogue for three weeks, and that a riot took place among the Jewish population because of the success of his preaching. Paul and Silvanus were expelled from the city (Acts 17:1–9). But from Paul's affection for the Thessalonian Christians, it would appear that he remained in the city for more than the brief period allowed by Acts. Paul's letter clearly suggests that Thessalonian Christians were mainly Gentiles, i.e. converts from paganism.

The letter

Where was it written?

According to Luke, Paul's Jewish opposition followed him to Beroea. Unaccompanied, Paul escaped to Athens (Acts 17:10–15). Silvanus and Timothy later joined Paul there, where he yearned to visit again the Thessalonians. Unable to do so, Paul sent Timothy in his place (1 Thessalonians 2:17–3:3). In the meantime Paul moved on to Corinth, where he was eventually joined by Timothy (Acts 18:5).

Why was it written?

Timothy brought good news about the situation of the church in Thessalonica but apparently indicated that there was some misunderstanding there about the fate of those who had died (4:13). This led to the writing of the letter.

When was it written?

It is virtually certain that it was written from Corinth almost immediately after Timothy's arrival there from Thessalonica. The impression given in Acts that the events of Paul's second mission journey were moving quickly at this point in his life is confirmed by 1 Thessalonians. Paul writes about being separated from the Thessalonians for a short while (1 Thessalonians 2:17). He frequently recalls his time spent in the Thessalonian community (2:1). It would seem, then, that only a short time, probably a few months, passed between Paul's evangelization of Thessalonica and his writing of 1 Thessalonians. Probably the letter was written in AD 50, but some scholars date it in AD 51.

Was it one letter?

Scholars have discussed whether it was one letter or two, and whether it is made up of several parts. It has also been widely believed that 2:13–16, because of its anti-Jewish tone, was added to the original letter.

Significance of the letter

> **creedal formulas** <
statements of Christian
belief, like the creeds used
today

The date at which 1 Thessalonians was composed makes it the earliest written book in the New Testament. Since it uses traditional material, particularly the **creedal formulas** (1:9–10; 4:14; 5:10), it serves as a significant witness to the gospel in the period between the death and resurrection of Jesus and the written works of the New Testament (i.e., AD 30–50). The letter provides the oldest literary evidence of the significance attached to the death and resurrection of Jesus by the early Christians.

Significance of its teaching

> **eschatological,
apocalyptic** <
see Chapter 19

It is the **eschatological** sections of the letter (4:13–18; 5:1–11) that are discussed most frequently. Paul has written about the Second Coming of Christ (4:13–18) and the Day of the Lord (5:1–11). These passages speak of the expectations of the early Christians, but they are in **apocalyptic** language, which is symbolic. There is considerable distance between the symbol and that to which the symbol points. Thus, the passages cannot be taken as a literal description of end-time events. Nonetheless, conservatives and fundamentalists understand the passages as if they provide literally a factual description of the end times.

From the literary standpoint, 1 Thessalonians is especially valuable as the oldest Christian document. After the death and resurrection of Jesus, a variety of historical, social, and religious factors prevented the development of a Christian literature. These factors did not prevent the writing of letters.

The structure of 1 Thessalonians is similar to the personal letters of the times, although the content is decidedly Christian and evangelical. Because it has the form of a personal letter, it must be read as a letter, i.e., a communication addressed to a particular audience.

Outline

(I) Opening formula (1:1)

(II) Thanksgiving (1:2–3:13)
   (A) *First thanksgiving period: the Thessalonians' reception of the gospel (1:2–2:12)*
   (B) *Second thanksgiving period (2:13–3:13)*

(III) Exhortation (4:1–12)
   (A) *On chastity (4:1–8)*
   (B) *On charity (4:9–12)*

(IV) Eschatology (4:13–5:11)
   (A) *First revelation: the Second Coming (4:13–18)*
   (B) *Second revelation: the end of time (5:1–11)*

(V) Final exhortation (5:12–22)
   (A) *First period: call for order in the community (5:12–13)*
   (B) *Second period: call for various functions (5:14–22)*

(V) Closing wishes and final greeting (5:23–28)

HIGHLIGHT

The Day of the Lord
1 Thessalonians 5:1–11

[1]Now concerning the times and the seasons, brothers and sisters, you do not need to have anything written to you. [2]For you yourselves know very well that the day of the Lord will come like a thief in the night. [3]When they say, 'There is peace and security', then sudden destruction will come upon them, as labour pains come upon a pregnant woman, and there will be no escape! [4]But you, beloved, are not in darkness, for that day to surprise you like

a thief; [5]for you are all children of light and children of the day; we are not of the night or of darkness. [6]So then let us not fall asleep as others do, but let us keep awake and be sober; [7]for those who sleep sleep at night, and those who are drunk get drunk at night. [8]But since we belong to the day, let us be sober, and put on the breastplate of faith and love, and for a helmet the hope of salvation. [9]For God has destined us not for wrath but for obtaining salvation through our Lord Jesus Christ, [10]who died for us, so that whether we are awake or asleep we may live with him, [11]Therefore encourage one another and build up each other, as indeed you are doing.

FORTY-SIX

The Letter to

the Galatians

For whom was it written?

The material in this
chapter is digested
from NJBC article
47, 'The Letter to
the Galatians', by
Joseph A. Fitzmyer,
SJ.

No one seriously queries whether Paul wrote Galatians, but
where were the 'churches of Galatia' (1:2)?

Galatia was a province of the Roman Empire. Territorially
it included the original 'Galatian country' in northern Asia
Minor, the area about Ancyra, Pessinus and Tavium; also a
large part of the south and centre as well. In the southern area
were situated Pisidian Antioch, Iconium, Lystra and Derbe. The
population of the whole area was quite mixed.

Paul went from Lystra and Iconium (i.e. southern Galatia)
into Phrygia and 'the Galatian country' (see also Acts 18:23).
Galatians 4:8; 5:2–3; 6:12–13 implies that Paul is writing to a
community of Gentile Christians that has become fascinated
with Jewish practices. All of this means that Paul has written
Galatians to the predominantly Gentile Christian churches of
northern Galatia, i.e. to the ancient 'Galatian country'.

Date

Galatians is not easily dated – 4:13 may suggest that it was
written after a second visit to Galatia (probably that of Acts
18:23 on his third missionary journey). Ephesus is the likely
place of writing. At any rate, Galatians belongs to the period of
Paul's major struggle with those who insisted on keeping all
Jewish customs in the early church. A likely date is *ca.* AD 54,
not long after Paul's arrival in Ephesus at the beginning of his
third missionary journey.

Why Paul wrote Galatians

Fragment of a papyrus, showing two kinds of handwriting. Paul's letters may have looked like this, part being by a scribe and part 'in my own hand'. Reproduced by courtesy of Cambridge University Library

Shortly after Paul's second visit to the churches of northern Galatia he learned in Ephesus that 'some agitators' (1:7) in Galatia were attacking his authority as an apostle (1:1, 12 – apparently saying that his commission did not come from Christ); they further claimed that he was not preaching the true gospel (1:7), because he did not insist on observance of Mosaic regulations: circumcision (even for Gentile Christians, 6:12), celebration of Jewish feasts (4:10, days, months, seasons, and years). Thus he was thought to be watering down the requirements of the gospel for the sake of Gentile converts.

Having learned of the activity of such agitators and the confusion that they were creating in the Galatian churches, Paul wrote this strong letter to warn his Christian followers there against this 'different gospel' (1:7) that was being preached to them by such people.

He defended his position as an 'apostle' and stoutly maintained that the gospel he had preached, without the observance of the Jewish practices, was the only correct view of Christianity, as recent events had shown. Galatians thus became the first example of Paul's teaching about justification by grace through faith apart from deeds prescribed by the law; it is Paul's manifesto about Christian freedom. Though he called the Galatians 'senseless' (3:1), he still found room in his heart for 'my children' (4:19) and 'brothers' (4:12; 5:11; 6:18).

The agitators in Galatia are best identified as Jewish Christians of Palestine, of an even stricter Jewish background than Peter, Paul, or James, or even the 'false brethren' (2:4) whom Paul had encountered at Jerusalem.

Outline

(I) Introduction (1:1–11)
  (A) Opening formula (1:1–5)
  (B) Paul's amazement (1:6–7), warning (1:8–9), transition (1:10–11)

246

(II) **Paul tells of his historic call to preach the gospel
(1:12–2:14)**
  (A) *Paul's gospel not of human origin (1:12–24)*
  (B) *Paul's gospel approved by Jerusalem church leaders
  (2:1–10)*
  (C) *Paul's gospel challenged Peter's inconsistency at
  Antioch (2:11–14)*

(III) **Paul's gospel set forth (2:15–21)**

(IV) **In God's plan humanity is saved by faith, not by the law
(3:1–4:31)**
  (A) *Proof 1: experience of the Galatians in first receiving
  the Spirit (3:1–5)*
  (B) *Proof 2: experience of Abraham and God's promises
  to him (3:6–26)*
  (C) *Proof 3: experience of Christians in baptism
  (3:27–29)*
  (D) *Proof 4: experience of Christians as children of God
  (4:1–11)*
  (E) *Proof 5: experience of Galatians in their relation to
  Paul (4:12–20)*
  (F) *Proof 6: the allegory of Sarah and Hagar (4:21–31)*

(V) **Encouragement to Christian behaviour (5:1–6:10)**
  (A) *Advice: preserve the freedom that you have in Christ
  (5:1–12)*
  (B) *Warning: walk not according to the flesh, but
  according to the spirit (5:13–26)*
  (C) *Advice: the right way to use Christian freedom
  (6:1–10)*

(VI) **Paul's 'signature' and reminder; farewell blessing
(6:11–18)**

HIGHLIGHT

The gospel as taught by Paul
Galatians 2:15–16

[15]We ourselves are Jews by birth and not Gentile sinners; [16]yet we
know that a person is justified not by the works of the law but
through faith in Jesus Christ. And we have come to believe in
Christ Jesus, so that we might be justified by faith in Christ, and
not by doing the works of the law, because no one will be justified
by the works of the law.

FORTY-SEVEN

The Letter to
the Philippians

THE NEW
JEROME
BIBLE
HANDBOOK

The material in this chapter is digested from NJBC article 48, 'The Letter to the Philippians', by Brendan Byrne, SJ.

> **colonia** <
a colony or settlement of Roman citizens

> **ius italicum** <
the same rights in Roman law as an Italian city

> **exorcism** <
casting out a devil

Philippi: the city and the Christian community

In the time of Paul, Philippi was a leading town in the Roman province of Macedonia. Veterans of Roman armies were settled at Philippi, and the city, made up of Romans and Macedonians, received the prized status of a Roman **colonia**, enjoying thereby the **ius italicum** – a dignity noted in Acts 16:12 and important for the understanding of Philippians.

In Philippi Paul began the European phase of his missionary work *ca.* AD 50 on his second mission journey. Acts 16:11–40 describes the foundation of the church. Since the city had no Jewish synagogue, Paul began his preaching at a 'prayer-place' by the river. His **exorcism** of a slave girl led to his being arrested, flogged and imprisoned. An earthquake during the night gave Paul an opportunity to escape. Instead, he publicly vindicated his cause by revealing his Roman citizenship. Women seem to have played a leading role in the community from the start (notably Lydia [Acts 16:14–15, 40]; Euodia and Syntyche [Philippians 4:2–3]). Personal names appearing in Philippians suggest that the community was predominantly Gentile Christian.

The letter itself

It is agreed that Paul wrote Philippians. There is today a widespread view that Philippians represents two or three originally separate letters put together.

- LETTER A 4:10–20: The Philippians had sent money to Paul in prison via one of their number, Epaphroditus. 4:10–20 represents Paul's immediate acknowledgement of this gift.

- LETTER B 1:1–3:1a; 4:4–7, 21–23: This letter followed some weeks after letter A. Epaphroditus had fallen ill but was now better and anxious to return to Philippi. Paul composes a more extended response to what he has heard about the situation in Philippi. The Philippians are experiencing considerable antagonism from their fellow citizens (1:28–30). Paul sees their capacity to withstand weakened by internal divisions, caused by self-seeking and pride. With great love he urges them to close ranks and find a deeper unity through unselfishness.

  At the same time, reflecting upon his own fate, he comforts them by teaching that, as they share in his suffering, they should share also in the joy coming from the deeper union with Christ that such suffering brings. The letter revolves around the idea of *koinōnia* ('common participation and sharing'). *Koinōnia* in Paul's writings means the union established between persons through their common sharing in something, such as the eucharist (1 Corinthians 10:16–17). In Philippians shared suffering intensifies the union between apostle and community; at the same time, the basic *koinōnia* in Christ should shape and determine their relationships.

- LETTER C 3:1b–4:3,8–9: This warning seems to come from a period after Paul's release from prison and to follow the visit to Philippi proposed in 2:24 (cf. 1:26; Acts 20:1–2). Paul sees a grave threat to the community posed by those who taught that the whole Jewish law must be kept. So he writes (possibly from Corinth: cf. Acts 20:2–6; Romans 15:24–26) to counter this danger, building his case upon his own discovery of what conversion to Christ means and wherein true 'perfection' lies.

Date

Letters A and B would date from the closing period of Paul's stay in Ephesus (AD 54–57) with Letter C following some months later (AD 57–58).

The letters in the setting of Paul's life

At least two of the letters contained in Philippians (A and B) presuppose that Paul is in prison. Most modern scholars assign the imprisonment to the apostle's lengthy stay in Ephesus in the course of his third missionary journey (Acts 19:1–20:1), because (1) we have no record of an imprisonment in Ephesus but he recalls multiple imprisonments (2 Corinthians 11:23) and speaks (doubtless metaphorically) of having 'fought with beasts in Ephesus' (1 Corinthians 15:30–32; cf. 2 Corinthians 1:8–10); (2) Philippi lay within easy reach of Ephesus.

Outline

(I) **Introduction (1:1–11) [Letter B]**
    (A) Opening formula – address and greeting (1:1–2)
    (B) Thanksgiving (1:3–8)
    (C) Prayer (1:9–11)

(II) **Part I: news and instructions (1:12–3:1a) [Letter B]**
    (A) Paul's own situation (1:12–26)
    (B) Exhortation for the community (1:27–2:18)
    (a) Unity and steadfastness (1:27–30)
    (b) Humility and selflessness (2:1–11)
    (c) Obedience and witness to the world (2:12–18)
    (C) Announcements about Timothy and Epaphroditus (2:19–30)
    (D) Conclusion (3:1a)

(III) **Part II: warning against false teachers (3:1b–4:1) [Letter C]**

(IV) **Part III: exhortations to unity, joy and peace (4:2–9)**
    (A) Call to unity (4:2–3) [Letter C]
    (B) Call to joy and peace of mind (4:4–7) [Letter B]
    (C) Call to imitation of Paul (4:8–9) [Letter C]

(V) **Part IV: acknowledgement of community's gift (4:10–20) [Letter A]**

(VI) **Conclusion (4:21–23) [Letter B]**

HIGHLIGHT

The Christ-hymn
Philippians 2:6–11

Paul supports his exhortation to unselfishness in community relations by quoting what appears to be a very early Jewish-Christian hymn. The hymn recalls the way in which the totally unselfish 'mind' or attitude of Christ, at all stages of his existence, stood at the centre of God's plan to reclaim and save the universe. Paul summons the Philippians to live out the same unselfish attitude. This should well up within them on the basis of their new life 'in Christ' (verse 5).

⁶Christ though he was in the form of God,
    did not regard equality with God
    as something to be exploited,
⁷but emptied himself,
    taking the form of a slave,
    being born in human likeness.
And being found in human form,
⁸ he humbled himself
    and became obedient to the point of death –
    even death on a cross.
⁹Therefore God also highly exalted him
    and gave him the name
    that is above every name,
¹⁰so that at the name of Jesus every knee should bend,
    in heaven and on earth and under the earth,
¹¹and every tongue should confess that Jesus Christ is Lord,
    to the glory of God the Father.

251

FORTY-EIGHT

The First Letter

to the

Corinthians

The material in this chapter is digested from NJBC article 49, 'The First Letter to the Corinthians', by Jerome Murphy-O'Connor, OP.

The city of Corinth

By the early 1st century AD Corinth had a thriving Jewish community. Other religious groups were also well represented. Temples dedicated to the cult of the emperor and to the various Greek and Egyptian gods highlight both the religious diversity and the ethnic mix of the city that Paul was to make one of the most important centres of early Christianity.

The church in Corinth

More data are available on the social makeup of the Corinthian church than of any other. The names of 16 members are known from Acts 18, 1 Corinthians 16, and Romans 16, and details given or implied about them can be analysed in various ways. There was a solid nucleus of Jews but many pagans. The social status of most is not simple; they rate high in some areas but low in others, e.g. rich but female (Phoebe), a city official but an ex-slave (Erastus), a skilled artisan but a Jew with a wife of higher social rank (Aquila). Such individuals did not cease to question and explore once they had accepted Christianity, and so led to a greater diversity of problems for Paul than any other church. In particular they welcomed other visions of Christianity and competed with one another for spiritual prestige.

When and where 1 Corinthians was written

Paul himself tells us that 1 Corinthians was written in the spring from Ephesus (16:8). When all of Paul's complex relations with the Corinthians are taken into account, the most probable date is the spring of AD 54, or possibly of AD 57.

Why Paul wrote the letter

1 Corinthians is a complex reaction to two sets of data about the situation in Corinth. In a letter (7:1), probably carried by Stephanas and others (16:17), the Corinthians brought to Paul's attention a series of problems on which they wanted his advice. Such official information was supplemented by gossip. Chloe's people (1:11), on their return to Ephesus from a business trip to Corinth, told Paul about those aspects of the life of the church there that surprised them, but that apparently did not worry the Corinthians. These observations revealed to Paul certain basic flaws in the Corinthians' understanding of Christian community. In consequence, he integrated his replies to their questions into an effort to bring them to a true appreciation of authentic life in Christ.

Outline

(I) Introduction: greeting and thanksgiving (1:1–9)

(II) Part I: divisions in the community (1:10–4:21)
    (A) *Rival groups in the community (1:10–17)*
    (B) *God has different standards (1:18–31)*
    (C) *The power of Paul's preaching (2:1–5)*
    (D) *True wisdom and the language of love (2:6–3:4)*
    (E) *The right attitude toward pastors (3:5–4:5)*
    (F) *How this applies to the Corinthians (4:6–13)*
    (G) *The visit of Timothy (4:14–21)*

(III) Part II: the importance of the body (5:1–6:20)
    (A) *A case of incest (5:1–8)*
    (B) *Clearing up a misunderstanding (5:9–13)*
    (C) *Lawsuits among Christians (6:1–11)*
    (D) *Casual sexual behaviour (6:12–20)*

(IV) Part III: responses to Corinthian questions (7:1–14:40)
    (A) Problems of social status (7:1–40)
    (a) Sexual relations in marriage (7:1–9)
    (b) Marriage and divorce (7:10–16)
    (c) Changes in social status (7:17–24)
    (d) Changes in sexual status (7:25–40)
    (B) Problems arising from pagan environment (8:1–11:1)
    (a) Food offered to idols (8:1–13)
    (b) Paul renounces his rights (9:1–27)
    (c) The dangers of over-confidence (10:1–13)
    (d) The significance of social gestures (10:14–22)
    (e) The scruples of the weak (10:23–11:1)
    (C) Problems in liturgical assemblies (11:2–14:40)
    (a) Dress at liturgical assemblies (11:2–16)
    (b) The eucharist (11:17–34)
    (c) The gifts of the Spirit (12:1–11)
    (d) The body needs many members (12:12–31)
    (e) Love the greatest gift (13:1–13)
    (f) Prophecy more important than tongues (14:1–25)
    (g) Order in the use of spiritual gifts (14:26–40)

(V) Part IV: the Resurrection (15:1–58)
    (A) The creed of the church (15:1–11)
    (B) The consequences of different beliefs (15:12–28)
    (a) The Corinthians' thesis (15:12–19)
    (b) Paul's thesis (15:20–28)
    (C) Other arguments for resurrection (15:29–34)
    (D) The resurrected body (15:35–49)
    (E) The need for transformation (15:50–58)

(VI) Conclusion (16:1–24)
    (A) The collection for Jerusalem (16:1–4)
    (B) Paul's travel plans (16:5–9)
    (C) Some recommendations (16:10–18)
    (D) Final greetings (16:19–24)

HIGHLIGHT

Love's supremacy
I Corinthians 13:1–13

[1]If I speak in the tongues of mortals and of angels, but do not have love, I am a noisy gong or a clanging cymbal. [2]And if I have prophetic powers, and understand all mysteries and all knowledge, and if I have all faith, so as to remove mountains, but do not have love, I am nothing. [3]If I give away all my possessions, and if I hand

over my body so that I may boast, but do not have love, I gain nothing.

⁴Love is patient; love is kind; love is not envious or boastful or arrogant ⁵or rude. It does not insist on its own way; it is not irritable or resentful; ⁶it does not rejoice in wrongdoing, but rejoices in the truth. ⁷It bears all things, believes all things, hopes all things, endures all things.

⁸Love never ends. But as for prophecies, they will come to an end; as for tongues, they will cease; as for knowledge, it will come to an end. ⁹For we know only in part, and we prophesy only in part; ¹⁰but when the complete comes, the partial will come to an end. ¹¹When I was a child, I spoke like a child, I thought like a child, I reasoned like a child; when I became an adult, I put an end to childish ways. ¹²For now we see in a mirror, dimly, but then we will see face to face. Now I know only in part; then I will know fully, even as I have been fully known. ¹³And now faith, hope, and love abide, these three; and the greatest of these is love.

FORTY-NINE

The Second

Letter to the

Corinthians

The material in this chapter is digested from NJBC article 50, 'The Second Letter to the Corinthians', by Jerome Murphy-O'Connor, OP.

2 Corinthians: two letters – or five?

(a) Authenticity

Apart from 6:14–7:1, which many consider a later addition, 2 Corinthians is accepted as composed by Paul. Its unity, however, is a matter of some controversy.

(b) Unity

Most commentators see it as a collection of letters from Paul. The most influential view divides 2 Corinthians into five letters dated in the following order:

(A) 2:14–7:4 apart from 6:14–7:1

(B) 10–13, the letter written in tears (see page 238)

(C) 1:1–2:13 plus 7:5–16, the letter of reconciliation

(D) 8:1–24, a letter to Corinth concerning the collection for Jerusalem

(E) 9:1–15, a circular letter to the region of Achaia about the collection.

Some scholars believe chapters 1 to 9 are one letter. Chapters 10–13, however, cannot be the continuation of chapters 1–9; it is psychologically impossible that Paul should suddenly switch from the celebration of reconciliation (1–9) to a savage reproach and sarcastic self-justification (10–13). Thus, 2 Corinthians is certainly a combination of at least two letters.

(c) Paul on the defensive

In both of the letters combined in 2 Corinthians, Paul is on the defensive. Outbursts of anger, stimulated by a sense of injury, replace the cool logic in 1 Corinthians. Themes are strung together by links that give rise to digressions and repetitions.

When and where was 2 Corinthians written?

It is probable that chapters 10–13 (Letter B) were caused by some development at Corinth after the dispatch of chapters 1–9 (Letter A). The seeds of the trouble that necessitated Letter B can be detected in Letter A. Letter A was written a year after 1 Corinthians (2 Corinthians 8:10; 9:2; cf. 1 Corinthians 16:1–4), therefore in the spring of AD 55, from Macedonia (2 Corinthians 2:13; 7:5; 8:1; 9:2), where Paul had wintered (at Thessalonica or Philippi). Titus had been the bearer of the sorrowful letter (2 Corinthians 7:6) because he had been at the Jerusalem conference (Galatians 2:1) and could report authoritatively on the attitude of the mother church to the Gentile mission; he was also entrusted with Letter A (8:16–17), which brought to a happy conclusion a distasteful episode in Paul's relations with Corinth.

Having spent the winter with the churches of Macedonia, there was little more for Paul to do there, so in the summer of AD 55 he moved on to new territory (2 Corinthians 10:16) in Illyricum (Romans 15:19). At some point news reached him there of a drastic deterioration in the situation at Corinth. Letter B was written in the heat of his disappointment and anger.

Paul's opponents at Corinth

Letters A and B reflect different stages of a developing situation at Corinth. Opposition to Paul that is only hinted at in Letter A is brought out into the open in Letter B. There is agreement on two points: the intruders were Jewish Christians, and they attacked Paul's authority as an apostle. The situation was further complicated by the fact that the Corinthian church, which had to decide between Paul and his rivals, tended to judge religious figures by the standards of the pagans around them. This in turn influenced not only Paul's opponents but Paul himself. They adapted their approaches to meet the expectations of the community.

Letter A (1–9)

Outline

(I) Introduction: greeting and blessing (1:1–11)

(II) Part I: a cancelled visit to Corinth (1:12–2:13)
  (A) *Paul's plan (1:12–22)*
  (B) *The consequences of a change of plan (1:23–2:13)*

(III) Part II: authentic apostleship (2:14–6:10)
  (A) *The apostolate: theory and practice (2:14–3:6)*
  (B) *Ministry: old and new (3:7–4:6)*
  (C) *Ministry and mortality (4:7–5:10)*
  (a) The manifestation of Jesus (4:7–15)
  (b) Facing the fear of death (4:16–5:10)
  (D) *Reconciliation in a new creation (5:11–6:10)*
  (a) The new creation (5:11–17)
  (b) The ministry of reconciliation (5:18–6:10)

(IV) Part III: relations with Corinth (6:11–7:16)
  (A) *An appeal for openness (6:11–7:4)*
  (B) *The results of the mission of Titus (7:5–16)*

(V) Part IV: the collection for Jerusalem (8:1–9:15)
  (A) *A challenging request (8:1–15)*
  (B) *The recommendation of representatives (8:16–9:5)*
  (C) *The rewards of generosity (9:6–15)*

Letter B (10–13)

Outline

(VI) Part I: an appeal for complete obedience (10:1–18)
  (A) *The consequences of disobedience (10:1–6)*
  (B) *Paul's authority as founder of the community (10:7–18)*

(VII) Part II: Paul speaks like a fool (11:1–12:13)
  (A) *His justification for being foolish (11:1–21a)*

(B) *Paul's boasts of himself (11:21b–12:10)*
(a) His sufferings (11:21b–33)
(b) His visions and revelations (12:1–10)
(C) *Further justification for his foolishness (12:11–13)*

(VIII) **Part III: a warning prepares for a visit (12:14–13:10)**
(A) *Again the question of financial support (12:14–18)*
(B) *The Corinthians must correct themselves (12:19–13:10)*

(IX) **Conclusion: final words and greeting (13:11–13)**

HIGHLIGHT

Paul's sufferings
2 Corinthians 11: 21b–33

But whatever anyone dares to boast of – I am speaking as a fool – I also dare to boast of that. [22]Are they Hebrews? So am I. Are they Israelites? So am I. Are they descendants of Abraham? So am I. [23]Are they ministers of Christ? I am talking like a madman – I am a better one: with far greater labours, far more imprisonments, with countless floggings, and often near death. [24]Five times I have received from the Jews the forty lashes minus one. [25]Three times I was beaten with rods. Once I received a stoning. Three times I was shipwrecked; for a night and a day I was adrift at sea; [26]on frequent journeys, in danger from rivers, danger from bandits, danger from my own people, danger from Gentiles, danger in the city, danger in the wilderness, danger at sea, danger from false brothers and sisters; [27]in toil and hardship, through many a sleepless night, hungry and thirsty, often without food, cold and naked. [28]And, besides other things, I am under daily pressure because of my anxiety for all the churches. [29]Who is weak, and I am not weak? Who is made to stumble, and I am not indignant?

[30]If I must boast, I will boast of the things that show my weakness. [31]The God and Father of the Lord Jesus (blessed be he forever!) knows that I do not lie. [32]In Damascus, the governor under King Aretas guarded the city of Damascus in order to seize me, [33]but I was let down in a basket through a window in the wall, and escaped from his hands.

FIFTY

The Letter to

the Romans

The material in this chapter is digested from NJBC article 51, 'The Letter to the Romans', by Joseph A. Fitzmyer, SJ.

Who wrote Romans?

It is now universally agreed that Paul wrote Romans. But there are still questions about whether it was all one letter written at the same time, and whether the last few verses (chapter 16, verses 25–27) were composed by Paul. Some parts may have been written separately: Romans 16:1–16 reads like a letter of recommendation for Phoebe, a deacon of the church of Cenchreae, and may have been sent to Ephesus. Most commentators, however, admit that it too is an integral part of Romans and was sent to Rome.

Date and place of writing

Chapter 15 suggests that Paul wrote Romans shortly before he made his last trip to Jerusalem (15:25). He probably wrote it in Corinth or in Cenchreae, some time in the winter of AD 57–58.

His purpose in writing

Paul was aware that his apostolate in the eastern Mediterranean was over, and he was planning to visit the Roman church for the first time, on his way to Spain. But first he had one task to attend to: to carry personally to Jerusalem the money collected in Gentile churches that he had founded (15:25; cf. 1 Corinthians 16:1) to show the Jewish-Christian mother church in Jerusalem the solidarity existing between the 'poor' in their community and the Gentile Christians of Galatia, Macedonia and Achaia. These Gentile Christians had contributed to the collection, realizing that they had 'shared in the spiritual blessings' of the mother church (15:27). So before he left for Jerusalem, Paul wrote to the Roman church to announce his coming visit, and to introduce himself to this church which did not know him personally. He took this chance to explain his understanding of the gospel (1:16–17), which he was eager to preach at Rome too (1:15).

The Roman church

Paul had established Christian communities in important cities of the empire (Philippi, Thessalonica, Corinth, Ephesus). Though eager to preach the gospel in Rome too he knew that its church had been founded by someone else (15:20; cf. 1:8, 13). Who it was he does not say. It is unlikely that he considered Peter its 'founder' (cf. Galatians 2:7–8). Most likely the community there was formed of converts who came from Palestine or Syria at an early date (cf. Acts 2:10). Peter probably did not arrive in Rome before the 50s; he was still in Jerusalem for the 'Council' (about AD 49). Scholars do not agree whether the church in Rome was predominantly Jewish or Gentile. Probably it was mainly Gentile Christian, as Paul includes his readers among the Gentiles to whom he had been sent as an apostle (1:5–7, 12–14; 11:11–13; 15:16).

Detail from the Arch of Titus in Rome showing the spoils taken from Jerusalem when it was destroyed by the Romans in AD 70

The significance of Romans

Romans has affected later Christian theology more than any other New Testament book. It has influenced other New Testament writings (1 Peter, Hebrews and James), and the works of early Fathers, the makers of the Reformation, and modern religious thinkers.

What is the letter about?

The letter does not cover the whole of Paul's teaching: some of his significant teachings (e.g. on the church, the eucharist, the resurrection of the body and eschatology) are missing from it. It presents his missionary reflections on the historical possibility of salvation, rooted in God's uprightness and love, now offered to all human beings through faith in Christ Jesus.

Paul had come to realize that justification and salvation did not depend on deeds prescribed by the law, but on faith in Christ Jesus. Through faith and baptism human beings share in the effects of Christ's work, in the plan of salvation conceived by the Father and brought to realization in the death and resurrection of Jesus Christ.

Some themes and questions in Romans

(a) Paul's concern about how the church in Jerusalem would react to him and to his collection for them: he was anxious that they should see that it was not just to help the poor but also to show the solidarity of his Gentile converts with the Jewish Christians in Jerusalem. He asks the Roman church to pray about this.

(b) Paul is writing to a church he does not know at first hand, so he is referring to problems which he has only heard about, and which are similar to problems he has met elsewhere. His advice to the 'weak' and the 'strong' (14:1–15:13) probably refers to conflict between the Jewish Christians and the Gentile Christians of Rome. For a time the edict of the emperor Claudius (AD 49) had forced Jews and Jewish Christians to leave Rome; when the Jewish Christians returned after Claudius's death (AD 54) they found that the Gentile Christians, who had stayed in

Rome, had developed a way of life which paid much less attention to Jewish traditions (e.g. about diet or the calendar). Paul
is probably referring to the Gentile Christians as the 'strong'
and the Jewish Christians (who were more anxious about rules)
as the 'weak'. He urges them to unity and love.

Outline

(1) **Introduction (1:1–15)**
  (A) *Address and greeting (1:1–7)*
  (B) *Thanksgiving (1:8)*
  (C) *Preface: Paul's desire to come to Rome (1:9–15)*

(II) **Part I: doctrinal section – God's gospel of Jesus Christ our
  Lord (1:16–11:36)**
  (A) *Through the gospel the uprightness of God is revealed
    as justifying the person of faith (1:16–4:25)*
  (a) The theme announced: the gospel is the powerful
    source of salvation for all, disclosing God's
    uprightness (1:16–17)
  (b) The theme negatively explained: without the gospel
    God's wrath is manifested toward all human beings
    (1:18–3:20)
    (i) God's wrath against the Gentiles (1:18–32)
    (ii) God's judgement against the Jews (2:1–3:20)
  (c) The theme positively explained: God's uprightness is
    manifested through Christ and apprehended by faith
    (3:21–31)
  (d) The theme illustrated: in the OT Abraham was
    justified by faith (4:1–25)
  (B) *The love of God assures salvation to those justified by
    faith (5:1–8:39)*
  (a) The theme announced: the justified Christian,
    reconciled to God, will be saved, sharing with hope in
    Christ's risen life (5:1–11)
  (b) The theme explained: new Christian life brings a
    threefold liberation (5:12–7:25)
    (i)   Freedom from sin and death (5:12–21)
    (ii) Freedom from self through union with Christ
      (6:1–23)
    (iii) Freedom from the law (7:1–25)
  (c) The theme developed: Christian life is lived in the
    Spirit and is destined for glory (8:1–39)
    (i)   Christian life empowered by the Spirit (8:1–13)
    (ii) Through the Spirit the Christian becomes a child
      of God, destined for glory (8:14–30)
    (iii) Hymn to the love of God made manifest in Christ
      (8:31–39)

(C) *This justification/salvation does not contradict God's promise to Israel of old (9:1–11:36)*
(a) Paul's lament for his former fellow-believers (9:1–5)
(b) Israel's plight is not contrary to God's direction of history (9:6–29)
(c) Israel's failure is derived from its own refusal (9:30–10:21)
(d) Israel's failure is partial and temporary (11:1–36)

(III) **Part II: encouragement to Christian behaviour – the demands of upright life in Christ (12:1–15:13)**
(A) *Christian life must be worship in the spirit paid to God (12:1–13:14)*
(B) *Charity is owed by the strong to the weak (14:1–15:13)*

(IV) **Conclusion (15:14–33)**

(V) **Letter of recommendation for Phoebe (16:1–23)**

(VI) **Doxology (16:25–27)**

HIGHLIGHT

Romans 3:21–31

[21]But now, apart from law, the righteousness of God has been disclosed, and is attested by the law and the prophets, [22]the righteousness of God through faith in Jesus Christ for all who believe. For there is no distinction, [23]since all have sinned and fall short of the glory of God; [24]they are now justified by his grace as a gift, through the redemption that is in Christ Jesus, [25]whom God put forward as a sacrifice of atonement by his blood, effective through faith. He did this to show his righteousness, because in his divine forbearance he had passed over the sins previously committed; [26]it was to prove at the present time that he himself is righteous and that he justifies the one who has faith in Jesus.

[27]Then what becomes of boasting? It is excluded. By what law? By that of works? No, but by the law of faith. [28]For we hold that a person is justified by faith apart from works prescribed by the law. [29]Or is God the God of Jews only? Is he not the God of Gentiles also? Yes, of Gentiles also, [30]since God is one; and he will justify the circumcised on the ground of faith and the uncircumcised through that same faith. [31]Do we then overthrow the law by this faith? By no means! On the contrary, we uphold the law.

The Letter to

Philemon

The man Philemon

The addressee was a young, well-to-do, respected Christian of a town in the Lycus valley of Asia Minor, probably Colossae (see Colossians 4:9). Paul greets him along with Apphia (probably Philemon's wife) and Archippus (their son?), and 'the church that meets in your house' (2). Philemon was apparently converted by Paul (19), possibly in Ephesus.

The occasion and purpose behind the letter

The slave **Onesimus** had run away, having caused his master considerable damage (11, 18). In his flight he came to where Paul was imprisoned, perhaps knowing of his master's respect for Paul. Somehow Paul managed to give him refuge and ultimately converted him to Christianity ('whose father I have become in my imprisonment', 10). Eventually, Paul learned that Onesimus was Philemon's slave, and though he wanted to keep him with himself for help in evangelization, he recognized Philemon's right and decided to send Onesimus back (14, 16).

In the letter Paul begged Philemon to take the runaway slave back, 'no longer as a slave, but ... as a beloved brother' (16). In effect, Paul asked Philemon not to inflict on Onesimus the severe penalties permitted by law. Paul also promised to restore the damage that Onesimus had caused – how he would do this from prison is not said. Paul further suggested that he would like Onesimus to come back to work with him (20). Did Paul mean by this that Philemon should free the slave? This may be implied.

The material in this chapter is digested from NJBC article 52, 'The Letter to Philemon', by Joseph A. Fitzmyer, SJ.

> **Onesimus** <
a name meaning 'useful one'

When and where was the letter written?

There is no need to question that Paul wrote Philemon from prison (1, 9–10, 13, 23), but it is almost impossible to say where that imprisonment was. The traditional view makes it his house arrest at Rome (AD 61–63). Some commentators, however, have preferred the imprisonment at Caesarea (*ca.* AD 58–60). More recently, the imprisonment at Ephesus (*ca.* AD 56–57) has been in favour; it has the advantage of keeping Philemon (in Colossae) and Paul (in Ephesus) within a range of about 108 miles and also explains more easily Paul's plan to visit Philemon (22), which would have been difficult from Rome.

The significance of the letter

Why did a private letter with little general pastoral concern become part of the Bible? Probably the letter was addressed to others than Philemon himself, even to a house-church. If Paul does not demand obedience of Philemon by his authority as an apostle (8), he does confront him with a plea for love (8–11, 21). Despite its surface character as a letter dealing with a private matter, Philemon embodies an attitude toward slavery that merits Christian attention.

First, it shows Paul's pastoral and warmhearted affection for Onesimus. Second, in sending him back to Philemon, Paul does not try to change the existing social structure. Modern Christians are repulsed by the idea of slavery, but this outlook is perhaps a development of a principle that Paul tries to advocate in this letter, while realizing the futility of trying to abolish the system of slavery at that time. Third, Paul's own solution was to transform or interiorize the social structure; recall 1 Corinthians 7:20–24; 12:13. He urges Philemon to welcome Onesimus back as a 'brother', for he is a 'freedman of the Lord' (1 Corinthians 7:22), especially in view of what Paul teaches in Galatians 3:27–28. Moreover, this plea is made 'for love's sake' (8), but it took centuries for the Pauline principle to be put into practice, even in the Christian West.

Outline

(I) Introduction: author's greeting (1–3)

(II) Thanksgiving: thanks to God for Philemon's faith and love (4–7)

(III) Body: appeal to Philemon's goodwill to welcome back Onesimus and a hint at his usefulness to Paul (8–20)

(IV) Conclusion: final instructions, greetings, and blessing (21–25)

HIGHLIGHT

Philemon 8–20

[8]For this reason, though I am bold enough in Christ to command you to do your duty, [9]yet I would rather appeal to you on the basis of love — and I, Paul, do this as an old man, and now also as a prisoner of Christ Jesus. [10]I am appealing to you for my child, Onesimus, whose father I have become during my imprisonment. [11]Formerly he was useless to you, but now he is indeed useful both to you and to me. [12]I am sending him, that is, my own heart, back to you. [13]I wanted to keep him with me, so that he might be of service to me in your place during my imprisonment for the gospel; [14]but I preferred to do nothing without your consent, in order that your good deed might be voluntary and not something forced. [15]Perhaps this is the reason he was separated from you for a while, so that you might have him back forever, [16]no longer as a slave but more than a slave, a beloved brother — especially to me but how much more to you, both in the flesh and in the Lord.

[17]So if you consider me your partner, welcome him as you would welcome me. [18]If he has wronged you in any way, or owes you anything, charge that to my account. [19]I, Paul, am writing this with my own hand: I will repay it. I say nothing about your owing me even your own self. [20]Yes, brother, let me have this benefit from you in the Lord! Refresh my heart in Christ.

The Second Letter to the Thessalonians

The material in this chapter is digested from NJBC article 53, 'The Second Letter to the Thessalonians', by Charles Homer Giblin, SJ.

It is not certain whether this letter was written by Paul; it was most probably composed by an author who wishes to appeal to Paul's authority. It was probably written in the last ten years of the first century, in Asia Minor. The author knew Paul's first letter to the Thessalonians well and was developing the same theme of the Second Coming of Christ, but in a different way, to respond to a different situation.

The problem

The author is countering false belief: this may be the idea that the Day of the Lord has already occurred, and so the Second Coming of Christ is irrelevant; or it may have been an expectation of an imminent Second Coming, with calculations of the day when this will happen.

How the theme is handled

In 1 Thessalonians Paul encouraged the Thessalonians to be prepared, and assured them that the faithful who had died will have priority over those who still wait for the Lord's Coming within their own lifetime.

In contrast 2 Thessalonians disapproves of excessive interest in the day and the hour of Christ's Coming, but points to the conditions that will be necessary for the Lord's triumphal Coming.

Outline

(I) Opening formula (1:1–2)

(II) Test of persecution leading to the Lord's glory in
judgement (1:3–12)
   (A) Thanksgiving (1:3–10)
   (B) Prayer (1:11–12)

(III) Proper understanding of the Second Coming (2:1–17)
   (A) The Lord's triumph over deception (2:1–15)
   (B) Prayer for strengthening (2:16–17)

(IV) Two sets of closing exhortations and prayers (3:1–5,
6–16)

(V) Final greetings (3:17–18)

HIGHLIGHT

2 Thessalonians 2:15–17

[15]So then, brothers and sisters, stand firm and hold fast to the
traditions that you were taught by us, either by word of mouth or
by our letter.
   [16]Now may our Lord Jesus Christ himself and God our Father,
who loved us and through grace gave us eternal comfort and good
hope, [17]comfort your hearts and strengthen them in every good
work and word.

The Letter to

the Colossians

The material in this
chapter is digested
from NJBC article
54, 'The Letter to
the Colossians', by
Maurya P. Horgan.

Introduction

Colossae was an important city in late antiquity. It had a flour-
ishing wood and textile industry, and its population included
native Phrygians, Greeks and a sizeable community of Jews. The
Christian community, made up principally of Gentiles (1:21, 27;
2:13), was probably founded by Epaphras (1:7; 4:12), who was
born and lived in Colossae. The slave Onesimus was also from
Colossae, and probably also his master, Philemon.

Colossians was not written by Paul

The language of Colossians contains many words which Paul
never uses, and some of Paul's favourite expressions – such as
the address 'brothers' or 'my brothers' – do not occur in the
letter. The style of this letter differs from Paul's usual way of
writing. Colossians does not have the debating features of
Romans and Galatians. This letter is in the style of worship; it
has frequent poetic repetitions (1:11, 22, 23, 26; 2:7; 3:8, 16;
4:12) and long and complicated sentences. The letter differs
from the undisputed Pauline epistles also in its teaching about
Christ, the last things, and the church. The many differences
from Paul's language and ideas have persuaded most modern
scholars that Paul did not write Colossians. It was probably
composed after Paul's lifetime, between AD 70 and 80, by someone who knew Paul's teaching.

Colossians is a carefully composed letter that incorporates
the main structural features of Paul's letters (greeting, thanksgiving, exposition, exhortation, messages, and closing) and also
blocks of traditional material as follows:

1:15–20 – a hymn
2:6–15 – baptismal teaching
3:5–17 – lists of vices and virtues
3:18–4:1 – a household code of behaviour.

Opponents of the faith in Colossians

The purpose of Colossians was to bolster the faith of the community (1:3–14; 2:2–3) and to correct errors reported about the church in Colossae (2:4, 8, 16, 18–22). One of the chief areas of study about Colossians has been the attempt to identify the opponents who were misleading the community in Colossae. According to the letter, the false teaching is a philosophy and an empty deceit (2:8), a human tradition (2:8); it concerns the elemental spirits of the universe (2:8) and angels (2:18); it demands observance of food regulations and festivals, new moons, and sabbath (2:14, 16, 20, 21); and it encourages practices of severe self-discipline.

Since the opponents are charged with 'not holding fast to the head', the error must have arisen within the believing community.

A complex of Judaism, paganism, Christianity, magic, astrology and mystery religion forms the cultural background of the letter; there is no way of identifying the opponents at Colossae with any one group. However, most scholars connect the error with Judaism in some form, since the elements that can be connected with pagan cults, mystery religion, and Greek philosophy can also be found somewhere in the Judaism of the time.

Outline

(I) Greeting (1:1–2)

(II) Thanksgiving and prayer (1:3–23)
    (A) *Thanksgiving (1:3–8)*
    (B) *Prayer (1:9–11)*
    (C) *Application and transition (1:12–14)*
    (D) *Hymn (1:15–20)*
    (E) *Application and transition (1:21–23)*

(III) Paul's ministry (1:24–2:5)
(A) *The apostle's hardships (1:24–25)*
(B) *The mystery revealed and preached (1:26–29)*
(C) *Application and transition (2:1–5)*

(IV) Life in the body of Christ in teaching (2:6–3:4)
(A) *The tradition of Christ Jesus (2:6–15)*
(B) *The human tradition (2:16–23)*
(C) *Application and transition (3:1–4)*

(V) Life in the body of Christ in practice (3:5–4:6)
(A) *Vices (3:5–10)*
(B) *Virtues (3:11–17)*
(C) *Household code (3:18–4:1)*
(D) *Application and transition (4:2–6)*

(VI) Messages and closing salutation (4:7–18)

HIGHLIGHT

Christ, the head of the body, the church
Colossians 1:15–20

[15]He is the image of the invisible God, the firstborn of all creation; [16]for in him all things in heaven and on earth were created, things visible and invisible, whether thrones or dominions or rulers or powers – all things have been created through him and for him. [17]He himself is before all things, and in him all things hold together. [18]He is the head of the body, the church; he is the beginning, the firstborn from the dead, so that he might come to have first place in everything. [19]For in him all the fullness of God was pleased to dwell, [20]and through him God was pleased to reconcile to himself all things, whether on earth or in heaven, by making peace through the blood of his cross.

The Letter to
the Ephesians

Did Paul write Ephesians?

The material in this
chapter is digested
from NJBC article
55, 'The Letter to
the Ephesians', by
Paul J. Kobelski.

Although some modern scholars believe Paul wrote Ephesians,
others argue for a core of the letter written by Paul which was
then expanded or altered by a disciple. But the author knew
Paul's letters very well. There are clear echoes of Paul's thought
throughout Ephesians (Ephesians 2:8 and Romans 3:28; Ephesians 2:17–18; 3:11–12 and Romans 5:1–2; Ephesians 4:28
and 1 Corinthians 4:12; Ephesians 3:14; 4:5 and 1 Corinthians
8:5–6). Like the author of Colossians, the author of Ephesians
may have belonged to a group of followers of Paul (in Ephesus?) that was committed to the thinking of Paul and the traditions that had developed in Pauline mission areas in the period
after Paul's mission.

*Statue of Artemis
(Diana) of Ephesus.
Her temple (see Acts
19) was one of the
Seven Wonders of the
World*

Arguments against Paul's authorship

The question of Paul's authorship is based on content, vocabulary and style, theological differences from the undisputed letters of Paul, and literary dependence on Colossians.

(a) Content
Although Paul is mentioned as the writer of the letter (1:1; 3:1)
and there are references to his personal experience, nevertheless
there are statements such as 'I have heard of your faith' (1:15)
and 'I am sure you have heard of the stewardship ... given to
me' (3:2), that suggest an audience that had no firsthand
acquaintance with the preaching of Paul (see also 3:5; 4:21).

(b) Vocabulary and style

There are terms such as 'heavenly places' (1:3, 20; 2:6; 3:10; 6:12) alongside Paul's more usual language of 'the heavens'; a different Greek word for 'devil' in 4:27 and 6:11; words that occur in late New Testament writings, and words that occur with meanings different from the undisputed letters of Paul.

A date for Ephesians

The author's use of the genuine letters of Paul and of Colossians suggests a date late in the 1st century (AD 80–100) after the collection together of Paul's writings.

The author's purpose

While Ephesians is like a letter in structure, it is more of a theological lecture, destined for several churches in the Roman province of Asia. It reminds its readers, in terms familiar to them from teaching and worship, of the exaltation of Christ and the church over all heavenly and earthly powers and the reconciliation of Jews and Gentiles in the church under the headship of Christ; and it encourages them to celebrate their unity by appropriate conduct.

The first half of the letter (1:3–3:21) is structured as an extended prayer of intercession with a pattern that can be seen in Jewish and early Christian devotional literature: blessing – thanksgiving – prayer of intercession – concluding **doxology**.

> **doxology** <
a formula of praise and glory to God

The second half (4:1–6:20) exhorts Christians to behaviour that is in keeping with their exalted status as children of light and members of the church – God's household and the bride of Christ.

The relationship to Colossians

Structural and verbal similarities are evident in the address (Ephesians 1:1–2; Colossians 1:1–2), in the thanksgiving (Ephesians 1:15–17; Colossians 1:3–4,9–10), and in the conclusion (Ephesians 6:21–22; Colossians 4:7–8). Certain doctrinal elements in Ephesians are developed in dependence on the thought of Colossians:

resurrection with Christ (Ephesians 2:5–6; Colossians 2:12–13);

putting off the old nature and putting on the new (Ephesians 4:17–24; Colossians 3:5–15);

Spirit-filled worship (Ephesians 5:17–20; Colossians 3:16–17);

household codes (Ephesians 5:22–25; 6:1–9; Colossians 3:18–4:1);

need for unceasing prayer (Ephesians 6:18; Colossians 4:2);

request for prayer for the preacher (Ephesians 6:19; Colossians 4:3).

Outline

(I) Introduction: address and greeting (1:1–2)

(II) Part I: God's plan revealed and accomplished (1:3–3:21)
- (A) *Blessing (1:3–14)*
- (B) *Thanksgiving and prayer of intercession (1:15–23)*
- (C) *Once dead, now alive with Christ (2:1–10)*
- (D) *Union of Jews and Gentiles (2:11–22)*
- (E) *Paul as interpreter of the revealed mystery (3:1–13)*
- (F) *Prayer (3:14–19)*
- (G) *Concluding doxology (3:20–21)*

(III) Part II: exhortations to worthy conduct (4:1–6:20)
- (A) *Unity and diversity in the church (4:1–16)*
- (B) *Christian and non-Christian conduct (4:17–5:20)*
- (C) *Code of conduct for the household of God (5:21–6:9)*
- (D) *Christian life as warfare with evil (6:10–20)*

(IV) Conclusion: personal news and blessing (6:21–24)

HIGHLIGHT

Marriage and its mutual obligations
Ephesians 5:21–31

[21]Be subject to one another out of reverence for Christ.

[22]Wives, be subject to your husbands as you are to the Lord. [23]For the husband is the head of the wife just as Christ is the head of the church, the body of which he is the Saviour. [24]Just as the

275

church is subject to Christ, so also wives ought to be, in everything, to their husbands.

[25]Husbands, love your wives, just as Christ loved the church and gave himself up for her, [26]in order to make her holy by cleansing her with the washing of water by the word, [27]so as to present the church to himself in splendour, without a spot or wrinkle or anything of the kind – yes, so that she may be holy and without blemish. [28]In the same way, husbands should love their wives as they do their own bodies. He who loves his wife loves himself. [29]For no one ever hates his own body, but he nourishes and tenderly cares for it, just as Christ does for the church, [30]because we are members of his body. [31]'For this reason a man will leave his father and mother and be joined to his wife, and the two will become one flesh.'

FIFTY-FIVE

The Pastoral

Letters

Introduction: 'Pastoral'

The material in this
chapter is digested
from NJBC article
56, 'The Pastoral
Letters', by Robert
A. Wild, SJ.

Because these letters are the only New Testament documents
addressed to 'pastors' of Christian communities and because
they deal with church life and practice (i.e., with 'pastoral'
theology), 1 Timothy, 2 Timothy, and Titus since the 18th century have been called the 'Pastoral Letters'.

Timothy and Titus

Timothy and Titus were two of Paul's closest companions.
According to Acts 16:1–3 Timothy, who was born of mixed
Jewish and pagan parentage, had become a Christian and
began to follow Paul after meeting him at Lystra. Timothy
served as Paul's representative on missions to Thessalonica
(1 Thessalonians 3:2, 6), to Corinth (1 Corinthians 4:17;
16:10–11), and probably also to Philippi (Philippians
2:19–23). He was in close contact with Paul during Paul's
imprisonment at Ephesus (Philemon 1) and was also with him
at Corinth when Romans was written (Romans 16:21).

He is listed as a coauthor of four of Paul's genuine letters
(2 Corinthians 1:1; Philippians 1:1; 1 Thessalonians 1:1; Philemon 1). (Acts 17:14–15; 18:5; 19:22; 20:4; Colossians 1:1; 2
Thessalonians 1:1; and Hebrews 13:23 also mention Timothy.)

Titus, a Gentile convert, came with Paul to the Jerusalem
conference *ca.* AD 49, and Paul subsequently claimed that he
had refused at that time to have him circumcised (Galatians
2:1, 3–5). Titus later accomplished a delicate mission to Corinth to patch up relations between Paul and that community (2
Corinthians 12:18; 2:13; 7:6–7, 13–16) and then served there

as Paul's delegate for the gathering of the Jerusalem collection (2 Corinthians 8:6, 16–24).

The order of the Pastoral Letters

The present order of the Pastorals, 1 Timothy–2 Timothy–Titus, almost certainly is not original but probably derives from a typical ancient way of organizing a group of related texts: those with more lines precede those with fewer (e.g. 1–3 John). Since 2 Timothy is in the form of a spiritual last will and testament and predicts the imminent death of Paul (2 Timothy 4:6–8), it must once have been the final letter. Brief as it is, Titus has a greeting (Titus 1:1–4) that is 65 words long. Of the New Testament epistles only Romans and Galatians have longer greetings (Romans 1:1–7; Galatians 1:1–5). This suggests that Titus was intended as the first letter in the Pastorals, a conclusion that is strengthened by the observation that 1 Timothy has no proper concluding section and so leads easily into 2 Timothy. The Pastorals, therefore, were originally read in the order: Titus–1 Timothy–2 Timothy.

Did Paul write the Pastoral Letters?

Since the early 19th century scholars have argued that these letters are the creations of a later follower of Paul. The arguments seem quite convincing. Although quite similar to one another in vocabulary, grammatical usage, and style, 1–2 Timothy and Titus diverge sharply in all these respects from the clearly genuine letters of Paul. Numerous key terms used in the Pastorals do not appear in Paul (e.g., 'piety', 'good conscience', 'epiphany', 'sound teaching', 'trustworthy word'), and many words important in Paul's writings are not found in the Pastorals even where they would be expected (e.g., 'body' [of Christ, etc.], 'cross', 'freedom', 'covenant').

Church order
The Pastorals also present a much more developed church order than is found in the clearly genuine letters of Paul, less expectation of an imminent Day of the Lord and a stress on Jesus' birth and resurrection but not, at least as much as in

Paul, his crucifixion. Although developments certainly occurred within Christianity even during Paul's lifetime, changes such as these, taken together, tend to point to a later period than Paul's own age.

The message of the Pastoral Letters

Although written by someone else under Paul's name, the Pastorals are not 'forgeries'. The writer sought to extend Paul's thought to the problems of a later day. The writer said in effect, 'Paul would surely have said this if faced with this set of problems or issues'. It is quite likely that the original readers of the Pastorals knew very well that Paul himself was not the 'actual' author and that the letters represented an effort to extend his teaching to a later generation.

The author of the Pastorals views Pauline Christianity as the only true philosophy or way of life. He calls church leaders, and, by extension, all Christians, to a renewed commitment and enthusiasm for this teaching. What Paul said and what Paul did are proposed as the example of this way of life; indeed, the Pastorals make no reference to the existence of any apostle except Paul.

What the author of the Pastorals did intend was to urge church leaders to value and maintain order. For him true Christianity (i.e., as taught by Paul) upheld the fundamental value of Roman society, 'piety', i.e., the due maintenance of proper relationships between the divine realm and the human and between the various orders of human society among themselves. He envisioned Christianity as a worldwide and fully unified movement that fulfilled the deepest aspirations of contemporary culture for harmony in the family and in society.

Titus and 1 Timothy each set forth procedures for the proper maintenance of 'God's household', the church (1 Timothy 3:15).

The false teachers

The 'false teachers' that appear so often in the Pastorals called themselves 'teachers of the law' (1 Timothy 1:7), and the author attacked them as too eager for 'legal debates' (Titus 3:9) and for 'human commandments' (Titus 1:14). He says they were also interested in 'Jewish myths' (Titus 1:14; see 1 Timothy 1:4). Although these features may point to some confused type of Jewish Christianity, other elements do not fit this picture as well. For example, the false teachers seem to have had a very negative view of our physical world and therefore opposed marriage and urged strict abstinence from food (1 Timothy 1:3–5). Probably the author was concerned about several different types of false teaching, or else wished to offer an all-purpose refutation of false teaching in general.

When and where were the Pastoral Letters written?

The Pastorals focus on Christian churches in the Aegean area and especially in Asia Minor. This has led most scholars to suppose that the Pastorals originated somewhere in this region, perhaps in Ephesus.

The dates proposed for these letters, however, have a very wide range (*ca.* AD 60 to AD 160). Both the more developed church order found in the Pastorals (an ordination ritual; rules for the appointment of bishops, deacons, and widows; etc.) and the use of language drawn from contemporary Greco-Roman philosophy suggest a later rather than an earlier date. On balance, a date before or around AD 100 seems the best estimate.

Sources used

The author of the Pastorals drew on the writings of Paul, although it is not certain that he knew all of his letters. The Pastorals offer clear allusions to Romans and 1 Corinthians and possibly have a reference or two to Philippians. Titus 3:3–7 makes use of Ephesians 2:3–12 or a closely related tradition. There are many allusions to and quotations of the Old Testament, and 1 Timothy 2:11–14 makes use of an extensive argument based on Genesis 2–3. Other early Christian texts are also drawn upon.

Outline

(I) Address and greeting (1:1–4)

(II) Leaders for the church on Crete (1:5–9)
    (A) The charge to Titus (1:5)
    (B) Qualities required of the presbyter (1:6–9)

(III) False teaching v. true teaching (1:10–3:8)
    (A) The nature of the false teachers (1:10–16)
    (B) What the true teacher is to teach (2:1–3:8)
    (a) Christian duties within the household (2:1–15)
        (i) The basic charge (2:1)
        (ii) Duties of the household members (2:2–10)
        (iii) Reason: God's saving action (2:11–14)
        (iv) The basic charge restated (2:15)
    (b) Christian duties within society (3:1–8)
        (i) Duties (3:1–2)
        (ii) Reason: God's saving action (3:3–8)

(IV) Strife and division to be avoided (3:9–11)

(V) Business matters and closing blessing (3:12–15)

1 TIMOTHY

Outline

(I) Address and greeting (1:1–2)

(II) Introduction: main themes of the letter (1:3–20)
    (A) Paul's command to Timothy (1:3–5)
    (B) The opponents as false teachers (1:6–11)
    (C) Paul as the true teacher (1:12–17)
    (D) Summary (1:18–20)

(III) Worship and leadership in the church (2:1–3:13)
    (A) The community's conduct at worship (2:1–15)
    (a) Prayer intentions (2:1–7)
    (b) How men should act (2:8)
    (c) How women should act (2:9–15)
    (B) Leadership for the community (3:1–13)
    (a) Basic principle (3:1)
    (b) Requirements for bishops (3:2–7)

   (c)   Requirements for deacons (3:8–12)
   (d)   Conclusion (3:13)

(IV) Purpose and theological perspective of 1 Timothy (3:14–4:10)
   (A) Purpose: conduct in God's household (3:14–16)
   (B) Perspective: the goodness of creation (4:1–10)
   (a)   The basic statement (4:1–5)
   (b)   These things must be taught (4:6–10)

(V) Teachings for different groups in the church (4:11–6:2)
   (A) Introduction (4:11)
   (B) Timothy as type of the church leader (4:12–16)
   (C) The leader and various age groups (5:1–2)
   (D) The widows (5:3–16)
   (E) The elders (5:17–25)
   (F) Slaves (6:1–2)

(VI) Summation (6:3 16)
   (A) The situation of the false teachers (6:3–10)
   (B) How Timothy is to act (6:11–16)

(VII) Supplementary reflection on the rich (6:17–19)

(VIII) Final exhortation to Timothy (6:20–21a)

(IX) Closing blessing for the community (6:21b)

2 TIMOTHY

Outline

(I) Address and greeting (1:1–2)

(II) Thanksgiving (1:3–5)

(III) Call to Timothy to renew the spiritual gifts of power, love, and ethical instruction (1:6–2:13)
   (A) Introduction: rekindle the divine gift (1:6–7)
   (B) The endurance of sufferings in the strength of God (1:8–12)
   (C) Fidelity to Paul (1:13–18)
   (D) The steadfast handing on of the gospel (2:1–10)
   (a)   Need to preserve the deposit of faith (2:1–2)
   (b)   Three examples for imitation (2:3–6)
   (c)   Paul's example of faithfulness to Christ (2:7–10)
   (E) Summary: the 'reliable saying' (2:11–13)

(IV) **True teaching v. false teaching (2:14–4:8)**
- (A) *Four ways to distinguish the true teacher from the false (2:14–26)*
- (B) *Resources available to the church leader amid the evils of the Last Days (3:1–17)*
- (a) The behaviour of the false teachers v. the virtuous example of Paul (3:1–12)
- (b) The errors of the false teachers v. the truth of scripture (3:13–17)
- (C) *Concluding exhortation (4:1–8)*

(V) **Paul's situation and needs (4:9–21)**
- (A) *Timothy is to come to Paul (4:9–13)*
- (B) *Paul's legal situation (4:14–18)*
- (C) *Greetings and other matters (4:19–21)*

(VI) **Closing blessings to Timothy and to the readers (4:22)**

HIGHLIGHT

I Timothy 4:1–5

¹Now the Spirit expressly says that in later times some will renounce the faith by paying attention to deceitful spirits and teachings of demons, ²through the hypocrisy of liars whose consciences are seared with a hot iron. ³They forbid marriage and demand abstinence from foods, which God created to be received with thanksgiving by those who believe and know the truth. ⁴For everything created by God is good, and nothing is to be rejected, provided it is received with thanksgiving; ⁵for it is sanctified by God's word and by prayer.

The First

Epistle of Peter

The material in this
chapter is digested
from NJBC article
57, 'The First Epistle
of Peter', by William
J. Dalton, SJ.

A pastoral document

1 Peter is a pastoral document. By emphasizing the dignity of the Christian vocation, which provides a God-given 'home' for the 'homeless' and the value of sharing the passion of Christ through persecution, the writer encourages his readers to remain faithful. These two themes run through the whole letter but reach high points in texts such as 2:4–10 (the 'spiritual house') and 2:18–25 (directly dealing with slaves but valid for all Christians). The climax of the letter seems to come in 3:18–4:6, where Christians' confidence in persecution is seen as based on the story of Christ's saving acts.

Arguments about whether Peter the Apostle wrote the epistle continue to be debated by scholars.

The situation in which 1 Peter was written

There is good reason for dating 1 Peter just before Peter's death, which took place probably in AD 65 in the persecution of Nero. The letter is addressed to 'visiting strangers' (1:1), 'resident aliens' (2:11), terms that indicate the precarious condition of Christians in the pagan world. They were mainly of pagan origin (see 1:14, 18; 2:9, 10; 4:3–4), probably recently converted (see 1:14; 2:2; 4:12), and in danger of giving up the Christian faith in the face of pagan hostility. There is no indication of an official state persecution: the letter encourages respect for government and emperor (2:13–17). By recalling the greatness of their vocation and by showing that persecution is a sign of their calling, the writer encourages and exhorts his readers to stand firm (5:12). Those who are regarded by the world as aliens and strangers have found a home in the Christian community.

Outline

(I) Introduction: address and greetings (1:1–2)

(II) Part I: the dignity of the Christian vocation and its responsibilities (1:3–2:10)
   (A) *The Christian vocation (1:3–25)*
   (a) Salvation wrought by the Father, through the Son, revealed by the Spirit (1:3–12)
   (b) Exhortation to holiness (1:13–25)
   (B) *Responsibilities of the Christian vocation (2:1–10)*
   (a) Exhortation: live as God's children (2:1–3)
   (b) The new household of God (2:4–10)

(III) Part II: witness of Christian life (2:11–3:12)
   (A) *Conduct in a pagan world (2:11–12)*
   (B) *Traditional instructions (2:13–3:7)*
   (a) Behaviour toward civil authority (2:13–17)
   (b) Domestic behaviour (2:18–3:7)
   (C) *Above all, love and humility (3:8–12)*

(IV) Part III: the Christian and persecution (3:13–5:11)
   (A) *The Christian approach to persecution (3:13–4:11)*
   (a) Confidence in persecution (3:13–17)
   (b) Christ is the basis for confidence (3:18–4:6)
      (i) Christ's victory over sin applied to Christians by baptism (3:18–22)
      (ii) The Christian through suffering renounces sin (4:1–6)
   (c) Christian life and the Second Coming of Christ (4:7–11)
   (B) *Persecution faced realistically (4:12–5:11)*
   (a) Joy in actual persecution (4:12–19)
   (b) Exhortation to elders and faithful (5:1–5)
   (c) Final exhortation: trust God, who brings you through suffering to glory (5:6–11)

(V) Conclusion: this is the true grace of God: stand firm in it; farewell (5:12–14)

HIGHLIGHT

1 Peter 2:4–10

[4]Come to him, a living stone, though rejected by mortals yet chosen and precious in God's sight, and [5]like living stones, let yourselves be built into a spiritual house, to be a holy priesthood, to offer spiritual sacrifices acceptable to God through Jesus Christ. [6]For it stands in scripture:

'See, I am laying in Zion a stone,
　　a cornerstone chosen and precious;
and whoever believes in him will not be put to shame.'

[7]To you then who believe, he is precious; but for those who do not believe,

'The stone that the builders rejected
　　has become the very head of the corner,'

[8]and

'A stone that makes them stumble,
　　and a rock that makes them fall.'

They stumble because they disobey the word, as they were destined to do.

[9]But you are a chosen race, a royal priesthood, a holy nation, God's own people, in order that you may proclaim the mighty acts of him who called you out of darkness into his marvellous light. [10] Once you were not a people,
　　but now you are God's people;
once you had not received mercy,
　　but now you have received mercy.

FIFTY-SEVEN

The Epistle of

James

Who was the author James?

The first verse says that this epistle is written by 'James, a servant of God and of the Lord Jesus Christ'. The most widely held view today is that a Christian who understood Greek culture and Judaism wrote the letter under the name of James of Jerusalem, 'brother of the Lord', in the latter part of the 1st century AD. The writer was probably a church official: he speaks with some authority.

A likely date would be the early or middle 60s, after Paul's teaching on faith and works, but before the destruction of Jerusalem in AD 70. In that case Jerusalem would well have been the place of origin. But if the letter dates from after the destruction of Jerusalem, then it would probably have been written in Antioch or Alexandria.

The material in this chapter is digested from NJBC article 58, 'The Epistle of James', by Thomas W. Leahy, SJ.

The purpose and destination of the epistle

It consists of a series of homilies, some long and some short. The main theme is that readers should express their faith in action, in every aspect of their lives. In a situation where there are many trials and temptations, where the poor suffer at the hands of the rich, it encourages joy, endurance, wisdom, confident prayer and faithful response to the liberating word of God, as they wait for the coming of the Lord. The readers would seem to be a group of Jewish Christian communities who were living outside Palestine, but who would respect the name of James.

Wall painting in Pompeii, showing a man holding a scroll of papyrus

Outline

(I) Opening formula (1:1)

(II) Opening exhortation (1:2–18)
   (A) *Joy in trials (1:2–4)*
   (B) *Unwavering prayer for wisdom (1:5–8)*
   (C) *Attitudes of the lowly and the rich (1:9–11)*
   (D) *Endurance gains the crown of life (1:12)*
   (E) *Origin of sin and death (1:13–15)*
   (F) *Our birth in God's word (1:16–18)*

(III) Be doers of the word (1:19–27)
   (A) *The proper attitude (1:19–21)*
   (B) *The precept: be doers, not mere hearers (1:22)*
   (C) *Illustration of the mirror (1:23–25)*
   (D) *Genuine religion (1:26–27)*

(IV) Avoid partiality (2:1–13)
   (A) *The precept (2:1)*
   (B) *Example (2:2–4)*
   (C) *Various arguments (2:5–13)*

(V) Faith without works is dead (2:14–26)
   (A) *Main thesis (2:14–17)*
   (B) *Various examples (2:18–26)*

(VI) Guard of the tongue (3:1–12)

(VII) Qualities of wisdom (3:13–18)

(VIII) Causes of strife: remedies (4:1–12)

(IX) A warning to merchants (4:13–17)

(X) Woe to the rich (5:1–6)

(XI) Patient waiting for the Coming of the Lord (5:7–11)

(XII) Directions for various circumstances; end of letter
   (5:12–20)

HIGHLIGHT

Faith without works is dead
James 2:17–26

[17]So faith by itself, if it has no works, is dead.

[18]But someone will say, 'You have faith and I have works.' Show me your faith apart from your works, and I by my works will show you my faith. [19]You believe that God is one; you do well. Even the demons believe – and shudder. [20]Do you want to be shown, you senseless person, that faith apart from works is barren? [21]Was not our ancestor Abraham justified by works when he offered his son Isaac on the altar? [22]You see that faith was active along with his works, and faith was brought to completion by the works. [23]Thus the scripture was fulfilled that says, 'Abraham believed God, and it was reckoned to him as righteousness,' and he was called the friend of God. [24]You see that a person is justified by works and not by faith alone. [25]Likewise, was not Rahab the prostitute also justified by works when she welcomed the messengers and sent them out by another road? [26]For just as the body without the spirit is dead, so faith without works is also dead.

The material in this chapter is digested from NJBC article 59, 'The Epistle of Jude', by Jerome H. Neyrey, SJ.

FIFTY-EIGHT

The Epistle of

Jude

Who was the author?

The author is said to be 'Jude . . . brother of James', who is presumably James 'the brother of the Lord' and leader of the Jerusalem church. Jude is not the Apostle Jude, since the letter is written at a late date, and speaks of the Apostles as though they were figures of the distant past.

When was Jude written?

Nothing in Jude indicates its date, but since it was used by 2 Peter (which was written about AD 100) Jude must have been written earlier, probably in the 90s.

To whom was it written?

This letter is not addressed to any specific church but to all churches, alerting them to a general problem: the conflicting viewpoints in the churches at that time. The author mentions the presence of scoffers who question central doctrines such as God's authority, and whose bad theology leads to immorality. It is not clear exactly what their wrong teaching was.

Outline

(I) Letter opening (1–2)

(II) Occasion of the letter (3–4)

(III) Judgement warnings (5–15)
    (A) *Past judgements of God (5–7)*
    (B) *Declaration of God's judgement (8–10)*
    (C) *Examples of judgement (11–13)*
    (D) *Prediction of judgement (14–15)*

(IV) Sinners and saints (16–23)
    (A) *Traits of sinners (16–19)*
    (B) *Characteristics of saints (20–23)*

(V) Letter closing: doxology (24–25)

HIGHLIGHT

Characteristics of sinners and saints
Jude, verses 16–23a

[16]These are grumblers and malcontents; they indulge their own lusts; they are bombastic in speech, flattering people to their own advantage.

[17]But you, beloved, must remember the predictions of the apostles of our Lord Jesus Christ; [18]for they said to you, 'In the last time there will be scoffers, indulging their own ungodly lusts.' [19]It is these worldly people, devoid of the Spirit, who are causing divisions. [20]But you, beloved, build yourselves up on your most holy faith; pray in the Holy Spirit; [21]keep yourselves in the love of God; look forward to the mercy of our Lord Jesus Christ that leads to eternal life. [22]And have mercy on some who are wavering; [23]save others by snatching them out of the fire; and have mercy on still others with fear.

The Epistle to
the Hebrews

The material in this
chapter is digested
from NJBC article
60, 'The Epistle to
the Hebrews', by
Myles M. Bourke.

The Apostle Paul is not the author of Hebrews

The identity of the writer of the Epistle to the Hebrews is
unknown; the epistle begins without a greeting mentioning the
writer's name. The tradition that it was written by Paul goes
back at least to the end of the 2nd century in the church at
Alexandria, but today the view of scholars, almost without
exception, is that Paul is not the author, as was the opinion of
Origen, quoted by Eusebius (*History of the Church* 6.25.14):
'who wrote the epistle, in truth, God knows'.

The differences of vocabulary and style from the letters of
Paul and the different manner of introducing Old Testament
references are two of the reasons for denying Paul's authorship.

The author was a Greek Christian who wrote to Jewish
Christians about the old covenant that had been superseded by
the sacrifice of Christ. Pleas not to abandon the Christian faith
are important parts of the epistle: 2:1–3; 3:12; 6:4–6.

Major theme: the priesthood of Christ

> **apostasy** <
deserting the faith

The author's purpose was to ward off **apostasy**, a real danger
for those to whom he wrote. The work is called a 'word of
exhortation' (13:22), a title used of a synagogue sermon in Acts
13:15. Probably, Hebrews is a written homily about fidelity to
Christ the high priest to which the author has given a letter
ending (13:22–25).

*Papyrus certificate
confirming that the
holder has sacrificed
to the gods; AD 250.
Reproduced by
courtesy of the
Director and
University Librarian,
the John Rylands
University of
Manchester*

The date of Hebrews

Many commentators favour a date later than the destruction of the Temple in AD 70, usually AD 80–90. The author wishes to show that the sacrifice of Jesus has replaced Old Testament sacrificial worship.

Outline

(I) **Introduction (1:1–4)**

(II) **The Son higher than the angels (1:5–2:18)**
   (A) *The Son's enthronement (1:5–14)*
   (B) *Exhortation to fidelity (2:1–4)*
   (C) *Jesus' exaltation through abasement (2:5–18)*

(III) **Jesus, merciful and faithful high priest (3:1–5:10)**
   (A) *Jesus, the faithful Son, superior to Moses (3:1–6)*
   (B) *A warning based on Israel's infidelity (3:7–4:13)*
   (C) *Jesus, merciful high priest (4:14–5:10)*

(IV) **Jesus' eternal priesthood and eternal sacrifice
   (5:11–10:39)**
   (A) *An exhortation to spiritual renewal (5:11–6:20)*

(B) *Jesus, priest according to the order of Melchizedek*
    (7:1–28)
(a) Melchizedek and the levitical priesthood (7:1–10)
(b) The levitical priesthood superseded (7:11–28)
(C) *The eternal sacrifice (8:1–9:28)*
(a) The old covenant, tabernacle, worship (8:1–9:10)
    (i) The heavenly priesthood of Jesus (8:1–6)
    (ii) The old covenant contrasted with the new
        (8:7–13)
    (iii) The old covenant tabernacle (9:1–5)
    (iv) The old covenant worship (9:6–10)
(b) The sacrifice of Jesus (9:11–28)
    (i) Sacrifice in the heavenly sanctuary (9:11–14)
    (ii) The sacrifice of the new covenant ((9:15–22)
    (iii) The perfect sacrifice (9:23–28)
(D) *Jesus' sacrifice, motive for perseverance (10:1–39)*
(a) The many sacrifices and the One Sacrifice (10:1–18)
(b) Assurance, judgement, recall of the past (10:19–39)

(V) **Examples, discipline, disobedience (11:1–12:29)**
    (A) *The faith of the ancients (11:1–40)*
    (B) *God's treatment of his sons (12:1–13)*
    (C) *The penalties of disobedience (12:14–29)*

(VI) **Final exhortation, blessing, greetings (13:1–25)**

HIGHLIGHT

Hebrews 1:1–5

[1]Long ago God spoke to our ancestors in many and various ways by the prophets, [2]but in these last days he has spoken to us by a Son, whom he appointed heir of all things, through whom he also created the worlds. [3]He is the reflection of God's glory and the exact imprint of God's very being, and he sustains all things by his powerful word. When he had made purification for sins, he sat down at the right hand of the Majesty on high, [4]having become as much superior to angels as the name he has inherited is more excellent than theirs.

[5]For to which of the angels did God ever say,
'You are my Son;
    today I have begotten you'?
Or again,
 'I will be his Father,
    and he will be my Son'?

The Gospel
According to
John

Who wrote the Fourth Gospel?

The material in this
chapter is digested
from NJBC article
61, 'The Gospel
According to John',
by Pheme Perkins.

The Beloved Disciple is identified as the witness behind the Gospel tradition in John 23:24, but John 21:20–23 contains a reference to his death. So clearly he cannot be the one and only author, even though he may be responsible for much of the Gospel, which is the result of several stages of editing.

The other question is: which John was the Beloved Disciple? Bishop Irenaeus of Lyons (who died in 202) said the Gospel was written by the Beloved Disciple, named John, at Ephesus, towards the end of his life. But passages in the Gospel itself (chapter 21) suggest that the Beloved Disciple was not John, son of Zebedee.

Although the Gospel could have been produced by one author or editor, what is important is that it came from the traditions of the community of believers known as the Johannine community.

For whom was the Gospel written?

It was written for the Johannine community, using traditions handed down in that community. The Johannine community was a group of house-churches which originated among the various sects of Judaism in Palestine.

(A) Two important sources of the Gospel go back to this period:

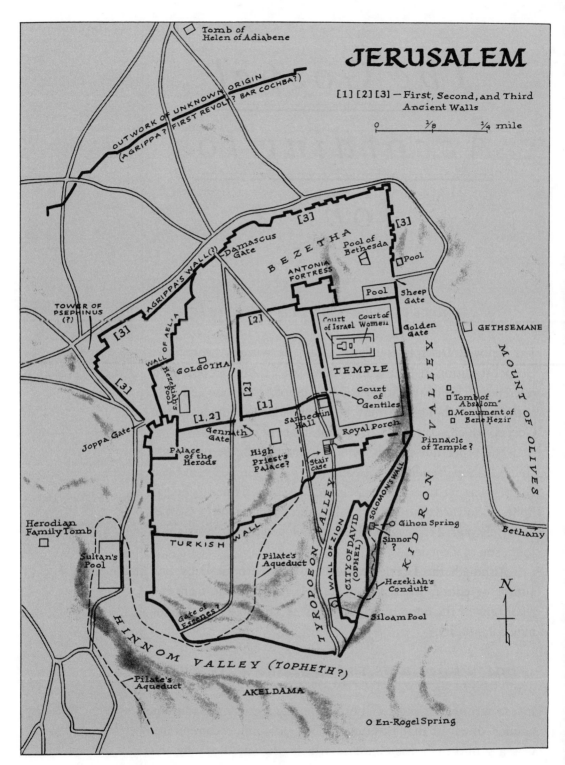

Plan of Jerusalem. The New Jerome Biblical Commentary

296

(a) the collection of Jewish titles for the Messiah and the affirmation that Jesus fulfils the Scripture, which now form the basis of John 1:19–51,

(b) the initial collection of the miracles of Jesus, which at this period were probably explained as evidence for belief in Jesus as Messiah and Son of God.

(B) At some point members of the Johannine community converted a number of Samaritans. The mission in Samaria may have coincided with the emphasis on Jesus taking the place of the Temple (2:13–22).

Jesus is the true source of the covenant blessings, the only one to have 'seen God', and the prophet who restores true worship of God.

(C) After expulsion from the synagogue, and possibly a move from Palestine to Ephesus, the missionary effort of the community is focused on Gentiles. John 7:35 and 12:20–22 may show that the mission was successful. This period (in the 90s) also sees the community's tradition in writing developing. The extensive expansion on the miracle traditions, the hymn to 'the Word' in the prologue, and the carefully crafted passion narrative were probably written before the account of Jesus' mission. Some of the teaching now preserved in chapters 15–17 may also have taken shape during this period.

Sources for the Gospel of John

The writer may have known one or more of the other three Gospels (Matthew, Mark or Luke), and certainly drew on traditions related to theirs. Several types of source seem to have been used:

- a collection of miracle stories (often called the Signs Source)
- a collection of sayings of Jesus different from that behind the other Gospels
- an earlier account of Jesus' passion, the empty tomb and resurrection appearances of Jesus.

Differences between John and the other Gospels

- Jesus' words no longer focus on the kingdom of God or use proverbs and parables. Instead he speaks in symbolic language.
- John presents the ministry of Jesus over three years.
- He puts the death of Jesus on the day of Preparation before Passover.
- He does not mention exorcism among the healings.
- In John the disciples recognize Jesus as Messiah from the beginning, while in other gospels this is the climax of Jesus' ministry in Galilee.

The message of the Fourth Gospel

Jesus, the Son of God, is the source of eternal life.

Believing in Jesus means seeing the special relationship between Jesus and the Father. In the 'I am' sayings Jesus takes over the great religious symbols of Judaism to show that he is the one who reveals God. The Prologue of the Gospel shows that Jesus existed from the beginning with God. He comes to reveal the Father.

The Prologue seems to be based on an early hymn. It may have been added after the Gospel was completed.

The plot

The plot of the Gospel is focused on the 'hour' of Jesus' glorification, his return to the Father at the crucifixion.

At the same time that the plot moves towards the glorification of Jesus, the story moves through cycles of acceptance and rejection.

- Chapters 1–4 are positive statements of Jesus' coming to those who receive him. The meetings with Nicodemus and the Samaritan woman introduce the reader to the 'double meaning' of Johannine teaching and the idea that Jesus is the key to salvation.

- Chapters 5–12, however, tell of conflicts over Jesus' identity and the beginning of rejection of him.
- Chapters 13–17 provide an interlude.
- After that, the events of the passion begin to unfold in a series of short scenes (18:1–19:42) until the dying Jesus pronounces his mission completed (19:30). The resurrection traditions added to the Gospel, especially chapter 21, carry the reader into the future mission of the disciples, and establish faith within the community.

The portrayal of 'the Jews' in John's Gospel

The narrator and Jesus speak of 'the Jews' as outsiders. Sometimes the phrase is used in a neutral way, and sometimes it is used as if they are enemies. Not all who are Jews in the narrative fall into these negative categories, since some do believe.

Jewish tradition behind the Fourth Gospel

The Gospel affirms that whatever a person's understanding of salvation is, it is fulfilled and corrected by the unique revelation of God in Jesus.

As scholars discover the diversity of 1st-century Judaism, the Jewish background of the Gospel comes more sharply into focus. Though John does not quote the Old Testament as much as the other Gospels do, allusions to Old Testament texts and images are woven into it.

In John's Gospel	In the Old Testament
Jesus' teaching on manna, and the Bread of Life, and the people murmuring against him	John reminds readers of Moses in the wilderness and the people murmuring against him
John reminds readers that Jesus is the prophet foretold in Deuteronomy 18:15	
John affirms Jesus as the Divine word active in creation	This reflects the traditional idea of God's Wisdom as active in creation
Jesus is rejected by his own people	Wisdom finds no dwelling among humans
Jesus identifies himself with God's name 'I am'. He said:	God told Moses 'I am who I am' and Isaiah uses this name of God
I am he (the Messiah)	
I am the bread of life	
I am the light of the world	
I am the door	
I am the good shepherd	
I am the resurrection and the life	
I am the vine	

Outline

(I) **Prologue: the Word coming into the world (1:1–18)**

(II) **Book of Signs: 'His own did not receive him . . .'
(1:19–12:50)**
  (A) Gathering disciples (1:19–4:54)
  (a) At John's testimony (1:19–51)
    (i) John is not the Messiah (1:19–28)
    (ii) Jesus is the Lamb of God (1:29–34)
    (iii) Andrew and Peter (1:35–42)
    (iv) Philip and Nathanael (1:43–51)
  (b) Cana: disciples see his glory (2:1–12)
  (c) Judea: Temple cleansing (2:13–25)
    (i) Sign of the resurrection (2:13–22)
    (ii) Comment: faith rejected (2:23–25)
  (d) Nicodemus: rebirth and eternal life (3:1–36)
    (i) Dialogue: receiving eternal life (3:1–15)
    (ii) Comment: God sent the Son to give life (3:16–21)
    (iii) John testifies to Jesus (3:22–30)
    (iv) Comment: God sent Jesus to give life (3:31–36)
  (e) Withdrawal to Galilee (4:1–3)
  (f) Samaria: Saviour of the world (4:4–42)
    (i) Dialogue: living water (4:6–15)
    (ii) Dialogue: the Messiah-prophet (4:16–26)
    (iii) Dialogue: the harvest (4:27–38)
    (iv) Samaritan believers (4:39–42)

(g)   Galilee: the official's son (4:43–54)
    (i)   Jesus' return to Galilee (4:43–45)
    (ii)   The official's son healed (4:46–54)

(B)   *Disputes over Jesus' deeds and words: is he from
    God? (5:1–10:42)*

(a)   Jerusalem: healing the cripple: life and judgement
    (5:1–47)
    (i)   A cripple healed on the sabbath (5:1–18)
    (ii)   The Son's authority to give life (5:19–30)
    (iii)   Testimony to Jesus (5:31–40)
    (iv)   Unbelief condemned (5:41–47)

(b)   Galilee: the bread of life (6:1–71)
    (i)   Feeding the five thousand (6:1–15)
    (ii)   Walking on water (6:16–21)
    (iii)   Dialogue: Jesus is bread from heaven (6:22–40)
    (iv)   Dispute over Jesus' origins (6:41–51a)
    (v)   The bread is Jesus' flesh (6:51b–59)
    (vi)   Dispute: Jesus loses disciples (6:60–66)
    (vii)   Peter's confession (6:67–71)

(c)   Jerusalem at Tabernacles (7:1–8:59)
    (i)   Galilee: rejects advice to go to the feast (7:1–9)
    (ii)   Jesus goes secretly to the feast (7:10–13)
    (iii)   Jesus teaches in the Temple (7:14–24)
    (iv)   Division: is this the Messiah? (7:25–31)
    (v)   Soldiers sent to arrest Jesus (7:32–36)
    (vi)   Jesus is the living water (7:37–39)
    (vii)   Division: is this the prophet? (7:40–44)
    (viii)   Authorities reject Jesus (7:45–52)
       [Woman taken in adultery (7:53–8:11)]
    (ix)   The Father testifies to Jesus (8:12–20)
    (x)   Jesus is returning to the Father (8:21–30)
    (xi)   The seed of Abraham hear the truth (8:31–47)
    (xii)   Before Abraham was, I Am (8:48–59)

(d)   Jesus restores sight to the blind (9:1–41)
    (i)   Healing a man born blind (9:1–12)
    (ii)   Pharisees question the man: Jesus is a prophet
       (9:13–17)
    (iii)   Jews question the parents: fear of being expelled
       from the synagogue (9:18–23)
    (iv)   Second interrogation and expulsion from the
       synagogue (9:24–34)
    (v)   Jesus is Son of Man (9:35–38)
    (vi)   Blindness of the Pharisees (9:39–41)

(e)   Jesus, the Good Shepherd (10:1–42)
    (i)   Parable of the sheepfold (10:1–6)
    (ii)   Jesus, the gate and the good shepherd (10:7–18)
    (iii)   Division: is Jesus possessed? (10:19–21)
    (iv)   Jesus' sheep know his identity (10:22–30)

HIGHLIGHT

The Prologue
John 1:1–18

[1]In the beginning was the Word, and the Word was with God, and the Word was God. [2]He was in the beginning with God. [3]All things came into being through him, and without him not one thing came into being. What has come into being [4]in him was life, and the life was the light of all people. [5]The light shines in the darkness, and the darkness did not overcome it.

⁶There was a man sent from God, whose name was John. ⁷He came as a witness to testify to the light, so that all might believe through him. ⁸He himself was not the light, but he came to testify to the light. ⁹The true light, which enlightens everyone, was coming into the world.

¹⁰He was in the world, and the world came into being through him; yet the world did not know him. ¹¹He came to what was his own, and his own people did not accept him. ¹²But to all who received him, who believed in his name, he gave power to become children of God, ¹³who were born, not of blood or of the will of the flesh or of the will of man, but of God.

¹⁴And the Word became flesh and lived among us, and we have seen his glory, the glory as of a father's only son, full of grace and truth. ¹⁵(John testified to him and cried out, 'This was he of whom I said, "He who comes after me ranks ahead of me because he was before me."') ¹⁶From his fullness we have all received, grace upon grace. ¹⁷The law indeed was given through Moses; grace and truth came through Jesus Christ. ¹⁸No one has ever seen God. It is God the only Son, who is close to the Father's heart, who has made him known.

The Johannine

Epistles

The relationship among the three epistles

The material in this chapter is digested from NJBC article 62, 'The Johannine Epistles', by Pheme Perkins.

2 John and 3 John are letters. They are untypical in not giving a personal name for the sender and, in 2 John, not stating where the church addressed is located. However, both letters address concrete problems. They should not be taken as 'fictional' letters. 2 and 3 John are short letters from a person called 'the presbyter' (elder) to other communities. 2 John forbids association between members of the church and a separatist group of Christians. 3 John seeks to secure hospitality for missionaries associated with the presbyter from Gaius after another leading Christian, Diotrephes, had refused it.

1 John is an appeal to Christians in the churches associated with John to be faithful to their tradition; the opponents fail to observe the commandment of love, are deceivers and antichrists; they do not believe in the coming of Jesus 'in the flesh'. The community does not seem to have established authorities, though they did have teachers and may have called them presbyters. But the writer of 1 John asks them to remember that his teaching represents what they have heard from the beginning.

The author

Comparison with the Gospel of John suggests that these letters were not by the author of the Gospel.

Date and relationship to the Fourth Gospel

If the Gospel was written about AD 90, the epistles would represent the situation of the communities for whom the Gospel was written, about AD 100. The power of many of the passages in 1 John depends on echoing the tradition established in the Gospel.

1 John echoes the relationships between God (Father, Son, Spirit) and the Christian: the Father loves the Christian (John 14:21; 1 John 4:16); the Son lives in the faithful Christian (John 15:4; 1 John 3:24); gift of the Spirit (John 14:16–17; 1 John 4:13). Important factors in the way in which the Christian relates to God are:

- mutual indwelling (John 14:20; 1 John 3:24);
- forgiveness (John 15:3; 1 John 1:9);
- eternal life (John 17:2; 1 John 2:29);
- righteousness (John 16:10; 1 John 2:29).

Basic conditions for Christian discipleship are reasserted: the believer is not 'in sin' (unlike the unbelieving 'world', John 16:8–9; unlike the false perfectionism of the dissidents, 1 John 1:8; 3:4–9); one must love Jesus, keep commandments (John 14:15; 1 John 2:3 ['know him' instead of love]; 3:10, 22–24); reject behaviour that is 'of the world' (John 15:18, world's hatred of believers; 1 John 2:15, not 'love the world'; 4:1, false spirits gone out into world); belief 'overcomes the world' (John 17:8–9; 1 John 2:13–14; 5:5).

The opponents

1 and 2 John mention persons who had been part of the fellowship but have now separated themselves from that community (1 John 2:19; 4:1; 2 John 7). The statement that persons have separated from the community is linked with a failure to 'confess' the truth about Jesus, and it is claimed that such persons are 'deceivers and antichrists', who must be overcome.

If some time has passed between 1 John and 2 John, the sharper tone might suggest that the situation had worsened.

It seems that the opponents proclaimed the believer sinless and regarded any representation of the death of Jesus as sacrifice useless. They also claim to have received 'knowledge of God' and of the Spirit. How such views led them to separate from the Christians addressed in 1 and 2 John, we do not know. By refusing to grant hospitality to those who come from the presbyter, Diotrephes appears to be turning the presbyter's rule for dealing with the dissidents (2 John 10–11) against him. 3 John does not imply that Diotrephes was sympathetic to the opponents. He is the leader of a local community, who has decided to exclude all travelling missionaries.

1 JOHN

Outline

(I) **Prologue (1:1–4)**

(II) **Walking in light (1:5–2:29)**
 (A) Two-way exhortation (1:5–2:17)
 (a) God is light (1:5)
 (b) Freedom from sin (1:6–2:2)
 (c) Keeping the commandments (2:3–11)
 (d) Address to three groups (2:12–14)
 (e) Reject the world (2:15–17)
 (B) Reject the antichrists (2:18–29)
 (a) Division as a sign of the last hour (2:18–19)
 (b) Anointing preserves true faith (2:20–25)
 (c) Anointing teaches the community (2:26–27)
 (d) Confidence at the judgement (2:28–29)

(III) **Love as the mark of God's children (3:1–24)**
 (A) The Father makes us children now (3:1–10)
 (a) We are God's children now (3:1–3)
 (b) Those born of God do not sin (3:4–10)
 (B) Christians must love one another (3:11–18)
 (a) Cain: hatred is death (3:11–15)
 (b) Christ's death: model for love (3:16–18)
 (C) Our confidence before God (3:19–24)
 (a) God is greater than our hearts (3:19–22)
 (b) God abides in those who keep the commandments (3:23–24)

(IV) **Commandments to love and believe (4:1–5:12)**
 (A) Reject the antichrists (4:1–6)
 (a) They do not confess Jesus (4:1–3)

    (b) They have not overcome the world (4:4–6)
    (B) God is love (4:7–21)
    (a) Christ has shown us God's love (4:7–12)
    (b) We know God's love through the Spirit (4:13–16a)
    (c) Our confidence: abiding in God's love (4:16b–21)
    (C) Belief in the Son (5:1–12)
    (a) Faith overcomes the world (5:1–5)
    (b) Testimony: the Son came in water in blood (5:6–12)

(V) Conclusion (5:13–21)
    (A) Confidence in prayer (5:14–17)
    (B) Three confidence sayings (5:18–20)
    (C) Keep yourselves from idols (5:21)

2 JOHN

Outline

(I) Opening formula (1–3)

(II) Body of the letter (4–11)
    (A) Faithfulness of the addressees (4–6)
    (B) Warning against the opponents (7–9)
    (C) Take action against the opponents (10–11)

(III) Letter closing (12–13)

3 JOHN

Outline

(I) Opening formula (1–2)

(II) Body of the letter (3–12)
    (A) Readers' hospitality to missionaries (3–8)
    (B) Diotrephes's refusal of hospitality (9–10)
    (C) Request for hospitality (11–12)

(III) Letter closing (13–15)

HIGHLIGHT

Our God is love
I John 4:7–14

[7]Beloved, let us love one another, because love is from God; everyone who loves is born of God and knows God. [8]Whoever does not love does not know God, for God is love. [9]God's love was revealed among us in this way: God sent his only Son into the world so that we might live through him. [10]In this is love, not that we loved God but that he loved us and sent his Son to be the atoning sacrifice for our sins. [11]Beloved, since God loved us so much, we also ought to love one another. [12]No one has ever seen God; if we love one another, God lives in us, and his love is perfected in us.

[13]By this we know that we abide in him and he in us, because he has given us of his Spirit. [14]And we have seen and do testify that the Father has sent his Son as the Saviour of the world.

The Apocalypse

(Revelation)

The material in this chapter is digested from NJBC article 63, 'The Apocalypse (Revelation)', by Adela Yarbro Collins.

What kind of book is the Apocalypse?

The Apocalypse (Revelation) narrates extraordinary visions that concern things normally unseen and unheard by human beings. It is unique in the New Testament, but not in the ancient world. There are similar texts in the Old Testament and in other Jewish and Christian literature (see Chapter 19).

Apocalypse
The book begins with the words 'The revelation (apocalypse) of Jesus Christ . . .'. The Greek word 'apocalypse' expresses the idea that God (through Jesus Christ, John, and this written text) has unveiled secrets about heaven and earth, past, present and future. The visionary does not receive the revelation directly from God, as an oracle, but only through a mediator, a heavenly being, an angel or the risen Christ, in a variety of forms: appearances of God, visions, hearing voices, other-worldly journeys, or a heavenly book. The revelation has two focuses: secrets of the cosmos and secrets of the future. Secrets are revealed in order to present a particular interpretation of the times and to persuade the hearers or readers to think and live in a certain way.

Revelation and prophecy, letters and drama
The book also has something in common with:

- prophecy: it refers to itself as prophecy (1:3; 22:7, 10, 18, 19), and the messages to the seven congregations are prophetic oracles.
- letters: it is not a letter, but it is put into the form of a

letter with a standard opening formula of a letter of its time.

- drama: it has some affinities with drama, particularly Greek tragedy because it excites fear. As it emphasizes the danger facing the faithful in this world, it also portrays the terrors of the next world for those who prove unfaithful.

Who is the author of the book?

In 1:1 the author is simply referred to as God's servant John. The case for the authorship of Revelation by one of the Twelve Apostles is not very strong. Conceivably, John the son of Zebedee moved to Asia Minor and survived until about AD 95 (see below); but it is not probable that he was the author.

The relationship between Revelation and the Gospel of John is also a complicated issue, but the differences between the two works are so great that it is unlikely that they were written by the same person.

It seems best to conclude that the author was an early Christian prophet by the name of John, otherwise unknown. The authority of the book lies in the effectiveness of the text itself and in the fact that the Church has included it in the Bible.

The date of the book

There is no reason to doubt the traditional dating of Revelation, at the end of the reign of the emperor Domitian (AD 95–96). There is a tradition that Revelation was written in response to a great persecution of Christians during Domitian's reign.

The overall shape and structure of the book

Its structure is problematic because of the presence of numerous parallel passages and repetitions within the book and because of occasional breakdowns in consecutive development. Particularly striking parallel passages are the seven messages, seven seals, seven trumpets, and seven bowls. The parallels between the trumpets and bowls are especially close. The events associated with the sixth bowl (16:12–16) seem to repeat those following the sixth trumpet (9:13–21). The sequence of one event logically following another breaks down especially between 11:19 and 12:1 and between 19:10 and 19:11. A fundamental question is whether these are part of the author's original literary plan or not.

The theological perspective of Revelation, its images and symbols, its language and style, is very consistent. There is an overall sense of unity which suggests that Revelation owes its present form to a single author, but it does not exclude other possibilities: that the author used oral or even written sources or that the work was edited by the author once or even more times. But, if the structure of Revelation is the author's literary design, then repetition and the number seven are important features of the shape.

Outline

(I) **Prologue (1:1–3)**
 (A) *Description of the book (1:1–2)*
 (B) *Promise to the reader (1:3)*

(II) **Letter framework (1:4–22:21)**
 (A) *Author and reader (1:4–6)*
 (B) *Two prophetic sayings (1:7–8)*
 (C) *Report of a revelatory experience (1:9–22:5)*
 (a) Setting of scene (1:9–10a)
 (b) The revelatory experience proper (1:10b–22:5)
 (i) First cycle of visions (1:10b–11:19)
 (1) Epiphany of Christ to John with seven messages (1:10b–3:22)
 (*a*) To Ephesus (2:1–7)
 (*b*) To Smyrna (2:8–11)
 (*c*) To Pergamum (2:12–17)
 (*d*) To Thyatira (2:18–29)
 (*e*) To Sardis (3:1–6)
 (*f*) To Philadelphia (3:7–13)
 (*g*) To Laodicea (3:14–22)
 (2) The scroll with seven seals (4:1–8:5)
 (*a*) The heavenly court (4:1–11)
 (*b*) The scroll and the Lamb (5:1–14)

(D) Isolated sayings (22:6–20)

(a)   Saying about the nature and origin of the book (22:6)

(b)   An oracle implicitly attributed to Christ which is an apocalyptic prediction (22:7a)

(c)   Promise to the readers of the book (22:7b)

(d)   Identification of the visionary by name (22:8a)

(e)   Reaction of the visionary and angel's reply (22:8b–9)

(f)   Directive to the visionary from the revealing figure (22:10)

(g)   Threat of judgement and promise of salvation (22:11–12)

(h)   Self-disclosing oracle implicitly attributed to Christ (22:13)

(i)   Promise of salvation and threat of judgement (22:14–15)

(j)   Self-identification of the revealing figure, Jesus (22:16)

(k)   Invitations to the water of life (22:17)

(l)   Threat of judgement against those who violate the integrity of the book (22:18–19)

(m) An oracle implicitly attributed to Christ which is an apocalyptic prediction (22:20a)

(n)   Response to the oracle (22:20b)

(E) Blessing at the end of the letter (22:21)

HIGHLIGHT

A new heaven and a new earth
Revelation 21:1–8

[1]Then I saw a new heaven and a new earth; for the first heaven and the first earth had passed away, and the sea was no more. [2]And I saw the holy city, the new Jerusalem, coming down out of heaven from God, prepared as a bride adorned for her husband. [3]And I heard a loud voice from the throne saying,
'See, the home of God is among mortals.
He will dwell with them as their God;
they will be his peoples,
and God himself will be with them;
[4]he will wipe every tear from their eyes.
Death will be no more;
mourning and crying and pain will be no more,
for the first things have passed away.'
[5]And the one who was seated on the throne said, 'See, I am making all things new.' Also he said, 'Write this, for these words are trustworthy and true.' [6]Then he said to me, 'It is done! I am the Alpha and the Omega, the beginning and the end. To the

thirsty I will give water as a gift from the spring of the water of life. ⁷Those who conquer will inherit these things, and I will be their God and they will be my children. ⁸But as for the cowardly, the faithless, the polluted, the murderers, the fornicators, the sorcerers, the idolaters, and all liars, their place will be in the lake that burns with fire and sulphur, which is the second death.'

SIXTY-THREE

The Second

Epistle of Peter

The material in this
chapter is digested
from NJBC article
64, 'The Second
Epistle of Peter', by
Jerome H. Neyrey,
SJ.

When was it written?

In spite of statements in the epistle (1:1, 12–15; 3:1) scholars do not consider this epistle to have been written by the Apostle Peter.

It includes parts of Jude, which makes it seem unlikely that it is an original letter. It speaks of a 'collection' of Paul's letters which did not exist until the end of the century; it also seems to follow the argument of a work by Plutarch, a Greek writer, dated to AD 96; it speaks of 'your apostles' as if the writer did not belong to that group.

It relies on traditions about Peter which would only have been brought together later. It does not address any local church, but is more of a general letter, confirming traditional doctrine for all churches everywhere for all times.

So the most likely date for its writing would be about AD 100.

For whom was it written?

It was written to a church of both Jewish Christians and Greek converts. The examples and arguments are chosen to be suitable for people of both Jewish and Greek cultures.

The relation of 2 Peter and Jude

Numerous blocks of material in 2 Peter are either identical with or similar to Jude:

2 Peter	Jude	2 Peter	Jude
2:1, 3b	4	2:13, 15	11–12
4, 6	6–7	17	12b–13
5	5	18	16
10–11	8–9	3:1–4	17–18
12	10	10–13	14–15
		14–18	20–25

Who depends on whom? It would appear that 2 Peter edited a
general document (Jude) to fit a specific situation. It is hard to
imagine how Jude would discard two-thirds of 2 Peter.

The message of 2 Peter

2 Peter addresses the problem of God's just judgement, along
with the delay of Christ's Second Coming. 2 Peter should be
viewed alongside 1st-century Greek and Jewish debates about
God's providence and judgement. Heretics were arguing that
God does not intervene in human life, there is no judgement, no
afterlife and therefore no rewards or punishment after death.
The epistle responds in a traditional way.

Outline

(I) **Letter introduction (1:1–11)**
   (A) Letter opening (1:1–2)
   (B) God's deeds (1:3–4)
   (C) Eschatology and ethics (1:5–11)
   (a) Good theology leads to good behaviour (1:5–7)
   (b) Two ways (1:8–11)

(II) **Letter setting: Peter's testament (1:12–15)**

(III) **First reason to believe: prophecy of the Second Coming
   (1:16–21)**
   (A) Mythmaking (1:16a)
   (B) Transfiguration and Second Coming (1:16b–18)
   (C) Transfiguration as prophecy (1:19)
   (D) Inspired interpretation (1:20–21)

(IV) **Argument with the heretics (2:1–22)**
   (A) God's sure judgement (2:1–11)
   (B) Error leads to vice (2:12–16)

(C) *False promises (2:17–19)*
(D) *Lapse from grace (2:20–22)*

(V) Second reason to believe: end of the world (3:1–7)
(A) *Faithful remembering (3:1–2)*
(B) *Attack on the predicted judgement (3:3–4)*
(C) *Rebuttal: proof from history (3:5–7)*

(VI) Third reason to believe: 'delay' as a gift (3:8–9)

(VII) Eschatology and ethics again (3:10–13)
(A) *Thief in the night (3:10)*
(B) *God's day (3:11–13)*

(VIII) Peter and Paul agree (3:14–16)

(IX) Letter closing (3:17–18)

HIGHLIGHT

The Second Coming
2 Peter 1:16–19

[16]For we did not follow cleverly devised myths when we made known to you the power and coming of our Lord Jesus Christ, but we had been eyewitnesses of his majesty. [17]For he received honour and glory from God the Father when that voice was conveyed to him by the Majestic Glory, saying, 'This is my Son, my Beloved, with whom I am well pleased.' [18]We ourselves heard this voice come from heaven, while we were with him on the holy mountain.

[19]So we have the prophetic message more fully confirmed. You will do well to be attentive to this as to a lamp shining in a dark place, until the day dawns and the morning star rises in your hearts.

General articles on the Bible

SIXTY-FOUR

Inspiration

The traditional teaching of the church

The material in this chapter is digested from NJBC article 65, 'Inspiration', by Raymond F. Collins. It has not been possible to reflect the full scope of that article.

Christians have always believed that the Scriptures are inspired by God, even though they have had different ways of understanding and expressing this belief.

Vatican II reaffirmed the traditional teaching of the Roman Catholic Church with these words: 'Those divinely revealed realities which are contained and presented in sacred Scripture have been committed to writing under the inspiration of the Holy Spirit.' God made use of the powers and abilities of chosen authors so that 'with him acting in them and through them, they, as true authors, consigned to writing everything and only those things that he wanted'.

This statement agrees with the views of many evangelical Christians, who look to the Scriptures, especially 2 Timothy 3:16–17 and 2 Peter 1:19–21, as providing the key witness as to how inspiration is to be understood. God is 'the inspirer and author of both Testaments'. Vatican II repeatedly gives inspiration as the ground for belief that the Scriptures are (or contain) the word of God.

The New Testament tradition

The two most important New Testament passages are 2 Timothy 3:16–17 and 2 Peter 1:19–21 (Revised Standard Version translation):

2 Timothy 3:16–17: 'All Scripture is inspired by God and profitable for teaching, for reproof, for correction, and for training in righteousness, that the man of God may be complete, equipped for every good work.'

321

2 Peter 1:19–21: 'We have the prophetic word made more sure ... First of all you must understand this, that no prophecy of Scripture is a matter of one's own interpretation, because no prophecy ever came by the impulse of man, but men moved by the Holy Spirit spoke from God.'

The early Christians believed that the Jewish Scriptures had begun to be fulfilled in Jesus Christ. This early Christianity shared with Jewish tradition the belief that the (Jewish) Scriptures were inspired.

Consequences of a doctrine of biblical inspiration

Vatican II stated: 'The books of Scripture must be acknowledged as teaching firmly, faithfully and without error that truth which God wanted put into the sacred writings for the sake of our salvation.'

Reflection on the nature of biblical 'truth' or 'error' must take into full consideration the literary form and the kind of language used, and its intention. Although the Bible is the inspired Word of God, the texts are formulated in human words. Nevertheless, in and through the human expression, the Scriptures present divinely revealed truths without error.

The Scriptures, therefore, have authority for both Christians and the church, which is why they are used for the personal piety and the spiritual growth of individual Christians, and in liturgical worship. The truth of the Bible is a saving truth. In the Scriptures God manifests his fidelity to his people, bringing them into loving union with himself.

Christians of various backgrounds should be able to approve and accept the language of Vatican II about Scripture's teaching without error that truth which God wanted put into the sacred writings for the sake of our salvation.

SIXTY-FIVE

Canonicity

Introduction

The material in this chapter is digested from NJBC article 66, 'Canonicity', by Raymond E. Brown, SS and Raymond F. Collins.

A 'canonical' book is one that the church acknowledges as belonging to its list (or 'canon') of sacred books. It recognizes these books as (a) inspired by God and (b) offering rules for life in terms of faith and morals.

In Roman Catholic terminology two groups of Old Testament books are considered canonical: (1) the 39 protocanonical books which are the same books as appear in the Protestant Old Testament canon; and (2) the 7 deuterocanonical books which are often listed in Protestant Bibles among the Apocrypha. These are Tobit, Judith, 1–2 Maccabees, Wisdom, Sirach (Ecclesiasticus), Baruch (plus parts of Esther and Daniel). Luther excluded the deuterocanonical books, retaining the 39 we see in Protestant Bibles today. Incidently, these 39 are the same books that St Jerome had listed 1,200 years earlier because they were written in Hebrew and Aramaic and so accepted by the Jews of his time. The deuterocanonical books were earlier accepted as well by the Jews of Alexandria; and some of them, although preserved in Greek, were originally written in Hebrew or Aramaic.

Noncanonical are the other Apocrypha which include *1–2 Esdras*, the *Prayer of Manasseh* and (sometimes) *3–4 Maccabees*; and the Pseudepigrapha (sometimes bearing the names of famous men of antiquity who did not write them), for example *Enoch, 2 Baruch*.

Canonicity and inspiration have different meanings:

(1) A book from the biblical period is canonical because it is part of a closed collection of books, the Bible, that has unique status in the church.

(2) A book is inspired because the Holy Spirit was its source.

There are enormous difficulties as to exactly how and why individual books were judged canonical: sometimes decisions favoured books of no great theological interest (Jude); some books were really anonymous collections (Malachi); many were not written by those whose names have been attached to them (all or most of the Gospels). Very diverse theologies are at work within the same canon. These and other factors make the study of the canon extremely complicated.

The canon of the Old Testament

The composition of the Old Testament was a process that took over 1,000 years. The first poetic compositions, e.g., the Song of Miriam (Exodus 15:1–18) and the Song of Deborah (Judges 5), probably go back to the 12th century BC. The latest books, 2 Maccabees and Wisdom, were composed *ca.* 100 BC. During this long period of composition there was a gradual gathering of material into books and then into collections of books.

The division of the Hebrew Bible accepted by Judaism is the Law, the Prophets, and the Writings. The Law consists of the five books of the Pentateuch. The Prophets are subdivided into the Former Prophets (Joshua, Judges, 1 and 2 Samuel and 1 and 2 Kings) and the Latter Prophets (Isaiah, Jeremiah, Ezekiel and the twelve Minor Prophets). The Writings are Psalms, Proverbs, Job, Canticles, Ruth, Lamentations, Ecclesiastes, Esther, Daniel, Ezra, Nehemiah and 1 and 2 Chronicles.

The generally accepted view is that each division or collection – Law, Prophets, and Writings – represents a stage in the development of the Bible, so that the Law was fixed before the Prophets, etc. There is another point of view that sees the three divisions growing more or less at the same time. Although it is true that individual books belonging to each of the three divisions were being composed at the same time, it is difficult to deny the evidence that one collection was fixed before another.

The deuterocanonical books were composed later and are not part of the Hebrew Bible.

The canon of the New Testament

General observations

Today, Roman Catholics, Protestants, and most Orthodox all accept the same canon of 27 New Testament books. From the beginning the followers of Jesus had Scriptures that they considered sacred, but these were writings that had come down to them from their Jewish heritage.

Once there were Christian writings, what factors determined which ones were to be preserved and were to be considered uniquely sacred? Some 1st-century writings were not preserved, and other early works that were preserved were not accepted as canonical. The following factors were important.

• (1) Origin from the apostles, real or claimed, was very important. The canonicity of Revelation and Hebrews was debated precisely because it was doubted whether they were written by John and Paul respectively.

• (2) Most of the New Testament works were addressed to particular Christian communities, and the history and importance of the community involved had much to do with the preservation and even with the ultimate acceptance of these works. The churches of Greece and Asia Minor seem to have preserved the largest portion of New Testament material, i.e., the writings thought to be by Paul, John and perhaps Luke. The church of Rome preserved Mark, Romans and perhaps Hebrews and the writings of Luke.

• (3) Conformity with the rule of faith was a criterion of acceptance. Doubts about the thousand-year reign of Christ caused suspicion of the Apocalypse (Revelation).

Composition and collection of New Testament works

All the works eventually accepted into the New Testament were probably written before AD 150. The dates for their collection into recognized groups are hard to specify. (See the chart on page 331.)

(A) WRITINGS THOUGHT TO BE BY PAUL Most of the letters and epistles truly written by Paul were instruction and encouragement to churches that Paul himself had evangelized (Romans is a notable exception).

In all, 13 letters or epistles came to bear Paul's name as author (a claim not made by Hebrews, which was eventually attributed to Paul as the 14th letter). Numerically this collection constitutes one-half the New Testament collection of 27 books. The Pastoral Letters (Titus, 1–2 Timothy), Colossians, Ephesians and 2 Thessalonians are thought by many scholars to be written by disciples of Paul rather than by Paul himself.

(B) THE FOUR GOSPELS These present a different picture. Written traditions about Jesus came before the canonical Gospels. Luke 1:1 says that many other people had already undertaken to compile a narrative of the things that had been accomplished by Jesus. Thus there is a line of development from Jesus himself, through pre-Gospel writings to the canonical Gospels.

The canonical Gospels were written between AD 65 and 100, with Mark most likely the earliest. (Besides a small amount of genuine Jesus material from the 1st century that survived into the 2nd century outside the canonical Gospels, there was much Christian imagination and theological reflection about Jesus that gave rise to the Apocrypha, a term covering works not eventually accepted by the church as part of the canon.)

The letters of Paul and the four Gospels, two separate books of early Christian literature, stemming from apostolic witness, were the nucleus of the New Testament.

(C) OTHER LITERATURE Other Christian works that eventually became part of the New Testament were known in the 2nd century: Acts, dealing with how the apostles, and especially Peter and Paul, were guided by the Holy Spirit to continue the work of Jesus; writings related to James, Peter, Jude and John were listed as the catholic, or universal, epistles; and a visionary book known as Revelation.

Gradually these were accepted as Scripture, so that by the end of the 4th century there was a wide acceptance of the 27-book canon of the New Testament.

Problems of authority

Even when it is agreed which books of Scripture are inspired and canonical, are some more authoritative than others? Obviously some have more value than others.

Obviously, too, some books claim to be more directly from God than others do; e.g., the prophets claim to convey the word of God that came to them, whereas the wisdom writers, although inspired, seem to be giving us the fruit of their own human experience.

In liturgy the church uses some biblical books extensively and others very seldom, thus forming an 'actual canon' within the formal canon.

This question has become more acute as we have recognized that there are differing outlooks and theologies in the books of Scripture. When these differences exist between the two Testaments, one can solve them in terms of new revelation, e.g., Job's formal and explicit denial of an afterlife (14:7–22), contrasted with Jesus' clear affirmation of it (Mark 12:26–27).

But, even within the New Testament, works of roughly the same period contain divergent theologies. The outlook on the law in Romans 10:4 certainly is not the same as the outlook in Matthew 5:18. One may explain that there is no *contradiction* between Romans 3:28 ('justified by faith apart from the works of the law') and of James 2:24 ('justified by works and not by faith alone'); but one can scarcely imagine that Paul's attitude was the same as that of James. The idea that there was a uniform and harmonious development of theological understanding from the time of Pentecost to the end of the apostolic era is not supported by the New Testament critically read.

But then the question arises: If there are two different views in the New Testament, which one is to be considered authoritative? Within the canon of Scripture and in particular within the New Testament, what books are most important in showing us what to believe? We should not press the differences in the Scriptures to the point of their being contradictory. We should also recognize that some New Testament books that seem less important at one period in Christian history, may seem very important at another time. Granted such qualifications, the church must be faithful to the whole New Testament, constantly being challenged by it as the voice of Christ.

A final caution is that the biblical writers spoke as people of their times, and not all their religious statements have enduring value. For instance the reader of the Bible must be careful about statements concerning the Second Coming of Christ. If the New Testament writers describe the future coming of the Lord in terms of trumpet blasts and celestial cataclysms, this is not necessarily revelation to be believed. The problem of distinguishing what is revelation and what is not becomes acute for delicate topics. The church, guided by and guiding scholarly investigation, helps to tell us what is God's revelation for his people.

A good practical rule for avoiding self-deception in this matter is to pay more attention to Scripture when it disagrees with what we want to hear than when it agrees. When the Bible disagrees with the spirit of our times, it is not always because the biblical authors are giving voice to a limited, out-of-date religious view; frequently it is because God's ways are not our ways.

Works of the Old Testament era: approximate dates of collection or composition

Centuries BC	The Law	The Prophets		The Writings	Deuterocanonical
		Former Prophets	Latter Prophets		
13th–11th	Career of Moses? Traditions underlying Pentateuch taking shape; early law codes. Early poetry (Exodus 15).	Stories of conquest of Palestine. Traditions underlying Judges and 1 Samuel. Early poetry (Judges 5).			
10th	J tradition put into writing.	Stories of David especially 'Court History' (2 Samuel 9–20, 1 Kings 1–2).		Use of Psalms in temple worship begins. Cultivation of proverbial wisdom in Jerusalem court under Solomon.	
9th	E tradition composed.	Preservation of royal annals of Judah and of Israel (source of 1–2 Kings, 1–2 Chronicles). Elijah and Elisha cycles (1 Kings 17–2, Kings 10).		Ruth? Marriage songs, later echoed in Canticles.	
8th	J and E merged (under Hezekiah, ca. 700)?	Preservation of royal annals of Judah and Israel.	Amos and Hosea in Israel. Isaiah and Micah in Judah.	Hezekiah is a traditional patron of proverbial wisdom (Proverbs 25).	
7th	Nucleus of Deuteronomy is made basis of Josiah's reform (ca. 622). Holiness Code (Leviticus 17–26) edited.	Preservation of royal annals of Judah.	Oracles of Isaiah collected by disciples and edited. Zephaniah, Nahum and Habakkuk. Jeremiah dictates to Baruch.		

329

Centuries BC	The Law	The Prophets		The Writings	Deuterocanonical
		Former Prophets	Latter Prophets		
6th	P is compiled from earlier sources and gives structure to emerging Pentateuch.	Deuteronomic History edited in exile.	Ezekiel in Babylon. Second Isaiah (*ca.* 550). Editing of pre-exilic prophetic corpus. Post-exilic oracles of Haggai, Zechariah (1–9), and Third Isaiah.	Lamentations. Job(?).	
5th	Completion of Pentateuch (*ca.* 400?).		Malachi. Obadiah(?).	Memoirs of Nehemiah and/or Ezra. Proverbs 1–9 written as preface to rest of Proverbs.	
4th–3rd			Jonah(?). Joel(?). Isaian Apocalypse (24–27[?]). Second Zechariah (9–14[?]).	Chronicler's History. Sayings of Qoheleth (Ecclesiastes) edited by students. Collection of Psalms(?).	
2nd				Esther(?). Daniel.	Sirach (*ca.* 190). Baruch. Tobit. Judith. Greek Esther. Greek parts of Daniel. 1 Maccabees.
1st					2 Maccabees. Wisdom.

Works of the New Testament: approximate dates of composition

Early 50s	Mid/Late 50s	Early 60s	Mid-60s	70s–80s	90s	After 100
1 Thessalonians	Galatians	Philemon (?)	MARK	MATTHEW	JOHN	2 Peter
2 Thessalonians (?)	1 Corinthians	Colossians (?)	Titus (?)	LUKE	Revelation	
	2 Corinthians	Ephesians (?)	1 Timothy (?)	Acts	1 John	
	Romans		2 Timothy (?)	Colossians (?)	2 John	
	Philippians		1 Peter (?)	Jude (?)	3 John	
	Philemon (?)		James (?)	James (?)	Jude (?)	
			Hebrews (?)	Hebrews (?)	2 Thessalonians (?)	
				1 Peter (?)	Ephesians (?)	
					Titus (?)	
					1 Timothy (?)	
					2 Timothy (?)	

PAULINE CORPUS			GOSPELS		CATHOLIC EPISTLES	
EARLY LETTERS	1 Thessalonians	51	Mark	65–70	1 Peter	64 or 70s–80s
	2 Thessalonians	51 or 90s	Matthew	70s–80s	James	62 or 70s–80s
			Luke	70s–80s	Jude	70s–90s
GREAT LETTERS	Galatians	54–57	John	90s	1 John	90s
	Philippians	56–57			2 John	90s
	1 Corinthians	57			3 John	90s
	2 Corinthians	57			2 Peter	100–150
	Romans	58				
CAPTIVITY LETTERS	Philemon	56–57 or 61–63				
	Colossians	61–63 or 70–80				
	Ephesians	61–63 or 90–100			OTHER WRITINGS	
PASTORAL LETTERS	Titus	65 or 95–100			Acts	70s–80s
	1 Timothy	65 or 95–100			Hebrews	60s or 70s–80s
	2 Timothy	66–67 or 95–100			Revelation	90s

(?) Date uncertain. This chart does not attempt to include datings proposed by a small minority.
Except for the early Pauline writings, an approximation of a decade governs most of the dating, e.g.,
Matthew and Luke could have been written in the 90s.

The material in this
chapter is digested
from sections
78–117 by
Raymond E. Brown,
SS in NJBC article
67, 'Apocrypha'.

> **wadi** <
a stream in winter, dry in
summer

> **scriptorium** <
a place where manuscripts
are written or copied

*The caves of the
Dead Sea Scrolls at
Qumran*

SIXTY-SIX

Qumran and the Dead Sea Scrolls

The discovery and nature of the Dead Sea Scrolls

The **wadi** called Qumran by the Arabs empties into the north-west corner of the Dead Sea, 10 miles south of Jericho. About a mile inland from the sea there are ruins that show evidence of the life of a community: rooms, a complete water system with conduits and cisterns; a kitchen, pantry, and large dining room; store rooms; a **scriptorium**; pottery workshops; and cemeteries holding 1,200 graves.

In 11 caves within a few miles of the Qumran buildings have been found the remains of some 800 manuscripts consisting of about ten complete scrolls and thousands of fragments.

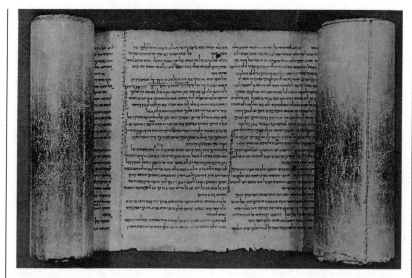

Isaiah. Scroll made by sewing together pieces of parchment; found in Cave 1 at Qumran

Indeed, it was the 1947 discovery of scrolls in cave 1 that focused the interests of archaeologists on the area. Seven of the scrolls from cave 1 and the Temple Scroll from cave 11 are in Jerusalem's Shrine of the Book; the rest of the material is at the Rockefeller Museum in East Jerusalem. An international team of scholars has been preparing material from caves 2–11 for publication.

About a quarter of the Qumran manuscripts are biblical, for instance, texts of Isaiah, the Psalms, parts of Leviticus and Ezekiel, Habakkuk and fragments from the (lost) Hebrew text of Sirach. There are also commentaries that study the biblical text verse by verse, searching for a meaning applicable to the life of the sect, to its past or present circumstances, and to its future hope. The members of the Qumran community seem to have believed that the ancient prophet or psalmist who wrote a biblical work addressed himself not to his own times but to the future, and that that future was the history of the Qumran community. When *ca.* 600 BC Habakkuk spoke of the righteous, he really meant the Righteous Teacher of the Qumran community. There are also many works that relate directly to the life of the Qumran community. For example:

THE MANUAL OF DISCIPLINE was written between 150 and 125 BC and was the essential rule book for the life of the community. Its theme is that the community represents the new covenant

Jar from Qumran, originally containing scrolls; 1st century AD. Reproduced by courtesy of the Trustees of the British Museum

between God and humanity prophesied by Jeremiah 32:37–41. Entrance into the community of the covenant is described. There is a graphic description of two opposing ways of life: the way dominated by the spirit of light and truth and the way dominated by the spirit of darkness and falsehood.

Then follow the actual rules that govern community life. The pattern is very much that of Israel during Moses' time in the desert wanderings, and the idea is that by withdrawing to the desert (Qumran) this community is preparing itself to be the nucleus of the new Israel that in God's time will be brought to the promised land. This is the first known example of what in Christianity would develop into rules for monastic life.

The history of the Qumran sect

The movement of religious and national reformation that would ultimately give birth to the Qumran sect, who are most often identified as Essenes, came to the fore about 167 BC.

In particular, the Qumran sect is probably to be related to the Hasidean branch of the Maccabean revolt against Antiochus. In 1 Maccabees 2:42 we hear that Mattathias, the father of Judas Maccabeus, was joined by the Hasideans ('pious ones'). For a while the Hasideans supported the Maccabees; but whereas the Maccabees became more and more politically oriented, ambitious to establish a **dynasty**, the interest of the Hasideans was primarily religious. (It has generally been assumed that these were the ancestors of the Pharisees; but Qumran documents indicate strong Sadducee elements. Perhaps the 'pious ones' were a mixed group, not yet distinguishable by the latter identifications of Pharisee and Sadducee.) But then God 'raised for them a Righteous Teacher to guide them in the way of his heart'. Seemingly the Qumran Essenes derived directly from those Hasideans who abandoned the Maccabees and followed the Righteous Teacher. The identity of the Righteous Teacher remains a mystery, but he brought his followers (perhaps at that stage no more than 50) to Qumran where he died before the turn of the century.

About 100 BC the Qumran complex was enlarged to hold up to 200 persons and the community flourished until destroyed by fire and an earthquake. Abandoned for 30–40 years, the settlement was re-established before the beginnings

> dynasty <
a royal family

Benches and desks from the scriptorium (where manuscripts were copied) at Qumran. Reproduced by courtesy of the Palestine Archaeological Museum, Jerusalem

of the Christian era. It was destroyed for the last time in the summer of 68 by the Romans. Before this destruction the community manuscripts were deposited in caves, especially in cave 4, and some coins were buried. Some of the Essenes seem to have gone south to join the last-ditch resistance at the stronghold of Masada. The Romans, who established military encampments in the ruins of Qumran, evidently stumbled upon the manuscript hoards, for many of the documents were brutally damaged in antiquity.

The Qumran community: how did they live?

The members of the community lived in huts (and caves?) around a communal centre. To join, it was necessary to be an

Israelite. The ceremony of entry involved taking an oath to observe the Law as interpreted by the Righteous Teacher and being ritually washed.

For the first year the initiates took no part in the solemn meals or the purificatory rites of the community. They retained their own possessions. At the end of the year there was another scrutiny, and the novices who passed it were asked to hand their possessions into the care of the 'supervisor'. They were not admitted to the community meals yet, and only when the second year had passed were they made full-scale members of the community. Then their possessions were added to the common fund. There were rules for punishing those who violated community rules and for expelling serious offenders.

> **celibacy** <
never marrying

How extensive was **celibacy** among the Qumran Essenes? Ancient authors mention Essene celibacy. This agrees with the discovery that there were only male skeletons in the main burial ground of the Qumran community. However, there is mention of women and children in some texts, and female skeletons were found on the fringes of the cemetery. Probably one group (the elite, or the priests, or the fully initiated) did practise celibacy, at least for periods of their life – the priestly line had to be continued – but the rest were married. Evidently, both in their constant ritual washings and in their celibacy, the full-scale members of the community imitated the purity that the Old Testament demanded of priests before sacrifice. Their dislike for divorce was close to that of Jesus.

Whether or not the Essenes practised animal sacrifice at Qumran is not clear. (Skeletons of animals have been found buried, but do they represent sacrifice or refuse?) Certainly there was a tendency on the part of the sectarians to regard their whole existence at Qumran as having sacrificial value.

Life at Qumran in the fierce heat of the Jordan valley must have been demanding. After their daily work, the sectarians assembled at night for prayer, study, and reading. Their meals were imbued with religious significance. Community meals were looked upon as spiritual foretastes of the messianic banquet.

The similarity between Qumran life and that of the Jerusalem church described in Acts has been noted by several scholars. At Qumran there was a Session of the Many very similar to the 'multitude' of the disciples in Acts 6:2, 5 and 15:12. Both had a special body of the Twelve. Moreover, the Christian bishop is an excellent parallel to the Qumran supervisor. The functions of the bishop described in the New Testament are much the same as those of the Qumran supervisor, e.g., shepherd of the flock, steward and manager of community property, and inspector of the doctrine of the faithful (1 Peter 2:25; Acts 20:28; Titus 1:7–9; 1 Timothy 3:2–7).

The community: its faith

The community believed that it was living in the last days. Throughout Israel's entire history, God had prepared for this community of the new covenant. Habakkuk had promised that the just man would live by faith/fidelity. The community represented all those who observed the Law because of their faith in the Righteous Teacher. Eventually all the just would join the sect.

The death of the Righteous Teacher showed that deliverance had not been achieved during his lifetime, but the community believed that they were living in a period before God's final intervention and his raising up the one(s) chosen or anointed (= messiah) to accomplish ultimate victory. The Qumran text speaks of 'the coming of a prophet and the Messiahs of Aaron and Israel'. The Messiah of Aaron would be the anointed High Priest, and the Messiah of Israel would be the anointed king of the line of David set aside by God to do his work.

The New Testament clearly presents Jesus as the Davidic Messiah, but there are also indications of a theology of Jesus as the anointed High Priest of **eschatological times**, e.g., in Hebrews. There are some echoes in **patristic writings** as well of Jesus as a twofold Messiah.

> **eschatological
times** <
the last days

> **patristic writings** <
the writings of the early
church Fathers

SIXTY-SEVEN

Texts and

Versions

Based on sections by
Kevin G. O'Connell,
SJ and Raymond E.
Brown, SS in NJBC
article 68, 'Texts
and Versions'.

Introduction

The first thing when discussing the hundreds of different texts and versions of the books of the Bible is to distinguish between:

(a) the date (actual or supposed) of the original composition of the book (see the charts in Chapter 65, pages 329–31);

(b) the oldest existing manuscripts of the original

(c) the dates when translations of the books of the Bible were made into other languages and the oldest existing copies of them.

It is convenient to study the resources available by distinguishing between:

(1) the Hebrew Old Testament

(2) the Greek Old Testament

(3) the Greek New Testament

(4) the Aramaic, Syriac, Latin and Coptic Old Testament and New Testament

(5) the Bible in English

(1) The Hebrew Old Testament

No manuscript actually written by the author or editor of any Old Testament book is still in existence; all existing copies are the work of later scribes. Not only this, but each book has its own separate history. By the 2nd century AD the Hebrew text of the Old Testament books had become standardized; previously, as we know from the Dead Sea Scrolls in particular, the texts had varied to a considerable degree.

A unique survival into the Middle Ages is the Samaritan Pentateuch: a Hebrew text not subject to the standardization of the late 1st century AD. It is now represented in European libraries by copies ranging in age from the 12th to the 20th century AD. The oldest exemplar (11th century AD) is kept by the Samaritan community at Nablus.

Beginning about AD 900 the ben Asher family produced carefully edited **codices** of the prophets and of the whole Old Testament that have been considered the model Hebrew Bibles for study ever since.

> **codices** <
manuscripts bound as
books, not scrolls

The 'modern' period begins with printing. Printed Bibles with complete rabbinic interpretative aids appeared in the early 16th century. The text of the edition of 1524/25, by Jacob ben Chayim, for better or worse, remained the norm for all printed Hebrew Bibles until recent years.

(2) The Greek Old Testament

The Hebrew Old Testament was translated into Greek between the years 300 and 130 BC and was subsequently revised or 're-worked'. This translation is given the name 'Septuagint' and commonly referred to by the Latin numbers LXX because of the legend that it was produced with one effort by 72 (rounded to 70) elders in Egypt. By the late 4th century AD, Jerome stated, there were three traditions of the LXX in use, associated with Egypt, Caesarea and Antioch.

In total, in addition to some fragmentary texts from before AD 100, there are approximately 1,800 LXX manuscripts of a later date. Some of the most famous are: Codex Vaticanus and Codex Sinaiticus from the 4th century. Septuagint manuscripts are classified on the basis of the material used (papyrus or parchment) or the writing style (uncial, i.e. capital letters, or minuscule, i.e. lower case letters). The great codices were uncials.

Copies of the LXX contain not only books translated from the Hebrew collection, but also Old Testament books composed originally in Greek or preserved in full only in Greek. These are the deuterocanonical books listed in Chapter 65 above.

Codex Sinaiticus, 4th century AD, *showing the beginning of the Gospel of John. Reproduced by permission of the British Library*

(3) The Greek New Testament

The New Testament was written in Greek. The New Testament books accepted as canonical (included in the Scriptures) were composed mostly in the 1st century AD and were collected together in the 2nd century (Pauline epistles, Gospels) and the 3rd century. However, until fairly recently the oldest complete copies available to scholars dated from the 4th and 5th centuries, and there were variations among them. Two questions arose from this: (a) Which of the copies contains the best text of the New Testament? (b) How much change took place in the 200 to 300 years between the writing of the New Testament and these later copies?

Two things have helped scholars work on these questions: (i) Since 1890 a large number of fragments and some copies of individual New Testament books have been found in Egypt, written on papyrus and dating from the 2nd to the 8th centuries.

Papyrus fragments of an unknown gospel; Egypt, ca. AD *150. Reproduced
by permission of the British Library*

(ii) Closer examination of quotations from the New Testament by the early Fathers of the church helps to establish the New Testament text in their time.

How does this affect the reader of an English translation? Clearly a more recent translation can take account of recent discoveries. For example Luke 22:19c-20 was put in a footnote of the first edition of the Revised Standard Version but has now been brought up into the text in new editions.

(4) The Aramaic, Syriac, Latin and Coptic Old and New Testaments

Early translations into these languages can also help in discovering the original text. Translations into Latin have had a special influence on Western Christianity. Latin texts of the New Testament were in use towards the end of the 2nd century and for the whole Bible in the 3rd century; all the early translations were made from Greek.

By 383–384 Jerome had revised the older Latin versions of the Gospels; to what extent he influenced the Latin of other books of the New Testament is unclear. From about AD 389 Jerome started work on translating into Latin the Hebrew Old Testament text preserved among the Jews. The whole Bible in Latin stemming from this period, incorporating Jerome's work, is known as the Vulgate.

(5) The Bible in English

● (1) Before 1066 parts of the Bible were translated into Anglo-Saxon by the Venerable Bede (d. 735) and others. After the Norman conquest of England a complete Bible was produced in Anglo-Norman.

The first complete translation into English is associated with John Wycliffe (and his supporters) and dates from about 1382–84.

● (b) The Reformation led to the chain of translations that were the background of the King James Version, among them:

Tyndale's Bible (1523–31)
Coverdale's Bible (1535)

The Great Bible (1539–41)

Geneva Bible (1560): this was the Bible of Shakespeare,
John Bunyan and the Puritans

Bishops' Bible (1568)

- (c) After the Authorized Version or King James Bible (1611)
was produced, no further version was attempted until the
Revised Version (1881–85) which greatly improved the New
Testament because of knowledge of better Greek copies.
- (d) The Revised Standard Version (1946–52) and the New
Revised Standard Version (1989) have been able to use more of
the findings of modern scholarship.

Outside the King James tradition is the New English Bible
of 1961–70, revised in 1989.

- (e) Roman Catholic translations. In 1582–1609 Catholic
scholars exiled from England worked on the Continent to
produce from the Latin Vulgate the Douay–Rheims English
translation, and this was modernized 150 years later. After the
Second Vatican Council translations into English from the original languages (Hebrew, Greek) came into use in the Jerusalem
Bible (1966) and the New American Bible (1952–70). Both of
these have appeared in new editions.

HIGHLIGHT

Luke 2:12–14

Authorized Version

And this shall be a sign unto you; Ye shall find the babe wrapped in
swaddling clothes, lying in a manger.

And suddenly there was with the angel a multitude of the
heavenly host praising God, and saying,

Glory to God in the highest, and on earth peace, good will
toward men.

Douay–Rheims

And this shall be a sign unto you: You shall find the infant wrapped
in swaddling clothes and laid in a manger.

And suddenly there was with the angel a multitude of the
heavenly army, praising God and saying:

Glory to God in the highest; and on earth peace to men of good
will.

Revised Standard Version
'And this will be a sign for you: you will find a babe wrapped in swaddling cloths and lying in a manger.' And suddenly there was with the angel a multitude of the heavenly host praising God and saying,
> 'Glory to God in the highest,
> and on earth peace among men with whom he is pleased!'

New Revised Standard Version
'This will be a sign for you: you will find a child wrapped in bands of cloth and lying in a manger.' And suddenly there was with the angel a multitude of the heavenly host, praising God and saying,
> 'Glory to God in the highest heaven,
> and on earth peace among those whom he favours!'

Revised English Bible
'This will be a sign for you: you will find a babe wrapped in swaddling clothes, and lying in a manger.' All at once there was with the angel a great company of the heavenly host, singing praise to God:
> 'Glory to God in highest heaven,
> and on earth peace to all in whom he delights.'

New Jerusalem Bible (1985)
'And here is a sign for you: you will find a baby wrapped in swaddling clothes and lying in a manger.' And all at once with the angel there was a great throng of the hosts of heaven, praising God with the words:
> Glory to God in the highest heaven,
> and on earth peace for those he favours.

New American Bible (1986)
'And this will be a sign for you: you will find an infant wrapped in swaddling clothes and lying in a manger.' And suddenly there was a multitude of the heavenly host with the angel, praising God and saying:
> 'Glory to God in the highest
> and on earth peace to those on whom his favor rests.'

Interpreting the

Scriptures

(Hermeneutics)

Introduction

The material in this
chapter is digested
from sections by
Raymond E. Brown,
SS in NJBC article
71, 'Hermeneutics'.

The Greek word *hermeneia* covered a broad scope of interpretation. As applied to the Bible, 'hermeneutics' covers the different methods scholars have used to interpret the Scriptures and
the different kinds of meaning (senses) they have found in them.
We may distinguish the literal sense and a group of meanings
that go beyond the literal sense.

The literal sense

(I) Definition of the literal sense
Most scholars who write commentaries on the Bible work with
a definition of the literal sense closely resembling the following:
*The sense which the human author directly intended and which
the written words conveyed.* Notice the basic parts of that definition.

(A) AUTHOR The ancient understanding of an author was wider
than the popular modern idea of a writer. By modern standards
most of the biblical books are anonymous (do not mention the
writer) or pseudonymous (attributed to a famous person who
did not himself write them). None of the writers of the Gospels
identified himself by name. Many biblical books were the result
of complex growth and collective contributors: written at one
period and edited later, once or many times.

An intelligent debate centres on how to apply 'author' in discussing books where two figures, the writer and the editor, were separated by considerable distance of time and/or outlook. During the 'biblical period' of composition we often find considerable alteration of earlier written work. The composition of the book of Isaiah covered a span of at least 200 years; not only were new sections added to the original parts that came from Isaiah's lifetime, but also some additions had the result of modifying the meaning of the original.

In instances like this the literal meaning includes both the meaning that the parts originally had before editing and the meaning of the book after editing.

(B) CONVEYED BY WRITTEN WORDS This part of the definition of the literal meaning looks at what is actually written, for the author's intention does not become a sense of Scripture until it is effectively conveyed by writing. (The distinction between the author's thought world and the message he conveys in writing is important.)

What Jesus himself intended by his words is important, but Jesus was not a Gospel writer and often we do not know the context in which he actually spoke his words; thus it may be impossible to tell exactly what the words meant when he actually spoke them. The literal meaning of a Gospel passage is the meaning of Jesus' words understood by the individual evangelist, with the result that the same words can have different meanings according to the different contexts in which the respective evangelists have put them.

The idea of 'conveyed by written words' includes what the author expected them to mean to the readers. Discovering what an ancient author meant is no simple task. It may become plain only after much effort. Can one think a Bible thousands of years old is going to be easier to read than the newspaper published this morning?

(II) Types of Bible readers

Nevertheless, reading the Scriptures profitably must not become an elitist privilege. So let us concentrate on two important groups of Bible students and readers: professional and general.

(1) PROFESSIONAL READERS Those who will preach and teach (clergy, catechists, leaders of Bible classes) – those whose

knowledge of the Bible can affect how they communicate God's words to others – have to make realistic efforts to grasp what the authors of Scripture were trying to communicate.

Extremely useful to them are certain types of specialized knowledge.

• *A knowledge of the history of the biblical era.* The story of God's action in the history of a particular people is largely unintelligible when isolated from Near Eastern history.

• *A knowledge of the biblical languages.* Only a small percentage of those who study the Bible can be experts at Hebrew, Aramaic and Greek; yet some familiarity with the structure and thought pattern of these languages is essential for a type of professional biblical knowledge. Some of the basic words of biblical theology defy adequate translations into English, e.g., 'covenant', 'kindness', 'mercy' in the Old Testament, 'truth' in the New Testament; modern translations catch only a part of a wider meaning. With English as one's only language it is possible to have a good acquaintance with the Scriptures but scarcely a professional one.

(2) GENERAL READERS who will not be called on to preach or to teach the Bible but wish to grasp its message for their own lives and for nourishing the faith they share with others must also make some effort in their reading. The Judeo-Christian religion is based on a belief that God has communicated with human beings and that the Bible is a privileged vehicle of that communication.

Considerable portions of Scripture are clear to all because they voice universal sentiments, e.g., some of the Psalms and some simple stories of Jesus. Spiritual help and insight may be drawn from the Bible by those who have no technical knowledge; their appreciation may be based on experience shared with what the Bible narrates. For the ordinary, intelligent Jew or Christian, however, reading the Scriptures should involve some understanding of what the original author meant, since the message that he directed to his times is certainly part of God's inspired communication.

What the author wrote communicates meaning to us today, but he did not understand our circumstances or write to us in our times. When we try to draw from his text a message for our circumstances, there is always the problem of whether we achieve true communication or only impose on the text what we want to find. But the basic background information enabling the ordinary reader to perceive the literal sense intended by the author is not difficult to acquire, since scholars write and lecture in order to make commonly accepted views available to the general public.

Translations of the Bible into truly contemporary English can to a certain extent give us the equivalent of biblical ideas and help understanding. But much of the biblical imagery cannot be modernized; and if it can be interpreted, it cannot be dispensed with, for it is an important part of the biblical message, e.g. the symbolism of Revelation. The difference between the world view of the biblical author and our own means that we must help modern readers to understand the ancient mentality.

It is important to distinguish between what a biblical passage meant and what it means, but such meanings are not totally separable or unrelated. The biblical authors were not writing for the theologian, the preacher, or the ascetic. As a witness to God's revelation they gave us a library of books dealing with relations between God and human beings on the scale of life itself. Sometimes we can recognize how past generations read the Scriptures in a biased way and how they distorted them to their own purposes. We must be careful not to do the same ourselves, for precisely what we do not find relevant to our times may be God's principal word to another generation.

(III) The different kinds of literature in the Bible

In a modern library, books are classified according to the type of literature: fiction, poetry, history, biography, drama, etc. Similarly, the Jews classified the books of the Old Testament as Torah, Prophets and Writings; the Christian division of these same books into Pentateuch, Historical, Prophetic and Wisdom literature is also close to a distinction of literary types. Only in modern times, however, with the discovery of the literatures of people contemporary with Israel, have we realized just how many types of literature existed in antiquity.

The Old Testament

• POETRY There are many kinds of poetry in the Old Testament. There is epic poetry (long poems telling the stories of heroes) underlying some of the stories in the Pentateuch and in Joshua.

Lyric poetry (poetry and songs expressing sentiments and emotions) can be found in the Psalms and Canticle of Canticles (Song of Songs). Didactic (teaching) poetry is found in Proverbs, Sirach and Wisdom.

- DRAMA Elements of drama are found in Job.
- PROPHECY AND APOCALYPTIC (revelations, dreams, visions and oracles) are found in the prophetic books.
- HISTORY There are many forms of history: a factual, penetrating analysis as if by an eye witness, in the court history of David (2 Samuel 11–1 Kings 2); stylized, short, court records in Kings and Chronicles; a romanticized and simplified national saga in Exodus; tales of tribal heroes in Judges; stories of great men and women in the accounts of the patriarchs (Abraham to Jacob).

There is even pre-history in the Genesis narratives of the origin of humanity and of evil, which borrow legends from other nations and use them to communicate the Hebrew vision of reality.

- OTHER FORMS In addition there are fictional tales, parables, allegories, proverbs, maxims, love stories etc. The way different forms are combined in one book affects our understanding of its meaning.

Readers can learn from the literary form used what the author intended: for example, if Jonah is a fictional parable, then it is easy to recognize that the author is *not* giving a history of the relations between Israel and Assyria and is *not* presenting the story of a prophet in a whale's belly as a factual happening; rather, the author is using an imaginative way of telling a profound truth about God's love for the Gentile nations.

If the statement that the sun stood still in Joshua 10:13 comes from a poetic description in a victory song, the reader will judge it as poetic licence, rather than strictly as scientific observation.

If the stories of Samson are folktales, readers will not give them the same historical credence as the almost eye-witness narrative of David's court.

Many difficulties about the Bible have come from not recognizing the different literary forms in it, and treating as scientific history parts of the Bible which were not intended in that way.

The Gospels

The Gospels were not written as scientifically historical biographies of Jesus; they were written accounts of what the early church preached and taught about Jesus. They must be judged as accounts of the church's preaching and teaching – but as accounts that have true historical value, since they have been developed from what Jesus actually did and said. See Chapter 69 below, where church teaching about three stages of this development shows what manner of historicity is involved in the Gospels.

Two common misconceptions

1. Some think it dangerous to apply the theory of literary forms to the more sacred sections of the Bible. But if one correctly classifies a certain part of the Bible as fiction, one is not destroying the historicity of that section, for it never was history; one is simply recognizing the author's intention in writing that section.

2. There is a feeling that somehow recognizing that certain parts of the Bible were written as fiction weakens or challenges their inspiration. Yet God could inspire any kind of literature that is good (e.g. not pornography or lies). Biblical fiction is just as inspired as biblical history.

(IV) Literary history

After one has determined the type of literature involved, another step is to find out the literary history of the book or section one is studying. This is a special problem in biblical study because of the long history of editing. In the Gospels it is important to know whether a particular saying of Jesus has come to Luke or Matthew from Mark, from Q, or from one of the sources peculiar to the respective evangelist. Such literary history tells us about the intention of an author who drew on previous sources in composing his own work. The joining and the adaptation of those sources may reveal something of the meaning of the final composition.

(V) Conclusion

The literal meaning of some 90–95 per cent of the Bible can be determined by the ordinary rules of interpretation. There are

> **Q** <
the name given to an early collection of sayings of Jesus, now lost, but believed to lie behind both Matthew and Luke

some passages whose meaning eludes us because the text has been damaged or garbled, because they use rare words, because the author expressed himself obscurely, or because we do not have sufficient knowledge about the context in which they were composed. But that is the exception.

Going beyond the literal meanings

From very early days, thoughtful Bible readers have seen and tried to express, in many different ways, biblical meanings beyond the literal ones, i.e. beyond what the human author directly intended and conveyed in his written words.

For example, when a biblical book was placed in the larger context of the Old Testament, or New Testament, or whole Bible, passages gained meaning through relationships that could now be seen. The Church Fathers who commented on Scripture detected parallels between Old Testament events and people and their New Testament counterparts, for instance, between the patriarch Joseph sold and abandoned by his brothers and Jesus sold by Judas and abandoned by the Twelve. In modern times those studying the Bible with a background in sociology, **rhetorical** techniques, psychology, etc., have suggested depths of meaning of which the original author may have been unaware. Judgement must always be exercised as to whether such suggestions remain faithful to the literal sense and are defensible developments of it.

In particular, today, in order to build the faith and vision of Christian communities struggling for freedom, some would argue that the only way to read the Scriptures is as liberation of the oppressed. Their interpretation is centred less on texts and more on the people whose story of liberation is remembered in the Bible. They appeal to the story of Exodus. Others seek what may be an inspiration for women who are struggling for liberation, upheld by their belief in the God of creation and salvation.

The biblical authors were unaware of some of the issues that seem important to us. This does not mean that the modern causes are less important, but they must be set in the context of history. Some issues that were very important to Paul or Matthew (like the question of whether Gentiles could become

> **rhetorical** <
to do with the art of using
the language effectively

351

Christians without also becoming Jews) seem irrelevant to us today.

This should warn us that our burning issues today may seem irrelevant in the future, and an interpretation of Scripture simply in terms of modern issues may have little meaning several decades from now.

It is fair, however, to end by saying that most biblical commentaries written up to now have concentrated almost exclusively on the literal sense. Part of the task of those who preach, teach or explain the Bible is to take that literal sense and show how it is relevant to modern issues.

Two related topics in the study of hermeneutics

(1) Accommodation

This is a technical term used when a sense or meaning that does not come from Scripture is given to Scripture, for example, when Gregory the Great told his audience that the Gospel parable of the five talents referred to the five bodily senses, he was accommodating. A very frequent use of accommodation is in sermons, e.g., when preachers eulogized Pope John XXIII by citing John 1:6, 'There was sent by God a man whose name was John'.

But accommodation must be only an occasional use of Scripture and not the principal use. Preachers may find accommodation easy and may resort to it rather than taking the trouble to draw a relevant message from the literal sense of Scripture.

(2) Authoritative interpretation

One must be careful about the often-made claim that Roman Catholics say that the church interprets Scripture, while Protestants believe in private interpretation. Among many Protestants, there is a strong church tradition, with no suggestion that each individual can interpret Scripture *authoritatively*. Since the correct interpretation of Scripture requires education and effort, the average Protestant is no more capable of picking up the Bible and determining at a glance what the author meant than is the average Catholic, whence the importance of Sunday schools, religious education, and sermons. The difference between Protestant and Catholic opinions is often centred not on the existence of a traditional interpretation of Scripture but on the binding value given to that tradition.

As for Roman Catholics, in 99 per cent of the Bible, the church has not commented officially on what a passage does or does not mean. The church is primarily concerned with what Scripture means to its people; it is not immediately concerned with what Scripture meant to those who wrote it or first heard it – the literal sense.

Occasionally the church has rejected a proposed interpretation of a biblical text because it runs against what has been understood as church doctrine. The logic behind that authoritative rejection is that Scripture was written out of the life experience of God's people. In particular, the New Testament represents the written tradition of the early church. Therefore, *in the crucial matters of Christian faith and practice (morals)*, the subsequent church, which is the people of God, can recognize what is a true or false interpretation.

Yet even then, notice how restrained is the area of claimed authority: faith and morals. The church claims no absolute or direct authority over matters of biblical authorship, geography, chronology, and many issues of historicity. Moreover, official church teachers do not come to their conclusion about what a biblical passage does or does not mean by some sort of mystical instinct or direct revelation from on high. Traditional faith, good theology, and scholarship all enter into the decision. Like the other churches, the Roman Catholic Church needs and uses its theologians and biblical scholars.

Recent

Pronouncements

by the Roman

Catholic Church

The material in this chapter is digested from NJBC article 72, 'Church Pronouncements', by Raymond E. Brown, SS and Thomas Aquinas Collins, OP.

Introduction

For Roman Catholics there are three types of ecclesiastical pronouncements that relate to the Bible:

(1) Decrees of Ecumenical Councils

(2) Papal encyclicals

(3) Decrees of Church Teaching Offices, especially the Pontifical Biblical Commission (PBC).

They are referred to as 'conciliar', 'papal' and 'curial' documents. They must all be evaluated in the light of the time in which they were issued and the problems to which they were addressed. A fundamentalism in interpreting them is just as objectionable as a fundamentalism in interpreting Scripture.

Between 1941 and 1965 there was a rebirth of Catholic biblical studies which has continued to the present day.

(a) In 1943 Pope Pius XII announced that Catholic scholars should use modern tools in their work. The study of literary forms involving historical problems and new translations of the Bible from the original languages enabled Catholic scholars to catch up with Protestant scholarship, which had greatly outdistanced them during the preceding years.

(b) In 1955 the Secretary of the Pontifical Biblical Commission stated that Catholic scholars had complete freedom in their interpretation of the Bible except where previous statements of the Commission touched on faith and morals (and very few of them did). This meant that Catholics were now free to adopt modern positions on authorship and dating.

(c) In 1964 the PBC issued an 'Instruction on the Historical Truth of the Gospels', an encouraging document opening the way to honest biblical criticism in the very delicate field of Gospel historicity.

The modern Catholic biblical movement, approved by the Pope, confirmed by Vatican II and supported by the PBC, is now too much a part of the church to be rejected.

What the Councils of the church have said

VATICAN I stated that the church holds the books of Holy Scripture as sacred and canonical, because 'having been written by the inspiration of the Holy Spirit, they have God as their author and, as such, they have been handed down to the church itself'.

VATICAN II insisted that the teaching office of the church authentically interprets the word of God but that this teaching office is not above the word of God but serves it. On the role of the Bible in the life of the church; it provides a wealth of truly pastoral counsel. We note only the following points: A close parallel is drawn between Scripture and the sacraments ('The church has always venerated the divine Scriptures just as she venerates the body of the Lord'); there is an insistence that preaching must be nourished and ruled by Scripture; the Bible should be translated *from the original languages* and, where feasible, with the co-operation of non-Catholics; explicit encouragement is given to biblical scholars to continue their work; the study of Scripture is the soul of theology; the clergy must be well trained in Scripture for preaching and catechizing; bishops have an obligation to see that the means are provided whereby the people can be instructed in Scripture, by way of both translations and commentaries.

What the encyclical letters of the Popes have said

For over 100 years the Popes have issued encyclicals encouraging the reading of the Bible and wrestling with the issues presented by modern biblical studies. Statements by Popes Leo XIII and Pius X were wary of the dangers; but when the times changed, Pope Pius XII gave very positive encouragement, as explained above.

What the Church Teaching Offices have said

Many decrees of the PBC before 1940 were very conservative about biblical authorship and dating. Recent documents, however, are obviously the most significant and reflect the growing progressive attitude toward Catholic biblical studies since Pius XII. Six pronouncements are of particular interest, all but one ((4) below) from the PBC.

(1) On Scripture in seminaries (1950)
The following points were stressed: (i) the difference between the training of biblical specialists and that of future shepherds of the Lord's flock; (ii) the Scripture professor must enjoy the freedom to dedicate himself entirely to his work and not be compelled to teach other important subjects at the same time; (iii) the proper method of teaching biblical subjects in seminaries and religious colleges. Students are to be taught in a strictly scientific manner and to be made conversant with current biblical problems. Difficulties and obscurities in the Old Testament must be faced squarely and reasonable solutions given.

(2) On biblical meetings (1955)
Biblical associations should be encouraged; there should be meetings, 'Scripture days and weeks'; subjects should be properly selected. The jurisdiction of the competent Ordinary over all such gatherings is stressed, and technical and scientific meet-

ings should not be open to outsiders who would be poorly prepared to evaluate and understand what was being said.

(3) On Gospel historicity (1964)

This 'Instruction on the Historical Truth of the Gospels' begins with praise of biblical scholars as 'faithful sons of the church', and repeats Pius XII's command that they be treated with charity by other Catholics; in a very significant development this document recognized that the Gospels were the product of the tradition of the early church.

The interpreter should pay attention to *three stages* by which the doctrine and life of Jesus have come down to us: (1) *Jesus* explained his doctrine, adapting himself to the mentality of his listeners. His chosen disciples saw his deeds, heard his words, and were thus equipped to be witnesses of his life and doctrine. (2) The *apostles* after the resurrection of Jesus clearly perceived his divinity and proclaimed the death and resurrection of the Lord to others. While preaching and explaining his life and words, they took into account the needs and circumstances of their listeners. The faith of the apostles did not deform the message; but rather, with the fuller understanding they now enjoyed, they were able to pass on to their audiences what was really said and done by the Lord. The modes of speaking with which these preachers proclaimed Christ must be distinguished and properly assessed: catecheses, stories, testimonia, hymns, doxologies, prayers, etc. – the literary forms in use at the time. (3) The *sacred authors* committed to writing in four Gospels this primitive instruction that had been passed on orally at first and then in pre-Gospel writings. From the many things handed down, the evangelists 'selected some things, reduced others to a synthesis, and still others they explicated, keeping in mind the situation of the churches'. They adapted what they narrated to the situation of their readers and to the purpose they themselves had in mind.

(4) Mysterium Ecclesiae (1973; written by the Holy Office)

While insisting on the church's ability to teach infallibly, it acknowledges that in expressing revelation, 'difficulties also arise from the historical condition': (1) The meaning of faith pronouncements 'depends partly on the power of language used at a certain ... time'. (2) 'Some dogmatic truth is at first expressed incompletely (but not falsely) and later ... receives a fuller and more perfect expression.' (3) Pronouncements usually have a limited intention 'of solving certain questions or removing certain errors'. (4) The truths being taught, while 'distinct from the changeable conceptions of a given epoch', are sometimes phrased by church authority 'in terms that bear the traces of such conceptions'. Accordingly, so as to present more clearly the same truth, church authority may need to reformulate them.

(5) On women priests (not published)

In 1976, after two years of study of the Bible as to whether women could be ordained to the priestly ministry of the eucharist, the confidential results were 'leaked' to the press. Reportedly the PBC member scholars voted 17–0 that the New Testament does not settle the question in a clear way, once for all; and voted 12–5 that neither Scripture nor Christ's plan alone excluded the possibility.

(6) On Christology (1983)

The document recognizes different evaluations of Christ in the New Testament which it interprets generally in accord with the historical-critical method, e.g., the Gospels are not necessarily historical in minute details, nor are Jesus' sayings preserved verbatim; Jesus' resurrection 'by its very nature cannot be proved in an empirical way'; 'it is legitimate to begin a historical investigation about Jesus considering him a true human being ... as a Jew'.

Postscript

Finally, John Paul II in 1986 issued a strong attack on fundamentalism: 'Attention must be given to the literary forms of the various biblical books in order to determine the intention of the sacred writers. And it is most helpful, at times crucial, to be aware of the personal situation of the biblical writer, of the circumstances of culture, time, language, etc., which influenced the way the message was presented. ... In this way, it is possible to avoid a narrow fundamentalism which distorts the whole truth.'

Biblical

Geography

Introduction

We study biblical geography to improve our appreciation of the country that is the setting of the Bible. Modern maps draw upon:

The material in this chapter is digested from NJBC article 73, 'Biblical Geography', by Raymond E. Brown, SS and Robert North, SJ.

(1) Ancient maps

The earliest map of Palestine is a mosaic from AD 560, still partly surviving on the floor of an Orthodox church in Madeba, in Jordan.

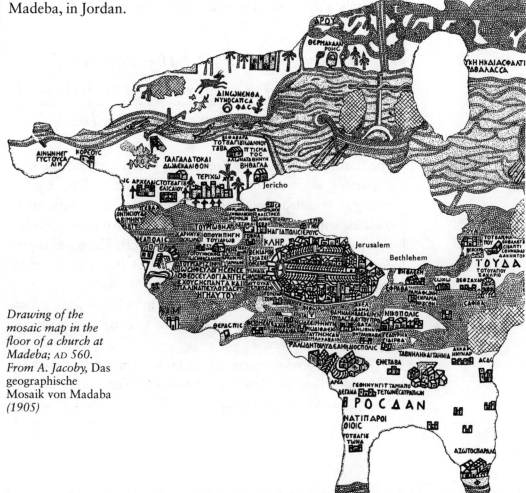

Drawing of the mosaic map in the floor of a church at Madeba; AD 560. From A. Jacoby, Das geographische Mosaik von Madaba *(1905)*

The only other truly ancient map is the Tabula Peutingeri-ana, a road map of the world reduced to a strip 25 feet long and 13 inches wide, divided into 12 sections. The original map may stem from the 3rd century AD, but the copy now existing is from 1265.

(2) Town lists in the Old Testament

These supply a genuinely biblical geography since they are expressed in the Bible's own terms and categories. They include Joshua 13–21; Genesis 10; 2 Chronicles 11:6–10; and the 'Threats against the Nations' in the Major Prophets.

(3) Classical and medieval writers

First, there are the classic authors, Herodotus, Strabo, Pliny, the geographer Ptolemy, and then Eusebius (AD 330), and Jewish and Muslim geographers. Data supplied by pilgrims and the Crusades are important, especially for New Testament sites (although, unfortunately, pilgrims were often shown alleged sites so identified because they were convenient to main roads rather than those based on real historical memories).

The geography of the countries surrounding Palestine in the biblical context before the Exodus

The narrow strip running from the Persian Gulf up the river Euphrates, westward toward the Syrian coast, and down again to Egypt is called the *Fertile Crescent* because it happens to coincide with a fringe of water sources that make food production possible around the edge of a vast desert. The water supply determined not only the farming centres but also the trade routes from one of the great export areas to another.

The movements of Abraham coincide with the major route from Babylonia to Egypt, i.e., from one tip of the Fertile Crescent to the other.

At the Babylonian end of the crescent stood *Ur*, which the Bible identifies as Abraham's homeland (Genesis 11:28–31). Near Ur was *Uruk*, the Erech of Genesis 10:10 (modern Warka) whose king Gilgamesh (*ca.* 2800 BC) became the hero of a flood story (cf. Genesis 6–9). From the excavations of this site have come the earliest known examples of writing.

From *ca.* 2500 on, Semites are found in Mesopotamia under the name of Amorites ('Westerners').

The greatest of the Semitic dynasties set up in this region was at *Babylon*, some 150 miles north-west of Ur and the site of a famous ziggurat, or temple tower, consisting of receding brick platforms (cf. Genesis 11:4–9 – the Tower of Babel).

A thousand years later Babylon once more became prominent in Israel's history when Judah was carried off into captivity to Babylonia (598 and 587 BC). From contact with this Babylonian region Israel knew the ancient mythology of creation, from which some of the imagery of Genesis 1–2 may have been borrowed.

Much to the east of this area is the mountainous region of *Persia*, whose king Cyrus liberated the Jews from Babylonian captivity in 538.

Haran (Harran), identified in the Bible as the place where Abraham lived after he migrated from Ur, is thought by many scholars to have been Abraham's original homeland. The towns of the region bear names that are variants of the names given by Genesis 11 to Abraham's relatives: Peleg (verse 16), Serug (verse 20), Terah and Nahor (verse 24), and Haran itself (verse 27).

Copper statuette of a goddess, ca. *1800–1700 BC, from Ras Shamra*

The topmost arc of the Fertile Crescent reaches from Haran west to the Euphrates. Where the river cuts the present Turkish frontier is the site of *Carchemish*. It became the scene of Nebuchadnezzar's decisive battle against Assyria.

From here the crescent route turns sharply south, along the line Aleppo–Hama–Damascus–Jerusalem. *Aleppo* was a very ancient city. On the seacoast, west of Aleppo, stood the city-state *Ugarit*, modern Ras Shamra. Archives found there since 1929 were written in Ugaritic and are very important for the study of the earliest form of Hebrew. Farther inland at *Ebla* (Tell Mardikh) excavations have unearthed tablets a millennium earlier than those of Ugarit, constituting the earliest attestations of written Semitic related to Hebrew (*ca.* 2300 BC). An even more important ancient city was *Damascus*. As a well-watered city on the fringe of the desert, it was a 'Last Chance' for travellers' supplies. Surprisingly, in describing Abraham's

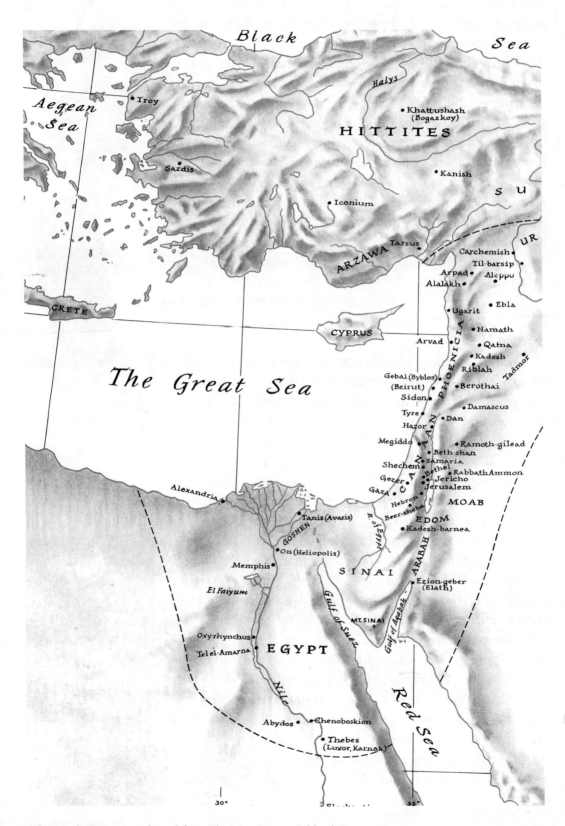

The Fertile Crescent. Adapted from The New Jerome Biblical Commentary

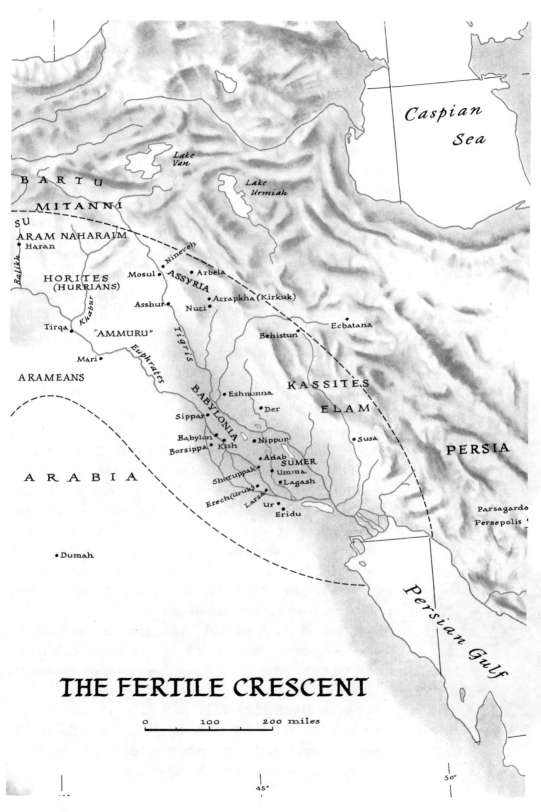

THE FERTILE CRESCENT

0   100   200 miles

passage (Genesis 12:5), the Bible makes no mention of these centres. It skips from Haran to the heart of Canaan, i.e., to what later would be called Samaria.

Canaan, the promised land, was small and off to the south-west corner of the Fertile Crescent. Yet it was in a strategic midposition between the rival merchant states: Arabia to the south, Egypt to the south-west, Hittites to the north, Babylon to the east. Hence, if the lines of traffic and population density are set in proper perspective, Canaan may be considered the 'hub' of the whole Fertile Crescent. Indeed, it was the hub of the whole universe known from Abraham's day down to Alexander the Great.

The Abraham clans, migrating from Mesopotamia, made no immediate claim to the land of Canaan. But Abraham personally is shown as getting a foothold in Canaan by the important experiences he had at the major centres of worship: Shechem, Bethel, Hebron, and Beersheba. In reality, his sojourn in the Holy Land is no more than a nomadic stopover on the route to the natural end of the journey, viz., Egypt.

In fact, Abraham does go on immediately to visit Egypt according to Genesis 12:10. But the migration to which he has given his name probably took place in successive waves over several generations, ending only with the descent of the Jacob tribes to join Joseph in Egypt (Genesis 46:7). Thus, the latter part of the Abrahamic migration turns out to be a part of what the historical records outside the Bible recognize as the movement of the Hyksos. 'Hyksos' is an Egyptian word meaning 'foreign rulers'. It refers to Asiatic immigrants who installed themselves in the north-east Delta and from there ruled Egypt between 1700 and 1560. In the eyes of some modern scholars, they were not an invasion but more a horde of peaceful infiltrators. They were mostly Semites.

It was in the north-east Delta, then, in the land that Genesis 47:6 calls Goshen, that Joseph's relatives settled. Here at the south-west tip of the Fertile Crescent the Bible sets the stage for the Exodus.

Ramses II (*ca.* 1290–1224) of the 19th Dynasty cluttered the whole Nile Valley with his building projects. In this land 'of Goshen' (Genesis 47:11) the descendants of the patriarchs were enslaved and put to work on the building projects.

Inscribed bases of Egyptian scarabs from the Hyksos period

The route of the Exodus

The much-disputed route of the Exodus according to most scholars is related to the problem of the location of Mount Sinai. Sinai and Horeb are not separate peaks, but names for the same place, occurring in different traditions of the Pentateuch.

Routes for the Exodus suggested by scholars include a northern and a southern direction. Indeed some scholars think of several exoduses, following different routes. The theory of the northern route suggests that the Israelites headed east directly across the north part of the 'Sinai' peninsula to Kadesh-barnea. This was the shortest and the natural route from Egypt to Canaan. It is marked on the map as the way of the Wilderness of Shur. It is explicitly excluded by Exodus 13:17, but in terms involving the Philistines who were not there at the time. Although they may have raided the coast of Canaan in the 13th century, they do not seem to have had firm control of the south Canaan coasts before 1180–1150, long after the Exodus.

The route of the Exodus. The New Jerome Biblical Commentary

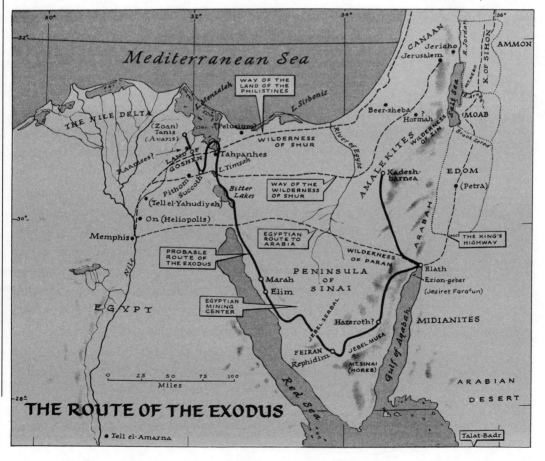

THE ROUTE OF THE EXODUS

Other biblical statements fit better with a southern route for the Exodus, involving a detour far to the south. At the traditional site of Mount Sinai, i.e. Jebel Musa itself, there is a steep precipice named Safsafa towering over a vast plain. The nearness of water and the rugged splendour of the surroundings have convinced most moderns that this is the mountain of Exodus 19:2. However, the Greek tradition related to St Catherine's Monastery focuses attention on the opposite east end of the Jebel Musa range.

After the appearance of God at Sinai, in a period of about 40 years, the Israelites under Moses are said to have moved on to Transjordan. The route from Mount Sinai to Edom is indicated twice in the Bible, once with remarkable minuteness in Numbers 33, and later more briefly in Deuteronomy 1. Yet the list of places is in effect unusable, for most of the sites are unknown to us. Further, there are discrepancies in the two biblical lists and in the descriptions of the route followed in the direction of Ezion-geber on the Gulf of Aqabah. Perhaps, as at the Exodus from Egypt, different routes were followed by different groups. Eventually the Israelites came to Mount Nebo at the north-east corner of the Dead Sea (Salt Sea on the map) where Moses died and was buried (Deuteronomy 34:5).

Climate of Palestine

The climate varies according to the main natural features of the land: the coast, the mountains, the Rift or Jordan Valley. Basically there are two seasons: the hot, dry summer and the cool, wet winter.

The temperature in the Palestinian mountains is about 10°F cooler than that of the coast. The summer in the mountains, at Jerusalem for instance, brings hot sunny days (average 85°F) and cool nights (65°F). Uncomfortable weather in the mountains is caused by windstorms, whether it is the wind that drives rain in from the Mediterranean or the burning wind (sirocco or khamsin) that sweeps in from the desert in May and October (Isaiah 27:8; Jeremiah 4:11). Jesus knew of both (Luke 12:54–55); and in the wintertime he circulated in the only porch of the Temple that offered protection from the prevailing wind (John 10:23). The part of the Rift Valley that is far below

Palm tree

sea level, e.g., at Jericho, bakes in intense heat in summer (over 100°F) but serves as an ideal winter resort.

The rainfall of Palestine also varies according to region. The land nearer the Mediterranean tends to get more rain, for the Palestinian mountain range acts as a barrier to storms coming in from the sea, forcing them to dump their water on the west side of the mountains. Correspondingly, the east slopes are much drier. A good year is one in which the autumnal or early rain falls in October at seedtime, and the late or spring rain falls in March and April just before harvest. Biblical references to these two rains are numerous: Deuteronomy 11:14; Hosea 6:3; Jeremiah 5:24; Joel 2:23. The rainfall made an extraordinary impression on the Israelites when they were fresh from Egypt, a land where water comes from the Nile and not from the heavens (Deuteronomy 11:10–25). Snow is not unusual in the Palestinian mountains; e.g., in Jerusalem, Bethlehem, or Hebron; and in the Transjordanian mountains snowfalls sometimes block the roads.

The seasonal character of the rain means that water has to be stored in cisterns for the dry season, unless a town is fortunate enough to be near a spring and thus have flowing or 'living' water (whence the imagery in Ezekiel 47:1; Zechariah 13:1; John 4:10–14). Characteristic of Palestine is the wadi, i.e., a valley that is dry in the summer but becomes a channel of flash floods and strong streams in the rainy season. When dry, these wadis serve as roads from the valleys into the mountains.

The geography of Palestine

Physical features

The biblical story was enacted on a small stage – the capitals of the divided monarchy, Samaria in the north and Jerusalem in the south, were less than 35 miles apart. The length of Palestine from Dan to Beer-sheba is only 150 miles and the width from the Mediterranean to the Jordan valley would be only some 30 miles in the north and 50 miles at the level of the Dead Sea.

The larger area of the Negeb and Transjordan (the land east of the Jordan), as well as Israel proper, lends itself to a

Cedar tree

367

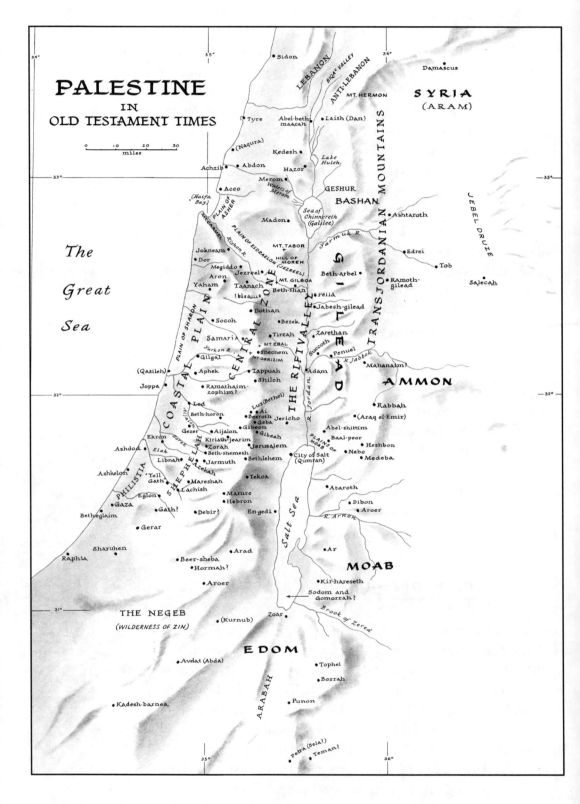

Palestine in Old Testament times, showing the chief geographical divisions. Adapted from The New Jerome Biblical Commentary

division of four roughly parallel strips running north to south. From east to west these strips are:

(1) The Transjordanian mountains
(2} the Rift Valley
(3) the Mediterranean coastal plain
(4) the Palestinian mountains and the central zone.

(1) TRANSJORDAN The Transjordanian mountains are higher than the Palestinian. They are cut across east–west by a series of tremendous canyons or gorges, through which flow streams. From south to north, the divisions of the Transjordan are:

(A) **Edom** The mountainous plateau of Edom, over 5,000 feet in height, is about 70 miles long and about 15 miles wide. The mountain dwellers of the Edomite plateau, who lived 'in the clefts of the rock' (Obadiah 3), could not support themselves simply by farming or herding flocks. They mined copper from the mountains, and they taxed the travellers on the King's Highway, which ran north–south along their plateau. This foreign contact may have given them their reputation for knowledge (Jeremiah 49:7).

(B) **Moab** The territory of the Moabite plateau is quite unlike the forbidding reaches of Edom to the south. True, crops like wheat and barley can be planted only in a small area; but the tableland offers rich grazing for flocks. Even today the black tents of the bedouin dot the land as they pasture their flocks – the economic descendants of Mesha, king of Moab, a sheep breeder, who 'had to deliver annually to the king of Israel 100,000 lambs and the wool of 100,000 rams' (2 Kings 3:4). The wealth of Moab may have accounted for the pride of which Jeremiah 48:29 and Isaiah 25:10–11 accuse its inhabitants.

(C) **Ammon** If the frontiers of Ammon were vague, its capital was indisputably Rabbah or *Rabbath Ammon*, the modern Amman, capital of Jordan. The formidable mountain citadel of this city gave strong resistance to David's army (2 Samuel 11:1, 14–21; cf. Amos 1:14). The most valuable possession of the Ammonites was the fertile valley of the upper Jabbok river, which begins near Amman and goes north before swinging west into the Jordan valley.

(D) **Gilead.** The Jabbok river, as it comes down from the Transjordanian mountains into the Jordan valley, divides Gilead into two parts. The terrain gave small forces an advantage over a large army, so that this territory became a place of refuge, e.g., for David when he fled from Absalom (2 Samuel 17:24).

(E) **Bashan.** The mountains of Gilead drop off to a fertile table-land. These are the rich plains of Bashan. The rainfall is adequate here, for the low hills of Galilee on the Palestinian side permit the storms from the Mediterranean to pass over and to water Bashan. In many areas of the plains the soil is rich volcanic alluvium. The combination of rainfall and fertility makes Bashan the great wheat granary of the region and very good pasture. The Bible speaks of the fatness of the animals in Bashan as proverbial (Psalm 22:12; Amos 4:1; Ezekiel 39:18). In eastern Bashan, sturdy oaks grew on the slopes of the Jebel Druze, so that Bashan could be grouped with Lebanon for the splendour of its trees (Isaiah 2:13; Nahum 1:4; Ezekiel 27:6; Zechariah 11:1–2). The forests of Bashan offered refuge to those in trouble (Psalm 68:15, 22; Jeremiah 22:20).

(2) THE RIFT VALLEY The great Rift Valley through which the Jordan river now flows from above the Huleh Basin in the north to the Dead Sea in the south, is a great cleft in the earth, which descends to 1,300 feet below sea level at the Dead Sea, and continues south of the sea as the barren valley of the Arabah that opens into the Gulf of Aqabah.

It is not certain that any of the Palestinian mountains was ever volcanic, although earthquakes are well attested in antiquity (Amos 1:1; perhaps in Joshua's damming of the Jordan in Joshua 3:16; a destruction at the Qumran settlement in 31 BC) and have also occurred in modern times (Safed in 1837; Nazareth, 1900; Jaffa, 1903; Jericho, 1927). **The sources of the Jordan** In the shadow of Mount Hermon the Jordan river is born of four streams fed by water from the mountains of Lebanon. This beautiful region of waterfalls and turbulent springtime torrents is eloquently lyricized in Psalm 42:6–7. The shrine of Dan, an important religious centre since the time of the judges (Judges 18:30; Amos 8:14), was one of the two official shrines of the Northern Kingdom (1 Kings 12:29; 2 Kings 10:29). The religious associations of the Dan territory carried over into New Testament times. The town was rebuilt as Caesarea Philippi; Jesus and his disciples visited it, and it was there that Peter acknowledged Jesus as the Messiah (Mark 8:27). Some have suggested that Mount Hermon, towering over Caesarea, was the 'high mountain' of the transfiguration in the next chapter of Mark (9:2).

Lake of Galilee As the Jordan flows down to 675 feet below sea level, we come to the centre stage of Jesus' ministry and truly one of the most beautiful places in Palestine – the heart-shaped lake, 12–13 miles long and 7–8 miles wide, at its broadest, called in Hebrew Chinnereth ('harp,' whence the plain of Gennesaret in Matthew 14:34, the Lake of Gennesaret in Luke 5:1).

The lake's blue waters are framed by cliffs on nearly every side except the north where green plains, especially in the north-west, provide an attractive border. Its beauty has never been lost on people.

Capernaum on the north-north-west shore was Peter's home (according to Mark 1:21, 29). This town became Jesus' headquarters, and its synagogue heard his preaching (Luke 4:31; 7:5; John 6:59). Some 4 miles away, across the Jordan and on the north-north-east shore, may have stood *Bethsaida*, connected with the multiplication of the loaves (Luke 9:10; John 6:1; but cf. Mark 6:45) and, according to John 1:44; 12:21, the home of Peter, Andrew and Philip. Mary Magdalene, once possessed by seven demons (Luke 8:2), seems to have come from *Magdala* on the western shore of the lake, while the demoniac of Mark 5:1 prowled in tombs on the eastern shore of the lake. There is little of Old Testament importance in this area.

Jordan valley Between the Lake of Galilee and the Dead Sea, a distance of 65 miles, the Jordan falls from 675 feet below sea level to 1,300 feet below. On both sides the mountains rise 1,000 feet and more above the rift that tore them apart.

Roughly through the centre of the Rift Valley runs the Jordan river, a narrow stream only 60–80 feet wide at the traditional spot for Joshua's crossing to Jericho. Little wonder then that Naaman the Syrian found the rivers of Damascus more impressive (2 Kings 5:12). As it twists and meanders, especially midway down from the Lake of Galilee and toward the south, the Jordan has worn into the Rift Valley floor a deep bed of its own, called the Zor. In places the Zor is a mile wide and 150 feet deep. Flooded in springtime when the melting snows of Hermon engorge the Jordan, the Zor is often an impenetrable thicket of shrubs and stunted trees, which in antiquity offered a habitat to wild animals, including lions (Jeremiah 49:19; Zechariah 11:3). Wisely does Jeremiah 12:5 stress the danger to those who fall down in the jungle of the Jordan (also 49:19).

About 8 miles north of the Dead Sea, on the western side set back from the river, stood the pearl of the south Jordan valley, the city of *Jericho*, one of the oldest cities on earth and the site of extremely important archaeological excavations.

Dead Sea The Jordan river comes to an end in the Dead Sea, the most dramatic feature of the Rift Valley. Fringed by mountains on both sides, roughly 50 miles long by 10 miles wide, the Dead Sea (Sea of the Arabah, Salt Sea) is the lowest point on the earth's surface, 1,300 feet below sea level with a water depth of another 1,300 feet in the north. The Dead Sea can claim to be the world's most unusual body of water. Over 27 per cent of its composition is solid chemical matter (salt, chlorides and bromides); its salt content increases constantly because the seven million tons of water that flow into it daily have no outlet, and the constant evaporation leaves residual solids. The 45 billion tons of chemical it contains are an attraction for the chemical-extraction industry both in Israel and in Jordan, but even this will not prevent the shallow southern end of the sea from being ultimately silted up. No fish can exist in such water – at least until Ezekiel's vision will be fulfilled and a life-giving stream will flow from Jerusalem to sweeten the Dead Sea as far as En-gedi (47:10). Neither the intense heat nor the parched terrain in this area is conducive to large-scale settlement (although the region serves as a winter resort).

On the north-west shore, near the spring called Ain Feshkha, stand the ruins of Qumran, the settlement of the community that produced the Dead Sea Scrolls. Halfway down on the west shore is the more celebrated water source of En-gedi (Canticles 1:14), where David sought refuge from Saul (1 Samuel 23:29). The isolated mountain fortress of Masada, two-thirds of the way down the sea, was the last stronghold in the Jewish struggle against the Romans in AD 73, and the valleys between En-gedi and Masada are dotted with caves that were outposts of Jewish resistance – caves that yielded additional Dead Sea Scrolls.

On the southern end of the western shore stands the great salt mountain Jebel Usdum, whose name recalls biblical Sodom and the pillar of salt that once was Lot's wife (Genesis 19:26). It is generally thought that *Sodom* and *Gomorrah* and the three other cities of the plain (Genesis 18:16ff.) lie under the waters at the southern end of the sea.

Arabah This valley, 100 miles long, went from the salt marshes at the end of the Dead Sea south to the Gulf of Aqabah. This was the focal point of Solomon's copper industry. Copper was mined from the hills and crudely smelted in the valley to meet the needs of Israel's greatest builder. At the southern end was Ezion-geber, the port built by Solomon for launching his fleet, and for trade with Somaliland, Arabia and the East.

(3) THE COASTAL PLAINS From Philistine Gaza in the south to Phoenician Tyre in the north, the Mediterranean coast is about 130 miles long. The southern part, Philistia, was dominated by 'Sea Peoples' or Philistines, who invaded (*ca.* 1200 BC) from the Mediterranean islands. Farther north, past modern Tel Aviv, is *Mount Carmel*, the most noticeable natural feature on the coast, jutting out into the sea and forming the large bay that harbours Haifa and Acco. The view from Carmel over Haifa Bay is breathtaking, and this was traditionally the place of the dramatic confrontation of Elijah and the priests of Baal (1 Kings 18:20ff., especially verse 43). Haifa itself is not a biblical site.

(4) THE CENTRAL ZONE OF PALESTINE This was the most important area of Palestine as far as biblical history is concerned. There are five main divisions.

(A) Negeb This is the southernmost area, called in the Bible the Wilderness of Zin (Numbers 20:1; 33:36). The region was important because commerce from Transjordan or from the Gulf of Aqabah (e.g. from Ezion-geber in Solomon's time) had to travel up the gorges and wadis of the Negeb in order to reach Beersheba and the rest of Palestine.

(B) Territory of the House of Judah. Under the first three kings, Saul, David and Solomon there was a united kingdom which included all the twelve tribes (see map on page 30). But in 922 BC the northern part of the kingdom broke away to become

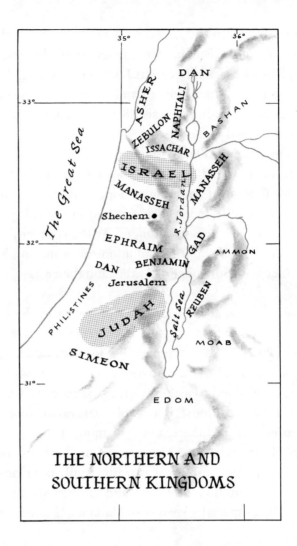

THE NORTHERN AND
SOUTHERN KINGDOMS

a separate kingdom: this is called the Northern Kingdom (or Israel, or Samaria). The territory of the House of Judah covered the Southern Kingdom (or Judah), and its chief cities were Hebron, Bethlehem and Jerusalem. (See the map above.)

Hebron was historically the centre of Judah's power; David was crowned there as Judah's first king (2 Samuel 2:1–4). Hebron was where Sarah and Abraham were buried (Genesis 23; 25:9). At the nearby shrine of Mamre Abraham received the divine promises and saw God (Genesis 13:14–18; 18). Isaac also died at Hebron (Genesis 35:27). Today the tombs of the patriarchs are venerated under the mosque, once a church, that stands in the middle of Hebron, adjacent to magnificent Herodian remains.

Bethlehem (or Ephrathah), 15 miles north of Hebron and

5 miles south of Jerusalem, was not in itself an important city of Judah (Micah 5:2), but it acquired importance as the ancestral home of David (Ruth 1:1; 4:22; 1 Samuel 16; Luke 2:4; Matthew 2:5; John 7:42). A church built by Constantine and modified by the Crusaders stands over the grotto traditionally associated with Jesus' birth, and fields east of Bethlehem are most suitable to have been the shepherds' fields of Luke 2:8, 15.

Jerusalem, 'the holy mountain, fairest of heights, the joy of all the earth' (Psalm 48:2), did not come into Judah's possession until David's time (*ca.* 1000). In a stroke of genius, after capturing Jerusalem (2 Samuel 5:6–10), he moved his capital from the provincial and clearly southern Hebron to this border city with no northern or southern affiliations. We read of its Canaanite prehistory as a shrine of El Elyon and perhaps of Zedek in Genesis 14:18.

The mount covered by Jerusalem in its era of greatness is

Meanders in the river Jordan

375

set off on three sides by valleys. On the east there is a sharp decline into the Kidron (Cedron), a wadi that has a swift stream when rainfall is plentiful. This valley separates Jerusalem from the higher Mount of Olives, from which one gains a splendid view of the city (2 Samuel 15:23, 30; 2 Kings 23:6; John 18:1). Despite its narrowness, the Kidron is traditionally identified as the Valley of Jehoshaphat where Joel 3:2–12 places the gathering of all nations for judgement. On the west of Jerusalem is the Valley of Hinnom. This valley (= Ge-Hinnom [Gehenna]) acquired an unpleasant reputation because it was used for the burning of rubbish and the worship of pagan gods (1 Kings 11:7; 2 Kings 16:3; 23:10), whence the derived meaning of Gehenna as 'hell' (Matthew 5:22).

The west hill of Jerusalem is the higher and more impressive, and for centuries was identified (e.g., by the ancient Jewish writer Josephus) as Zion or ancient Jerusalem. Today it is universally recognized that the city of David and Solomon was on the east hill. The general area of the Temple is occupied today by the superb Muslim mosque of 'the Dome of the Rock'.

(C) Territory of the House of Joseph This was a mountainous strip some 45 miles long, running north from Judah to the Plain of Esdraelon. It was dominated from about 1220 to 720 BC by the tribes descended from Joseph: Ephraim and half of Manasseh (Genesis 49). In 992 BC this became the Northern Kingdom. These tribes were rivals of the House of Judah for power. We note particularly some cities of this area running from south to north and north-west.

(A) EPHRAIM *Bethel* was just inside the border of Ephraim when it was strong (Joshua 16:1). Once called Luz (Joshua 18:13), Bethel was a sanctuary figuring in both the Abraham and Jacob cycles of narratives (Genesis 12:8; 13:3–4; 28:10–22; 35:1–16). Excavations at Bethel show that it was spectacularly destroyed in the 13th century, information that may correspond with the statement in Judges 1:22: 'The house of Joseph went up against Bethel.' Bethel served as a shrine and a rallying place in the time of the judges (Judges 20:18); and Jeroboam I, after the division into Northern and Southern kingdoms in 922, made Bethel, along with Dan, one of the national shrines of the Northern Kingdom. Worship at Bethel (just as worship at Jerusalem) became corrupt and superstitious; Amos (7:10–17) castigated the people there, and Hosea (4:15; 5:8; see gloss in Joshua 7:2) mockingly changes its name from Bethel ('House of God') to Beth-aven ('House of Wickedness').

Shiloh, standing on a rocky plain in the heart of Ephraim's territory, had its greatest importance in the period of the judges. It was a place of assembly for the tribes (Joshua 22:9, 12; Judges 21:19ff.), and the Ark of the Covenant came to rest there in a permanent building.

(B) MANASSEH (SAMARIA) From the time of the formation of the Northern Kingdom (922), the area controlled by Manasseh emerged into greater importance.

Shechem. In south Manasseh, as one descends from Ephraim, the broad plain of Mahneh is singularly beautiful. The west of the plain is hemmed in by the high mountains of Gerizim (2,910 feet) and Ebal (3,100 feet). Between these two mountains, going from east to west, is a valley designed by nature to be the main thoroughfare for traffic from Judah and Ephraim to the north. At the mouth of this valley stood Shechem (Sichem, modern Balatah), the most important Palestinian biblical city after Jerusalem.

It was at Shechem that the northern tribes rejected Rehoboam son of Solomon in favour of Jeroboam I as king (1 Kings 12:1–25). This king made Shechem his temporary capital; and even when the centre of administration and power in the Northern Kingdom moved to Samaria, Shechem remained the focus of the covenant renewal ceremony (from which Deuteronomy drew its legal code). In New Testament times Jesus stopped at the well of Shechem for a drink and talked with a Samaritan woman (John 4:4–42). This story reminds us that Mount Gerizim's slope overlooking Shechem was the holy place of Samaritan worship and the site of the Samaritan temple. Today the Samaritans survive at Nablus (Roman Neapolis) built two miles farther west in the same valley; and at Passover they proceed to Gerizim's summit to slaughter animals for their celebration – the only remnant of the blood-sacrifice of Israel.

Samaria. Cutting west through the Gerizim–Ebal valley and then north we find before us the majestic hill of Samaria, the greatest capital of Israel. (We have an idea of the short

377

distances in this area if we realize that Samaria is only 7 miles from Shechem.)

An isolated hill, crowned by the magnificent buildings of Omri and his son Ahab, Samaria must have been the most beautiful city in Israel. For 150 years this city so dominated the Northern Kingdom that Israel could be called 'Samaria', just as Judah was sometimes called 'Jerusalem' (Ezekiel 16:46 – thus it is important for the reader of the Bible to distinguish between the city of Samaria and the district of Samaria; the latter means the territory of Manasseh or sometimes the whole Northern Kingdom). Even after its fall to the Assyrians in 722, the city retained its strategic importance as the capital successively of an Assyrian province of Samaria, of a Persian province (Ezra 4:17; Nehemiah 3:33–34), and of a Syrian district (1 Maccabees 10:30). Herod the Great rebuilt the city as Sebaste in honour of the emperor Augustus (Greek *sebastos*), but the district retained the name of Samaria.

(D) Plain of Esdraelon (Jezreel) (i) INTERNATIONAL IMPORTANCE. Esdraelon was the plain through which ran the main route between Egypt and Syria. The plain's south side is flanked by the Carmel mountain range, and armies or commerce that came up the coast from Egypt through Philistia and along the fringes of the Plain of Sharon had to go through one of the four passes in the Carmel range to reach the plain. Consequently, four fortresses guarding these passes were built on the southern edge of Esdraelon: Jokneam, Megiddo, Taanach, and Ibleam. The route past *Megiddo* was strategically the most important, as corroborated by an ancient Egyptian report: 'The capture of Megiddo is as the capture of a thousand towns.' The book of Revelation (16:16) places the final world battle at Armageddon (Mount Megiddo).

(ii) NATIONAL IMPORTANCE. Esdraelon was important also on the scale of internal Israelite history. As long as it remained in Canaanite hands (Judges 1:27), the northern tribes (Issachar, Naphtali, Zebulun and Asher) were cut off from the house of Joseph. Consequently, in the period of the judges, there was a series of battles for control of the plain.

When Omri and Ahab made Samaria the capital of the Northern Kingdom, they paid both the beauty and the importance of the Valley of Esdraelon a tribute by keeping a palace at

Seal of Shema, servant of Jeroboam, found at Megiddo

the town of *Jezreel*, standing at the west entrance to the corridor leading to Bethshan (called the Valley of Jezreel). The tragic incident of Naboth's vineyard and the bloody death of Jezebel took place here (1 Kings 21:1; 2 Kings 9:30; 10:11). The prophet Hosea named his son Jezreel as a threat of divine punishment for the crimes committed there: 'I will break the bow of Israel in the Valley of Jezreel.' Yet, playing on the meaning of the name Jezreel ('May God sow'), Hosea also saw in this name a divine promise of fertility: 'The earth shall respond to the grain and wine and oil, and these shall respond to Jezreel, and I will sow him for myself in the land' (Hosea 1:4–5; 2:22–23).

In New Testament times Jesus was in the Plain of Esdraelon when he raised to life the son of the widow of *Nain* (Luke 7:11–17), a town on the north slope of the hill of Moreh.

(E) Galilee When we cross the Plain of Esdraelon on our journey north, we come to an area which figures surprisingly little in Old Testament history but which for Christians was to crown the expectations of that history; for on the north side of Esdraelon rise the hills of Galilee, and just three miles into these hills stands *Nazareth*, the home of Jesus.

Galilee seems to have been outside the mainstream of Israelite life as it is preserved in the biblical records. Galilee fell to the Assyrians after the Syro-Ephraimite war of 735 (2 Kings 15:29); yet Isaiah (9:1–2), speaking of the land of Zebulun and Naphtali as 'Galilee of the Gentiles', promised that the people there who walked in darkness would see a great light. In Hellenistic times there was a heavy population of Jews in Galilee (1 Maccabees 5:9–23).

The terrain of south Galilee is marked by a series of basins watered by drainage from the surrounding hills. The floors of the basins are fertile alluvium and lend themselves to farming, while the towns climb the adjacent hillsides. This was the region described so vividly in Jesus' parables: fields separated by hedgerows and stone fences; flocks pastured on the hills; towns set on mountain tops; etc. Two towns of south Galilee mentioned in the New Testament, Nazareth and *Cana*, are built on the sides of rich basins.

The material in this
chapter is digested
from NJBC article
74, 'Biblical
Archaeology', by
Robert North, SJ
and Philip J. King.

SEVENTY-ONE

Biblical

Archaeology

Introduction

Archaeology is one way of learning 'more about the Bible from
outside the Bible'.

Great names in the history of biblical archaeology

Among the most famous 19th- and 20th-century biblical
archaeologists are Félicien de Saulcy, Charles Clermont-Gan-
neau, William Flinders Petrie, Fr L.-Hughes Vincent, Gottlieb
Schumacher, William F. Albright, Kathleen Kenyon, Yigael
Yadin and G. Ernest Wright. The pioneering work of Heinrich
Schliemann in Greece and Turkey was also important.

*Letter from Yapahu,
ruler of Gezer in
Palestine, asking the
Pharaoh for help
against the Hapiru
(?Hebrews). Baked
clay tablets, 14th
century* BC.
*Reproduced by
courtesy of the
Trustees of the British
Museum*

(1) SCHLIEMANN proved that successive settlements of the past could be dug up out of the ground, one from beneath the other. This was basically an application of excavation techniques developed in Italy, especially by the rediscovery of Pompeii in 1790.

(2) DE SAULCY performed, in 1863, the earliest Palestinian excavations in north-west Jerusalem. He discovered 'Royal Tombs' containing several sarcophagi, one with an inscription. The burial chambers belonged to a Persian queen, Helen of Adiabene, who embraced the Jewish religion at the time of Christ, rather than to King David and his sons, as de Saulcy thought.

(3) CLERMONT-GANNEAU made some of the most important early discoveries in the Holy Land. He found the first of two surviving stone inscriptions threatening death to any non-Jew who entered the Temple area.

(4) PETRIE made the first stratified excavation in Palestine at Tell el-Hesi near Ashkelon in 1890. There he brilliantly exemplified the principle that was to become normative for all Palestine digging: 'Broken pottery, even without an inscription, is a sure clue to dating.' His contributions have been brilliantly continued by other British archaeologists in the Holy Land.

(5) FR VINCENT, a Dominican, went to Palestine in 1891 and stayed until his death in 1960. He performed the unique function of interpreting and *correlating* all the excavations that were to be carried on in Palestine. No less significant were his own original researches at Hebron, Emmaus-Nicopolis, and what was thought to be the 'Stone Pavement' (John 19:13) in Jerusalem.

(6) SCHUMACHER excavated Megiddo in 1903 and published important researches on the Gadara region.

(7) ALBRIGHT, an American, came to Jerusalem in 1920. He was a prodigious linguist and sparked international co-operation, especially through the (Journal of the) Palestine Oriental Society, the early presidents of which include a French Jesuit and an Arab Franciscan. His diggings at Gibeah (1922), Bethel (1927), Bethzur (1931) and at Tell Beit Mirsim, south of Hebron (1926–32) were significant.

(8) KATHLEEN KENYON in 1952 reopened excavations at Jericho. She showed that the brick walls which Joshua was

thought to have destroyed were in fact 1,000 years older; and that the Jericho mound called Tell es-Sultan was almost completely abandoned throughout all dates possible for the major biblical references, from 1500 BC through the periods of Joshua and of Hiel (860 BC; 1 Kings 16:34). Only *ca.* 800 was the site reoccupied. She then did equally important work at Jerusalem.

(9) YADIN was the outstanding representative of the immense boom in archaeological research encouraged by the Zionist movement in Israel. His father, Eleazar Sukenik, had also been an archaeologist. Sukenik and Yadin bought many of the Dead Sea Scrolls for Israel. From 1960 Yadin explored the En-gedi desert and Masada; but his greatest work was the excavation of Hazor, sponsored by the Hebrew University.

(10) WRIGHT was second only to Albright in his influence on the archaeology of Palestine. Today there is hardly an American dig that does not bear the stamp of Wright, either directly or through his students.

Where to dig

The pioneer archaeologists tended to dig at or near big centres like Jerusalem. The very fact that a centre has remained important through the centuries makes it more difficult to excavate. Such a settlement has grown by the gradual addition of new buildings. Those of an earlier period either continue in use, or their materials have been transformed into the buildings of later periods. Even debris from the rubbish-heap has been pressed into service or used for fill. The situation is better at cities like Nablus, where the population centre has gradually moved off a mile or two, so that a protective layer from 1,000 years' disuse has sealed off the biblical settlement of Shechem. There are many such abandoned or sidetracked villages in Palestine, and the name given to them is 'tell'. A tell has a very distinctive truncated-cone shape. One of the most conspicuous is at Megiddo.

In the past, archaeologists intent upon studying **stratigraphy** confined their digging to narrow trenches (usually five-metre squares). This method is still useful for dating events of political history, such as destruction of cities. To understand the ancient environment, however, archaeologists must dig broad,

Bronze Age vase in the shape of a bird, found at Jericho

> stratigraphy <
studying cities in layers, with the oldest buildings in the bottom layer

lateral areas. This so-called horizontal approach is helpful for gaining insight into the everyday life of ancient people.

A site must always be seen in its setting. Today archaeologists conduct surface surveys and regional studies as means of understanding such phenomena as settlement and trade patterns, population shifts, social structures, ecology, and economics in antiquity. Our own concern for the modern environment has made archaeologists conscious of the ancient environment and the human response to it.

Specialists from the natural and social sciences, including geologists, physical and cultural anthropologists, **hydrologists**, **palaeoethnobotanists** and zoologists, collaborate in the field with archaeologists. The vast reservoir of new evidence amassed through this co-operative effort is extremely useful in reconstructing both the history and the cultural process of past society. At the same time, techniques of retrieval, recording, and analysis have improved substantially.

> **hydrologists** <
experts on the distribution of water

> **palaeoethno- botanists** <
experts on ancient plants

Pottery and dating

Apart from buildings, the most frequently encountered 'artefact' or product of human industry found in Palestine excavation is broken pottery, or 'sherds'. A rare amulet or brief inscription and fairly numerous flints, stone grinders, bone

Iron Age pottery, ca. 7th century BC, found near Bethlehem. Reproduced by permission of the Trustees of the British Museum

tools, and seeds are also uncovered. It is natural that clay should be found, whether in the form of unbaked bricks and mortar or in the form of kiln-bricks and pottery. In biblical times, most utensils in an ordinary house were made of clay. Canisters, glasses, and spoons were pottery of various shapes. Bread was baked in the form of a plate, and other food was served on it, so that no table was needed: if company came, a mat served the purpose.

There was furniture, too, but organic material such as wood is not usually preserved. Blankets and mats were often piled up or spread in various ways and ultimately served as clothing. The source of heat and light was fire, often inside a jar. The plumbing and refrigeration were usually a porous jar whose 'sweat' evaporation cooled the water inside. But we do have evidence of drains, sewers, and even a toilet (in the City of David).

Pottery has a unique value for dating not only because it is so universal but because it is both the easiest and the most difficult of all things to destroy! It is easily broken in the sense that the complete vessel is smashed and thus loses its form. But to break down the fragments into an unrecognizable, that is, a non-pottery state would be an expensive engineering project even with the machines of today. And from any part of the rim or certain other small fragments, the size and shape of the original jar can be very accurately inferred.

Since the broken vessels were easily replaced – virtually with the mud in the front yard – there was a tremendous turn-over. Thus pottery styles were as fluctuating as fashions in clothes today. Some good grey styles in storage jars or cooking pots were retained unchanged through 1,000 years. But per-fume bottles or hip flasks enjoyed changing fashions. Such ware can sometimes be dated to an interval as exact as 50 years. Even those styles that lasted 300 years overlapped, so that the combi-nation of various styles found at a single site can narrow down the time range. Being so breakable, pottery would not be pre-served as a family heirloom or carried along when the famiky moved to a distant place. Because of this, it is a far better dating criterion than are art objects or even coins (which came in only after 500 BC).

Philistine pottery bowl

The 'ceramic clock'

The growth of Palestine archaeology is reflected in the combined achievement of scholars in working out the 'ceramic clock'. By this we mean a table giving pottery types characteristic of each successive 100-year period. Although the major periods have been named after metals (bronze, iron) or predominant cultures, actually the styles of pottery enable us to determine any given period. Not only the shape of the pots but also the composition of the clays is carefully studied. When the source of the clay beds can be located, much is learned about trade and commerce. Neutron activation analysis is used today for establishing the origin of the clay used in particular pottery.

Radiocarbon dating

The radiocarbon-dating technique was devised about 1948. Its point of departure is that all organic compounds (materials that were once alive), as they disintegrate, lose one half of their Carbon-14 isotopes every 5,700 years, more or less. Since the number characteristic of each compound is known, the date of its death can be determined. This is a brilliant discovery that is of great usefulness for archaeological dating, although it has its limitations. Since the material to be tested is completely destroyed in the process, a significant amount must be available. Also the material must never have been contaminated by contact with other organic materials. These conditions are hard to verify.

As well as radiocarbon, several other sophisticated dating techniques, such as potassium–argon, thermoluminescence, fluorine testing, **dendrochronology**, and pollen analysis are available today. There seems to be no end to what nuclear and computer sciences can contribute to archaeology.

> **dendrochronology** <
dating wooden objects by
studying trees' annual
growth rings

Examples of an excavation:
discoveries at Megiddo

Twenty separate strata were recognized. The long duration and careful subdivision of these Megiddo strata make them a fine framework for synchronizing Palestinian sites occupied for less time.

THE STABLES The most characteristic find at Megiddo was a stone half-column, 3 or 4 feet high with rectangular faces, repeated in endless rows, as many as 400 in all. Many of the stone posts had a hole pierced diagonally near a corner. It is thought that the Megiddo posts, which also supported wooden beams for the roof, were hitching posts for horses. We know that the town was a district capital of Solomon, who is repeatedly reported as trading in horses (1 Kings 4:12; 9:19; 10:26).

CITY GATES At the north of the mound is a sequence of monumental gates. The stone wall (*ca.* 3000 BC) was the most massive fortification ever erected on the site, originally 15 feet wide, later thickened to an impressive 28 feet. In the course of the centuries the stone wall was covered over and replaced by one of mud brick. Later a gateway of cut-stone facing, filled in with rubble, was erected. This lasted from *ca.* 1300 until it was destroyed about 1050 BC. In its place a small unimposing gate was put up, only to be destroyed, probably by David. Then a few yards further east the finest fortified gate in Palestine was erected by Solomon *ca.* 950. After Solomon the quadruple gate was transformed into a triple gate, presumably by the armed forces of the Egyptian Pharaoh.

SHAFT AND TREASURY The Megiddo water system consisted of a vertical shaft and a horizontal tunnel, which conducted the springwater from a natural cave to the bottom of the vertical shaft. The earliest part of the water system was called the 'gallery', leading outside the city to a spring located at the southwestern slope of the tell. Yadin demonstrated that the gallery was constructed during the reign of Solomon, while the water system dates to the 9th century.

STONE BIN Another noteworthy feature visible today is the stone bin for grain storage under Jeroboam II (750 BC). Megiddo was doubtless one of the towns used for storage of taxes collected 'in kind', as attested by jar handles from all over Palestine bearing the inscription 'For the King'.

TREASURES At an earlier stage in its history (*ca.* 1150), Megiddo held treasures of a different kind, the ivory carvings contemporary with similar Phoenician examples from the Guadalquivir

Pottery from the Hyksos period, found at Megiddo

valley in Spain. At the end of the Lower Bronze Age ivory plaques and other luxury items were in use.

And speaking of treasure, we must note that the Megiddo diggers overlooked a fragment of the Babylonian 'Flood Epic' named after its hero Gilgamesh. This was picked up on a debris heap by a shepherd in 1956.

Archaeological periods in Palestine from 1550 BC to AD 1918

(This chart ignores the prehistoric ages which, except for Genesis 1–11, may be judged to be pre-biblical.)

Late Bronze	1550–1200 BC
LB I	1550–1400 BC
LB II	1400–1200 BC
Iron	1200–539 BC
Early	1200–900 BC
Late	900–539 BC
Persian	539–332 BC
Hellenistic	332–64 BC
Roman	64 BC–AD 324
Early	64 BC–AD 135
Late	AD 135–324
Byzantine	AD 324–640
Early Islamic	AD 640–1174
Crusader	AD 1099–1291
Late Islamic	AD 1174–1918

(The dates in the table are approximate.)

Jerusalem

Jerusalem is perhaps the most excavated city in the world. However, it is not so well known archaeologically as other cities in Palestine because continuous occupation from the Bronze Age has impeded intensive excavation. Explorers and pilgrims have been visiting Jerusalem for centuries, but the city became the object of systematic investigation only in the second half of the 19th century.

Terracotta coffin, ca. 1200 BC, from Beth-shan. Reproduced by courtesy of the Palestine Archaeological Museum, Jerusalem

Among the discoveries are the fortifications of the City of David from the Middle Bronze Age to the Byzantine period, the nature of dwellings from the Early Bronze to the Early Iron Age on the terraces of the eastern slope and the three interconnected water systems emanating from the Gihon spring: Hezekiah's tunnel, the Siloam channel, and Warren's shaft (named after its discoverer). Anticipating Sennacherib's attack on Jerusalem in 701 BC, Hezekiah brought the waters of the Gihon spring inside Jerusalem by means of a 1,750–foot tunnel. The Siloam channel serviced reservoirs and provided irrigation water. Warren's shaft, consisting of a vertical shaft and connecting tunnels, enabled the Jerusalemites to draw water from the Gihon spring without exposure to hostile attack. Early explorers considered Warren's shaft, the earliest of these water systems, to be the conduit of 2 Samuel 5, providing David's soldiers access to Jerusalem in their attempt to capture it. But this water system in fact dates to the Israelite occupation of the 10th and 9th centuries. Also discovered were a hoard of 51 clay 'bullae' used to seal papyri. These sealings were lying in a layer of a house burnt when the Babylonians attacked Jerusalem in 597/587 BC.

Solomon's Temple

There is information from excavations elsewhere about the probable structure of Solomon's Temple. In the same style is the much later complete temple of Edfu in southern Egypt. We know that Solomon had not only a marriage alliance but other close cultural contacts with Egypt. The temple of Baalbek in Lebanon, built about the same time as that of Edfu, though it is partially destroyed, was built by an architect of the same Phoenician nationality as the one who drew Solomon's blueprints.

The remains of these temples show that the innermost 'Holy of Holies' was approached from an outer sanctum, which in turn was shielded by an imposing porch. The Jerusalem Temple was a long-room temple with its entrance at the end or short side of the rectangular form. (See the description in Chapter 73 below.)

A recent discovery in northern Samaria relating to Iron Age worship is a bronze bull figure, the largest ever found in Israel. This may help in understanding the cult of the golden calf in the Bible.

When the northern tribes broke off from subjection to the house of David, they had no permanent capital city for a while. In 876 Omri became king and built an entirely new city, calling it Samaria. Excavations have revealed a most imposing building at the top of a hill, underneath the remains of a temple to Augustus built by Herod. (See the description of Samaria in Chapter 70 above.)

The building of the hilltop palace seems to have been begun by Omri and continued by his son Ahab (869–850), and also by Jeroboam II (786–746). It contained beautifully carved ivories. Similar ones, Phoenician in origin, have been discovered at various points of the Fertile Crescent. The luxury these ivories represent helps us to understand the frequent tirades against social inequalities by the first of the writing prophets, Amos, in whose book we find several contemptuous references to ivory (3:15; 6:4). (See pages 68, 83 and 391.)

Another precious insight is afforded by an archive of tax receipts from the Samaria palace. They are in the form of ostraca, i.e. potsherds with writing in ink, dated over a period of some 17 years during the long reign of Jeroboam II.

New Testament period

Interest in the sites of the life of Jesus has been understandably great. Unfortunately, in many instances there are rival claimants for sites, two or even three, with alleged archaeological evidence. Supporting the identifications of the incarnation and nativity sites of *Nazareth* and *Bethlehem* is the virtual absence of any rival claimant. The earliest monumental remains in the basilicas erected over these sites go back to approximately 300 years after the events they commemorate. *Nain* (Luke 7:11) too is an uncontested little hamlet, and a few tombs there have been traced back to New Testament times. *Caesarea Philippi*

(Matthew 16:13) is uncontested, but near the Lake of Galilee are three possible sites for *Bethsaida*.

Tell Hum on the north-north-west shore of the Sea of Galilee has been identified as *Capernaum*. The date of the synagogue there is in dispute, but all agree that this most famous limestone synagogue of Galilee is a magnificent structure. The ruins of a more ancient basalt building lying beneath are probably of the synagogue where Jesus preached.

The site commemorating Jesus' baptism at the Jordan near Jericho, not really claimed to be authentic, is located at the most conveniently accessible point *near* a site supported by an ancient tradition.

There is no argument about where the Temple area was in Jerusalem. Here took place a large number of the most important events in the life of Jesus, from his presentation and finding, down through his public ministry to the evening before his death. The Mount of Olives is similarly important and undisputed.

The ancient tradition of localizing Calvary in the Church of the Holy Sepulchre has shown itself to be strong. An important issue is the Praetorium with the Pavement (John 19:13), traditionally identified with the Antonia fortress built by Herod the Great. Upon it depends the validity of the basic arrangement of the Way of the Cross (which, however, is founded on devotion more than on history). The alternative site on the other side of Jerusalem is Herod's citadel; and many maintain that the Praetorium where Pilate condemned Jesus was located there.

Despite the fact that thousands of crucifixions took place in Palestine, archaeological evidence of this was discovered for the first time in 1968. In the Jewish tombs at Givat ha-Mivtar, north-east of Jerusalem, were the remains of a crucified man, a Jew in his twenties who had lived in Jerusalem before AD 70. The man's wrists were tied to the crossbeam; his legs straddled the upright, with a nail attaching each heel to the side of the cross.

SEVENTY-TWO

A Time Chart of

the History of

Israel

I The Patriarchal period, *ca.* **2000–1700** BC

Abraham

Isaac

Jacob

Joseph

II The Exodus and the conquest of Palestine, *ca.* **1300–1050** BC

Moses

Joshua

The Judges

III The Monarchy, *ca.* **1020–587** BC

Saul (*ca.* 1020 BC)

David (1000–962 BC)

Solomon (961–922 BC)

This chart is based
on outlines of
sections by Roland
E. Murphy, OCarm
and Joseph A.
Fitzmyer, SJ (and a
chart on the
monarchy by
Raymond E. Brown,
SS) in NJBC article
75, 'A History of
Israel'.

*Winged creature with
a human head. Ivory
decoration from the
palace of Ahab.
Reproduced by
courtesy of the
Palestine
Archaeological
Museum, Jerusalem*

The divided monarchy (922–587 BC)			
JUDAH		ISRAEL	
Rehoboam	922–915	922–901	Jeroboam I
Abijah (Abijam)	915–913	901–900	Nadab
Asa	913–873	900–877	Baasha
		877–876	Elah
		876	Zimri
		876–869	**Omri**
Jehoshaphat	873–849	869–850	**Ahab**
		850–849	Ahaziah
Jehoram (Joram)	849–842	849–842	Jehoram (Joram)
Ahaziah	842		
Queen Athaliah	842–837	842–815	**Jehu**
Jehoash (Joash)	837–800	815–801	Jehoahaz (Joahaz)
Amaziah	800–783	801–786	Jehoash (Joash)
Uzziah (*Azariah)	783–742	786–746	**Jeroboam II**
[Regency of Jotham	750–742]	746–745	Zechariah
		745	Shallum
		745–738	Menahem
Jotham	742–735	738–737	Pekahiah
Ahaz (Jehoahaz I)	735–715	737–732	Pekah
		732–724	Hoshea
		721	FALL OF SAMARIA
Hezekiah	715–687		
Manasseh	687–642		
Amon	642–640		
Josiah	640–609		
Jehoahaz II (*Shallum)	609		
Jehoiakim (*Eliakim)	609–598		
Jehoiachin (*Jeconiah)	597		
Zedekiah (*Mattaniah)	597–587		
FALL OF JERUSALEM	587		

The names of the most important kings are in **bold** type. Variant or alternative names are put in brackets; an asterisk marks possible original names of kings whose names as kings are given first.

IV The exile (587–539 BC)

V The Persian era (539–333 BC)

VI The Greek era (333–63 BC)
Alexander the Great (333–323 BC)
The Maccabean revolt (175–135 BC)
The Hasmonean rulers (134–63 BC)

VII Roman influence in Palestine exercised through Jewish high priests (63–37 BC)

VIII Herod the Great (37–4 BC)

IX Herod's heirs and Roman prefects (4 BC–AD 39)

JUDEA AND SAMARIA	GALILEE AND PEREA (TRANSJORDAN)	EAST AND NORTH OF LAKE OF GALILEE
Archelaus (4 BC–AD 6) Roman prefects (AD 6–41), especially Pontius Pilate (AD 26–36)	Herod Antipas (4 BC–AD 39)	Philip (4 BC–AD 34)

Coin of Herod Antipas ('that fox': Luke 13:32)

X Herod Agrippa I, AD 37–44. Extended rule gradually over whole of Palestine

XI Roman procurators, AD 44–66. Ruled whole of Palestine

XII First Jewish revolt, AD 66–70. Led to Titus's capture of Jerusalem and destruction of the Temple

XIII Between revolts, AD 71–132

XIV Second Jewish revolt, AD 132–135

In the 18th year of his reign (134–135) the emperor Hadrian demolished Jerusalem to build Aelia Capitolina. He decreed: 'that the whole [Jewish] nation should be absolutely prohibited from that time on from entering even the district around Jerusalem, so that not even from a distance could it see its ancestral home'.

Shekel and half-shekel coins

SEVENTY-THREE

Religious

Institutions of

Israel

The material in this chapter is digested from NJBC article 76, 'Religious Institutions of Israel', by John J. Castelot and Aelred Cody, OSB.

What was the function of the priest in Israel?

(1) Care of the sanctuary. The priest was attached to the sanctuary or temple, the house of God. Until the use of priestly ritual was limited to Jerusalem, priests served in sanctuaries throughout the land.

(2) Oracular consultation. Those who wished to ask God which course of action to take went to a priest who used objects called Urim and Thummim to show the will of God in the form of a yes or no. There is no way of knowing what the Urim and Thummim looked like. Later priests gave answers by casting lots.

(3) Torah. By the mid-8th century some priestly decisions had been put down in writing, and this developed into codes like the Law of Holiness (Leviticus 17–26). In Deuteronomy priests handle all disputes.

(4) If a sacrifice was made at a sanctuary the priest would be involved. Later the altar came to be reserved to priests. By the end of the royal period sacrifice was considered an activity characteristic of priests.

(5) Priests were not always Levites (members of the tribe of Levi), but the tribe of Levi did claim that they were priests by right. Later, after the exile, all priests were reckoned as levitical, but a separate class of Levites existed who had no hope of advancement to the priesthood. When the other sanctuaries

were abolished, priests could function only in Jerusalem. They alone could officiate at the altars, they blessed the people, and gave moral and legal pronouncements. The Levites were responsible for the liturgies of praise and thanksgiving twice daily and on special days, the purifications of objects, making of the ritual bread, care of the Temple's courtyards and supply rooms. They could help the priests with sacrifices and with the administration of the Temple and its finances and buildings.

The tent or tabernacle and the Ark

With the Temple, these distinctive institutions of Israelite worship span the history of Israel from the Exodus to the destruction of Jerusalem in AD 70.

(1) The tent or tabernacle
The Israelites had this portable sanctuary with them during the Exodus. It was a place where Moses consulted Yahweh to know his will (Exodus 33:7), and it represented the abiding presence of Yahweh among his people. There are two descriptions of the tent: first, when Yahweh gives the specifications for its construction (Exodus 26), and again when Moses has it built (36:8–38).

(2) The Ark ('of the Testimony' or 'of the Covenant')
What the tent sheltered (Exodus 26:33; 40:21) was the Ark; the two 'tables of the testimony' given at Sinai (31:18) were kept inside it (25:16; 40:20). According to 25:10–22; 37:1–9, the Ark was a box 4 feet × 2.5 feet × 4 feet made of acacia wood, gold-plated without, and furnished with rings through which poles were passed when it had to be transported. The Ark was the centre of Israelite worship during the wandering in the desert, and it continued to be such until the destruction of the Temple in 587.

The Ark of the Covenant. From a stone carving at Capernaum

The significance of the Ark
The Ark was believed to be the place where God was present. When the Israelites brought the Ark into their battle camp, the Philistines were frightened and said: 'God has come into their camp' (1 Samuel 4:7). It was also the place where the tablets of

the Ten Commandments were kept. It made sense that the Law of God should be kept in his presence.

The Temple of Jerusalem

Introduction
It took approximately seven years to build Solomon's Temple (1 Kings 6:37–38).

The interior (see plan below) was divided into three sections: the Ulam or vestibule; the Hekal (palace; temple), later called the Holy Place or Sanctuary; and the Debir (back room), later called the Holy of Holies. The most sacred part was the Holy of Holies, for in it was kept the Ark of the Covenant.

The history of the first Temple
The first or Solomonic Temple suffered in the same way as the nation itself. It was altered, defiled, restored, and eventually reduced to rubble in 587 BC.

SOLOMON'S TEMPLE

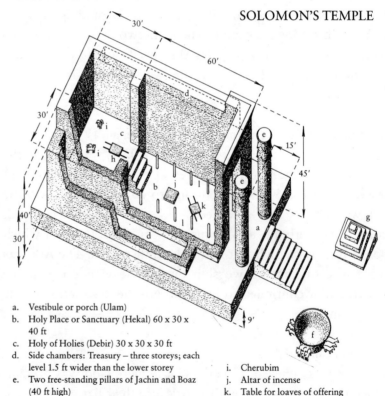

a. Vestibule or porch (Ulam)
b. Holy Place or Sanctuary (Hekal) 60 x 30 x 40 ft
c. Holy of Holies (Debir) 30 x 30 x 30 ft
d. Side chambers: Treasury – three storeys; each level 1.5 ft wider than the lower storey
e. Two free-standing pillars of Jachin and Boaz (40 ft high)
f. Bronze sea (15 ft diameter)
g. Bronze altar
h. Ark of the Covenant

i. Cherubim
j. Altar of incense
k. Table for loaves of offering
l. Ten candlesticks – five on each side

N.B.: Flat roof, no towers.

Solomon's Temple. Adapted from The New Jerome Biblical Commentary

The history of the second Temple

When, in 538, the Jews returned from the exile, they brought with them Persian authorization to rebuild the Temple. Cyrus restored to them the precious utensils that Nebuchadnezzar had pilfered. But the work of reconstruction proceeded at a snail's pace. The first to return erected a new altar (Ezra 3:2–6) and began to rebuild the Temple (5:16). They had hardly removed the rubble from the area when they were interrupted by the hostile tactics of the Samaritans (4:1–5). Another reason is suggested by Haggai 1:2, viz., their own discouragement and flagging enthusiasm. Work was resumed in 520 under the energetic direction of Zerubbabel and Joshua, and with the urging of Haggai and Zechariah (Ezra 4:24–5:2; Haggai 1:1–2,9; Zechariah 4:7–10). The task was completed in 515.

Theological significance

The Temple played an important part in the life of Israel, because the Temple was considered God's own house in the midst of his people. At the entrance of the Ark into Solomon's new Temple, God symbolically took possession of his house; and according to 1 Kings 8:10, a cloud signifying the divine presence filled the Temple (Exodus 33:9; 40:34–35; Numbers 12:4–10).

One sanctuary

In early times there were many shrines throughout the land, at places where God had appeared. But not all these sanctuaries were equally important. During the period of the judges, when the tribes met to worship together, it was always at the shrine where the Ark was kept, particularly at Shiloh and later at Gibeon.

When David took the Ark to Jerusalem, this was the beginning of the importance of Jerusalem; and with the building of the Temple in Solomon's time Jerusalem became the focal point of worship and attracted thousands of pilgrims from all over the country.

Sacrifices in Israel

Like the Temple, the altar had deep religious significance for the Israelites, much of it received from ancient Near Eastern cultures but modified conceptually to bring it into harmony with the theological views of orthodox Israelite religion. The central act of Israelite worship, the sacrifice, took different specific forms:

(A) HOLOCAUST OR BURNT OFFERING The most solemn of the Israelite sacrifices was the holocaust, or burnt offering. In it, the victim was completely burned.

(B) COMMUNION SACRIFICE OR PEACE OFFERING The ritual of the communion sacrifice is described in Leviticus 3, and its characteristic feature is that the victim is shared, with portions going to God, to the priest, and to the offerer.

(C) SACRIFICES OF EXPIATION There are two: the sin offering and the guilt offering.

(D) THE 'GIFT' (*MINHA*): CEREAL OFFERINGS The victim in the sacrifices so far discussed was an animal, but the Israelites also commonly offered various cereals. This offering was known by the name 'gift', and several kinds are listed in Leviticus 2. There was one of fine wheat flour mixed with oil; the ritual called for an offering of incense as part of this sacrifice.

(E) THE SHOWBREAD Related to the cereal offerings was the showbread, which is called in Hebrew, 'the bread of the face' (of God) or 'the bread of the Presence'.

This consisted of twelve cakes of fine wheat flour arranged in two rows on a table before the Holy of Holies; fresh cakes were put on the table every sabbath (Leviticus 24:5–9). The priests ate the old cakes at the time of the renewal, and the incense that had been placed alongside each row was burned on the altar of incense. The twelve loaves were a perpetual reminder or pledge of the covenant between Yahweh and the twelve tribes.

(F) PERFUME OFFERINGS Incense played a large part in the sacrificial ritual of Israel. The word means 'that which goes up in smoke' and in this wide sense may be applied to anything burned on an altar. In the liturgy, it refers to perfumed offerings.

*Branch of a
frankincense tree*

The meaning of sacrifices in Israel

What was the Israelite notion of sacrifice? The answer must begin with an appreciation of Israel's notion of God. He was unique, transcendent, all-powerful, supremely self-sufficient, personal; and because he was personal, he called for a response on the part of his people. This response had to be correspondingly personal, rational. Sacrifice, then, was the external expression of a personal response to a personal God. It was not a mechanical, magic gesture unrelated to the attitude of the one offering it.

Other ritual acts in Israelite worship

(A) Liturgical prayer

The Bible gives formulas for blessing (Numbers 6:22–27) and for cursing (Deuteronomy 27:14–26). It prescribes a formula to be used in the rite of the 'bitter water' (Numbers 5:21–22) and in the situation resulting from the murderer being at large (Deuteronomy 21:7–8). It gives the formulas to be used in the offering of the firstfruits (Deuteronomy 26:1–10) and in the payment of the tithe that was due every three years (Deuteronomy 26:13–15). It specifies the scriptural reading for the Passover celebration (Deuteronomy 6:20–25; see Exodus 12:26–27).

Amos (5:23) refers to the singing of the hymns to instrumental accompaniment.

Standing seems to have been usual for prayer during the Old Testament period. Solomon, however, is said to have knelt down (2 Chronicles 6:13), and in Nehemiah 9:3–5 the people stood for the reading; then they fell to their knees for the confession of sins. It is not surprising to read of people kneeling in prayer (1 Kings 8:54; Isaiah 45:23; Daniel 6:11) with arms raised toward heaven (1 Kings 8:22, 54; Isaiah 1:15; Lamentations 2:19). Other texts suggest the Muslim custom of falling to the knees and pressing the forehead to the ground (Psalms 5:8; 99:5).

(B) Purifications

Modern minds find the Old Testament concepts of 'cleanness' and 'uncleanness' strange, but legislation served a sublime purpose by putting Israel in a class apart. The pagans might touch this or that and eat anything with impunity, but not the people of Israel. They belonged to an all-pure, transcendent God and had to reflect his holiness.

The sabbath

(A) Origin

Exodus 16:22–30 suggests that the sabbath existed before the covenant, and Genesis 2:2–3 traces it to the time of creation itself.

(B) Significance

The role that the sabbath played in Israelite life and thought made it unique. It was not just a holiday on which to rest up for another week of work. It was related to the covenant that God had made with his people and was a day consecrated to him in a special way.

(C) Observance

As a sign of the covenant, observance of the sabbath indicated fidelity to the covenant and was an assurance of salvation (Isaiah 58:13–14; Jeremiah 17:19–27); non-observance was tantamount to apostasy (Exodus 31:14; 35:2; Numbers 15:32–36). If the people as a whole neglected the sabbath, God would punish them severely (Ezekiel 20:13; Nehemiah 13:17–18).

In the early days the sabbath was a joyful, relaxed holiday, predominantly religious but not overly restrictive. Manual labour and business were suspended, but the people could move about freely. They made pilgrimages to nearby sanctuaries (Isaiah 1:13; Hosea 2:13) or went to consult their prophets (2 Kings 4:23).

Then during the exile, when celebration of the other feasts was impossible, the sabbath came into prominence as the distinctive sign of the covenant.

After the exile, although the sabbath continued to be a day of pleasurable relaxation, it was subject to tighter restrictions. All business and travel were forbidden (Isaiah 58:13); the people could not carry anything from their homes or do any work (Jeremiah 17:21–22, a post-exilic addition).

Pre-exilic feasts in Israel

Apart from the great feasts, the Israelites observed everyday Temple services. According to Exodus 29:38–42 and Numbers 28:2–8, two lambs were to be offered daily as sacrifices, one in the morning and the other in the evening. Along with them went an offering of flour mixed with oil, a libation of wine, and an incense offering (Exodus 30:7–8).

On the sabbath the same ritual was observed, but in each sacrifice two lambs were offered rather than one as on ordinary days (Numbers 28:9–10). On the first day of each month, the day of the new moon, there was a special ritual calling for a sacrifice of two bulls, a ram, and seven lambs, together with offerings and libations, and the sacrifice of a goat as a sin offering (Numbers 28:11–15).

The three annual pilgrimage feasts are: (1) the Passover, joined to the feast of Unleavened Bread of the earlier codes; (2) the feast of Weeks, with the explanation that it takes place seven weeks after the beginning of the grain harvest; and (3) the feast of Tabernacles or Tents, corresponding to the fruit harvest festival of the earlier codes of law.

Ram's horns

(1) The Passover

HOW WE KNOW ABOUT THE PASSOVER FESTIVAL The biblical texts relevant to Passover come from different traditions, formulated at different times; so it is possible to use them as guides to the development of the great Jewish feast. These are the passages in the Bible from which we learn about the way the feast was celebrated in later times: Leviticus 23:5–8; Numbers 28:16–25; Exodus 12:1–20.

From them we learn that the Passover was to be celebrated in conjunction with the full moon of the first month of the year (March–April). On the tenth of this month each family was to select an unblemished, male, one-year-old lamb. At twilight on the 14th, the lamb was slaughtered and the blood sprinkled on the lintels and doorposts of the house. During this night of the full moon the lamb was roasted and eaten; not one of its bones could be broken, and whatever was left over after the meal had to be burned. Unleavened bread and bitter herbs were eaten also, and those who partook of the meal had to be dressed as if ready for a journey. If a family was too small to consume a whole lamb, it joined some neighbours. Slaves and resident aliens could take part, so long as they were circumcised.

On the 15th of the month, the week-long feast of Unleavened Bread began. All leftover leavened bread had to be destroyed and for the following week only unleavened bread could be eaten.

The restriction of the Passover celebration to Jerusalem was a later innovation; with the disintegration of tribal unity Passover became a family feast.

ORIGIN OF PASSOVER No other Israelite rite resembles so closely those of the ancient nomadic Arabs. Passover required no priest, no altar, and the blood of the victim played an important role. Originally a young animal was sacrificed to obtain fertility for the whole flock, and the blood was put on the tentpoles to drive away evil powers (see Exodus 12:23: the Destroyer). This ritual has all the appearance of a rite celebrated when the tribe broke camp to head for the fresh spring pastures. The nomadic character of Passover is further suggested by several features: the victim was roasted; the meat was eaten with unleavened bread and bitter (wild, not cultivated) herbs; and the participants were to be dressed for immediate departure, with their shepherd's crooks in hand. The later texts that fix the dates for the celebration of the Passover reflect the pastoral, nomadic origin of the feast. They specify the 14th–15th of the first month (Abib: later Nisan; our March–April), precisely at the time of the full moon. In the desert life, a brightly lit night would be the logical choice for such a festival. All the evidence, therefore, points to the fact that the Passover went back to the days when the Israelites were leading a semi-nomadic existence, even to the time before the Exodus. This may be the feast that the Israelites, while still in Egypt, wanted to celebrate in the desert (Exodus 5:1), permission for which was refused by the Pharaoh.

ORIGIN OF UNLEAVENED BREAD This feast marked the beginning of the barley harvest. For the first seven days of the harvest the only bread eaten was with flour from the new grain, prepared without leaven. Containing nothing of the 'old year', it symbolized a fresh start. Furthermore, there was an offering to Yahweh from the new crops, but there was a later more formal offering of firstfruits on the feast of Weeks that marked the end of the grain harvesting season, 50 days after the beginning of the barley harvest. The feast of Unleavened Bread was an agricultural feast and was not celebrated until after settlement in Canaan (Leviticus 23:10). The Passover became a pilgrimage feast, and its proximity to the feast of Unleavened Bread led to an eventual combination of the two some time between the reform of Josiah (621), and the exile (587–539). Whereas the date of the Passover was determined by the full moon, the feast of Unleavened Bread had depended on the harvest and was supposed to begin and end on a sabbath. As it turned out, the Passover took precedence: on whatever day it occurred, the feast of Unleavened Bread began on the next day and lasted a week. The two feasts took on a profound new meaning as commemorations of God's deliverance of his people from Egypt, which had taken place at the same time of the year.

(2) The feast of Weeks (Pentecost)
Like all harvest feasts, it was a joyful occasion (Deuteronomy 16:11; Isaiah 9:2). The complete ritual for its celebration is given in Leviticus 23:15–21. The ceremony consists in offering two leavened loaves made from the new wheat flour. The use of unleavened bread at the beginning of the harvest, 50 days before, had marked a fresh start; but now that the harvest was over, normal customs were resumed. There was thus a sort of organic unity between the feast of Weeks and the earlier feast of Unleavened Bread, and through the latter, with the Passover.

(3) The feast of Tents – Tabernacles
This is the 'feast of the Ingathering' mentioned in the two most ancient calendars (Exodus 23:16 and 34:22).

Of the three annual pilgrimage feasts, this was the most important and the best attended. Like the feasts of Unleavened Bread and of Weeks, the feast of Tents was an agricultural feast, indeed the climax of the agricultural year. It marked the ingathering of all the produce of the fields (Exodus 23:16), the products of the threshing floors and of the wine and oil presses

(Deuteronomy 16:13). When the earth had yielded all its bounty for the current year, and that bounty had been gathered and stored, the people gave joyful thanks to God (the analogy with Thanksgiving Day is obvious). There was dancing, singing, and general merriment (Judges 21:19–21), including, apparently, a generous sampling of the new wine (1 Samuel 1:14–15).

As for the ritual of the feast, it is described as a pilgrimage to the Temple, and it lasted seven days. We learn from Numbers 29:12–38 what sacrifices were offered. In Leviticus 23:40–43 we read that for seven days the people are to live in huts, in memory of how the Israelites lived after their liberation from Egypt, and to 'gather foliage from majestic trees, branches of palms, and boughs of myrtles and of valley poplars' and 'make merry before the Lord'. Later historical texts make it clear that the foliage was carried in procession, as in the Palm Sunday ceremony.

The feast began as a harvest festival, as its earliest name (Ingathering) suggests, and as the ancient texts (Exodus 23:16; 34:22) indicate. Even after it had taken on a name inspired by an accidental part of the ritual (Huts = Tents or Tabernacles or Booths), it remained essentially an agricultural feast.

Later Old Testament feasts

(1) The Day of Atonement

The ritual of Yom Kippur is given in Leviticus 16. It is not a feast, but a day of complete rest, penance and fasting.

There are two distinct rituals. The first had the high priest offering a bull for his own sins and those of the priesthood. Then (and only on this day in the year) he entered the Holy of Holies and sprinkled the cover of the Ark with the blood. The second was related to two goats, which the community presented. Lots were then cast: one became the goat 'for Yahweh', the other the goat 'for Azazel'. The goat chosen for Yahweh was sacrificed for the sins of the people. The high priest then laid hands on the goat for Azazel; by this symbolic gesture he transferred to the goat all the sins of the community. This goat was sacrificed neither to Yahweh nor to the demon. It was led into the desert, and with it were removed the sins of the people

(Leviticus 16:8–10, 20–22).

(2) The feast of Hanukkah

The origin of the feast of Hanukkah is described in 1 Maccabees 4:36–59. The tyrant Antiochus Epiphanes had desecrated
the Temple and its altar and had put up on the site of the altar
of sacrifices a pagan altar. This was the Abomination of Desolation (1 Maccabees 1:54; Daniel 9:27; 11:31); upon it he offered
the first sacrifice to Zeus Olympios on the 25th of Kisleu
(December) 167 BC. Just three years later, on this same date,
Judas Maccabeus purified the sanctuary, erected a new altar,
and dedicated it (2 Maccabees 10:5). It was agreed that the
event be commemorated annually (1 Maccabees 4:59).

(3) The feast of Purim

This feast was celebrated in February–March in memory of the
victory of the Jews of Persia over their would-be exterminators.

The story of Esther gave this feast its existence and its
name. According to 3:7 Haman cast lots to determine the fate
of the Jews, which was to be extermination; but his scheme
backfired and he himself was hanged.

SEVENTY-FOUR

Aspects of Old Testament Thought

The material in this chapter is digested from NJBC article 77, 'Aspects of Old Testament Thought', by John L. McKenzie (died March 1991).

The name of God

(a) *El*. This is the common name for a god in Semitic languages.

(b) *Elohim*. This is a plural in Hebrew, meaning 'gods'. But when it is used of the God of Israel, it is used as if it were a singular noun.

(c) In certain places God was worshipped with extra titles which spoke of his qualities:

> at Jerusalem: El Elyon (God most High)
> at Beer-sheba: El Olam (God Eternal)
> at Shechem: El Berith (God of the Covenant).

(d) *Yahweh*. This is the personal name of the God of Israel. It was written in the Hebrew Bible with the four consonants YHWH. Out of reverence Jews in the period before Christ began not to say this name, but instead said 'Adonai' (Lord). The combination of the consonants YHWH plus the vowels of 'Adonai' gives in written Hebrew the form rendered as 'Jehovah', which is not a real word or name of God. Modern scholars think that originally YHWH was pronounced 'Yahweh'. This divine name was not known before Moses, and the story of the revelation of the name is told in Exodus 3:13–14 and 6:3.

One God

Yahweh is unique and the Israelites were to worship no other god and were to make no images of God. We know of no other ancient Near Eastern god who could not be represented in pictures or statues.

Israel, the people of Yahweh

God chose Israel and made a covenant with Israel. God's saving acts and his personal relation to Israel demand a personal response.

The word of God

The divine word was a creative force bringing the world into existence.

Creation

In the Old Testament, creation is the beginning of history – the first of the saving deeds of Yahweh. There is nothing in the beliefs of other ancient Near Eastern peoples that corresponds to Yahweh as creator, in spite of the fact that the Old Testament exhibits several ways of conceiving the creative process.

(I) CREATION AS COMBAT Probably the oldest approach to creation, now reflected only in some Old Testament allusions, related it to a combat between Yahweh and an adversary representing chaos.

(II) CREATION ACCORDING TO GENESIS In Genesis 1:1 we are probably not dealing with creation from nothing or creation in the strictest sense, but with God's ordering of chaos into a fixed universe.

The structure of the material universe seen in Genesis 1 and in almost all allusions to creation is on three levels: heavens, earth, and subterranean abyss of waters. The earth is a flat disc that floats upon the waters, and the heavens above are the divine dwelling. The entire structure rests on pillars. The heavenly bodies move across the sky; and rain, snow, hail and wind are stored in chambers above the sky.

(III) CREATION ACCORDING TO PSALM 104 The dominant theme is the care of the creator for living beings, both animals and humans. The poem is very optimistic, as are the other creation accounts. In all of them the work of creation is seen as good in its origin, without defect or any element hostile to humanity.

(IV) CREATION FROM NOTHING This concept appears clearly in the late Old Testament period, as Jews came into contact with Greek thought (2 Maccabees 7:28).

The covenant

The Old Testament describes the relationship between Yahweh and Israel in various ways: it is like father and son, like marriage, like king and subject, but above all, it is a covenant.

A covenant was originally a verbal agreement in a culture that did not keep written records; in the Old Testament covenants cover all social transactions.

The covenant between Yahweh and Israel dominates the last four books of the Pentateuch (Exodus, Leviticus, Numbers, Deuteronomy) and recurs in the historical books. The covenant is initiated by Yahweh through an act that is often called election, especially in Deuteronomy. Israel is the people of Yahweh through the choice of Yahweh. From love for his chosen people Israel Yahweh saved them from Egypt and gave them the land of Canaan; in return Israel is responsible for recognizing Yahweh alone as God and keeping his commandments. Later, Jeremiah sees the future of Israel in terms of a new covenant.

Recent studies have shown that the covenant was the principle of Israel's unity as a people made up of a number of groups of different origins.

The covenant and law

There are several law collections in the Pentateuch, especially:
- the Decalogue (Ten Commandments) in Exodus 20 and Deuteronomy 5
- the Book of the Covenant (Exodus 20:22–23; 19)
- the Deuteronomic Book of the Law (Deuteronomy 12–26)
- the Holiness Code of Leviticus 17–26.

The covenant and worship

The saving event told in Jewish worship is the saving deed of Yahweh in history, when he delivered Israel from Egypt to the promised land. The major festivals of the Israelite calendar commemorate events in the history of Israel (see Chapter 73). It has been thought strange that no actual covenant festival has been found; some think that it may have been connected with the New Year. By the first century the feast of Weeks was being celebrated as the anniversary of the revelation of the law, which is part of the covenant.

It is God's love for Israel that initiates the covenant; it is the dominating motive for the acts of Yahweh.

The relations between God and Israel

(1) ANGER in the Old Testament occupies the place that justice occupies in modern thinking about God. Yahweh is angered by unbelief, distrust, rebellion and worship of false gods, as well as by human injustice.

(2) REVELATION is the way Yahweh is known, through speech, through acts, through history, through the institutions of Israel, through the law, through the prophets, and through his creative works. At some times people had a clearer vision than at others.

(3) YAHWEH IS THE LORD OF HISTORY The Old Testament is a unique collection of historical documents, detailing Israel's encounter with Yahweh. The very idea that history is a process with beginning, middle and end, rather than cyclical, originates with Israel.

(4) THE MORALITY of the Old Testament rises above the morality of other ancient Near Eastern religious documents. The moral will of Yahweh is revealed in the covenant, and the covenant obliged Israel to a particular way of life. This is shown particularly in two areas:

(a) the morality of sex is far more rigorous in Israel than among its neighbours;

(b) respect for the honour and dignity of the human person.

The *limitations* of Israelite morality have often been pointed out; they include the acceptance of slavery, polygamy and divorce, the double standard of sexual morality (stricter on women), a remarkably intense hatred of foreigners, inhumanity in war, and a certain laxness in regard to lying and theft. But the remarkable feature of Israelite morality is that it contained the principles by which its limitations could be overcome.

Personal morality in the Old Testament is principally the concern of the wisdom literature. The maxims of wisdom, often paralleled in other ancient wisdom literatures, instruct the young man on how to manage his life.

(5) SIN AND GUILT are emphasized in the Old Testament, though not as strongly as in the New.

The paradise story of Genesis 3 is an account of the first sin and of its consequences, viz., the curse of those processes of fertility by which human life is sustained, and death as the inevitable end of the struggle for survival. But the paradise story is also a splendid psychological study of the sinful act, unparalleled elsewhere in the Old Testament. In a brief, simple dialogue the writer traces with masterful art the self-deception of the sinner, the rationalization of the action in one's own mind, the desire to be something greater than one really is, and the sinful choice made under the personal pressure of another. Almost every Hebrew word for sin is illustrated in the steps by which the man and the woman rebel against the restraint of the will of Yahweh.

(6) FORGIVENESS To obtain forgiveness *conversion* is necessary: to seek Yahweh, to ask for him, to humble oneself, to direct one's heart to Yahweh, to seek good, to hate evil and to love good, to learn to do good, to obey, to acquire a new heart, to circumcise one's heart, to plough a new furrow, to wash oneself from wickedness. Conversion is conceived of as a genuine interior change of attitude that issues in a revolution in personal conduct.

The assurance of forgiveness reposes on the forgiving character of Yahweh.

(7) JUDGEMENT For the pre-exilic prophets the judgement of Yahweh is accomplished in history. Amos (5:18–20, 26–27; 7:1–9; 9:1–8a) speaks of the coming downfall both of foreign nations and of Israel; nothing suggests that he is thinking of anything other than the historical factors as the weapons of Yahweh's judgement. Hosea (4:8–14; 8:7–10; 13:4–14:1)

speaks less clearly of a day or even of an event; but the doom of Israel is clearly announced and surely threatened. The judgements of Yahweh are much more prominent in Isaiah's thought (1:2–9; 5:26–30; 10:5–19). They are against both Israel and Judah and against various social classes, particularly against those in power.

Jeremiah and Ezekiel, at the time of the fall of Jerusalem, are perhaps pre-eminently the prophets of judgement. They are certain of an imminent judgement and of its justice.

(8) SALVATION in earlier times was often linked with deliverance from Egypt, victory over enemies, peaceful dwelling in Israel's own land, and prosperity.

Later, Isaiah saw it in more elevated terms, as the end of injustice and as the security that comes from government administered in righteousness. It is seen as the establishment of a new, saved community.

(9) THE REIGN OF YAHWEH is the acceptance of his will by all. This cannot happen until all know him. This must work a revolutionary change in humankind; and since the struggle against nature arises from human disobedience to God, there must be a corresponding revolution even in material nature.

God's future plans for his people

(1) THE MESSIAH The word means 'anointed'; the Greek is *christos*, thus 'Christ'. The Messiah came to be understood as the anointed king of the Davidic dynasty who would establish in the world the reign of Yahweh: such a conception was the product of a long development.

The expectation of the Messiah in the strict sense appears in post-exilic Judaism.

(2) LIFE AFTER DEATH It is generally held by scholars that no hope of individual survival after death is expressed in the Old Testament before some of its latest passages, which were probably written in the 2nd century BC.

There are passages in the Old Testament which seem to express a striving for some form of afterlife. In Psalms 49 and 73 the psalmist expresses his faith that God will deliver him from death; but he does not make clear just what he hopes for – he is relying on communion with Yahweh, and he may believe that this communion cannot be destroyed by death. If the punishment for the wicked is death, then the psalmist does not accept that the same death comes also to the righteous. The first clear expression of the hope of resurrection occurs in the Maccabean period in Daniel 12:2. See also Isaiah 26:19, a relatively late part of Isaiah.

There is no history of the development of the idea. Attempts to trace the belief to Iranian influence have not been successful. This distinctively Israelite idea arises from the Israelite conception of God and of the human being. Resurrection is not just a continuation of life on earth, like the Egyptian form of survival. It involves a new life in a new world. Nor is there merely a resurrection of the righteous; the dignity of the human person means that even the wicked will rise again.

The spirit of God

The same Hebrew word serves to signify both *wind* and *spirit*. The wind is the breath of God; it is a perceptible manifestation of the divine presence and power. It moves suddenly and unpredictably; we can neither foretell nor control its direction or its strength. We cannot determine its source or its destination (John 3:8). It is subtle, universal and irresistible in its scope. Hence, the wind is an extremely apt symbol of the divine.

In the Old Testament the spirit is not a personal being. It is a principle of action.

Paul

Sources and chronology of Paul's life

The material in this chapter is digested from NJBC article 79, 'Paul', by Joseph A. Fitzmyer, SJ.

What little is known about Paul comes to us from two main sources: (1) passages in his genuine letters, principally 1 Thessalonians 2:1–2, 17–18; 3:1–3a; Galatians 1:13–23; 2:1–14; 4:13; Philippians 3:5–6; 4:15–16; 1 Corinthians 5:9; 7:7–8; 16:1–9; 2 Corinthians 2:1, 9–13; 11:7–9, 23–27, 32–33; 12:2–4, 14, 21; 13:1, 10; Romans 11:1c; 15:19b, 22–32; 16:1; and (2) Acts 7:58; 8:1–3; 9:1–30; 11:25–30; 12:25; 13:1–28:31.

The two sources mentioned, however, are not of equal value. In the reconstruction of Paul's life, preference must be given to what Paul has told us about himself, for Luke's story of Paul's missionary activity is coloured by his literary and theological concerns. In what follows, what Paul reports of himself is kept in the past tense; what Luke reports is in the present tense.

Possible information from outside the Bible

Five events in Paul's career that are mentioned in Acts can be linked with events known of from sources outside the Bible.

(1) Paul was brought before the **proconsul** L. Junius Gallio Annaeus in Corinth (Acts 18:12). This is 'the one link between the Apostle's career and general history that is accepted by all scholars'. Gallio was Roman proconsul in the twelfth year of the reign of Claudius, that is AD 52.

> **proconsul** <
a senior Roman governor

(2) The expulsion of Jews from Rome by the emperor Claudius (Acts 18:2) is related by Luke to the arrival in Corinth of Aquila and Priscilla, with whom Paul stayed. Roman historians date this in AD 49.

(3) The famine in the reign of Claudius (Acts 11:28) lasted several years and is dated by historians in AD 46–48.

(4) Porcius Festus succeeded Felix as **procurator** of Judea (Acts 24:27), probably in AD 60. On the arrival of Festus Paul appealed to Caesar for a trial.

(5) The recall of Pontius Pilate to Rome in AD 36 to answer for his conduct. This was probably the time when persecution broke out against the Christians, with the lynching of Stephen (Acts 7:58–60) and the conversion of Paul.

Paul's name

In his letters the apostle calls himself *Paulos*, the name also used in 2 Peter 3:15 and from Acts 13 on. Prior to that in Acts he is called *Saulos*, the Greek form of the name of the first king of ancient Israel, Saul (see 1 Samuel 9:2, 17; cf. Acts 13:21). It means 'asked'. The name *Paulos* is the Greek form of the well-known Roman name Paul(l)us. Many Jews of the period had two names, one Hebrew (Saul) and the other Greek or Roman. There is no evidence that Saul was changed to Paul at the time of his conversion; the change is probably due to Luke using a different source of information.

The sequence chart on page 416 gives only a relative idea of Paul's career. In Paul's own letters the only event for which a date can be found outside the Bible is his Damascus escape (2 Corinthians 11:32–33), when he was let down in a basket through a window in the city wall (see Acts 9:24–25). That occurred at the end of Paul's three years in Damascus (Galatians 1:17–18). This happened after direct Roman rule of Damascus ended in AD 37; so Paul's escape must have occurred in the period AD 37–39 and his conversion was three years earlier.

Paul's career

Youth

The date of Paul's birth is unknown. He called himself an 'old man' in Philemon 9, i.e., someone between 50 and 56 years of age; this would mean that he was born between AD 1 and 10.

St Paul. 6th century mosaic from the church of San Vitale, Ravenna

Luke depicts Saul as a 'youth' standing at the stoning of Stephen, i.e., as between 24 and 40.

Paul never tells us where he was born, but his name, Paulos, would connect him with some Roman town. He boasted of his Jewish background and traced his lineage to the tribe of Benjamin (Romans 11:1; Philippians 3:5; 2 Corinthians 11:22). He was an 'Israelite', 'a Hebrew, born of Hebrews . . ., as to the law a Pharisee' (Philippians 3:6), one 'extremely zealous for the traditions of my fathers' and one who excelled his peers 'in Judaism' (Galatians 1:14). In calling himself a 'Hebrew' he may have meant that he was a Greek-speaking Jew who could also

415

> **Aramaic** <
the language of Palestine
in Jesus' time, related to
Hebrew

speak **Aramaic** and could read the Old Testament in the original. Paul's letters, however, reveal that he knew Greek well and could write it and that in addressing Gentile churches he usually quoted the Old Testament in Greek. He had a Greek education.

Luke also presents Paul as 'a Jew', as 'a Pharisee' born in Tarsus, a Greek-speaking town of Cilicia (Acts 22:3, 6; 21:39), as having a sister (23:16), and as a Roman citizen from birth (22:25–29; 16:37; 23:27). If Luke's information about Paul's origins is correct, it helps explain both the Greek and the Jewish background of Paul. Paul himself never mentions that he was brought up at Jerusalem as Acts 22:3 claims.

Sequence chart of Paul's movements	
Letters	**Acts**
Conversion near Damascus (implied in Galatians 1:17c)	Damascus (9:1–22)
To Arabia (Galatians 1:17b)	
Return to Damascus (1:17c): 3 years	
Flight from Damascus (2 Corinthians 11:32–33)	Escape from Damascus (9:23–25)
To Jerusalem (Galatians 1:18–20)	To Jerusalem (9:26–29)
'The regions of Syria and Cilicia' (Galatians 1:21–22)	Caesarea and Tarsus (9:30)
	Antioch (11:26a)
	(Jerusalem [11:29–30; 12:25])
	MISSION I: Antioch (13:1–4a)
	Seleucia, Salamis, Cyprus (13:4b–12)
Churches evangelized before Macedonian Philippi (Philippians 4:15)	South Galatia (13:13–14:25)
	Antioch (14:26–28)
'Once again after 14 years I went up to Jerusalem' (for 'Council', Galatians 2:1)	Jerusalem (15:1–12)
Antioch incident (Galatians 2:11–14)	Antioch (15:35); MISSION II
	Syria and Cilicia (15:41)
	South Galatia (16:1–5)
Galatia (1 Corinthians 16:1) evangelized for the first time (Galatians 4:13)	Phrygia and north Galatia (16:6)
	Mysia and Troas (16:7–10)
Philippi (1 Thessalonians 2:2 [= Macedonia, 2 Corinthians 11:9])	Philippi (16:11–40)
Thessalonica (1 Thessalonians 2:2; cf. 3:6; Philippians 4:15–16)	Amphipolis, Apollonia, Thessalonica (17:1–9)
	Beroea (17:10–14)
Athens (1 Thessalonians 3:1; cf. 2:17–18)	Athens (17:15–34)
Corinth evangelized (cf. 2 Corinthians 1:19; 11:7–9)	Corinth for 18 months (18:1–18a)
Timothy arrives at Corinth (1 Thessalonians 3:6) probably accompanied by Silvanus (1 Thessalonians 1:1)	Silas and Timothy come from Macedonia (18:5)
	Paul leaves from Cenchreae (18:18b)
	Leaves Priscilla and Aquila at Ephesus (18:19–21)

Sequence chart of Paul's movements

Letters	Acts
Apollos (in Ephesus) urged by Paul to go to Corinth (1 Corinthians 16:12)	Apollos sent to Achaia by Priscilla and Aquila (18:17)
	Paul to Caesarea Maritima (18:22a)
	Paul to Jerusalem (18:22b)
	In Antioch for a certain amount of time (18:22c)
Northern Galatia, second visit (Galatians 4:13)	MISSION III: north Galatia and Phrygia (18:23)
Ephesus (1 Corinthians 16:1–8)	Ephesus for 3 years, or 2 years 3 months (19:1–20:1; cf. 20:31)
Visit of Chloe, Stephanas, etc. to Paul in Ephesus (1 Corinthians 1:11; 16:17), bringing letter (7:1)	
Paul imprisoned (? cf. 1 Corinthians 15:32; 2 Corinthians 1:8)	
Timothy sent to Corinth (1 Corinthians 4:17; 16:10)	
Paul's 2nd 'painful' visit to Corinth (2 Corinthians 13:2); return to Ephesus	
Titus sent to Corinth with letter 'written in tears' (2 Corinthians 2:13)	
(Paul's plans to visit Macedonia, Corinth, and Jerusalem/Judea [1 Corinthians 16:3–8; cf. 2 Corinthians 1:15–16])	(Paul's plans to visit Macedonia, Achaia, Jerusalem, Rome [19:21])
Ministry in Troas (2 Corinthians 2:12)	
To Macedonia (2 Corinthians 2:13; 7:5; 9:2b–4); arrival of Titus (2 Corinthians 7:6)	Macedonia (20:1b)
Titus sent ahead to Corinth (2 Corinthians 7:16–17), with part of 2 Corinthians	
Illyricum (Romans 15:19)?	
Achaia (Romans 15:26; 16:1); Paul's third visit to Corinth (2 Corinthians 13:1)	3 months in Greece (Achaia) (20:2–3)
	Paul starts to return to Syria (20:3), but goes via Macedonia and Philippi (20:3b–6a)
	Troas (20:6b–12)
	Miletus (20:15c–38)
	Tyre, Ptolemais, Caesarea (21:7–14)
(Plans to visit Jerusalem, Rome, Spain [Romans 15:22–27])	Jerusalem (21:15–23:30)
	Caesarea (23:31–26:32)
	Journey to Rome (27:1–28:14)
	Rome (28:15–31)

Paul's conversion

Paul wrote of the crucial turn in his life in Galatians 1:16: 'God was pleased to reveal his son to/in me so that I might preach him among the **Gentiles**.' This revelation followed upon a career in Judaism and a persecution of 'the church of God' (1:13). After it he withdrew to 'Arabia' and then 'returned' to Damascus (Galatians 1:17). Three years later he escaped from Damascus (*ca*. AD 39) and went up to Jerusalem (1:18). Thus *ca*. 36 Paul the former Pharisee became a Christian and an 'apostle to the Gentiles' (Romans 11:13).

> Gentiles <
non-Jews

Paul clearly regarded the experience near Damascus as the turning point in his life and in that sense a 'conversion'. It was for him an encounter with the risen Lord that he never forgot. When his apostolate was subsequently challenged, he used to exclaim, 'Am I not an apostle? Have I not seen Jesus our Lord?' (1 Corinthians 9:1; cf. 15:8). As a result of that 'revelation of Jesus Christ' (Galatians 1:12), he became 'a servant of Christ' (Galatians 1:10), someone with a compulsion (1 Corinthians 9:16) to preach the gospel of Christ, and for it he became 'all things to all human beings' (1 Corinthians 9:22).

Paul's conversion should not be regarded as the result of the human condition described in Romans 7:7–8:2, as if that were an autobiographical account of his own experience. Paul as a Christian looked back on his Jewish career with a good conscience: 'As for righteousness under the law, I was blameless' (Philippians 3:6b). He was not crushed by the law.

Luke also associates Paul's conversion with a persecution of the church – in Jerusalem, because of which Christians scattered to Judea and Samaria (Acts 8:1–3) and farther (9:2; 11:19). Luke tells the Damascus experience three times in Acts: once in a narrative that depicts Paul eventually staying for several days in Damascus (9:3–19 – but with no mention of a withdrawal to Arabia); and twice in speeches, before a crowd in Jerusalem (22:6–16) and before Festus and King Agrippa (26:12–18). Each of these accounts stresses the overwhelming and unexpected character of the experience which occurred during Paul's persecution of Christians.

Paul's visits to Jerusalem

According to Paul's letters he visited Jerusalem twice after his conversion, once after three years (Galatians 1:18) and 'once again during fourteen years' (Galatians 2:1). In Romans 15:25 he planned another visit, before going to Rome and Spain.

According to Acts, however, Paul visits Jerusalem after his conversion five or possibly six times: (1) 9:26–29, after his flight from Damascus; cf. 22:17; (2) 11:29–30, Barnabas and Saul bring a collection from Antioch to the brethren of Judea – related by Luke to the famine in the days of Claudius; (3) 12:25, Barnabas and Saul go up to Jerusalem; (4) 15:1–2, the visit of Paul and Barnabas at the 'Council'; (5) 18:22, after

Mission II, Paul goes up and greets the church before going down to Antioch; (6) 21:15–17, the visit at the end of Mission III, when Paul is arrested.

It seems best to put Paul's and Luke's information together in this way. After Paul escaped from Damascus in AD 39, he came to Jerusalem for the first time 'to get information from **Cephas**' or 'to visit Cephas'. During his 15 days there he met James, 'the Lord's brother', but none of the other apostles; he was otherwise personally unknown to the churches of Judea. According to the Lucan version of this visit Barnabas introduces Paul to the 'apostles' and tells them how he has preached boldly in Damascus in the name of Jesus. Paul circulates in Jerusalem among them, continuing to preach boldly and provoking the **Hellenists,** who seek to kill him (Acts 9:27–29).

After the 15 days in Jerusalem, according to Galatians 1:21, Paul retired to Syria and Cilicia – for how long he does not say. About this time he must have had the vision to which he refers in 2 Corinthians 12:2–4; it occurred 14 years before 2 Corinthians was written but is scarcely to be equated with the conversion experience. According to Acts 22:17–21 Paul has an ecstasy while praying in the Jerusalem Temple during visit 1. It is the danger presented by the provoked Hellenists that leads the brethren to bring Paul from Jerusalem to Caesarea and to send him off to Tarsus (Acts 9:30). Acts does not specify how long Paul stays there, but the sequence makes a number of years not improbable (perhaps AD 40–44). The stay ends with a visit from Barnabas, who brings him back to Antioch where he remains a whole year (11:25–26), engaged in evangelization. Luke relates visit 2 to Jerusalem, the 'Famine Visit', to this period.

> **Cephas** <
Peter

> **Hellenists** <
Greek-speaking Jews

Mission I (AD 46–49)

The story of this pre-'Council' mission is recounted solely by Acts (13:3–14:28) and is confined to essentials to suit Luke's literary purpose (cf. 2 Timothy 3:11). Paul has given us no details about his missionary activity in the pre-'Council' period of 14 years (Galatians 2:1). For a time he was in 'the areas of Syria and Cilicia' (1:21) and was 'preaching the faith' (1:23) 'among the Gentiles' (2:2). When later he wrote Philippians he

recalled that 'at the beginning of the evangelization, no church
except you shared with me in the matter of giving and receiving, when I left Macedonia' (4:15). As he left Macedonia, then
(*ca.* AD 50), there were other churches, presumably evangelized
by Paul.

Moved by the Spirit, prophets and teachers in Antioch
impose hands on Barnabas and Saul and send them forth in the
company of John Mark, Barnabas's cousin (Colossians 4:10).

They depart from Seleucia, the port of Syrian Antioch,
head for Cyprus, and pass through the island from Salamis to
Paphos. There the proconsul Sergius Paulus is converted
(13:7–12). From Paphos the missionaries sail for Perga in Pam-
phylia (on the southern coast of central Asia Minor), where
John Mark deserts Barnabas and Paul and returns to Jerusalem.
Barnabas and Paul make their way to towns in south Galatia:
to Pisidian Antioch, Iconium, Lystra, and Derbe.

In Antioch Paul preaches first to Jews in their synagogue;
and when he encounters resistance, Paul announces his turning
henceforth to the Gentiles (13:46). After evangelizing the area
and meeting opposition from Jews in various towns (even stoning in Iconium), Paul and Barnabas retrace their steps from
Derbe through Lystra, Iconium and Pisidian Antioch to Perga
and sail from Attalia for Syrian Antioch, where Paul spends 'no
little time' with Christians (14:28).

One of the issues that surfaces in Mission I is the relation
of the new faith to Judaism, and more specifically the relation
of Gentile Christians to older Jewish converts. Are the Gentile
converts to be circumcised and required to observe the Mosaic
law?

Questions facing the early church

(1) Was the gospel to be preached to Jews or Gentiles?

(2) When Gentiles become Christians should they be circumcised and keep the law of Moses, like the Jews?

(3) Surely the Christian faith gives freedom from the 'law'?

(4) Can Jewish Christians eat with Gentile Christians?

(5) Should Jewish Christians go on keeping the Jewish laws about food?

(6) Should Christians eat meat sacrificed to idols?

(7) Should Christians eat only kosher meat, like the Jews?

(8) Should Christians be like the pagans in sexual behaviour?

(9) Should the Gentile churches care about the poor in Jerusalem?

'Council' visit (AD 49)

According to Luke, during Paul's stay in Antioch (end of Mission I) converts from Judea arrive and begin to insist on circumcision as necessary for salvation (15:1–3). When this leads to a dispute between them and Paul and Barnabas, the Antioch church sends Paul, Barnabas and others up to Jerusalem to consult the apostles and elders about the status of Gentile converts. This visit (Luke's number 4) results in the so-called Council of Jerusalem.

In Galatians 2:1–10 Paul told of this visit he went up to Jerusalem with Barnabas and Titus 'once again during 14 years' (to be reckoned from his conversion in AD 36, i.e., in the year 49–50). Paul spoke of this visit as the result of 'a revelation' (2:2), and he laid before 'those of repute' in Jerusalem the gospel that he had been preaching to the Gentiles, and they 'added nothing' to it. James, Cephas and John realized the grace given to Paul and Barnabas and extended to them the right hand of fellowship, uninfluenced by the 'false brethren' who had slipped in to spy out the freedom (from the law) gained in Christ and to whom Paul had not yielded 'so that the truth of the gospel might be preserved' (2:4–5). The issue settled on this occasion was circumcision: it was not obligatory for salvation; and Titus, though a Greek, was not forced to be circumcised.

The first part of Acts 15 (verses 4–12) deals with this same doctrinal issue. Those whom Paul labelled 'false brethren' are here identified as 'some believers from the sect of the Pharisees'

(15:5). When the matter is debated by the apostles and elders, Peter's voice seemingly prevails; and the assembly acquiesces in his decision (based on his own experience in Acts 10:1–11:18). The Jerusalem 'Council' thus frees the church from its Jewish roots and opens it to the world apostolate then confronting it. Paul's position is vindicated.

Antioch incident (AD 49)

After the Jerusalem 'Council' Paul went down to Antioch, and before long Peter followed. At first both of them ate with Gentile Christians, but soon 'some people from James' (Galatians 2:12), i.e., Christians with pronounced Jewish leanings, arrived and criticized Peter for eating with Gentile converts. Yielding to their criticism, Peter separated himself; and his action led other Jewish Christians, even Barnabas himself, to do the same. Paul protested and opposed Peter to his face, because he was 'not walking according to the truth of the gospel' (2:11). It may be implied that Paul was successful in his criticism, but even so the disciplinary question of Jewish dietary regulations for Gentile converts was now posed.

Jerusalem decree on dietary matters

Paul's opposition to Peter did not solve the dietary problem at Antioch. Emissaries seem to have been sent again to Jerusalem, presumably after Paul's and Peter's departure from Antioch. James convenes the apostles and elders again, and their decision is sent as a letter to the local churches of Antioch, Syria and Cilicia (Acts 15:13–19). Paul himself says nothing about this decision, and even in Acts he is only subsequently informed about it by James on his arrival in Jerusalem after Mission III (21:25).

As a result of the consultation James sends a letter to Antioch, Syria and Cilicia (15:22–29), recommending that Gentile Christians in such mixed communities abstain from meat sacrificed to idols, from blood, from the meat of strangled animals, and from illicit marital unions. It would have been sent with Judas Barsabbas and Silas (15:22) to Antioch and to Paul and Barnabas presumed to be still there. Acts 15:35–36 mentions Paul and Barnabas preaching in Antioch; but this should be understood of their stay immediately following the 'Council', after which Paul would have left Antioch for Mission II. Paul learns about the letter later (21:25).

Mission II (AD 50–52)

According to Acts 15:37–39 Paul refuses to take John Mark with him on Mission II because of his earlier desertion. Instead Silas accompanies Paul, and setting out from Antioch they make their way through Syria and Cilicia to the towns of south Galatia, Derbe and Lystra (where Paul takes Timothy as a companion, having had him circumcised, Acts 16:1–3!). From there he passes through Phrygia to north Galatia (Pessinus, Ancyra and Tavium) and founds new churches. Hindered from moving to Bithynia, he goes on from Galatia into Mysia and Troas. Here he seems to have been joined by Luke – or at least data from Luke's diary begin at this point (Acts 16:10–17, the first of the 'We-sections' – see Chapter 43 above).

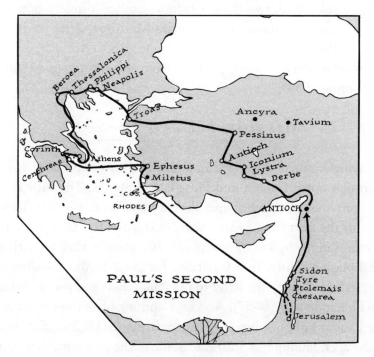

Paul's second mission. The New Jerome Biblical Commentary

In response to a dream-vision Paul passes over to Neapolis, the port of Philippi, and the latter becomes the site of his first Christian church in Europe. After imprisonment and flogging at Philippi for having exorcized a slave girl who had been the source of much gain for her masters, he passes on to Thessalonica via Amphipolis and Apollonia (Acts 17:1–9). His short stay in Thessalonica is occupied by evangelization and controversy with Jews; it ends with his flight to Beroea (17:10), and eventually to Athens (17:15). Here Paul tries to interest Athenians, renowned for their love of new ideas, in the gospel of the risen Christ (17:22–31). But he fails: 'We'll listen to you on this topic some other time' (17:32). After this disappointment Paul moves on to Corinth (AD 51), at that time one of the most important towns in the Mediterranean world. Here he lives with Aquila and Priscilla (18:2–3), Jewish Christians recently come from Italy and tentmakers by trade like Paul. During his stay in Corinth, which lasts for 18 months, he converts many Jews and Greeks and founds a vigorous, predominantly Gentile Christian church. In AD 51 Paul wrote his first letter to the Thessalonians. Near the end of his stay (AD 52), Paul is brought before the proconsul L. Junius Gallio, who dismisses the case as a matter of words, names, and Jewish law (18:15). Some time later Paul withdraws from Corinth, sailing from its port of Cenchreae for Ephesus and Caesarea Maritima. After paying a visit to the Jerusalem church (18:22), he goes to Antioch, where he stays well over a year (possibly from late autumn of 52 until the spring of 54).

Mission III (AD 54–58)

Leaving Antioch (Acts 18:23), Paul travels overland once again through north Galatia and Phrygia to Ephesus. The capital of the province of Asia becomes the centre of his missionary activity for the next three years (Acts 20:31), and for 'two years' he lectures in the hall of Tyrannus (19:10). Shortly after his arrival in Ephesus, Paul wrote Galatians (*ca.* 54). To this missionary period also belong the letter to the Philippians and possibly that to Philemon (*ca.* 56–57). Acts says nothing of an imprisonment of Paul at Ephesus, but see 1 Corinthians 15:32; 2 Corinthians 1:8–9; cf. Philippians 1:20–26. Some of the problems that Paul experienced and has described in 2 Corinthians 11:24–27 may well have happened to him in this period of missionary activity.

During this time reports came to Paul about the situation of the Corinthian church. To cope with the situation there – doubts, factions, resentment toward Paul himself, scandals – he

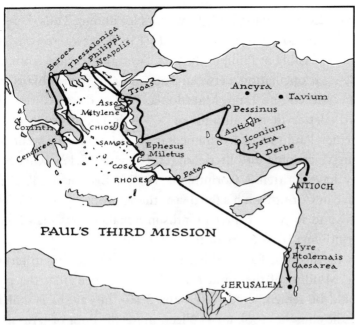

PAUL'S THIRD MISSION

wrote at least five letters to Corinth, of which only two survive (one of which is made up of more than one letter). One letter preceded 1 Corinthians (see 1 Corinthians 5:9), warning the Corinthians about associating with immoral Christians (and probably also recommending a collection for the poor of Jerusalem, a question about which the Corinthians sent a subsequent inquiry [see 1 Corinthians 16:1]). Then, to comment on reports and to answer questions sent to him, Paul wrote 1 Corinthians shortly before Pentecost (probably in 57). This letter, however, was not well received, and his relations with the faction-torn church of Corinth worsened. The situation called forth a hasty visit to Corinth (2 Corinthians 12:14; 13:1–2; 2:1 ['a painful visit']; 12:21), which really accomplished nothing. On his return to Ephesus, Paul wrote to the Corinthians a third time, a letter composed 'with many tears' (2 Corinthians 2:3–4, 9; 7:8, 12; 10:1, 9). This letter may have been taken by Titus, who visited the Corinthians personally in an attempt to smooth out relations.

Probably during Titus's absence the revolt of the Ephesian silversmiths occurs (Acts 19:23–20:1). Paul's preaching of the new Christian 'Way' incites Demetrius, a maker of miniature shrines of Artemis of Ephesus, to lead a riotous mob into the theatre in protest against Paul and the spread of Christianity.

This experience prompted Paul to leave Ephesus and go to

425

Troas (2 Corinthians 2:12) to work. Not finding Titus there, he decided to go on to Macedonia (2:13). Somewhere in Macedonia (possibly at Philippi) he met Titus and learned from him that a reconciliation between Paul and the Corinthians had been worked out. From Macedonia, Paul wrote to Corinth his fourth letter in the autumn of 57. It is not possible to say whether Paul proceeded immediately to Corinth or went first from Macedonia into Illyricum (cf. Romans 15:19), whence he may have written 2 Corinthians 10–13. Eventually, Paul did arrive in Corinth, on his third visit there, probably in the winter of 57 and stayed for three months in Achaia (Acts 20:2–3; cf. 1 Corinthians 16:5–6; 2 Corinthians 1:16).

By this time Paul had been thinking of returning to Jerusalem. Mindful of the injunction of the 'Council' that the poor should be remembered (Galatians 2:10), he saw to it that his Gentile churches took up a collection for the poor of Jerusalem. This was done in the churches of Galatia, Macedonia and Achaia (1 Corinthians 16:1; Romans 15:25–26). Paul planned to take the collection to Jerusalem and thus finish his evangelization of the eastern Mediterranean world. He wanted to visit Rome (Romans 15:22–24) and from there go on to Spain and the West. During the three-month stay in Achaia Paul wrote the letter to the Romans (probably from Corinth, or its port Cenchreae [Romans 16:1]) at the beginning of 58.

When spring arrives, Paul decides to sail from Corinth (Acts 20:3) for Syria. But as he is about to embark, a plot against him is hatched by some Jews; and he resolves to travel overland, by way of Macedonia. Disciples from Beroea, Thessalonica, Derbe and Ephesus accompany him. They spend Passover of 58 in Philippi (where Luke rejoins him – Acts 20:5, a 'We-section'). After the feast they leave by ship for Troas and journey overland to Assos, where they take ship again for Mitylene. Skirting the coast of Asia Minor, Paul sails from Chios to Samos, then to Miletus, where he addresses the elders of Ephesus summoned there (Acts 20:17–35). He is not deterred by their prediction of his coming imprisonment, but sails on to Cos, Rhodes, Patara in Lycia, Tyre in Phoenicia, Ptolemais, and Caesarea Maritima. An overland journey brings him to Jerusalem, which he has been hoping to reach by Pentecost of 58 (20:16; 21:17).

Paul's last imprisonment

For the rest of Paul's career we are dependent solely on Luke's information in Acts; it covers several years after 58, during which Paul endures a long captivity.

Last visit to Jerusalem and arrest (AD 58)

Arriving in Jerusalem, Paul and his companions pay their respects to James in the presence of the elders of that church (Acts 21:18). James immediately realizes that Paul's presence in Jerusalem might cause a disturbance among Jewish Christians. So he counsels Paul to join four men who are about to go through the **Nazirite** vow ceremony and to pay the expenses for them as a gesture of goodwill toward Jewish Christians. Paul consents, and the seven-day ceremonial period is almost over when he is seen in the Temple precincts by Jews from the province of Asia. They accuse him of advocating violation of the Mosaic law and of defiling the sanctity of the Temple by bringing a Greek into it. They set upon him, drag him from the Temple, and try to kill him. He is saved, however, by the **tribune** of the Roman **cohort** stationed in the **Fortress Antonia**. The tribune eventually puts Paul under protective arrest (22:27) and brings him before the **Sanhedrin**. But fear of the Jews makes the tribune send Paul to the procurator of Judea, Antonius Felix, residing in Caesarea Maritima (23:23–33). Felix, who expects Paul to bribe him (24:26), keeps Paul in prison for two years (58–60).

Appeal to Caesar; journey to Rome (AD 60)

When the new procurator, Porcius Festus, arrives (possibly *ca.* 60), Paul 'appeals to Caesar', i.e., requests trial in Rome (25:11), in virtue of his Roman citizenship. Festus has to grant this request.

Escorted by a Roman centurion (and probably by Luke, as the 'We-sections' indicate), he sets sail from Caesarea Maritima for Sidon and passes Cyprus to come to Myra in Lycia. In the late autumn of 60 (27:9) they leave Myra on an Alexandrian ship bound for Italy, expecting bad weather. Their route takes them first to Cnidus (on the southern coast of Asia Minor), then southward 'under the lee of Crete off Salmone' as far as Fair

> **Nazirite** <
someone following a Jewish custom by which he could consecrate himself to God for a period of time, during which he must avoid all alcohol, leave his hair uncut and avoid all contact with a corpse. At the end of the period of time he offered a sin offering and a sacrifice, shaved his head and burnt his hair, and then returned to normal life (see Numbers 6)

> **tribune** <
a junior officer in the Roman army

> **cohort** <
a division of the Roman army

> **Fortress Antonia** <
the barracks of the Roman garrison in Jerusalem near the Temple (see Chapter 71)

> **Sanhedrin** <
the administrative body of Judea

427

Havens, near the Cretan town of Lasea (27:7–8). When they try to reach the harbour of Phoenix, a northeaster blows up and carries them for days across the Adriatic to Malta, where they are finally shipwrecked (28:1).

After spending the winter on Malta, Paul and his escort sail for Syracuse in Sicily, then for Rhegium (modern Reggio di Calabria), and lastly for Puteoli (modern Pozzuoli, near Naples). Their overland journey to Rome takes them through Appii Forum and Tres Tabernae (28:15). Paul arrives in the capital of the empire in the spring of 61 and for two years is kept in house arrest (61–63) with a soldier to guard him. This situation, however, does not deter him from summoning Roman Jews to his quarters and evangelizing them (28:17–28). Traditional interpretation ascribes Paul's writing of Philemon, Colossians and Ephesians to this imprisonment.

End of Paul's life

Acts ends with the brief account of Paul's house arrest. His arrival in Rome and his unhindered preaching of the gospel there form the climax of the story of the spread of the word of God from Jerusalem to the capital of the civilized world of the time – Rome symbolizing 'the end of the earth' (Acts 1:8). But this was not the end of Paul's life. The mention of 'two whole years' (28:30) does not imply that he died immediately thereafter, no matter what interpretation is given to the end of Acts.

Eusebius in the fourth century is the first writer to mention Paul's second imprisonment in Rome and his martyrdom under Nero: 'After defending himself, [Paul] was again sent on the ministry of preaching, and coming a second time to the same city suffered martyrdom under Nero. During this imprisonment he wrote the second epistle to Timothy, indicating at the same time that his first defence had taken place and that his martyrdom was at hand.' Eusebius further quotes Dionysius of Corinth (*ca.* 170), who stated that Peter and Paul 'were martyred at the same time'. Tertullian compares Paul's death with that of John (the Baptist), i.e. by beheading.

Eusebius's testimony about Paul's death in the persecution of Nero is widely accepted. This persecution lasted, however, from the summer of AD 64 to the emperor's death (9 June 68);

and it is hard to pinpoint the year of Paul's martyrdom. The notice of Dionysius of Corinth that Peter and Paul 'were martyred at the same time' has often been understood to mean in the same year, but the preferred year for the death of Paul is 67, toward the end of Nero's persecution, as Eusebius's account seems to suggest.

Paul is said to have been buried on the **Via Ostiensis**, near the site of the modern basilica of St Paul's Outside the Walls. In 258, when Christian tombs in Rome were threatened with desecration during the persecution of Valerian, Paul's remains were transferred for a time to a place called *Ad Catacumbas* on the Appian Way. Later they were returned to their original resting place, over which Constantine built his basilica.

> **Via Ostiensis** <
the road to Ostia, the seaport of Rome

The Church in

the New

Testament

The material in this chapter is digested from sections by Raymond E. Brown, SS in NJBC article 80, 'Early Church'.

Introduction

The church is not the central topic of any New Testament writing, although Colossians and Ephesians direct attention to the church as body of Christ, and 1 Timothy and Titus discuss local church structure. The joining of those who accepted the proclamation of Jesus into churches and the gradual separation of Christians from the Jewish synagogues have to be reconstructed from scattered references in the New Testament and other texts written between AD 30 and 150.

In the four Gospels *ekklēsia*, 'church', 'community', appears on Jesus' lips only twice. Since Matthew 18:17 clearly refers to the local community, only once is Jesus remembered to have spoken about the church in the larger sense: 'Upon this rock I will build my church' (Matthew 16:18). Yet within a half century Ephesians 5:25 claims: 'Christ loved the church and gave himself up for her.' Some 30 years later (*ca.* 110) Bishop Ignatius of Antioch can refer to 'the catholic church'.

Jesus' public ministry (to ca. AD 30)

In what are commonly accepted as historical memories from his ministry, Jesus is surprisingly silent on foundational or structural issues. This is understandable if we see Jesus interested not in founding a separate religion but in renewing Israel, which already had worship, priests, sacrifices – Jesus did not need to plan such structures.

The choice of the Twelve is no exception to this image, for they represent the twelve patriarchs at the beginning of Israel and are expected at the end of the world to sit 'on thrones judging the twelve tribes of Israel' (Matthew 19:28; Luke 22:30 – Jesus' only recorded words about his purpose in choosing the Twelve). In the tradition of Jesus' sayings before the crucifixion there is never a reference to a mission outside Israel; indeed, in Matthew 10:5 he instructs his disciples, 'Go nowhere among the Gentiles and enter no town of the Samaritans.' Of course, his vision of the renewed Israel included the Gentiles' *coming* (Matthew 8:11) as did the vision of the prophets of Israel (Isaiah 2:2–3; 49:12); but that is quite different from a mission going to them.

Although some did leave their work (fishing, tax collecting) or home to follow Jesus during his ministry and be with him, many who accepted his proclamation of the kingdom seem to have remained where they were without a visible change in their lifestyle.

The apostolic period (ca. AD 30–66)

(A) The community and its life

Granted that Jesus showed little interest in a formally distinct society, it is remarkable how quickly the Christians became community-minded. Although Acts 19:1–5 indicates that there were followers of Jesus who had not received Christian baptism, the unanimity of Matthew, Acts, Paul and John suggests that this baptism very quickly became a standard feature of Christian life. As a visible action it helped to designate those who 'belonged' – a distinction not made in Jesus' ministry. The wide distribution of the term *koinōnia*, 'community', 'communion', in the New Testament shows that those who were baptized felt very strongly that they had much in common.

An early name for the Christian group may have been 'the Way', e.g., Acts 24:14: 'According to the Way ... I worship the God of our Fathers' (also Acts 9:2; 19:9, 23; 22:4; 24:22; cf. 16:17; 18:25–26). Preparing 'the Way of the Lord' describes the Jewish community responsible for the Dead Sea Scrolls, echoing Isaiah 40:3.

The word that became most popular, i.e. *ekklēsia*, 'church',

431

echoes the Greek Old Testament (Deuteronomy 23:2) where it described the assembly of Israel in the desert on the way to the Promised Land. The 'church of God' was used by Paul to remind regional Christian communities that they were patterned on the church in Judea. Thus, just as in the case of 'the Twelve', so also the various terms of early Christian self-understanding reflect continuity with Israel. And that may be the original symbolism of the Pentecost theme in Acts 2 as well, because we know that among some Jews this feast (Weeks) celebrated the renewal of the Sinai covenant; and at Qumran it was the occasion of the entry of new members into the community. The tradition reflected in Acts portrays that, amid Sinai-like wind and fire, God renewed his covenant for Israel, a covenant now based on what he had done in Jesus of Nazareth.

The life pattern of the Christian *koinōnia* also showed a strong heritage from Israel. Acts 2:42 mentions some features.

(1) PRAYER Jews who came to believe in Jesus continued to say prayers they had known previously: the basic Jewish prayer, the Shema: 'Hear, O Israel, the Lord our God, the Lord is One' (Mark 12:29). Christian hymns such as the Magnificat and the Benedictus (Luke 1:46–55, 68–79) are filled with Old Testament references. The Benedictus celebrates what God has done in the context of David, Abraham and the prophets. The Lord's Prayer also echoes synagogue prayers. Other hymns, some of them later, speak of Jesus in quite specific terms (Philippians 2:5–11; Colossians 1:15–20; John 1:1–18).

(2) BREAKING BREAD Acts portrays early Christians like Peter and John as going frequently, or even daily, to the Temple to pray at the regular hours (2:46; 3:1; 5:12, 21). There seems little reason to doubt this information, which implies that the first Jews to believe in Jesus saw no rupture in their ordinary worship pattern. The 'breaking of bread', presumably the eucharist, was in addition to and not in place of the sacrifices and worship of Israel. Paul, writing in the mid-50s (1 Corinthians 11:23–26), mentions a eucharistic pattern that was handed on to him (presumably, therefore, from the 30s) and says, 'As often as you eat this bread and drink this cup, you proclaim the Lord's death until he comes.'

(3) TEACHING OF THE APOSTLES Authoritative for all Jews were the Scriptures, in particular the Law and the Prophets; this would

have been true for the first followers of Jesus as well. Thus, early Christian teaching would for the most part have been Jewish teaching (a fact often overlooked by those who search out New Testament theology or ethics: the points of unique importance mentioned in the New Testament are like the tip of an iceberg, the bulk of which is the teaching of Israel). Points where Jesus differed from the law were remembered and became the nucleus of a special teaching. As they passed this on, the Christian preachers would have made their own application to situations that Jesus had not encountered; and the Jesus content in the teaching would have been expanded by apostolic teaching. When apostolic teaching, which was considered very authoritative, was eventually written down, those writings had within themselves the possibility of becoming a second set of sacred Scriptures (the New Testament). Those who believed in Jesus thus wrote supplements to the Law and the Prophets, even as did other Jews who produced sacred Jewish writing (the Mishna).

(4) COMMON GOODS An important aspect of *koinōnia* in Acts 2:44–45; 5:1–6 was a voluntary sharing of goods among the members of the community. This idealism of common goods was important. It bound communities together, as one had to support the other. A Christian ethic developed of giving up goods for the poor and of condemning wealth as an obstacle (Luke 1:53; 6:24; Mark 10:23; 2 Corinthians 8:9; James 5:1).

(B) Diversity within the community
Administration of common goods was the occasion of the first recorded dispute within the Christian community, i.e., between Jews of Hebrew upbringing ('Hebrews') and Jews of Greek culture ('Hellenists', who perhaps spoke only Greek) in Acts 6:1–6. The Greek-speakers were neither forced into conformity nor expelled from the *koinōnia*. Implicitly, cultural and theological differences that existed between the Hebrews and the Greek-speakers must have been thought less important than their common belief in Jesus, and the Greek-speakers were given their own administration, i.e., the Seven. The administrative structure emerged as an answer to problems like divisions and increased numbers. New Testament thought saw such structure as part of God's guidance through the Spirit for the church in response to prayer (6:6).

THE NEW
JEROME
BIBLE
HANDBOOK

The decision to preserve pluralism within the Christian *koinōnia* affected the missionary thrust of the group. Acts 5:34–40 indicates that, although at first the Twelve were persecuted by the Sanhedrin authorities, eventually they won a grudging tolerance (especially in the eyes of the Pharisees personified by Luke in the famous Gamaliel). This picture gets indirect confirmation from Paul, who seems to have been able to go to Jerusalem in the 30s and in the 40s and find James and Peter there without any hint of persecution. Presumably, the fact that there were different sects of the Jews in pre-70 Palestine enabled the Christians to find a certain tolerance even if they did not consider themselves a sect (Acts 24:14).

The persecution that broke out over Stephen (*ca.* 36?) described in 7:54–8:1 was a selective persecution of Greek-speakers, not of Hebrew Christians, and therefore presumably was motivated less by belief in Jesus than by Stephen's attack on the Temple. This persecution caused the Greek-speaking believers to leave Jerusalem for Samaria (where they converted many Samaritans: Acts 8:4–5) and for Antioch (where they converted Gentiles: 11:19–20).

The conversion of whole groups of Gentiles brought a showdown among the most famous Christian spokesmen. These included Cephas/Peter, the first among the Twelve; James, the brother of the Lord and the main authority in the Jerusalem community; and Paul, the apostle to the Gentiles. By the late 40s, the Gentile issue had produced at least four different attitudes within the Christian *koinōnia*, reflecting theological differences.

FOUR DIFFERENT ATTITUDES TO THE GENTILE QUESTION (1) No Gentiles may be accepted unless they are circumcised and become Jews. (2) Gentile Christians may be accepted but must keep some purity laws. (3) Paul's view: he insists that Gentile Christians need not keep the Jewish Law but nowhere does he state that Jewish Christians need not. (4) The institutions of Judaism (Temple, sacrifices) are no longer meaningful (see Acts 7:47–51; Hebrews 8:13; 10:8–9).

These different views could be found among Jews who believed in Jesus in the period before 65. Since all these Jews made Gentile converts, the oft-used designation Jewish Christianity and Gentile Christianity does not effectively differentiate attitudes toward the Jewish law and worship in this period. On the whole, Gentile Christians would have shared the attitude of the respective Jewish Christians who converted them.

It is remarkable that the Christian *koinōnia* seems to have withstood this wide range of differences. Acts 6 bears witness that the Greek-speakers were not expelled from the *koinōnia* even if given their own administrators; Acts 8:14 has the Twelve in Jerusalem (who were Hebrews) showing concern for the mission to those who spoke Greek. Even though Paul demeans James and Cephas/Peter as so-called pillars who were of no importance to him (Galatians 2:6, 9), they certainly showed concern about his views and mission. After dispute, they extended to him and Barnabas the right hand of *koinōnia* (2:9). If subsequently Paul opposes Peter and the men from Jerusalem face to face for the truth of the gospel (2:11–14), this does not imply broken *koinōnia*; for two or three years later when Corinthian Christians were forming separate parties, Paul cites Cephas and James, declaring solidarity with them about the gospel: 'Whether it was I or they, so we preach, and so you believed' (1 Corinthians 15:5, 7, 11).

Chi-Rho monogram, from a 1st-century tomb on the Mount of Olives. Chi and rho, the first two letters of Christos in Greek, formed an early Christian symbol

We have already mentioned Paul's collection of money for the Jerusalem church of James to stress the *koinōnia* of his Gentile churches with the churches of God in Palestine, which they are encouraged to imitate (1 Thessalonians 2:14).

The picture given thus far of Christianity before 65 is highly apostolic (a term wider than the Twelve), for the Gospels, Acts, and Paul all indicate the importance of apostles as a group or as individuals in this formative period. Was there a wider early Christianity not influenced by the apostles known to us?

Despite the lack of evidence, scholars have posited a Galilean Christianity distinct from Jerusalem Christianity, and bands of wandering preachers proclaiming Jesus in less-structured situations than those evidenced in Acts and Paul. Texts like Mark 9:38–41 and Acts 19:1–3 indicate that there was a proclamation of Jesus beyond what is known to us directly in the New Testament books. Good sense, however, warns us against elevating this unknown Christianity as the norm, and seeing the New Testament as a conspiracy to eliminate memories of a purer following of Jesus.

Here we concentrate on what can be learned from the New
Testament books written after AD 65 without entering into the
debate about their precise dating.

(1) By AD 65 the three best-known figures of the early church
(James, Peter and Paul) had died as martyrs respectively in
Jerusalem and Rome. Our documentation for the years 65–100
gives few new names for Christian leaders. Rather, there is a
tendency to speak in the name of the deceased apostles indicating what they would have said to a new generation. For
instance, if Colossians, Ephesians and the Pastoral Epistles
were written after Paul's death, each writer continues to speak
in Paul's name. It is doubtful that Matthew, one of the Twelve,
or Luke, a disciple of Paul, wrote the Gospels attributed to
them; but these Gospels preserve apostolic tradition.

(2) The age after the apostles is less missionary (fishing) and
more pastoral (shepherding), as the care for the ongoing communities founded between the 30s and the 60s becomes a major
concern. This development is illustrated in an emphasis on
shepherd imagery for Peter and Paul (1 Peter 5:1–4; John
21:15–17; Acts 20:28–30).

(3) Another transition was from Jewish to Gentile dominance.
Before 65, known leaders were Jews. After 100, when new
names become prominent (Ignatius, Polycarp), many of them
were not. In the 65–100 period, probably the majority in Christianity changed from Jews to Gentiles. The destruction of Jerusalem by the Romans had the side effect that the Jerusalem
church no longer had its central role.

Christianity now more clearly appeared as a new religion.
The religious institutions of Israel were regarded as finished (in
themselves and for Christians). What was permanently worth-
while was simply taken over as pertaining to Christians, not to
'unbelieving Jews'. 1 Peter 2:9–10 tells Gentile Christian readers: 'You are a chosen race, a royal priesthood, a holy nation,
God's own people' – privileges of Israel in the Old Testament.
By the end of the 1st century the eucharist was beginning to
take the place of the sacrifices of Israel – a Christian pure
oblation magnifying God's name among the Gentiles as 'foretold' by Malachi 1:11.

Yet there were also Jewish believers in Jesus who did not take this route. Christianity loyal to the institutions of Judaism survived into the 2nd century.

Paul stood against the imposition of the law on Gentile Christians: 'A human being is justified by faith apart from the works of the Law' (Romans 3:28). But James 2:24 shows how Jewish Christians would correct this slogan (perhaps misrepresented to them): 'A human being is justified by works and not by faith alone.' Even if 'faith' and 'works' do not have the same meaning in the two affirmations, a different outlook is obvious.

The church in the late 1st century

The passing of the great apostles in the 60s, the destruction of Jerusalem, and the increasing separation from Judaism produced various Christian reactions. Four characteristics may be considered.

(a) Church structure

Although there was incipient church structure in the pre-65 period, it was neither uniform nor greatly emphasized.

In a setting where the apostle is disappearing from the scene (2 Timothy 4:6–7) and false teachers are making an appearance (1 Timothy 4:1ff.; Titus 1:10–13; 2 Timothy 3:1–9; 4:3–4), the remedy is regularized church order.

Presbyteroi (presbyters, elders) are to be appointed in every town and they are to have the *episkopos* function (bishop, overseer, supervisor). Certainly that includes checking the religious and ethical behaviour of community members, caring for the needy out of common goods, and above all ensuring sound doctrine. They are to hold on to what they received (Titus 1:5–9), correcting false teachers. Thus they constitute a chain preserving apostolic teaching and authority.

The virtues demanded of the presbyter/bishops are 'institutional' (to be sensible, dignified, temperate), so as to make them both models for the community (able to manage their own household; married no more than once; having well-behaved Christian children; not recent converts) and examples of respectability to outsiders (not drunken, or violent, or lovers of money).

Deacons are also part of the structure, subject to most of the same requirements; yet we are not clear as to what deacons did as distinct from presbyters. As for women, seemingly there were women deacons (not simply the wives of male deacons: 1 Timothy 3:11) and an official class of widows (1 Timothy 5:3–16).

(b) Idealizing the church

The early Jewish Christians understood themselves as the renewal of Israel, so that there was a unified concept at the beginning. Nevertheless, in the period 35–65 the most frequent use of *ekklēsia* was for a local church, sometimes in a region (1 Corinthians 1:2; 16:1, 19), sometimes in a house when there were several house-churches in a region (Romans 16:5, 4, 15). Yet a passage like 1 Corinthians 12:28 indicates that there was a more universal usage as well. In the last third of the century, this becomes very frequent; see Acts 9:31; Matthew 16:18; and the female symbols in Revelation 12:4–5; 19:7; 21:9. In Colossians and Ephesians it dominates completely. For Ephesians 2:19–20 the church is 'the household of God built upon the foundation of apostles and prophets with Christ Jesus himself being the chief cornerstone'.

The church is the kingdom of God's beloved Son free from the dominion of darkness, in which Christians share the inheritance of the holy ones in light (Colossians 1:12–13). Most often the church is identified with the body of Christ, 'the fullness of him who fills all in all' (Ephesians 1:22–23). The church is the spotless bride whom Christ loved and for whom he gave himself (Ephesians 5:23–27). Christ has made known 'the plan of the mystery hidden for ages in God who created all things, that through the church the manifold wisdom of God might now be made known' (Ephesians 3:9–10).

(c) The Spirit guiding the church

Acts places little emphasis on church structure and does not identify the church as the body of Christ. Rather, it offers a view of history in which God's Spirit promised by Jesus guides the Christian community every step of the way. Peter and Paul and other human actors in the decisions of Christian history are but instruments of the Spirit. The crucial Pentecost scene employs the creational image of the wind as the Spirit of God (Genesis 1:2) to describe a renewal of the covenant that will now affect all peoples. Receiving the Spirit is part of the baptismal entry into the *koinōnia* of believers (Acts 2:38; 8:15–17; 9:17; 15:8; 19:5–6). The Spirit directs new steps in the mission as Samaritans and Gentiles are converted (8:29, 39; 10:38, 4–47; 11:12, 15; 13:2, 4).

When the great decision pertinent to the Gentiles is taken at Jerusalem in the presence of Paul, Peter and James, that decision is phrased thus: 'It has seemed good to the Holy Spirit and to us' (15:28). In steps significant for the spread of Christianity, the Spirit prevents Paul from taking a detour that would have delayed his planting Christianity in Europe (16:6–7); Paul's decision that he must go to Rome is a resolve in the Spirit (19:21); and when Paul bids farewell to Asia, the Holy Spirit has been provident by making presbyters who are overseers (bishops) of the flock (20:28).

Thus, every essential step in the Acts' story of how witness was borne to Christ from Jerusalem to the end of the earth is guided by the Spirit, whose presence becomes obvious at the great moments where human agents would otherwise be hesitant or choose wrongly.

(d) Discipleship animated by Christ

Jesus was often portrayed as the builder, founder or cornerstone of the Church, but in John's Gospel John portrays Jesus not as a past founder, but as a living presence, still 'alive and well' among Christians.

In John baptismal and eucharistic hints are associated with the signs of Jesus' ministry like the opening of the eyes of the blind (John 9) and the multiplication of the loaves (John 6), and conversations of Jesus about water (3:5; 4:10, 13–14). After the ministry, Jesus continues to make present these realities among his followers through the water and bread signs of baptism and the eucharist. As God's Son he has God's life (6:57); he gives that life to all who believe in him in a birth of water and Spirit, and he nourishes that life through the food and drink of his flesh and blood. For John the eucharist, never mentioned at the Last Supper, is primarily the food of eternal life.

The gift of life is the really important element for Christians; John shows no interest in a diversity of church functions or charisms. On the vine all are branches if they get life. In Johannine thought, all are disciples and primacy is constituted by the closeness to Jesus; there is no mention of an authority of supervision. No chain of human teachers is ever suggested to preserve the message of Jesus. That is the work of the Paraclete – a form of the Spirit that is the enduring presence of Jesus in each believer – who guides the Christian in the way of truth (16:13–15). If not teachers, Christians can be witnesses through whom the Paraclete bears witness (15:26–27).

This approach did not offer an answer to situations where Johannine Christians disagreed among themselves. 1 John gives the first evidence of the fellowship of Johannine Christians being broken. All the writer could recommend to people who claimed they were following the Spirit, was to 'put these spirits to the test to see which belongs to God. . . . Anyone who does not belong to God refuses to listen to us. That is how we can know the Spirit of Truth from the Spirit of Deceit' (1 John 4:1, 6).

The situation described in 1 John occurred at the end of the New Testament period. As the 1st century ended and the 2nd century began there was a clear breaking of *koinōnia* or communion among some of the followers of Jesus to the point where one group no longer recognized the other as Christian. Discouraging as that is, we should recognize that the four characteristics just discussed (church structure, idealism about the church, the role of the Spirit, and the relationship to Jesus as disciples), which were already explicit in New Testament Christian life, gave the church the ability to survive the death of the apostles and a rupture of unity. Those characteristics have kept the church alive from the 2nd century to our own times.

Index

OT = Old Testament
NT = New Testament
References to illustrations are in *italic* type. Most important references are in **bold** type.

WITHDRAWN